Services Management

The New Paradigm
in Hospitality

Services Management

The New Paradigm in Hospitality

Jay A. Kandampully

Upper Saddle River, New Jersey 07458

Library of Congress Cataloging-in-Publication Data

Kandampully, Jay.
   Services management : the new paradigm in hospitality / Jay Kandampully.
      p. cm.
   Includes bibliographical references and index
   ISBN 0-13-191654-8
   1. Hospitality industry—Management. I. Title.
   TX911.3.M27K364 2006
   647.94068—dc22

2005027190

Director of Development: Vernon R. Anthony
Senior Editor: Eileen McClay
Production Editor: Patty Donovan, Pine Tree Composition
Production Liaison: Jane Bonnell
Director of Manufacturing and Production: Bruce Johnson
Managing Editor: Mary Carnis
Manufacturing Manager: Ilene Sanford
Manufacturing Buyer: Cathleen Petersen
Senior Cover Design Coordinator: Miguel Ortiz
Cover Designer: Anthony Gemmellaro
Cover Image: Ray Kachatorian, Getty Images/The Image Bank
Executive Marketing Manager: Ryan DeGrote
Senior Marketing Coordinator: Elizabeth Farrell
Marketing Assistant: Les Roberts
Interior Design and Composition: Pine Tree Composition
Printer/Binder: R. R. Donnelley & Sons Company

A previous edition entitled *Services Management: The New Paradigm in Hospitality* was published by
Pearson Australia in 2002.

Pearson Education LTD.
Pearson Education Australia PTY, Limited
Pearson Education Singapore, Pte. Ltd.
Pearson Education North Asia Ltd.

Pearson Education Canada, Ltd.
Pearson Educación de Mexico, S.A. de C.V.
Pearson Education—Japan
Pearson Education Malaysia, Pte. Ltd

10 9

ISBN 0-13-191654-8

This book is dedicated to my father, Achan, and my mother, Amma, for instilling in me the courage to follow my conviction—even in the face of seemingly insurmountable challenges.

Contents

CONTENTS

CONTENTS

Preface

Customers demand service quality. Of all the challenges facing hospitality establishments today—including intense competition, globalization, and technological innovation—the single most pervasive and pressing challenge is the ever-increasing demand of customers for service quality. This has forced hospitality managers to discard traditional management thinking in favor of a new paradigm of hospitality management. Services management is the new paradigm of hospitality.

This book addresses hospitality management from the perspective of services management. The fact is that hospitality establishments offer *services* to fulfill the needs of customers. They do not merely sell accommodation, food, beverage, and entertainment. Because the quality of hospitality services is constituted by *the experience of the customer,* a services management perspective is entirely appropriate for hospitality management. Hospitality providers are essentially in the business of providing services rather than goods; their management orientation should therefore be that of services management rather than that of goods management.

Hospitality providers of all types will benefit from adopting the management philosophies and practices described in this book—philosophies and practices that have proven so effective in other service sectors. For example, it is well recognized in services that marketing and operations are simultaneous functions—the person providing the service is simultaneously marketing that service. This one example highlights a general point made repeatedly in this book—that in all services, including hospitality services, the *human element* (both employees and customers) is absolutely crucial. In selling services, hospitality enterprises are "selling" personal relationships.

This book thus addresses issues in the hospitality industry from a services management perspective, offering the reader a series of management concepts—covering operations, marketing, and human resources—all of which are capable of being effectively incorporated into any hospitality operation. Hospitality managers who conceptualize their hospitality offerings as being essentially *service offerings* will gain a new understanding of their business, and will be well placed to design, re-engineer, and market their offerings to meet the demands of their customers.

Apart from its emphasis on the new paradigm of services management, this book also deals with related topics of importance to the modern hospitality manager. These include value-added packages, strategic alliances and networks, and the challenges posed by globalization and technology.

Hospitality enterprises today cannot survive by selling only accommodation, food, and beverages. They must offer travelling offices for business customers, meeting places for conference customers, sophisticated in-room services for guest rooms, and sports and fitness facilities for all manner of people. The traditional core offerings of accommodation, food, and beverages now represent only small components of a total "package of experience" demanded by discerning customers. The new nontraditional service components (conference facilities, technology centers, in-room services, and so on) present hotels and other hospitality business with an opportunity to differentiate themselves from the competition using various value-added service packages.

Today's hospitality industry is global in nature, with producers and consumers spread around the world. In many cases, the holistic requirements of customers cannot be effectively fulfilled by the products or services of a single firm. Strategic alliances and partnerships with other firms enable hospitality providers to procure the extra competencies they require.

The complex nature of hospitality business today demands that firms adopt modern technology to ensure instantaneous interaction and provision of services to their customers and business partners—often across international borders. But with the increased use of technology, it has become increasingly important for firms to offer traditional "high-touch" service within a "high-tech" environment.

This book thus aims to guide hospitality managers away from the traditional management paradigm of a departmentalized organization selling physical products to a new paradigm, which sees hospitality as essentially a *services* business requiring a holistic cross-functional approach to meeting customers' needs within the context of personal relationship and experience. Creating and maintaining long-term, loyal relationships with customers is a consistent theme of this book.

The book is intended for hospitality management students at undergraduate and postgraduate levels, and for practitioners in the hospitality industry. The book assumes that readers have a basic understanding of hospitality operation, marketing, and management.

Acknowledgments

Many people have given their time and energy in contributing their wisdom, skills, and experience during the writing of the initial manuscript, and during the subsequent development of this book to its final form.

I thank my partner, Ria, for her unquestioning love, understanding, and encouragement in all of the numerous endeavors I undertake. To my mother, Amma, and my two brothers, Vijattan and Pachattan, I also express my gratitude—your ever-present love has always been an inspiration throughout my life. Ria, Amma, Vijattan, and Pachattan—your love is my strength; nothing is more important to me.

I am grateful for the opportunity to have worked with Dr. Ross Gilham, the project editor and copy editor for this book, who has helped me in myriad ways with his enormous effort and contribution. Through his outstanding editing skills, Ross has transformed my initial manuscript into a comprehensive textbook.

I would also like to take this opportunity to thank my friends, colleagues, and students, who have encouraged, supported, and assisted me during the preparation of this book. In particular, I would like to thank Linda Shea, Chris Roberts, H. G. Parsa, Clayton Barrows, Debby Cannon, Martin O'Neill, Gill Maxwell, Gillian Lyons, Kevin Baker, Jeremy Huyton, and Khanh Val La for their contribution of case examples to provide practical illustrations of the theory.

I am grateful to the "gurus" whose shoulders I stand upon, and the teachers who have shaped so much of my philosophy, thoughts, and passion. My sincere gratitude is also extended to a number of educational institutions that have contributed to my understanding, and that have supported and encouraged me in various ways to instill in me the dedication and passion that I have today for this field of study. In this regard I thank the Institute of Tourism and Hotel Management, Salzburg, Austria; the Birmingham College of Food, Tourism and Creative Studies, UK; the University of Exeter, UK; the University of Alaska, Fairbanks, Alaska; Lincoln University, New Zealand; the University of Queensland, Australia; and The Ohio State University, USA.

I am especially thankful to all my past and present students who have provided me with an opportunity to discuss pertinent issues and thus gain their perspective of the teaching and study of services management. I have learned much from you, and I acknowledge your contribution to this work. I am particularly grateful to my postgraduate students, Khanh Val La, Sunita Baker, and Sandy Lee, who have spent many long hours researching numerous issues to assist me with the preparation of the information used in this book.

Several publishing firms have also assisted me by kindly granting permission to publish materials that originally appeared, albeit in a different form, in various papers and book chapters published in their excellent journals and books. In this regard, I would like to thank Emerald Group Publishing, Haworth Press, and Continuum Publishing.

I also thank various hotels and other service firms for permission to use photographs of their firm and their services.

And last but not least, my special thanks to Mary Egan and Gerard Reid and their staff at Egan-Reid, New Zealand, for their design skills, which helped so much to make this book into an attractive and inviting volume.

About the Author

Dr. Jay Kandampully is an internationally recognized leader in the management and marketing of hospitality services. Jay is a professor in services management and hospitality at The Ohio State University. He also serves as a visiting professor at numerous other universities in Europe and in Asia. Jay is also Editor in Chief of the international journal *Managing Service Quality;* he also serves as the services management columnist for the Columbus, Ohio, business periodical *Business First.* He holds a PhD in service quality management, and an MBA, specializing in services marketing, both from the University of Exeter, England. His undergraduate degree was in Hotel Management from Salzburg, Austria and he holds a professional qualification in Hotel Catering and Institutional Management from the Birmingham College of Food and Creative Studies, England. His educational qualifications have been well supported by nine years managerial experience in Europe, India, and the United States. Additionally, he speaks six languages.

Jay Kandampully was the lead editor of the book *Service Quality Management in Hospitality, Tourism and Leisure,* which is being translated into Chinese, Korean, and Arabic. Additionally, he has published over 70 articles and has presented numerous papers at international conferences on issues relating to services management and marketing, service quality and service innovations. Jay serves on the editorial board of ten international refereed journals.

As an internationally recognized expert in the field, he enjoys close alliances with leading service organizations in the United States, United Kingdom, Austria, Australia, New Zealand, Singapore, Malaysia, France, Spain, Thailand, Mauritius, and India, where he is often invited to conduct management seminars to update managers with nascent service strategies.

Apart from his academic and practical experience in the field of services management in hospitality, Jay is an experienced and well-respected professor having received Excellence in Teaching awards in 1997, 1998, and 2001.

Jay's many years of study, writing, teaching, and practical experience in the field have led to his producing this landmark book on services management as the new paradigm in hospitality.

Part I

The Service Paradigm

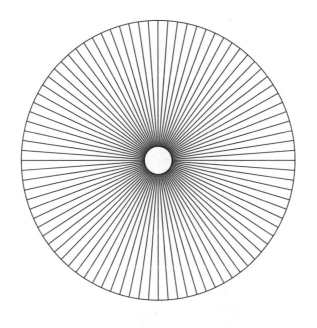

chapter one
The Metamorphosis
of Services

Study objectives

Having completed this chapter, readers should be able to:

✳ understand the growing importance of service industries in the modern economy, with particular emphasis on the hospitality and tourism sectors;

✳ understand the role of networking among service firms in providing customers with the desired benefits; and

✳ understand the concept of a "service package" and its application in the hospitality industry.

The framework of this chapter

This chapter is set out as follows:

* Introduction

* The service economy

* Growth in services

* The service advantage

* Global tourism and hospitality

  - The growing importance of tourism
  - Changing patterns of tourism
  - Developing countries
  - More choices for tourists
  - Parallel growth in hospitality

* Interdependency of services

  - Coordinated benefits
  - Components of a tourist service
  - Service interrelationship

* Hospitality as a service industry

  - Understanding hospitality services
  - Applying services management theory
  - The nature of a service

* Service packages

  - Tangible and intangible together
  - Visualizing a structured system
  - Travel packages
  - Core services and peripheral services
  - Designing an attractive package
  - Packaging to enhance customer benefit
  - Packaging to enhance business efficiency

* Tangible and intangible aspects of service offers

  - The tangible–intangible continuum
  - Managers and the continuum
  - What really matters to customers

* Summary of chapter

Introduction

People today live in a service-dominated economy. Services permeate the daily existence of every person. Within the past few hours, it is likely that the readers of this book will have listened to the radio, watched television, or been to the movies, traveled in a plane, bus, or cab, made or received a telephone call, consumed a restaurant meal, used a bank or automatic teller machine for their financial needs, used a gym or observed a sporting event, made an appointment with a doctor or dentist, contacted an insurance agency, or bought the weekly groceries from the store. In all of these cases, the ultimate end result for the consumer is a *service*. Indeed, the majority of the world's workforce is now employed in service-related activities.

As a major component of this dominant service sector, the tourism industry has enjoyed rapid development and now constitutes a global industry. Through its close association with tourism, the hospitality sector is also one of the fastest-developing industries worldwide. This chapter serves as an introduction to the wider context in which these industries operate and develop.

If they are to compete in the marketplace, commercial hospitality enterprises must first satisfy their customers. And if they are to tailor their service offerings successfully to meet the expectations of customers, it is essential that hospitality managers understand the perceptions of those customers. This chapter therefore also identifies the relationships created by hospitality firms—within a network of associated service providers—to enhance customer satisfaction. In addition, the chapter outlines the service dimension of the hospitality business from a managerial perspective.

The service economy

Services play a significant role in the economy of every nation in the world. The national economy of every country depends on its service infrastructure—including transportation, communication, education, health care, and various government services.

In the decades since World War II, economically developed nations have undergone extensive social and economic transformation, accompanied by a significantly increased rate of spending on services. In the early 1950s, service expenditure accounted for approximately one-third of personal consumption expenditure. It now accounts for about one-half of household expenditure, and is expected to continue to rise. This trend is apparent in both developed and developing countries in the past 30 years (Yu, 1999).

See the box "Engel's Seminal Research". Engel's research showed that prosperity and an increase in service infrastructure go together. More businesses undertake service-oriented activities—offering services either directly to the final customer, or to other business operations. The majority of the population within a community subsequently becomes employed in service-related activities. Services thus lie at the very hub of the economic activity of society. And we are only just beginning to understand the significance of this change in the way we live and work.

Services today employ more than twice as many people as the manufactured goods sector and the agricultural sector combined. The influence of this growing service sector permeates every part of the economy. It is estimated that one-third of worldwide international trade is generated from service activities. Most of the gross domestic product (GDP) of almost all developed countries is derived from the performance of services, rather than from the production of tangible goods, with services now accounting for around 70% of the GDP of developed nations (Lovelock, Patterson, & Walker, 1998). In the United States, for example, services are estimated to represent 75% of the product sector (Rust, Zahorik, & Keiningham, 1996).

Engel's seminal research

Ernst Engel (1857) showed that an increase in family income has the following effects on spending behavior:

* the percentage spent on food decreases;

* the percentage spent on housing and household operations remains constant; and

* the percentage spent on other purchases (e.g., education, health care, entertainment, recreation, and transportation) increases rapidly.

On the basis of Engel's work it is apparent that, as an economy develops, services become increasingly significant.

Growth in services

The dominance of service industries over the traditional "primary" and "secondary" industries (of raw materials and manufacturing) has become a global economic phenomenon. Most developed economies have transformed from being farming, mining, and manufacturing economies into service economies. The service sector in most of the developed economies (the U.S., U.K., Canada, Germany, France, Italy, and Australia) contributes more than 70% of GDP (services contribution to U.S. GDP, see Figure 1.1A) and offers employment to more than 75% of the population (services contribution to U.S. employment, see Table 1.1, Figure 1.1B). There is a consensus that economic growth, a higher disposable income, and technological advances have contributed to the rapid growth of services. Moreover, this growth in services has not been at the expense of mining, farming, or manufacturing. In fact, services have become an enabling factor in assisting these primary and secondary industries to achieve global competi-

Figure 1.1A *U.S. gross domestic product*

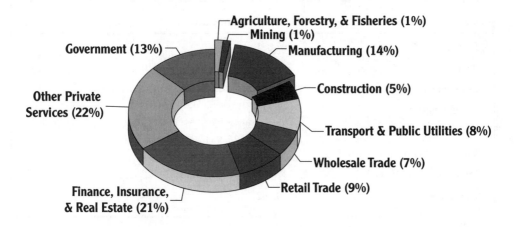

Source: http://www.ita.doc.gov/td/sif/Charts102002/Page1.htm

Figure 1.1B *U.S. employees on nonagriculture payrolls*

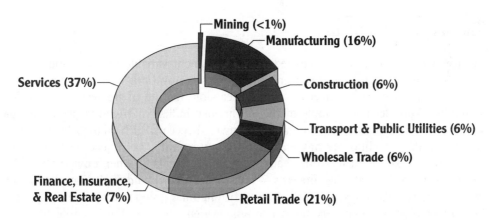

Source: http://www.ita.doc.gov/td/sif/Charts102002/Page1.htm

Table 1.1 *U.S. Employment*

Industry	2003 Employment
Service	107,891
Retail Trade	14,981
Government	21,495
Manufacturing	14,744
Professional and Business	15,999
Education and Health	16,498
Leisure and Hospitality	12,036
Construction	6,782

Source: http://stats.bls.gov/news.release/empsit.nr0.htm

tiveness. The internationally competitive market has compelled primary and secondary industries to transform themselves into truly customer-oriented, service-focused enterprises, irrespective of the products that they actually produce and sell.

The service advantage

Services have become the recognized value-assessment variable in predicting a firm's success in the marketplace. However, technological innovations have rendered services no longer a choice but a necessity—an inescapable feature of domestic and professional life. Consider the example of the automobile industry. Fifteen years ago people were able to attend to minor engine problems in their cars, such as adjusting the carburetor. Today's technology has replaced carburetors with fuel injectors, and owners now have to take their cars to mechanics for tuning. Similarly, when buying a washing machine or a dishwasher the concerns of consumers now extend to the various support services provided by the seller in the event of something going wrong. The competitive advantage of services has become increasingly evident—because there is little to differentiate competing products from the customer's perspective. The service component has thus become an integral part of most manufactured products, with the result that various types of industries have recognized the potential development of *service* as one of the few sustainable competitive advantages. This phenomenon is increasingly becoming evident in the tourism and hospitality industries.

Global tourism and hospitality

The growing importance of tourism

The tourism industry has become a crucial component of national economic development worldwide (Shaw & Williams, 1990), with enormous potential to generate local income and employment. Government agencies in many countries therefore actively encourage tourism-related entrepreneurial projects, resulting in an increasing number of individuals and organizations venturing into tourism-related services.

During the past 20 years or so, tourism has undoubtedly become a major industry worldwide. Forecasts by the World Tourism Organization (WTO) and by academic researchers continue to predict strong growth into the 21st century (WTO, 1991; Williams & Shaw, 1992; Smith & Eadington, 1992).

Tourism now stands as one of the world's leading industries. According to the World Travel and Tourism Council (WTTC), travel and tourism in the early years of this century is expected to generate direct and indirect employment for more than 200 million people—or one in every 12 workers worldwide (WTTC, 2001). The council has also forecast that, by 2011, the travel and tourism economy will constitute 11% of global GDP.

Changing patterns of tourism

From the mid-1990s, there was a gradual change in the patterns of tourism consumption worldwide. These changes have had a marked influence on tourism-related sectors, especially in the Western hemisphere. A massive shift in what might be called "value structure" has emerged, with the traditional perspective of sun, sea, and amusement becoming less popular, and the seeking of knowledge through cultural, environmental, and educational tourism becoming more common (Elliott, 1991; Wood, 1992).

Sociodemographic changes, marked by an active aging population with high spending power, have created a significant change in habits (Hall & Page, 1999; Hall & Weiler, 1992). New patterns of tourism consumption have developed (Krippendorf, 1999), and the influence of technology, demographics, and lifestyle patterns are expected to continue and accelerate these trends in the present century (Goeldner, 1992, 2000).

Developing countries

One of the most important factors contributing to the growth of tourism as a global business has been the effect of economic growth in developing countries. In the past, most tourism consumers were from a small number of developed Western nations. However, through economic growth and political freedom, consumers from an increasing number of countries have entered the global market—China, Thailand, Taiwan, Korea, and India being prime examples.

Tourism now constitutes a global business in which both consumers and producers are dispersed worldwide. During the 1990s and early 2000s there has been an exponential growth in various tourist destinations worldwide, and this has provided consumers with a greater variety of choices while simultaneously promoting healthy competition among tourist destinations.

More choices for tourists

The accelerated growth in worldwide demand for tourism products has caused a rapid proliferation of tourism ventures as these have increasingly been recognized as sound long-term business opportunities.

This growth in tourism ventures has been facilitated by the fact that tourism products cannot be patented by the establishing firm, thereby allowing other entrepreneurs to enter the market with ventures of a similar nature. This multiplication in the number of tourism service providers has resulted in increased choices for consumers.

"Special interest tourism"

According to Pearce (1988:219), "future trends for tourism seem to suggest that travellers will be especially concerned with not just being 'there,' but with participating, learning and experiencing the place they visit." Some of these rapidly growing tourism interests include:

* cultural and heritage tourism (Zeppel & Hall, 1992; Zeppel, 1999);

* ecotourism (Aston, 2000; Lawrence, Wickens, & Phillips, 1997);

* educational tourism (Kalinowski & Weiler, 1992; O'Rourke, 1990); and

* nature-based, environmental, and sustainable tourism (Aronsson, 2000).

All of these can be categorized under the umbrella term of "special interest tourism," and activities of this type will doubtless constitute the majority of tourism consumption in the future.

Readers with a special interest in any of these areas should consult the references given above.

The growth of the transport industry and associated technological developments have also had major effects on the growth of tourism. Access to destinations by air, sea, and land at affordable prices within a relatively short time has enabled tourists to travel to new destinations, often far from home. As travel has become less time-consuming and tedious, destinations that were once considered to be long-haul tourist treks now offer short-haul holidays and convention facilities. Improved transport has thus significantly affected tourism, and the offer of transport services as part of a package has become a major component of tourism services.

Apart from technological improvements in transport, technological innovations in every field of the tourist industry have affected the way in which the tourism business is conducted and marketed. This, of course, offers benefits to both suppliers and consumers. Just as technological innovations have made it possible for remote locations (such as Alaska and Antarctica) to become increasingly attractive and accessible tourism destinations, technology also helps tourism organizations to "maintain nature"—in the form of artificial snow on ski slopes, barriers to protect beaches from sea erosion, and so on.

Technological innovations in telecommunication also have wide implications in the tourism business. Some involve the personal needs of tourists (such as in-room services of various kinds), whereas others assist tourism organizations in a variety of tasks to do with the general running of the business (including reservations, marketing, conference facilities, internal communication functions, and so on). These matters are discussed in greater detail in Chapter 10.

Parallel growth in hospitality

In parallel with the global development of the tourism industry, the hospitality industry has also become a truly global industry. Economic growth in most countries around the world has contributed to this growth in the hospitality industry, with economic prosperity contributing to dramatic changes in social habits.

Socializing outside the family circle has become more common, with gatherings in restaurants, pubs, bars, and so on becoming part of everyday life for many people. Going out with friends and family has become a popular form of social entertainment. Changes in work schedules have produced changes in lifestyles. Whereas most people in previous generations lived very close to their workplaces, with their nearby homes providing food and lodging, people today tend to commute longer distances to work, requiring them to eat and seek lodging outside their homes.

Many people maintain more then one job to sustain their newly acquired expensive habits. These changes in social and working habits have contributed directly to changes in eating habits, as has the introduction of fast food, convenience foods, and international cuisine. In keeping with these developments, rail catering, sea catering, and airline catering have adapted to serve changing dietary requirements during travel—both for pleasure and for business. Catering for these changing requirements has spawned global businesses associated with the hospitality industry.

There has thus been an exponential growth in the need for hospitality services in almost every country in the world. In response to this global need, and to take advantage of these changing social phenomena, hospitality firms have expanded nationally and internationally. Firms, customers, and employees have all become international and multicultural. Indeed, it is difficult today to name a city that does not have an international hotel, restaurant, or other tourist facility.

Interdependency of services

Coordinated benefits

Services are benefits offered to customers, and these benefits are usually offered in sequences or in "bundles." These are of two main types:

* ✳ a single service provider might offer a number of services in sequence to any given customer; or

* ✳ a single customer might receive additional services from *other* providers before and after the service currently being rendered.

Although each of these services can be seen as an isolated benefit, they must be compatible, complementary, and coordinated.

Let us consider, as an example, a tourist or business traveller staying in a hotel. This traveller might have received services from an airline, a taxi company, or a limousine hire service before arriving at the hotel. After leaving the hotel, the traveller might take a taxi or a tour coach to receive the next service. From the customer's perspective, although these services are experienced separately, they are interrelated. The linkage between them is important if the traveller's itinerary is to run smoothly. The needs of customers can thus extend beyond the capabilities of one company's product or service offering.

Service firms cannot and do not exist in isolation. Through partnerships and collaborations with other firms, bundles of services are offered to satisfy the various needs of individual customers. These partners might or might not be involved in serving the customers directly. The entire system, however, is internally organized by an interactive web of relationships in which the customer participates at various stages—in both the production and consumption of the various services.

Components of a tourist service

The tourism service product is thus a composite product that, from the perspective of a traveller, is viewed as a total experience made up of individual units. This poses a major challenge in maintaining a superior service. The overall service product is comprised of a combination of services that, although fundamentally independent, are consumed by tourists in a continuous chain, one after the other, from the time they leave home, until the time they return.

Tourism can thus be understood as a system comprised of:

* services received at the tourist's place of origin—for example, travel agents, insurance, advice, and so on;

* en route services—for example, transport and food while travelling; and

* services at the destination—for example, accommodations, food, and attractions at the holiday site.

Thus, the tourist industry is made up of a network of independent, but interrelated, functions operating in a range of service sectors. Poor performance within one sector, or by one service provider, affects the other service providers in the chain. For example, a tourist losing his or her baggage during a flight is likely to perceive every other service negatively, or at least less favorably.

Service interrelationship

This concept of *service interrelationship* is critical to the management of services. It reflects the importance of *all* services involved in the relationship. And it must be understood that service interrelationship applies within a single organization, as well as across collaborating organizations.

Within any service organization, almost all service needs are cross-functional in nature. Cross-functional *systems* are therefore required within an organization—that is, systems capable of fulfilling customer needs in a coordinated fashion. Thus, within any service organization, all departments and functional units must be interdependent and coordinated, with their cross-functionality managed and coordinated effectively.

Essentially this means that, in any service interface, every employee should be capable of going beyond departmental boundaries to assist the customer.

Hospitality as a service industry

As noted above, hospitality is one of the fastest-growing service sectors throughout the world. In many respects, the hospitality industry is very closely associated with the tourism industry. In almost all circumstances, the growth of the tourism industry has fueled the growth of hospitality, resulting in its development as a global industry. It must be emphasized that hospitality is essentially a *service* business enterprise. The hospitality business must therefore be studied within a service industry framework, and services management theory is required to understand and explain hospitality management and operations.

Understanding hospitality services

Hospitality, as a generic service term, can be seen as being comprised of three main functional areas—accommodation, food and beverage, and entertainment—as illustrated in Figure 1.2.

Figure 1.2 *The three main functional areas of hospitality*

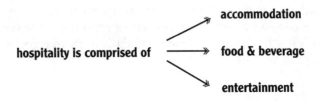

Author's presentation

These three functions within the hospitality sector might be offered separately by individual businesses (e.g., motels offering accommodation only, restaurants offering food and drinks only, and bars and nightclubs offering entertainment only). Alternatively, and more commonly, some businesses might offer various combinations of the three elements (e.g., hotels offering accommodation, food and beverage, and entertainment). The degree of specialization, or the combination of functions that a firm offers, determines the type of clientele it wishes to attract, and the image that the firm wishes to communicate to its customers.

However, as noted above, hospitality organizations operate within a network of service organizations that, to a large extent, are interrelated and interdependent.

They include:

* tour operators, travel agents, and tourism organizations;

* travel and transport operators;

* leisure, recreation, and entertainment venues;

* restaurants, bars, clubs, and cafés; and

* hotels, resorts, motels, camping grounds, bed & breakfast (B&B) establishments, and hostels.

It is becoming increasingly difficult for any hospitality firm to operate without being in association with a network—either at the production end or at the supply end. Hospitality networks benefit both the customer and the firm, and they often extend beyond national boundaries, depending on the firm and what is being offered to the customer. Through global networks, hospitality firms are able to enhance the perceived value of their offer. For further discussion on this, see "Designing and Managing Service Networks" (in Chapter 5).

Applying services management theory

As noted in the box "The Core Philosophy of This Book," the primary hospitality function should be on providing *service to the customer.*

Hospitality organizations are *not* in the business of offering accommodations, food and beverage, or entertainment in themselves. In the marketplace, what the customer receives from a hospitality establishment is *service.* What is important to the customer is the outcome—that is, the service—not simply the accommodation product, the food and beverage product, or the entertainment product. Indeed, the customer pays for the end result (the service) and not for the intermediary (the ostensible product being purchased).

It is extremely important that hospitality managers grasp this concept—that, through their hospitality establishments, they are offering *services.* As hospitality managers, it is therefore crucial that they understand in depth what they are offering, and how it should be offered, to create the best experience for their customers. This perspective of hospitality necessitates a reexamination and readjustment of ideas, concepts, systems, and methods. Fundamentally, this new perspective calls for a better understanding of the real hospitality product—that is, the nature of a service.

The core philosophy of this book

This book is essentially about applying the principles of service management to hospitality management. Two essential principles of this approach are:

* that hospitality organizations are business organizations and hence their focus should primarily be on the customer; and

* that hospitality organizations are service organizations and hence their primary orientation should be on service.

These two core principles combine to produce an emphasis on service to the customer.

Because hospitality is essentially a services business enterprise, the hospitality business must therefore be studied within a services industry framework, and services management theory is required to understand and explain hospitality management and operations.

This book thus aims to guide hospitality managers away from the traditional management paradigm of a departmentalized organization selling physical products to a new paradigm, which sees hospitality as essentially a services business requiring a holistic, cross-functional approach to meeting customers' needs within the context of personal relationship and experience.

The nature of a service

Services have been described as a "deed, act or performance" (Berry, 1980) or as "encounters in time, rather than physical objects" (Brunell, Kelley, & Ramesan, 1992). Hospitality services can similarly be described as various combinations of activities, benefits, and interactions (Figure 1.3). Thus services are subjective outcomes achieved through time, motion, and emotion—but achieved in the presence of, and with the assistance of, tangible products and information.

Figure 1.3 *Hospitality services involve activities, benefits, and interactions*

Author's presentation

For example, from a customer's perspective, a hotel's services consist of:

* *activities*—a variety of activities such as conferences, banquets, nightclubs, sports and games, health-related activities (gyms, spas, and so on), entertainment, social interactions, and so on;

* *benefits*—such as parking services, concierge services, laundry services, transport, business office services, room service, and so on; and

* *interactions*—all the interactions to which the customer is exposed while participating in the above activities and receiving the listed benefits.

Thus, from the customer's point of view, hotel services can be understood as a total experience. Moreover, it is an experience in which the hotel guest encounters and interacts at an intimate level with the service provider, other guests, the physical environment, and the process of service delivery. On a conceptual level, this experience can be termed a bundle, a package, or an assemblage—a concept that was developed by Normann (1984, 2000). See Figure 1.4.

Figure 1.4 *Hotel services as a "bundle" or "package"*

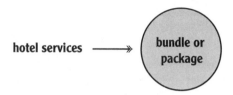

Author's presentation

Service packages

Tangible and intangible together

Although it is theoretically possible to make a distinction between services and goods, the reality is that most services are associated with some physical items and most products are accompanied by some aspects of service. For example, waiter service in a restaurant involves a significant service component (looking after the guest) as well as a physical product (the food itself). Even in a take-out restaurant, the product (the "fast food") is still accompanied by a definite service element (the carefully planned friendly and efficient service).

In theory, each of these components—the intangible service component and the tangible product component—constitutes only one part of the competitive package that the firm offers. But, in reality, from the perspective of the customer, the two components do not exist independently. A service firm offers a "package" or a "bundle" that includes a mixture of services, physical items, image, and experience. Neither services nor goods are marketed on their own. What is marketed is a "bundle of satisfaction."

Visualizing a structured system

The service package is the sum total of all the goods, services, and experiences offered to the customer (Albrecht & Zemke, 1985, 1990). The concept of a service "package," if expressed on paper as a visual framework of interlinked services, provides a basis for everyone in the service organization to comprehend the service components, and the overall service outcome, as experienced by the customer. This enhances the ability of every member of the team to think systematically about the delivery system.

An organization's service offer (in the form of a service package) follows logically from the direction of the service strategy. The service package constitutes the service value that the organization is willing to offer to the customer. Once the organization is clear as to the components of the service offer, it is then possible to develop the appropriate system for its production and delivery. Thus, the various services offered in a hotel can be conceptualized as bundles or packages on sale to its customers.

Service systems are discussed in more detail in Chapter 5.

Travel packages

The idea of a travel "package" has had an enormous influence on the tourism and hospitality industries in recent decades. The range of tour and accommodation packages available today is almost limitless. The concept of a service package in this case allows hotel managers to group a variety of service offerings within a hotel, and to combine this with travel services to cater for the individual and group needs of customers.

For example, for a business traveller, a hotel could offer a package of special accommodation rates, breakfast, and special services (such as a fax machine, a laptop computer, and a photocopier). See Figure 1.5.

As another example, a hotel might offer accommodation, breakfast, lunch, and dinner to a conference customer, together with entertainment, sightseeing trips, and rail or flight tickets at a special package rate (see Figure 1.6).

Figure 1.5 *A package for a business traveller*

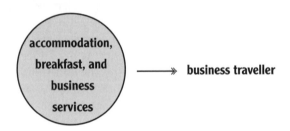

Author's presentation

Figure 1.6 *A package for a conference customer*

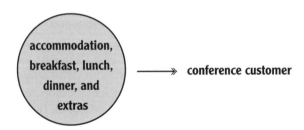

Author's presentation

Packaging thus entails making up a combination of services that are appealing, convenient, and complementary, and then presenting these as a single price offering.

Special packages can also be arranged for a marriage group or a function in which the customer's need is for nonaccommodation services such as food, beverage, and entertainment with a particular focus on the needs and expectations that go with a wedding reception (see Figure 1.7).

But packages do not have to be sophisticated, tailor-made packages catering for every whim of the guest. For example, a straightforward tourist package might consist, simply, of accommodation, breakfast, and one main meal of the day (see Figure 1.8).

Core services and peripheral services

According to Normann (1984, 2000), most service offerings or service packages consist of:

* a *core service*—the major benefit that the consumer is seeking; and

* *peripheral services*—the little things offered as added bonuses.

Figure 1.7 *A package for a marriage party*

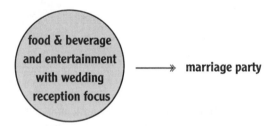

Author's presentation

Figure 1.8 *A simple tourist package*

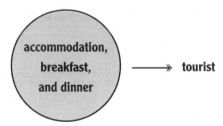

Author's presentation

For example, in a tour package, the core service is the visit to a specific location, whereas the peripheral services are the comfortable bus, the friendly tour guide, and the clean toilets at the location.

The core service is the centerpiece of the service offering—the basic reason for being in business. Without the core service, a business enterprise makes no sense. The peripheral services are a naturally compatible set of goods, services, and experiences that, when combined with the core service, serve to create an impression of high value in the customer's mind. See Figure 1.9.

Figure 1.9 *Customer needs and the design of the offer*

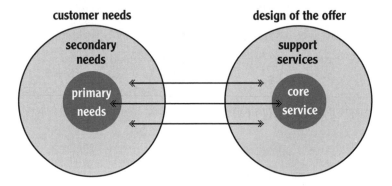

Adapted from Edvardsson and Gustavsson (1992)

The peripheral service should support, complement, and add value to the core service. The peripheral service, in most cases, is intended to provide the "leverage" that helps build the value of the total package in the eyes of the customer. Using a hotel as an example, the core service includes a clean, properly equipped room, whereas the peripheral service package includes services additional to accommodation—such as a wake-up call, morning tea, coffee, newspaper, laundry service, shoe-shining service, transport to and from the airport, and so on.

Bell and Zemke (1990) argued that satisfaction really comes from the peripherals that surround the core service—how the food is served in the restaurant; how the waiting staff interact with the customer; how the receptionist assists the customer when a credit card is not accepted; how the bellboy arranges dress hire for the party; and so on.

Companies commonly compete in similar markets and offer comparable core services. For example, two five-star hotels might be located in a city center, with the services and products offered by the two hotels being virtually indistinguishable from one another in the eyes of the consumer. Given these circumstances, the only way in which either of these hotels can gain a competitive edge is by offering added value.

Thus, from a managerial perspective, the differentiation between core service and peripheral service can be crucial. Once a core service has proved to be effective—that is, able to meet the primary needs of the customer—it is the peripherals of the service package that act as the key factors in a customer's final judgment of the value of the total service product. In many situations, the only possible difference between competitors lies with these peripherals (Albrecht & Zemke, 1985, 1990). The strongest company in the marketplace will be the one that offers the best-designed package of peripherals.

Defining the service package thus calls for:

✳ a clear understanding of the wants, needs, and expectations of the customer;

✳ a clear strategy for delivering service; and

✳ a great deal of creative thought and market judgment.

Designing an attractive package

Once a firm has a clear definition of the service package, it can then design (or re-design) the existing services and system, with a view toward maximizing the firm's competitive position.

To refer back to Figure 1.3, these packages or assemblages are manifested as *services* by the individual elements being formed into various combinations of activities, benefits, and interactions. In the hospitality industry, packaging helps to combine core services and peripheral services not only within the hotel, but also outside the hotel, extending into the local business environment, with packages often being provided by more than one participating organization. For example, many hotels in Orlando, Florida, offer theme-park entrance tickets to Disneyworld or Sea World as part of their packages.

The best packages are carefully planned and coordinated to fit the customer's needs as closely as possible. Club Med provides a good example of a successful service packaging concept involving sports activities, instruction, and entertainment in a combination that allows tourists to relax completely. All arrangements are preplanned with precision to provide an enjoyable experience for the customer—from the arrival and welcoming ceremony by the club's employees to the seating arrangements that ensure that the guests get to know each other (see box).

Service packages are often used by organizations to differentiate their offering from those of their competitors, incorporating different packages of varying combinations of core and peripheral services. This strategy allows an organization to deviate from its standardized service offering without disrupting its essential system for service delivery. In other words, by adopting the concept of packaging, a firm is able to offer a selection of services to suit the individual requirements of the customer.

The concept of packaging also allows firms to offer price variability according to customer need. For example, hotel business customers who require only a night's sleep, and who will leave early in the morning, can be offered a special rate on the basis that such guests will not receive food service. Such a price reduction will be attractive to business customers, and might make the difference between their accepting or rejecting the offer. By using service packaging, firms have many opportunities to offer personalized or customized services according to customers' needs. However, Gourville and Soman (2001) have argued that packaging services can hurt consumption. They found that packaging tends to mask the costs incurred by the firm in offering individual items within a bundle. This, they claimed, can cause customers to undervalue the individual items within the package.

Packaging to enhance customer benefit

Because many services offer off-peak reduced rates, packages can make hospitality and travel services more affordable to customers. For example, airline companies working in conjunction with hotels might offer domestic airfare and hotel rates for weekend holidays, or city center hotels that have low demand during weekends can effectively use a package to boost sales while, at the same time, benefiting customers.

As a result of collaborative bargaining, hotels are able to offer cheaper flights to their customers, and airlines are able to offer cheaper hotel accommodations to their customers. Similarly, cheaper entrance fees to theme parks, cinemas, operas, and concerts are often offered to hotel customers as part of a package. By using various combinations of packages, hotels have an opportunity to offer new entertainment, special events, and activities to their customers. This, in turn, encourages repeat visits.

Packages are often "all-inclusive" offers. This practice allows customers to know how much money to allocate for the holiday. For example, Club Med offers an all-inclusive priced holiday, which includes a return trip, accommodations, food, and free wine with meals. Such all-inclusive packages reduce customers' anxiety about how much they will have to spend, and what they will receive for their money.

Packaging to enhance business efficiency

A well-conceived, well-designed, and well-marketed package is of substantial benefit to customers, with positive long-term benefits through word-of-mouth referrals and repeat business. In this way, packages help to build customer volume and profitability. Creating off-peak demand through a creative and attractive package offer is of great benefit to hotels and travel organizations. Good packages that offer exceptional value for customers through the collaborative efforts of various organizations will, in fact, benefit every organization involved.

Specialized packages can assist hoteliers to hone in on selected target markets.

Skiing packages, tennis packages, bridge club packages, and so on are all good examples of this practice.

Finally, because most packages are booked and paid for well in advance, hotels and associated organizations are able to forecast demand more accurately. Strategic plan-

Club Med packages tailored for all

The success of the package holiday firm Club Med in becoming a household name in the holiday business is no accident. Everyone at Club Med, from the CEO to the kitchen porter, is committed to the ideal of customer satisfaction through every element of the package. Every member of the staff is aware that guests are coming to experience a combination of the resort location, the excellent facilities, and the all-important element of personal interaction. Guests come for a total experience—not just to have a few days away from home and work.

Club Med's success can be attributed to the creative inclusive packages it has developed—all combining the basic mix of location, facilities, and personal interaction. A typical Club Med inclusive package is comprised of three meals a day, beer or wine with lunch and dinner, a swimming pool and gymnasium, sailing, kayaking, snorkeling, tennis, water exercise, rock climbing, archery, aerobics, volleyball, basketball, table tennis, billiards, picnics, evening entertainment and dancing, a nightclub, and conference facilities.

Club Med offers different holiday plans—a budget plan, a moderate plan, and a deluxe plan—from which customers can choose in accordance with their expectations and expenditure. Within these categories they offer various packages—packages primarily for couples, packages primarily for singles, and packages primarily for families. The family package incorporates subpackages selected by parents for their children according to age—Kids Club, Petit Club, Mini Club, and Baby/Nursery Club.

With these various packages, Club Med offers not merely a holiday, but a hassle-free vacation package.

In the 1970s and 1980s Club Med was in vogue as "the" holiday destination for many single people in Europe. As these customers grew older, got married, and began having children, their needs changed. In response, Club Med extended its services and packages—thereby successfully maintaining the loyalty of its original customers for many years.

Using various specialized packages, Club Med has maintained its basic customer base while simultaneously extending its market demand to other customer groups.

ning of operations to enhance quality of service is thus facilitated. (For further information on this, see "Managing and marketing service demand," Chapter 7.)

Tangible and intangible aspects of service offers

The tangible–intangible continuum

As noted above, almost all services and products are offered to customers as a combination of service elements and product elements. There are very few "pure" services that do not utilize some form of product element in their service offering and, conversely, there are very few "pure" products that do not have a service element as a component of their delivery to the customer.

Services exist on a continuum—those that have very little tangible product component are at one end of this continuum, and those with a larger tangible element are at the other end (Shostack, 1977). For example, some of the services in a hotel can be depicted as illustrated in Figure 1.10.

Figure 1.10 *The service–product continuum*

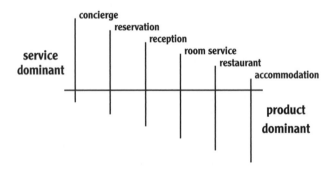

Adapted from Shostack (1977)

Managers and the continuum

The hospitality sector is an excellent example of a service offering that is comprised of tangible and intangible components in the core service. Hospitality managers must have a good understanding of the tangible and intangible mix of the services and products offered by their firms. Moreover, it is important to know how the service and product elements interact and complement each other and, more importantly, how they should be produced, marketed, and managed.

Figure 1.11 *Tangibles and intangibles of a service package*

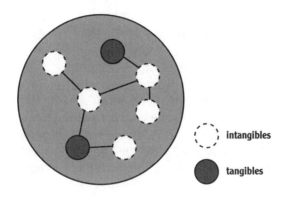

intangibles

tangibles

Adapted from Shostack (1977)

This configuration of tangible and intangible elements can be illustrated as shown in Figure 1.11. For example, the onboard services of an airline consist primarily of the core intangible service. This, however, consists of various onboard intangible elements (such as in-flight entertainment, telephone, Internet, and other communication facilities), as well as tangible elements (such as food, drinks, and comfortable seating).

Illustrating onboard services in the style of Figure 1.11 assists managers and employees to clarify the various functions of the components of the service package. Moreover, an illustration (in this style) of each and every service package within an organization also assists employees to understand the importance of the intangible nature of the package, and their own crucial role in service delivery.

What really matters to customers

In service organizations such as hotels, the customer's perception of quality, and the subsequent image (position) generated of the firm is often influenced more by the intangible elements of the offer than by its tangible elements. In the competitive marketplace, firms find difficulty in maintaining superiority based on the tangible components of the service offer—because these components are easily replicated by competing organizations. However, positive personal interaction with an obliging employee readily demonstrates a firm's superior service. Competitors have more difficulty emulating this sort of intangible element of service.

Differentiating and understanding the tangible and intangible elements components of the service assist management to focus on those components that require special attention to enhance the customer's perception of quality.

Summary of chapter

The emerging global economy, and the competitive forces inherent in globalization, are changing the nature of competition in the international hotel industry. Because hotel products are easily replicated by various establishments, traditional competitive strategies based on product features have been rendered inappropriate for sustainable long-term growth. Hotel operators have therefore been forced to search for new ways to differentiate themselves from competitors. Hospitality education has traditionally been viewed as a distinct subject area that focuses primarily on the technical aspects of hotel operations—such as knowledge of lodging products, and knowledge of food and beverage skills.

In the present marketplace, the practical value of this approach is limited by competitive forces and by changes in customers' needs, expectations, and perceptions of value. A new managerial perspective that views hospitality firms as service providers—rather than purely as retailers of accommodation and food and beverage products—is an appropriate strategy to cope with these emerging trends. This represents a major shift in the focus of hospitality management—a change in focus that allows managers to form a new basis of competition.

A market-oriented perspective is required, by which competition is based on customer value rather than on the quality of hotel products *per se*. This enables hoteliers to include customers' expectations and perceptions in the design of their own offerings, as well as in the design of various collaborations with other service providers. The aim is to form a strategic network that can provide customers with a total service experience.

Customers benefit by being able to choose from service packages that satisfy their holistic needs rather than being forced to choose on the basis of traditional hotel products that place more emphasis on technical features. From the firm's perspective, this approach opens a new competitive advantage with enormous potential, and offers an opportunity to improve business efficiency, profitability, and long-term growth.

The rest of this book explores these basic issues in further detail. The intelligent application of service management theory is essential to success in the modern competitive marketplace.

Review questions

1. Tourism is among the fastest-growing industries in the world, and is recognized as a leading industry in many countries. What are the factors that have produced such developments?

2. What is the importance of networking in service industries? Why do service firms need to operate in collaboration?

3. Briefly describe the concept of service packaging. Why is it important, and how might hospitality managers manipulate the different elements of a service package to gain a competitive advantage?

Suggested reading for this chapter

This is a list of suggested further reading on topics covered in this chapter. For a separate list of full reference citations quoted in the chapter, see "References," Chapter 1, at the end of the book.

Berry, L., Shostack, G. L., & Upah, G. D. 1983. *Emerging Perspectives on Services Marketing*, American Marketing Association, Chicago.

Fitzsimmons, F. A., & Fitzsimmons, M. J. 1998. *Services Management for Competitive Advantage*, McGraw-Hill, New York.

Kasper, H., van Helsdingen, P., & de Vries, W. (Jr) 1999. *Services Marketing Management, an International Perspective*, John Wiley & Sons, West Sussex, England.

Lovelock, C. H., Patterson, P. G., & Walker, R. H. 1998. *Services Marketing*, Prentice Hall, Sydney, Australia.

Normann, R. 2000. *Service Management*, John Wiley & Sons, West Sussex, England.

Rust, R. T., Zahorik, A. J., & Keiningham, T. L. 1995. *Service Marketing*, HarperCollins, New York.

chapter two
The Nature of Services

Study objectives

Having completed this chapter, readers should be able to:

* ✳ understand the differences between service products and manufactured goods from a marketing perspective;

* ✳ understand the distinctive process of services marketing, and the challenges faced by service managers; and

* ✳ apply these understandings in the context of hospitality management.

The framework of this chapter

This chapter is set out as follows:

* Introduction

* How services differ

  — Intangibility
    What is "intangibility"
    The special importance of intangibility

  — Inseparability of production and consumption
    What is "inseparability"?
    Inseparable during consumption
    Inseparable during production
    Inseparability and marketing
    Inseparability and quality
    Inseparability and "multiple consumption"

  — Heterogeneity
    People are heterogeneous
    Heterogeneity at various levels
    Technology not always helpful
    Heterogeneity not always a bad thing

  — Perishability
    What is "perishability"?
    Supply and demand
    "Ownership" of services

* Management implications

  — General problems and possible solutions

  — Particular problems with intangibility
    Intangibility and the customers' perspective
    Intangibility and the manager's perspective

  — Particular problems with heterogeneity

  — Particular problems with perishability

* Summary of chapter

Introduction

This chapter addresses the nature of services, and compares them with the products of manufacturing industries. Service products differ from physical products in their composition, production process, delivery, and consumption. The management and marketing of services therefore require approaches that are quite different from those traditionally used in the management and marketing of manufactured goods.

These different approaches stem largely from the four distinctive features of services:

* intangibility;

* inseparability (of production and consumption);

* heterogeneity; and

* perishability.

These characteristics lead to different consumer perceptions and behaviors—making it more difficult for service providers to ensure customer satisfaction and to establish a competitive advantage. The distinctive characteristics also present significant challenges in the management of supply and demand, in ensuring consistent service quality, and in achieving operational efficiency.

Services managers must understand and cope with these challenges if they are to compete successfully in the complex service environment. This chapter analyzes the distinctive characteristics of service products, and identifies some of the implications for services managers.

How services differ

Although the differences between products and services have been well established for more than two decades, many services today are still designed, produced, and marketed with little understanding of the true nature of services and the implications for production, consumption, marketing, and management. Even though services are comprised of a package of tangible and intangible components (see Chapter 1), many practitioners and academics continue to address services in a traditional management style—a style that is based, predominantly, on knowledge gained from the goods-manufacturing industry.

Such an approach is inappropriate because the service outcome is intangible in nature. The "product" is essentially an *activity* conducted by people, for people, in the presence of people. Services are thus distinctly different from products in their composition, production process, delivery, and consumption. The management and marketing of services requires a different approach from that of products.

Several writers have detailed the characteristics that distinguish services from products, and the ramifications of these differences for management and marketing (see, e.g., Lovelock & Wright, 1998). Although service industries are quite heterogeneous (including businesses as different as beauty salons, hotels, adventure tours, electrical utilities, and so on), they do have distinctive features in common about which it is possible to generalize. Understanding and applying this knowledge is valuable in every aspect of hospitality management.

Four of the most commonly cited distinctive features of services are:

* intangibility;

* inseparability (of production and consumption);

* heterogeneity; and

* perishability.

Each of these distinctive features is discussed in this chapter.

"Hear, read, mark, learn, and inwardly digest them ..."

Quotations are quotable! People remember and quote the words of others because something has been said in an especially memorable way. The quotation that heads this box is taken from the *Book of Common Prayer* of the Church of England (1662). The words give wise advice on how to take note of, and remember, things that are really important.

"Hear, read, mark, learn, and inwardly digest them ..."

One of the most important themes of this book is that services differ from physical goods in ways that have widespread implications for all aspects of services management. This matter is so fundamental to everything that follows in this book that the four distinctive features of services are highlighted in this box to ensure that readers "hear, read, mark, learn, and inwardly digest them." They must be remembered!

The four distinctive features of services are:

* intangibility;

* inseparability (of production and consumption);

* heterogeneity; and

* perishability.

These four distinctive features of services affect everything in services management.

Intangibility

What is "intangibility?"

Virtually all authors agree that the most distinctive feature of services is their *intangibility* (see, e.g., Shostack, 1977; Walker, 1995; Kasper, van Helsdingen, & de Vries, 1999). That is, most services are *performances* as opposed to objects—they cannot be seen, felt, tasted, or touched as goods can be. Although the effects of services might be felt for some time, the services themselves essentially go out of existence at the very moment that they are rendered.

> ## *Intangibility—the distinctive characteristic of services*
>
> Intangibility is *the* distinctive characteristic of services. Although there are said to be four distinctive characteristics of services (intangibility, inseparability, heterogeneity, and perishability), intangibility is *the* critical difference between services and physical goods. This intangibility is the factor from which all other differences between goods and services emerge (Bateson, 1979, 1992).

A service is the result of a deed, a performance, an effort, or an encounter in time. Services cannot be displayed, physically demonstrated, or illustrated. Services therefore have few of the characteristics technically described as "search" qualities, "experience" qualities, and "credence" qualities—that is, unlike manufactured goods, services cannot be physically examined ("search" qualities), checked ("experience" qualities), or tested ("credence" qualities).

The special importance of intangibility

Shostack (1977) highlighted the special importance of *intangibility* as a distinctive characteristic of services, even when the rendering of the service involves some physical goods. Although such services are accompanied by physical objects, these objects cannot be categorized as true product elements.

Tangibility exists along a continuum, and all products exhibit some tangible and intangible qualities (see Figure 2.1 and Figure 2.2). For example, in the case of a taxi service, the intangible service (the journey to a desired destination) obviously involves a necessary physical object (the taxi cab itself). But the service remains the primary product offering. Similarly, the services offered at a restaurant involve the combined effect of numerous intangible activities—including the acquisition of supplies, the preparation

Figure 2.1 *Tangible and intangible elements in hotel service*

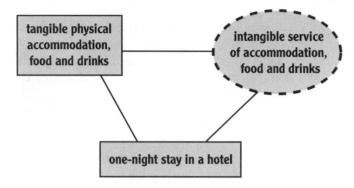

Author's presentation

Figure 2.2 *Continuum of tangibility and intangibility*

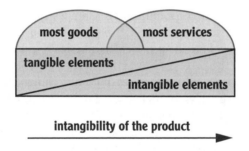

Adapted from Rushton & Carson (1985)

of meals, and the serving of those meals. The tangible components behind all this—the building, the interior decor, the kitchen equipment, the food items, and so on are obviously necessary for the service. However, the intangible service activities make up the key product offering.

Thus, although there are said to be four distinctive characteristics of services, intangibility is *the* critical difference between services and physical goods. This intangibility is the factor from which all other differences between goods and services emerge (Bateson, 1979, 1992).

Inseparability of production and consumption

What is "inseparability?"

The inseparability of production and consumption refers to the fact that most services are characterized by simultaneous production and consumption (Kurtz & Clow, 1998). Goods and services are quite different in this respect. Typically goods are first produced, then sold, and then consumed. In contrast, a typical service is first sold, and then produced and consumed simultaneously.

Inseparable during consumption

Simultaneous production and consumption means that the service provider is often physically present when consumption occurs. A hotel receptionist has to be present before a guest is able to check in; a barman has to prepare and serve drinks for guests at the bar; a dentist is present when examining a patient; an airline steward is present when serving an in-flight meal; and so on. In contrast, a physical good, such as a washing machine, might be manufactured in Germany and consumed in London.

Inseparable during production

Simultaneous production and consumption also implies the presence of the customer during the production of services. A diner is present during restaurant service; a customer is in the chair for a haircut; a patient is physically examined during a medical consultation; and so on.

Inseparability thus forces the buyer into intimate contact with both the process of production and the process of delivery. And, in most cases, there is no time lapse between production and consumption. But service providers are human, and client–provider interaction is spontaneous and simultaneous—whether it is face to face or via a telephone. Control of service output thus becomes a difficult and complex issue.

Inseparability and marketing

As we have seen, the production and consumption of services occur virtually simultaneously. The same could be said of *marketing*. For example, when a receptionist offers assistance to a customer, the information is certainly being consumed at the same time and in the same place as it is being produced. But the service is also being *marketed* at the same time. The receptionist is effectively "selling" the service (convincing the customer of its value) at the very same time as the service is being produced and consumed. The three elements—production, marketing, and consumption—are inseparable.

Produced, then sold, then consumed? Not in services!

Typically goods are first produced, then sold, and then consumed. This seems logical enough. But it doesn't apply to services. A typical service is first sold, and then produced and consumed simultaneously.

The idea of the "inseparability" of services thus changes the way we think about the apparently logical progression from production to sale to consumption.

And it doesn't stop there! The "inseparability" of services also means that traditional ideas of marketing and quality require radical reappraisal. As the service is being delivered to the customer, the product is effectively being marketed, consumed, and judged simultaneously.

The traditionally separate management functions of production, consumption, marketing, and quality are *inseparable* in services.

The presence of both service provider and service customer during the production and consumption of the service critically alters the traditional concepts of production and marketing as they have been applied to goods. In the marketing of goods, great emphasis is placed on distributing goods where and when customers desire them—that is, the key to goods marketing is to get goods to the *right place* at the *right time*. However, in the case of services, the emphasis shifts from attempting to ensure the *right place* and the *right time* to attempting to ensure that services are produced and delivered (i.e., distributed) in the *right way*. A service customer's main concern is not so much about *what* is being offered but *how* it is being offered. The way in which a waiter, a mechanic, a physician, a lawyer, a teacher, a bank teller, and so on *behaves* in the presence of the customer influences decisions on future patronage (Grönroos, 2000). As Schuler (1996:17) observed: "service companies win or lose during the moments of contact ('moments of truth') between employee and customer."

Inseparability also means that the producer and seller are represented in a single entity, and, in the majority of cases, only direct distribution is possible. Typical examples include medical services, education, and training. This feature of services demands highly interactive marketing and production (Grönroos, 2000). In effect, this means that service providers are required to have expertise in two fields simultaneously—production and marketing.

Inseparability and quality

In services that rely on personal contact and interaction between service deliverer and customer, quality is determined by service delivery. Service providers are therefore simultaneously involved in production, marketing, and quality control.

The concept of "inseparability" also has implications for the involvement of the consumer in quality control (Solomon, Surprenant, Czepiel, & Gutman, 1985). Service customers participate in a more or less active fashion, cooperating in the process of production and delivery, and therefore participating in determining the quality of the service received. For example, in medical services, the patient assists the doctor's diagnosis by providing information about symptoms. Similarly in legal services, the client collaborates with the lawyer by providing evidence. A customer in a bank also participates in the service when filling out documentation. In insurance services, completing elaborate questionnaires for policies involves the participation of a customer in the production of services. In a restaurant a customer selects food, napkins, and cutlery according to needs; indeed, a restaurant patron might even partially cook his or her own meal (in the case of a fondue, for example). In all these cases, the input from the recipient of the service is crucial to the quality of the service (Farber, 1997).

The degree of customer involvement varies from service to service. For example, the role played by a customer in an elegant restaurant is very different from that played in a fast-food restaurant. In the fancy restaurant, the customer is deeply involved in determining how the service works out. In a fast-food outlet, the consumer is much more of a passive recipient. In services where customer input is crucial, the customer's involvement effectively dictates the final quality of the service rendered. For example, the description of an incident in a legal case, or the relating of disease symptoms in a medical consultation, have enormous implications for the quality of the final service.

This has implications for the overall question of quality control in services—a subject considered in more detail in Chapter 3. The involvement of customers in the service-production process significantly affects a service firm's managerial control over its own service quality (Parasuraman, Zeithaml, & Berry, 1985).

Inseparability and "multiple consumption"

Finally, in considering the inseparability of production and consumption in many service interfaces, it should be noted that many services are delivered in a setting of "multiple consumption"—that is, the service is consumed by more than one person simultaneously. A typical example is a music concert, in which each member of the audience enjoys the music in the presence of others, but without having to "share" the services with others.

However, although the music is not "shared" (in the sense of any one consumer not receiving all of the "product"), the presence of others *does* influence the perception of the quality of the service. In such cases, the perception of quality is influenced by two types of interaction—the interaction between the customer and the service provider, and the interactions among customers. More will be said about "multiple consumption" later in this chapter.

Heterogeneity

People are heterogeneous

Service industries differ in the extent to which they are "people-based" or "technology-based." There is a larger human component involved in performing some services (e.g., restaurant meals) than there is in others (e.g., telecommunication services). The outcomes of people-based service operations tend to be more heterogeneous (i.e., more variable) than the outcomes of technology-based operations. Standardized and uniform outcomes are more difficult to ensure.

Heterogeneity in service delivery poses a major problem for management in labor-intensive services because there is potential for significant variability in the performance of services. Numerous employees are in contact with any one individual customer, thus raising the problem of inconsistency of behavior (Kandampully, 1997).

"... delivered by people to people"

The problems posed by heterogeneity in services were well expressed by Knisely (1979:47):

> In a service business, you're dealing with something that is primarily delivered by people to people. Your people are as much of your product in the consumer's mind as any other attribute of that service. People's performance day in and day out fluctuates up and down. Therefore, the level of consistency that you can count on and try to communicate to the consumer is not a certain thing.

Services and people are inextricably linked. There's no getting away from it! Heterogeneity is a fact of life in services management.

Heterogeneity at various levels

This variability of service performance occurs at various levels:

* the quality of service performance varies from one service organization to another;

* the quality of service performance varies from one service performer to another; and

* the quality of service performance varies for the same performer on different occasions.

For these reasons, what the firm has promised to deliver might be quite different from that actually received by the service customer. The "bottom line" is that uniformity of service delivery is difficult to ensure because there is no guarantee of consistent behavior from service persons (Hartline & Ferrell, 1996).

Technology not always helpful

Although heterogeneity is essentially a "people problem," the advent of increased technology does not necessarily improve matters. If a service firm attempts to decrease heterogeneity by replacing people with technology, the firm might inadvertently introduce yet another form of heterogeneity in its service delivery. That is, customers might perceive a significant difference between a firm's "new" services (as delivered via technology) and its "traditional" services (as delivered by persons). In this way, the advent of information technology has, in fact, increased the potential for heterogeneity.

For example, the variation between interaction conducted face-to-face ("high-touch") and interaction via the Internet ("high-tech") can be significant, and service companies that use the Internet extensively must be aware of this when using this medium. This has implications for customers' perceptions of the firm's quality and image.

This sort of problem is a common complaint from customers in such service industries as banking. Technology might offer the possibility of reducing variability among different service personnel (because every customer receives the same treatment from an impersonal machine), but customers might be more concerned about the much starker difference between dealing with a machine and dealing with a person. The introduction of technology might "fix" heterogeneity at one level, but exacerbate it at another level. This is summed up in the common complaint: "I don't like talking to a machine! I want to talk to a *real* person!"

Heterogeneity not always a bad thing

Having observed that heterogeneity is all but inevitable in services delivery, it must also be noted that heterogeneity in services is not always a bad thing. As noted above, some customers prefer services from persons (even if variable) to services from machines (even if more uniform).

In a similar way, variation can be beneficial in the case of specially customized services. In these cases, variability (at least from customer to customer) is an accepted part of good service (McLaughlin, 1996).

In addition, heterogeneity exists when customers form personal relationships with particular members of staff. Although there are potential problems in this (if staff members start "playing favorites" to the disadvantage of others), well-trained staff members should be able to utilize this form of heterogeneity to the advantage of the firm. Customers who receive "special" treatment feel wanted as individuals. This sort of "heterogeneity" is no bad thing.

Management usually strives for uniformity of service, and therefore usually strives to eliminate heterogeneity. But this is not always a desirable outcome for all customers in all situations.

Perishability

What is "perishability"?

Perishability is a distinctive characteristic of most services, and is closely related to intangibility. Perishability means that services cannot be stored, and are therefore produced only when needed by the customer. Service production is thus dictated by demand at any given time.

Within the hospitality industry, good examples of perishable items are a room in a hotel or a seat in a restaurant. If not used at the time, the opportunity for sale is lost. Similarly, if an aircraft takes off without its seats being filled, the revenue from the empty seats constitutes a nonrecoverable loss (Kandampully, 2000). Even if all subsequent flights are full due to a sudden surge in demand, lost revenue from the previous flight can never be recovered. In general, capacity not profitably utilized in service production represents a nonrecoverable loss.

Supply and demand

Unlike most goods, services are highly perishable and cannot be stored for future sale. Demand thus plays an especially significant role in the production and delivery of services.

A car producer who is unable to sell a company's total output during one period of sale can carry the stock forward to sell during a subsequent period. A service supplier does not have that "luxury." In contrast to manufactured goods, services must be produced at the exact time and place demanded by the customer. For example, food is needed when the customer is hungry. The fact that food was available in the restaurant a few hours previously is of no consolation to a hungry customer now. Similarly, a fireman is required when there is a fire—not at any other time. Immediate access is thus crucial in most service businesses.

The perishability of services does not pose a problem when demand is steady. In such circumstances, it is relatively easy to predict requirements and arrange for the services to be adequately staffed. But when demand fluctuates, service firms encounter problems. The breakfast rush in a hotel restaurant is an example of fluctuation in demand on a daily basis. The high seasonality of some resorts is an example of fluctuation over a longer time period. Some of these fluctuations are relatively predictable. Others are more difficult to manage.

The perishability of services, and the meeting of supply and demand, is a significant problem for service managers. (For further discussion on this issue, see "Capacity Management versus Demand Management," Chapter 7.)

Perishability, ownership, and control

Perishability of services is a distinctive characteristic closely related to intangibility. Unlike physical goods, services cannot be "possessed." They cannot be stored, taken away, or used at a later time. Services "disappear" as quickly as they are delivered.

Perishability thus forces services managers to reappraise the ideas of *ownership* and *control* of their products. This sort of reappraisal has significant implications for two fundamental management tasks:

* the management of supply and demand; and

* the management of patents, rights, and risks.

It is difficult to own and control products that "disappear" as quickly as they are delivered.

"Ownership" of services

The perishability and intangibility of services renders "ownership" impossible—by either the producer or the customer. Essentially, there is no "ownership" of services.

When purchasing physical goods, buyers acquire a title to the goods. However, when a service is performed, there is no corresponding transfer of ownership. Buyers of services are buying only the *right to a service*—and then only at a designated time. Consumers do not buy the service itself to take away and use as they see fit at a time of their choosing. For example, a dinner ticket for a New Year's gala function, a theater ticket for a particular performance, or an appointment for a specified portion of an accountant's time are all instances of the consumer securing the right to enjoy a service at a designated time. The consumer never "owns" the service in any real sense.

The fact that perishability and intangibility prevent "ownership" in any meaningful sense has implications for both suppliers and customers.

For suppliers, there is a problem with patenting. Services cannot be "owned" and patented in the way that physical goods can be, and there is always a possibility that services can be copied by competitors.

For consumers, the lack of "ownership" increases the perception of "risk" in purchasing services. At the end of the transaction, the consumer does not actually "possess" anything. In marketing services, managers must be aware of this heightened perception of risk among their customers.

"This is Lord Melberry's table"

In the British television comedy classic *Fawlty Towers,* the madcap hotelier Basil Fawlty (played by John Cleese), believes that a new guest, whom he has never seen before, is a Lord of the Realm. In his frantic attempts to impress "Lord Melberry," Basil rudely shifts guests who are already comfortably seated at a desirable table with a window view.

"This is Lord Melberry's table," asserts Basil untruthfully, going on to "explain" that Lord Melberry "always" sits at this table "whenever" he visits the hotel. The guests who are shifted are, understandably, not impressed! They thought that the table was, at least for the time being, "their table," not "Lord Melberry's table"!

In fact, it turns out that the so-called "Lord Melberry" is a "con-man" imposter who is in town attempting to conduct a scam on various citizens, including stealing some cash and a coin collection from Basil himself. Basil is extremely embarrassed and angry when he discovers that "Lord Melberry" has fooled him.

For our purposes, the interesting aspect of the story is the supposed "ownership" of the table. The guests who were already seated thought that it was "their table." Basil stated that it was "Lord Melberry's table," In fact, neither of these was true. All along, it was, and remained, "Basil's table." And anyway, the table was never the product on offer. Guests do not actually "own" a table in any meaningful sense when they sit at it for a restaurant meal. They are purchasing the service (and the food of course). The service and the food are both perishable, and promptly disappear. The guests do not gain ownership or title of any physical object (such as the table)—at least not in the sense that they are entitled to call it their own, lift it up, and take it away to use as they wish. It is not "theirs" in any real sense.

The perishability and intangibility of services makes "ownership" impossible. Essentially, there is no "ownership" of services.

Management implications

The general characteristics of services (as compared with manufactured goods), present many challenges to managers of service companies. Some of these challenges have been mentioned above. Let us now examine these in more detail.

General problems and possible solutions

The distinctive differences between services and products—intangibility, inseparability, heterogeneity, and perishability—pose challenges for service managers. Table 2.1 summarizes some of these challenges, and lists some possible solutions.

Table 2.1 *Management Implications of Distinctive Characteristics of Services*

Distinctive characteristics of services	Implications for management	Possible means to manage the effects
Intangibility	Difficult to calculate the cost or price	Focus on benefits
	No patents possible	Increase tangibility of services (e.g., physical representations of the service)
	Sampling difficult; not easy to promote	Use of brand names
	Customer has access to service but has no owner-ship of activity or facility	Use personalities to personalize services
Inseparability	Requires the presence of the producer	Train more competent service providers
	Most services depend on direct sale	Learn to work in large groups
	Limited scale of operation at one location by one server	Work faster
Heterogeneity	Standard of service is dependent on the service provider, the time of the day, and the day of the week	Careful personnel selection and training
	Consistent quality of service is difficult to manage	Ensure standards are monitored; prepackage service; mechanize part of the services; quality control
Perishability	Cannot be stored	Match supply and demand
	Service volume is dependent on demand	Manage demand as opposed to managing supply
	Demand fluctuates	Unbundle back-office operations

Author's presentation

Some of the more important problems and solutions are explored in greater detail in the rest of this chapter.

Particular problems with intangibility

Intangibility and the customers' perspective

From the customers' perspective, the intangibility of services is an especially significant problem, and managers must be sensitive to this. Intangibility means that:

* customers have difficulty in discriminating between one service offering and another;

* customers perceive the service purchase as involving high levels of risk;

* customers seek personal information regarding the reliability of service; and

* customers have difficulty assessing the quality of service before consumption— meaning that assessment is frequently price-based.

Each of these is discussed below.

Difficulty in discriminating between one service offering and another

Because customers have difficulty in discriminating between one service offering and another, management needs to develop a means of offering "cues" with which customers are able to associate the additional benefits. This does not alleviate all problems associated with intangibility, but it does provide reinforcement of the organization's commitment to fulfilling the needs of the customer.

This approach can be effectively communicated to the customer using various types of package deals. For example, a hotel can offer special packages to a business traveller inclusive of air travel, taxi service, and secretarial services. These recognizable benefits assist the customer to evaluate the service benefit before consumption, thus providing a means of assessing the service on the basis of individual need.

Perceiving the service purchase as involving high levels of risk

Reducing the customer's perceived risk is the most effective way in which an organization can market its services. This is particularly pertinent in the case of new services, or if customers are availing themselves of an organization's services for the first time. Research has shown that explicit service guarantees reduce the perceived risk. Although this is not a common practice in the service industry as a whole, it is rapidly being adopted by many leading service organizations. For more on this subject, see "Service Guarantees," Chapter 8.

Detailed information about the service and the benefits that customers are entitled to receive also reduces the perceived risk. Those responsible for advertising information (in all its forms) should bear this in mind. Customers are able to foresee and evaluate the service outcome by referring to such information. They also do this by recalling their previous experiences of a similar nature.

Reassuring, not just alluring

Hospitality service providers must be aware that advertising certain "promises" and "guarantees" is not just about attracting attention to themselves or alluring potential customers to the service. Because services are intangible, customers have a greater perception of risk than they experience when buying tangible goods. Advertising and promotions should be designed with this in mind. Advertised "promises" and "guarantees" should aim to minimize customer perceptions of risk. For example, in making guarantees of food quality or promises of superior room facilities, the advertiser should realize that customers want genuine reassurance regarding what they will get. They do not want empty promises that are merely designed to attract attention and allure people to the service.

Service industries must do more than attract attention to themselves. They must design their guarantees and promotions with the express intention of providing reassurance and reducing perceptions of risk. The distinctive intangible nature of services demands this extra dimension to services marketing.

Seeking personal information regarding the reliability of service

Because services are intangible experiences that cannot be picked up and taken away for examination by consumers, word-of-mouth recommendation among consumers is necessarily one of the most common means of comparing and judging services. The fact that potential customers rely on word-of-mouth opinion more than any other form of marketing message means that this form of "advertising" must be acknowledged and addressed as a significant management tool.

Service managers thus need to design systems and approaches to enhance word-of-mouth advertising by customers who have already used the services. Offering incentive sales to existing customers is a useful means of enhancing word-of-mouth recommendation. For example, a holiday resort might offer accommodation for a free second holiday to customers able to recommend and substantiate five further bookings. Moreover, the recommended guests might receive a 10% discount on their accommodation bill. Similar systems, in varying combinations, are very successfully used by many service organizations.

Assessing the quality of service before consumption

In goods manufacturing, price is often used by marketers as a guide to the quality that consumers might expect. Cheaper goods indicate poorer quality and more expensive goods indicate better quality. There is a simple correspondence between the two variables, and this is recognized and understood by consumers.

However, in the case of services, the situation is more complex. It is a well-accepted truism in marketing circles that service organizations possess limited opportunities to compete on the basis of price variability. This is because services, to a large extent, are personally offered. A service professional cannot easily offer services at a cheaper price and hope to make up the difference by selling more services. There is a limit to the number of personal services that can competently be provided per hour or per day. Service organizations, unlike goods producers, are therefore restricted in their ability to reduce price by selling a greater volume—so-called "economy of scale."

In addition, using price to differentiate the quality of service might not be appropriate in every case. For example, in educational services, expensive school or university fees might not necessarily produce a high student evaluation of the experience (process) undertaken. Rather, the evaluation of quality is intensely personal, and depends less on price and more on the student's needs, expectations, and perceptions, together with an assessment of the numerous service providers (teachers) with whom the student interacts. Similar comments apply to hotel services. Quality is a personal experience.

In services, therefore, price is not an especially useful guide to expected quality. As noted above, previous experience of the service and word of mouth are much more important. Customers' personal assessments become paramount.

Service managers thus have the difficult challenge of trying to control not only the quality of service offered but also the *customers' assessments* of that quality. Service managers cannot claim that the service quality was good if the customer does not think it was good. Controlling both the quality of service *and* the customer's assessment of quality is difficult to manage. The focus should therefore extend beyond the quality of service offered to encompass the enhancement of value of the final result as perceived by the customer. Value can be added through many facets of the service that are more controllable than quality alone. The little "touches" that enhance satisfaction (a complimentary gift or an extra personal service) become especially important in marketing an intangible "good."

Intangibility and the manager's perspective

Just as the intangibility of services can be an especially significant problem from the customers' perspective, intangibility also poses special problems from a management perspective. For the manager, intangibility means that:

* in many services, customers take an active role in the production process and, essentially co-produce the service;

* other customers co-consume the services and affect the perceived outcome; and

* the service must be provided at specified locations.

Each of these is discussed on the next page.

Customers taking an active role in the production process

The fact that consumers take an active role in the service-production process is an excellent opportunity for staff members to develop personal relationships with their customers. Systems can be devised, and service personnel can be trained, with a view to providing customers with opportunities to make immediate changes or requests—thereby enhancing the perceived quality of service.

The active involvement of customers enables management to ascertain those aspects of the service with which customers are satisfied or unhappy, and allows management to involve the customers in the co-production and modification of the production process in an appropriate fashion. Staff members must be alert to feedback, and must be trained to encourage and invite such feedback—including complaints. The idea of *encouraging* complaints might seem strange, but it is a logical implication of the fact that customers play an active part in the production process. If they are involved, they must be constructively involved.

Other customers co-consuming and affecting the perceived outcome

Management has to make every effort to plan both the production process and the "multiple-consumption" stage (see earlier in this chapter) if the desired effect is to be achieved.

Consider, for example, how a hotel might manage this aspect of service consumption in its nightclub, as compared with its formal restaurant. In the nightclub situation, the services should be designed and offered in a way that facilitates customer-to-customer interaction and generates a lively, crowded atmosphere. It is this atmosphere that, from a customer's perspective, actually constitutes the service. In contrast, in a formal restaurant, the emphasis is on balancing one customer's need for social interaction with another's need for privacy.

Co-consumption is not a neutral phenomenon. It is not something to be tolerated or ignored. It has enormous capacity to influence customer perceptions, and it must be managed effectively and creatively to the advantage of the service firm.

Providing the service at specified locations

Many types of services (such as a restaurant meal) can be received by a customer only at a specific location. This effectively limits the number of customers served at a specific time. The limit is the capacity of the restaurant. However, management might be able to offer selective components of the service away from the main location—such as take-out food from a specific outlet. Similarly, a hotel or restaurant might offer a dinner banquet at a customer's preferred location. In this case, the food is prepared at the hotel or restaurant, but the service is provided at another location.

The service-delivery system can thus be designed in a way that allows numerous services to be offered, at least in part, at different locations.

Particular problems with heterogeneity

Two management problems particularly associated with heterogeneity are:

✳ customers experience the same service differently, according to the time, day, and service producer; and

✳ variability can pose problems in maintaining brand standards at different service locations.

Each of these is discussed below.

Variability according to the time, day, and service producer

In a service business, many employees are required to perform similar services in a similar manner. For example, receptionists at a hotel are expected to conduct their service in a broadly similar style. However, customers commonly perceive differences in the services provided by different employees.

Management needs to establish training that facilitates consistency in the service offering and that supports the delivery process. In addition to such specific training of employees, service procedures and systems can be streamlined to reduce variability in task performance.

However, in some situations, variability can present opportunities for personalized service. This is particularly pertinent in professional services where professionals from different disciplines are involved to meet a customer's various needs. In these cases, variability constitutes an asset to the organization.

Variability in brand standards at different locations

In large service organizations in which services are offered from a number of outlets, maintaining a comparable service at all outlets is an ongoing management concern. The delivery of services is so dependent on individual personalities and attitudes that consistency in service interactions at different sites is extremely difficult to maintain.

Creating a company-wide culture to maintain standards has been successfully adopted by many leading service organizations; examples include Marriott, Hyatt, and Ritz-Carlton. This requires a carefully constructed company policy by which all staff members are not only aware of the "customer-centric" philosophy of the firm, but also trained and empowered to implement it. (For more on empowerment, see "Empowerment" Chapter 8.)

Particular problems with perishability

The Perishability of services is one of the most obvious management concerns. The problem with perishability is not an inability to offer the service at all, but an inability to offer the service when required by the customer. The problem is essentially the inability to store services and offer them when needed.

Because services cannot be stored, the focus must be on managing demand—as opposed to managing supply. In fact, the successful management of demand must be the guiding principle in the design of any system or process in the service industry.

Strategies that can be utilized to manage demand fluctuations are discussed further in "Managing and Marketing Service Demand" Chapter 7.

Summary of chapter

From a services marketing perspective, the main objective of hospitality management is to provide guests with a *superior service experience*. It is thus imperative that hotel managers understand the nature of their service offerings and be able to ensure customer satisfaction with the services rather than with the *technical features* of various hotel products.

The four basic differences between service products and manufactured goods—intangibility, inseparability, heterogeneity, and perishability—are well established in the literature. The four characteristics are well described, but the *ramifications* of these characteristics have not been as well explored. The fact is that the management and marketing of service products have been significantly influenced by theories from the manufacturing sector and/or by the intuitive judgments of individual service managers. This is really not good enough. Theory from the manufactured goods sector is inappropriate for services marketing, and a reliance on such theory can significantly decrease customer satisfaction with a firm's services, and thereby affect that firm's overall business performance.

The ramifications of the distinctive characteristics of service products present significant challenges to service firms. However, service providers who can meet these challenges will significantly improve customer satisfaction, maintain the firm's competitive advantage, and lift its overall profit performance.

It is therefore important that hospitality managers understand these distinctive characteristics of services, and the implications that flow from them—not only from a managerial perspective but also from the customers' point of view.

Managers must be able to design and implement appropriate strategies to overcome the challenges and thus maximize the potential for competitive advantage.

Review questions

1. Briefly describe the four distinctive characteristics of services.

2. Briefly describe the managerial implications of each of the characteristics described above.

3. Based on the four unique characteristics of services compare the hospitality industry with other service sectors (e.g., airlines, health services, etc.). Can you think of any special features that characterize the hotel business that are not found in other service businesses? For example, whereas airlines can adjust their schedules, allocate their aircraft to other routes, and hire additional aircraft in response to demand, hotels cannot change their locations or rent additional rooms to meet seasonal demand. As a result hotels generally have less flexibility than airlines in managing their capacity, which makes it more difficult for hotel managers to adjust their supply according to the demand. Can you think of other special features affecting the hotel industry?

Suggested reading for this chapter

This is a list of suggested further reading on topics covered in this chapter. For a separate list of full reference citations quoted in the chapter, see "References," Chapter 2, at the end of the book.

Grönroos, C. 1982. *Strategic Management and Marketing in the Service Sector*, Chartwellbrat Ltd., England.

Kandampully, J., Mok, C., & Sparks, B. 2001. *Service Quality Management in Hospitality, Tourism and Leisure*, Haworth Press, New York.

Palmer, A., & Cole, C. 1995. *Services Marketing: Principles and Practice*, Prentice Hall, Upper Saddle River, New Jersey.

Zeithaml, V. A., & Bitner, M. 2000. *Services Marketing*, McGraw-Hill, New York.

Part II

Services of Quality

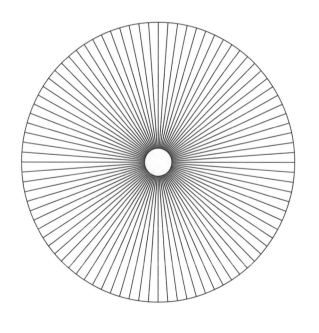

chapter three

Quality — the Core Service

Study objectives

Having completed this chapter, readers should be able to:

∗ understand the basic concepts of quality management;

∗ understand the need for, and challenges of, quality measurement and management in service industries; and

∗ have a thorough understanding of the various service quality models and their application in the hotel industry.

The framework of this chapter

This chapter is set out as follows:

✳ Introduction

✳ A historic perspective on quality

  − From shoddy mimicry to quality leadership
  − The early days of quality control
  − Postwar developments
  − Different ideas and different terminology
  − Total quality control, quality assurance, and "zero defects"

✳ Economic impact of quality

  − Product differentiation and competitive advantage
  − Market share and profitability
  − Overall corporate performance

✳ The cost of quality

  − Is it worth it?
  − Prevention is better than cure

✳ The quality "qurus"

  − W. Edwards Deming (1900–1993)
  − Joseph M. Juran (1904–)
  − Philip Crosby (1926–2001)

✳ The core ideas of TQM

✳ The special case of service quality

  − Lacking a philosophy of service quality
  − But services are different
  − Looking to the consumer

✳ Understanding service quality theory

  − Intangible and personal
  − Comparing expectations and performance
    Choosing a service
    Confirmation and disconfirmation of expectations
    Expectations–what *will* happen or what *should* happen?
    Expectations–what causes them?
    Meeting or exceeding expectations

✳ Service-quality concepts

– No easy task
– Grönroos: technical quality and functional quality
– The effect of multiple consumption
– Instrumental performance and expressive performance
– Lehtinen's process quality and output quality
Process quality
Output quality
Two types of output
Service production process
– Service quality gap
– The five-factor american model
– Rust and Oliver's three-dimensional model
– Multilevel models

✳ Summary of chapter

Introduction

In all industries, quality has long been recognized as essential to business survival. This chapter begins with an outline of the history and development of quality management and the contribution of quality "gurus" to the formation and promotion of quality-control principles.

Although these general principles of quality management in the manufacturing industry do have relevance to service industries, it must be recognized that services are characterized by distinctive features not found in manufactured products (see Chapter 2). Service quality is therefore not the same as product quality, and the management of service quality is not the same as the management of goods quality.

Service quality is difficult to define and difficult to control, and various measures of service quality have been proposed. However, in the final analysis, the *expectations and perceptions of customers* are what matters in any assessment of service quality. Ultimately, the needs and expectations of customers guide the design of quality strategies in services.

As service academics have recognized a need to define service quality accurately, and as service practitioners have felt the need to manage it effectively with a view to a sustainable competitive advantage, various ways of defining and measuring service quality have been introduced. This chapter presents some of the most significant quality-management theories in services marketing, together with their implications for hospitality managers.

A historic perspective on quality

From shoddy mimicry to quality leadership

In the early decades after World War II, Japan's 5,000-year-old society produced goods that had an international reputation for shoddy mimicry. Today, however, things have changed, and goods from Japan have a well-deserved reputation for delighting the customer with excellence. The workers who produce them are among the highest-paid workers in the world, and their managers are the most efficient in the world. Despite some difficulties in the general Japanese economy in recent times, this hard-won reputation for quality excellence is undiminished.

What has made this difference to Japanese goods in the past 30 years or so? The answer is *quality*—or, more specifically, the elevation of *quality management* to being a matter of the highest priority. Japan faced up to its industrial shortcomings and committed itself to the production of quality goods (Porter, Takeuchi, & Sakakibara, 2000).

In July 1950, the Union of Japanese Scientists and Engineers (JUSE) invited an American statistician and government consultant, Dr. W. Edwards Deming, to Japan. Deming held a series of lectures during which he taught the basic principles of statistical quality control to Japanese executives, managers, and engineers. His teachings made a deep impression and provided great impetus to the implementation of quality control in Japan. In appreciation, JUSE created a prize in 1950 to commemorate Deming's contribution, and to promote the continued development of quality control in Japan. Annual awards of the Deming Prize are still given each year (Deming Institute, 2002).

More than five decades following the award of the first Deming Prize in Japan, the concept of quality management has become the recognized guiding strategy for almost all firms around the world. Quality ultimately gives firms a competitive advantage and customer acceptance. This emphasis has been felt across all lines of business, whether profit making or nonprofit making, including the public services.

The early days of quality control

Quality control was first developed in manufacturing by engineers and statisticians during the 1920s, with control focusing on the physical production of goods and internal measurements of the production processes. Quality control was originally seen as a means of ensuring consistency among the parts produced by different sections of a single company, so that parts could be interchanged with confidence. At first this was achieved by inspecting 100% of all outputs. In those days it was relatively common for engineers to design the products, for manufacturing people to build them, and for quality personnel to inspect them as they came off the line. If a problem existed, manufacturing was expected to correct it.

A breakthrough occurred with the introduction of the concept of *statistical* quality control—the idea that only a random sample of output warranted inspection to ensure an acceptable quality level. Modern quality control began in the 1930s when Walter Shewhart, a physicist employed at Bell Labs, invented *process control,* using control charts and the "Plan–Do–Check–Act" cycle of continuous improvement. During arms manufacturing in World War II, American industry used a combination of Shewhart's process control and the statistical sampling methods of Deming, who had become an early disciple of Shewhart. The combination became known as *statistical process control.*

Postwar developments

In 1951, another significant development in the story of quality management came with the publication of the first edition of Joseph Juran's *Quality Control Handbook*—a publication that became the 'bible' of the quality-control movement. Also in 1951, Armand V. Feigenbaum took Juran's ideas a step further by proposing a concept of "total quality control" (TQC). Feigenbaum's ideas were based on his observation that all new products moved through three stages of activity—design control, incoming material control, and product (or shop floor) control—and that TQC required quality control at all stages.

While these new concepts were slowly gaining acceptance in Western countries, crucial changes were taking place in Japan following World War II. These changes resulted in Japan playing a vital role in the historic development of the quality movement. At the end of World War II, Japan's economic recovery was dependent on its only plentiful resource—people—and on their ability to export manufactured goods produced from imported raw materials and energy. Japan's likelihood of success at that time seemed remote. It had a largely unskilled and illiterate labor force and its industries had been devastated by war. This was exacerbated by the policy of the occupying forces under General Douglas MacArthur, who removed all prewar managers over 40 years of age from positions of authority, replacing them with younger men. At that time, Japan had a universal reputation as a producer of cheap and unreliable goods.

As noted previously, Deming was invited to Japan in 1950 to hold a series of lectures and seminars. This was followed by a meeting with the presidents of 21 major Japanese companies, including the present-day world giants Sony, Nissan, Mitsubishi, and Toyota. Much of the credit goes to General MacArthur, who initiated the invitation to Deming.

Different ideas and different terminology

A confusing array of terms and acronyms has developed to describe various aspects of the general idea of quality control. It is believed that this confusion of phrases started when the Japanese adopted statistical process control in the early 1950s as a result of Deming's teachings. The translation of terms from English to Japanese, and back again, produced shades of meaning and variations in usage. But these variations actually reflected a real difference in philosophy and attitude.

In the Japanese language, the word "control" has a similar connotation to that of the word "management" in English—that is a more general concept of "overseeing" rather than a more narrow idea of "checking." Consequently, the Japanese definition of "quality control" was far removed from the traditional Western interpretation. The Japanese understanding was more akin to a general management philosophy, whereas the Western idea had a more narrow emphasis on "inspection."

The Japanese idea of "control" as a management philosophy was markedly pervasive in Japanese culture. Indeed, by 1954, "quality control" had gone beyond being a major theme in Japanese management thinking to have become a national preoccupation exalted in the time-honored Japanese fashion with slogans and festivals that celebrated November as "National Quality Month."

Total quality control, quality assurance, and "zero defects"

Thus, although quality "control" was not invented in Japan, its seeds fell on fertile ground in that country. In 1956 a Japanese team of quality experts visited the U.S. and discovered Feigenbaum's concept of total quality control (TQC). As noted previously, Feigenbaum believed that quality efforts should be implemented in *all* areas of a company, not just in its manufacturing plants. This struck a chord with the Japanese, many of whom already had company-wide quality programs, and they were quick to adopt the term "TQC."

In 1958, another team of Japanese businessmen visited the U.S. and encountered yet another "quality" term—"quality assurance" (QA). This term was used by Bell Labs, where employees worked in groups to: (1) determine quality standards; (2) establish proper production procedures; (3) measure conformance to standards; and (4) establish procedures for handling defects. However, the Japanese considered these activities to be less extensive than their own programs of total quality control, and they adopted neither the term "QA" nor the method, although many U.S. firms adopted it.

Noting the discrepancies among the terms and the methods used in the United States and those adopted in Japan, Joseph Juran, Deming's peer, recommended at the first worldwide Quality Conference in 1969 that the all-encompassing concept of "TQC" be renamed "company-wide quality control" (CWQC). This new phrase, and the concept behind it, received fairly wide acceptance in Japan, although many firms have stuck with TQC.

In the late 1970s and early 1980s, another American quality "guru," Philip Crosby, through his book *Quality is Free,* proposed a controversial program called "zero defects" (Crosby, 1979, 1984). No other program defined quality as stringently as this—a total absence of failure! Crosby had a major impact on general management in the early 1980s, both in attracting attention to quality and in influencing management executives to commit themselves to quality.

As a result of these and other developments, total quality management, as a management system and philosophy, has gained acceptance all over the world, and it is now widely practiced in both the manufacturing and service environments.

Economic impact of quality

Product differentiation and competitive advantage

Conventional theory recognizes two generic strategic alternatives for developing a sustainable competitive advantage. The first is *product differentiation,* and the second is *overall cost leadership* (Porter, 1985). Quality control is a crucial element of the first of these.

Although product differentiation can take many forms, superior quality is the most common basis of differentiation (Kiechel, 1981; Crosby, 1979, 1984; Deming, 1982). If customers see a clearcut quality advantage, they usually favor that product, without trying to weigh all other factors. Quality rules.

During the past 30 years or so, this preoccupation of customers with quality has become increasingly recognized, and quality has become the key to gaining competitive advantage. Firms today know that they cannot afford to ignore quality; it has become essential to their survival. The so-called "Far-Eastern Machine" (i.e., Japanese firms in the first instance, and other East Asian countries later) have set the challenge and standard for European and other Western manufacturing industries. Japanese domination of the market in the second half of the 20th century, through the manufacture of exceptional quality products, has had a significant effect on the balance of payments in Western Europe and the U.S. It has became crucial, therefore, for manufacturers to lift competitiveness in Europe and North America to meet the quality of the reliable products offered by Japanese competitors.

This became even more apparent with the rapid development of so-called "globalization." In a competitive global market, with its fragmented and deregulated markets, it soon became apparent to management that companies could not survive without quality. Profitability depended on it.

Market share and profitability

This apparent link between quality and profitability was subsequently confirmed by numerous careful studies (see, e.g., Peters & Waterman, 1982). Quality soon became established as the means by which firms sustained their position among competing firms over time, and the means by which they therefore maintained market and profit share. In particular, the profits of Japanese firms surged in the postwar period as Japanese products (such as cars, motorcycles, watches, cameras, and electronics of every description) earned a reputation for unmatched quality and reliability at competitive prices.

Studies conducted by Garvin (1984) confirmed the apparent strong positive association between quality and market share. Similarly, subsequent studies of profit impact of market share (PIMS) indicated that improved quality increased the market share of firms five or six times faster than those that declined in quality (Buzzell & Gale, 1987; Kordupleski, Rust, & Zahorik, 1993). The link between quality of product (or service) and market share was confirmed in subsequent studies by Gale (1992) and Zeithaml (2000), who also found a positive association between quality and profitability.

It had therefore become established that quality improved market share, and that this then translated into overall company profitability. This was confirmed by research using the American Customer Satisfaction Index (ACSI; Ittner & Larcker, 1996). This clearly showed a positive correlation between customer variables (satisfaction, repurchase intention, perceived quality, perceived value, and loyalty) and financial output.

Overall corporate performance

The proven significance of quality had thus moved from apparent competitive advantage, to increased market share, to improved profitability. Easton and Jarrell (1998) completed the picture when they demonstrated that good quality not only increased profit, market share, and competitive advantage, but also improved overall corporate performance in virtually every aspect of company activity.

The pursuit of quality had thus become a total corporate philosophy—a concept far removed from the original idea of checking for faulty goods at the end of an assembly line!

Today, very few products and services exist as a monopoly. Firms and countries have realized that protecting market share through patents and other restrictions can seldom hold back competition. In this evolving global market, there is only one effective competitive weapon available to an organization that wishes to distinguish its products or services from its competitors. That weapon is quality. The strategy for deploying the weapon in the marketplace involves the pursuit of quality in every aspect of corporate life.

The cost of quality

Is it worth it?

The concept of the "cost of quality" is a relatively new phenomenon in the business world. Quality costs. It costs money to achieve quality. But, more significantly, it costs money *not* to achieve quality.

The cost of poor quality is well recognized (see, e.g., Early, 1991). Grönroos (1991) noted that it is not too much quality that really costs, but too much low quality—a point that had been made earlier by the "guru" Crosby (1979) who coined the startling phrase "quality is free" to emphasize the general point that the presence of poor quality is the real drain on resources, rather than the costs of attempting to fix the lack of quality. For example, a study of Chrysler in 1988 found that every fourth worker at Chrysler was an unnecessary cost because the only thing done by that worker was correction of mistakes made by others (Iacocca, 1988).

Indeed, according to the literature on operations management, quality and costs have been proven to be inversely related. That is, quality saves more than it costs. Or, to put it another way, the costs of improving quality are less than the resulting savings that would have otherwise been lost in rework, scrap, and warranty expenses. This is a view widely held among Japanese manufacturers, and explains much of their dedication to the goal of "continuous improvement."

Quality is synonymous with the absence of defects, and the costs in question are quality costs. These quality costs include:

* prevention costs;

* appraisal costs;

* internal failure costs;

* external failure costs:

* the cost of exceeding customer requirements: and, finally,

* the cost of lost opportunities.

Crosby (1979) argued that, taken together, these various costs can drain a company of 20–30% of its revenue or turnover. In service industries, this total cost can be as high as 40–45% of revenue or turnover.

Prevention is better than cure

Feigenbaum (1956) was one of the first to point out that the high price tag of quality is caused by money being spent in the wrong way—that is, allocating quality-control resources toward sorting bad products from good, and rectifying mistakes *after* they have been made, rather than spending that money on *preventive* measures to ensure that goods are manufactured correctly in the first place.

To understand this better, it is necessary to explore Feigenbaum's idea of there being three cost segments in quality management. According to Feigenbaum, these three cost segments are:

* *failure costs*—caused by defective materials and products that do not meet company quality specifications; these include loss elements such as scrap, spoilage, rework, and field complaints;

* *appraisal costs*—include the expenses for maintaining company quality levels by means of formal evaluations of product quality; these include inspection, tests, quality audits, laboratory acceptance examinations, and outside endorsements; and

* *prevention costs*—these prohibit defects from occurring in the first place; these costs include quality control in engineering, employee training, and the maintenance of patterns and tools.

By analyzing these three cost segments, Feigenbaum (1956) showed that the overall cost benefit of total quality control is derived from the fact that it cuts the first two major cost segments of quality (failure costs and appraisal costs) by a significant amount, and that it does this by means of a much smaller increase in the third cost segment (prevention costs). In other words, prevention *is* better than cure.

The quality "gurus"

The historic evolution of the quality movement has been led by three American experts on quality who have become known as the quality "gurus"—W. Edwards Deming, Joseph Juran, and Philip Crosby. Their emergence was predominantly a response to changes in American and Japanese markets, and the need to adapt to survive. The contributions of the "gurus" extend from the mere theory of overall management philosophy to the development of the practical tools of quality management.

W. Edwards Deming (1900–1993)

Dr. W. Edwards Deming is generally considered to have been the "father" of the Japanese quality revolution. William E. Conway described him as the "father of the third wave of the industrial revolution," and regarded Deming as the originator of quality control (Conway, n.d.). Deming was the first of the American quality "gurus" to arrive in Japan, and his rise to fame was closely linked to the development of quality within postwar Japanese industry.

Deming's message to the Japanese was really quite simple. It was encapsulated in his famous "chain reaction" (Figure 3.1).

Figure 3.1 *Deming's chain reaction*

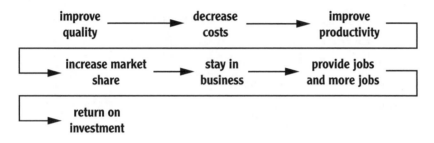

Author's presentation based on Deming (1982)

Although Deming did not introduce the Japanese to statistical quality control (these concepts and their importance having been well known in Japan long before he went there), the Japanese were struggling with the problem of conveying the mathematical concepts to their managers and staff. Deming's contribution was to help his hosts cut through the academic theory, such that the essential ideas were presented in a simple way that was meaningful—right down to the level of production workers (Hutchins, 1990).

Once the Japanese accepted his new approach, Deming concentrated on showing them how to improve quality by the use of statistical control of the process. The main thrust of Deming's philosophy was the *planned reduction of variation*. He demonstrated how productivity improves as variability decreases and, since all things vary, the need to use statistical methods to control work processes. According to Deming, statistical control did not imply absence of defective items; rather, it was a state of random variation, in which the limits of variation were predictable.

Deming was strongly opposed to motivational programs. He believed that such programs had little lasting effect, and that they misunderstood the role of the worker. Deming argued that a man could not be expected to do it right the first time if the incoming material was off gauge, off color, or otherwise defective, or if his machine was not in good order.

Deming's views on the role of management and the participating workforce were summarized in his oft-repeated "14 points" (see box).

With regard to the last point in his list—the commitment of top management—Deming felt that it was imperative to create a structure in management that facilitated, every day, the implementation of the other 13 points.

Deming's "fourteen points"

The famous "14 points" of Dr. W. Edwards Deming (1900–1993) were the basis of his approach to quality management. For Deming, quality was not merely a matter of inspection and checking. It was a whole management philosophy.

Deming's fourteen points can be expressed in the following terms:

1. Institute constancy of purpose (for continual improvement).
2. Embrace the new philosophy (that is, the economic age of quality).
3. Cease dependence on inspection.
4. End lowest-tender contracts.
5. Improve every process.
6. Institute training on the job.
7. Institute leadership.
8. Drive out fear (encourage two-way communication).
9. Break down barriers (between departments and staff).
10. Eliminate exhortation (slogans and posters).
11. Eliminate arbitary numerical targets (avoid setting numerical goals).
12. Permit pride of workmanship.
13. Encourage education.
14. Provide top management commitment.

Adapted from Deming Institute (2002)

Although he was primarily a statistician, Deming was clearly involved in more than the mere teaching of statistics in his 14 points. He was, in fact, proclaiming a whole management philosophy. However, at that time (and, sadly, even today), Deming's approach represented the complete antithesis of conventional management thinking.

As a result of Deming's influence in the early 1950s, various quality-control methods were developed, and many good results were achieved. However, three major defects remained:

* too much reliance on statistical methods;

* too much formality in the promotion of standardization; and

* top management lagging behind in the progress toward effective quality control.

Joseph M. Juran (1904–)

W. Edwards Deming was not the sole instigator of the Japanese "conversion," and nor was he the only "prophet" on quality in the immediate postwar period. Another American, Dr. Joseph M. Juran, visited Japan in 1954. He emphasized that quality control should be conducted as an integral part of overall management control. Like Deming, Juran had a huge impact on Japanese thinking, a fact that was later acknowledged when the Japanese emperor, Hirohito, awarded Juran the prestigious Order of the Sacred Treasure in 1981 in recognition of his contribution to "the development of quality control in Japan and the facilitation of US and Japanese friendship" (Juran Institute, 2002).

The background to Juran's approach in Japan was his work in the United States in the 1940s when he had been highlighting managerial responsibility for quality and emphasizing that quality was achieved through *people* rather than through *techniques.* Although a statistician himself, he did not limit his work to statistical analysis. Juran pointed out that companies could have a comprehensive knowledge of the technical aspects of quality, such as statistical process control, but that this did not help them to *manage* quality. He was the first of the "gurus" to emphasize that achieving quality was all about communication, management, and people. His message was clear—quality did not happen by accident; it had to be planned and executed by enlightened management. Juran believed that the majority of quality problems were the fault of poor management rather than poor workmanship on the shop floor. In fact, he argued that defects controllable by management accounted for more than 80% of all quality problems (Juran, 1989; Costin, 1994).

Juran detailed three basic steps to quality improvement:

* structured annual improvement plans;

* massive training programs involving the whole workforce; and

* leadership by senior management.

Juran was at one with Deming in maintaining that the majority of quality problems were systemic, and therefore the responsibility of management. Juran felt that the pursuit of departmental goals could sometimes undermine a company's overall quality mission. Like Deming, Juran was vehemently against campaigns to motivate the workforce to solve a company's quality problems. In his view, slogans and motivation failed to set specific goals, failed to establish specific plans to meet these goals, and failed to provide the needed resources. These motivation approaches merely suited the desire of executives to shift responsibility for quality to others in the organization.

Juran's "Quality Planning Road Map" consisted of nine steps.

1. Identify the customers.
2. Determine the needs of these customers.
3. Translate these needs into our language.
4. Develop a product that can respond to these needs.
5. Optimize the product that can respond to these needs.
6. Develop a process that is able to produce the product.
7. Optimize the process.
8. Prove that the process can produce the product under operating conditions.
9. Transfer the process to operations.

The concepts taught by Juran are, today, part of the standard lexicon of TQM. Juran was undoubtedly the first to bring a series of disconnected approaches into the cohesive whole that we now label "TQM," although he called it "quality control." "Control" has many meanings, but Juran used it in a universal sense as the totality of all the means used to establish and achieve standards.

Juran related company-wide quality management to the systemic methods used to meet business or financial goals. Company-wide quality control is concerned with the effectiveness of a company's design and manufacturing system. It commences with market research and continues through design and manufacture to after-sales service and the evaluation of data obtained from user experience. It has the combined objectives of (1) producing customer satisfaction; (2) providing value for money; and (3) increasing profits. Juran outlined the systemic approach to company-wide quality management as follows:

* establish policies and goals for quality;

* establish plans for meeting these quality goals;

* provide the resources to evaluate progress against the goals and take appropriate action; and

* provide motivation to stimulate people to meet the goals.

Juran did not believe that "quality is free" (as Crosby's rather provocative book title was later to proclaim). Juran explained that, because of the law of diminishing returns, there is an optimum point of quality, beyond which conformance is more costly than the value of the quality obtained.

Quality "gurus" tend to express their core ideas in a series of memorable steps or basic points. Joseph Juran was no exception. His "10 steps" are shown in the box.

Juran's "ten steps"

Joseph Juran was the first to bring a series of disconnected approaches into the cohesive whole that we now label 'total quality management' (TQM), although he called it 'quality control'. His message was clear—quality did not happen by accident; it had to be planned and executed by enlightened management.

Juran, like other quality 'gurus', suggested certain steps for quality improvement. He listed the following ten steps.

1. Build awareness of the need for improvement, and provide opportunity for it.
2. Set goals for improvement.
3. Organise to reach the goals (establish a quality council, identify problems, select projects, appoint teams, designate facilitators).
4. Provide training.
5. Carry out projects to solve problems.
6. Report progress.
7. Give recognition.
8. Communicate results.
9. Keep score.
10. Maintain momentum by making annual improvement part of the regular systems and processes of the company.

Adapted from Juran Institute (2002)

Philip Crosby (1926–2001)

Philip Crosby has probably done more to alert Western management to the need for quality improvement, and management's responsibility for it, than all the other "gurus" and experts combined. Beginning with *Quality is Free* (1979), his books, speeches, and broadcasts have influenced thousands of executives to change their behavior and commit themselves to quality. Crosby's best-known ideas have been the exhortation to achieve "zero defects" and the concept of "do it right first time." Crosby's thoughts, expressed in his book *Quality Without Fears* (1984), exerted a major influence on management in the early 1980s and initiated a growing body of research and literature in the field.

Crosby believed that, since most companies allow a certain deviation from specifications, manufacturing companies spend approximately 20% of their revenue doing things wrong, and then having to correct the errors. According to Crosby, for service companies this cost could amount to 35% of revenue. He did not believe that workers should take prime responsibility for poor quality; the reality, he said, was that management had to be improved.

Crosby's concepts and methodology were clear, easy to communicate, and appealing to management. In many cases, Crosby's books or videos were the first contact that executives had made with the concepts of quality management. Many companies that started implementing the Crosby approach became interested, read more widely, and thus came to be also heavily involved in the Deming approach and the Juran methodology. Indeed, many of these companies believe that they would not have been able to start the process of change without the inspiration of Crosby.

The essence of Crosby's teaching was contained in what he called the "Four Absolutes of Quality," and in a 14-step process of quality improvement. Although not included in the kernel of his concepts, his continual admonition that the job of management is "to help people" is at the heart of the TQM movement.

Crosby argued that effective quality management required:

* a definition of quality that can be readily understood by all; that is, the beginning of a common language that will aid communication;

* a system by which to manage quality;

* a performance standard that leaves no room for doubt or fudging by any employee; and

* a method of measurement that focuses attention on the progress of quality improvement.

These points provided the premise for Crosby's "four absolutes" for managing quality.

1. Quality is defined as conformance to requirements, not as "goodness" or "elegance."

2. The system for producing quality is prevention, not appraisal.

3. The performance standard must be *zero defects,* not that which is close enough.

4. The measurement of quality is the price of nonconformance, not indices.

The Crosby methodology for implementation was contained within a 14-step quality-improvement process. This process was clearly based on his experience in implementing quality improvement through the multidisciplined environment at the American firm ITT Industries in the 1970s. These steps have proved successful in many companies and therefore demand careful examination (see boxes).

Crosby's "four absolutes" and "fourteen steps"

Philip Crosby became well known for his somewhat provocative (but very effective) approach to quality management—for example, his uncompromising statement that the real aim of quality management should be "zero defects" and his proclamation that "quality is free." Crosby's ideas were very influential as a result of the clear and uncompromising manner in which they were communicated.

Like other "gurus" Crosby listed his core philosophy in a series of memorable points. He expressed these as "four absolutes for managing quality" and "14 steps to quality management."

Crosby's "four absolutes" were as follows:

1. Quality is defined as conformance to requirements, not as "goodness" or "elegance."

2. The system for producing quality is prevention, not appraisal.

3. The performance standard must be *zero defects,* not that which is close enough.

4. The measurement of quality is the price of nonconformance, not indices.

Crosby's 14 steps toward effective quality management were listed as follows.

1. *Management commitment*—top-level view on quality shown to all.

2. *The quality-improvement team*—to pursue the quality regime throughout the business.

3. *Quality measurement*—analysis of business quality performance in a meaningful manner; for example, late deliveries, budgeted to actual sales, deliveries, costs, and so on keep it simple for all to understand.

4. *The cost of quality*—make sure everyone in the business understands the need for a quality system, and the costs to the business if there is no quality system in place.

5. *Quality awareness*—make everyone in the business aware of the impact of quality systems.

6. *Corrective action*—ensure a system is in place for analyzing defects in the system and for applying simple cause-and-effect analysis, to prevent recurrence.

7. *Zero-defects planning*—look for business activities to which zero-defect logic should be applied.

8. *Supervisor training*—train supervisors in both quality logic and zero-defect appreciation that they can apply to their business activities.

9. *Zero-defects day*—a quality event by which all members of a section become aware that a change has taken place.

10. *Goal-setting*—once a change has been implemented in a section of the business, the next step is to get the employees and supervisors in that section to set goals to bring about continuous improvement.

11. *Error cause removal*—communication process by which management is made aware that set goals are difficult to achieve; then follows a reappraisal of the goals or assistance by management to achieve the goals.

12. *Recognition*—management must recognize the employees who participate in the quality schemes.

13. *Quality councils*—using both specialist knowledge and employee experiences to bring about a focused approach to a business quality regime.

14. *Do it over again*—continuous improvement means starting from the beginning again and again.

Department of Trade & Industry (2002); ecommerce-now.com (2002)

The core ideas of TQM

From the above discussion, it is apparent that there is no single entity called "total quality management" (TQM). TQM is an overall management philosophy that has been influenced by numerous academics and practitioners since the term "total quality control" was first introduced by Armand Feigenbaum in a 1956 issue of the *Harvard Business Review*. Some more influential figures in this "TQM movement" have been, among others, Feigenbaum, Deming, Juran, Crosby, Ishikawa, Kano, Imai, and Mizuno (see box).

Because this movement has had input from many people over several decades, and because the idea is difficult to define with any precision, there is little consensus in the literature regarding the core ideas of TQM. Everyone seems to have a different set of essential principles.

"Gurus," "fathers," "prophets," and others

The contributions of Deming, Juran, and Crosby to the pursuit of quality have been immense. Many organizations have developed a mixture of different methods and concepts from all the gurus without in-depth experience of any one of them. The applicability of the various approaches is dependent on the culture and nature of a particular business, and each business must make use of what suits it best.

Deming and Juran are rightfully acknowledged as the "fathers" of the Japanese revolution. However, it is not generally recognized that Crosby's concepts (more commonly associated with American industry) are also taught and practiced by Japanese management.

Apart from Deming, Juran, and Crosby, there are many other individuals, both American and Japanese, who have contributed to the theory on quality without quite attaining the eminence of the three main "gurus." Most notable among these is Armand Feigenbaum, who was something of a prophet in being the first to start using the word "total" in relation to quality. Among other thinkers on the subject, especially valuable contributions have been made by William E. Conway, H. James Harrington, Masaaki Imai, Kaoru Ishikawa, Shigeru Mizuno, Richard J. Schonberger, and Genichi Taguchi.

The following points (based on Marchese, 1991) provide a useful guide to the sorts of "core ideas" often put forward in an attempt to describe the essence of TQM.

1. *Customer-driven*—excellence is achieved by customer-driven organizations that systematically integrate customer feedback into their strategic planning, and into the delivery of products and services.

2. *Focus on Quality*—customer-driven organizations have a strong focus on quality, with quality being defined both in terms of the measurable objective qualities of products and services, and in terms of the perceptions of customers.

3. *Continuous improvement in systems*—continuous improvement results from such a focus on quality, and continuous improvement requires fundamental changes to manufacturing of service processes.

4. *Collaboration*—TQM requires a change to existing "mindsets" involving a paradigm shift in which organizational and individual success is perceived to be a result of collaboration rather than cut-throat competition.

5. *Objectivity*—decisions should be objective and data-driven. Previous experiences need to be systematically documented and analyzed to achieve continuous improvement.

6. *Teamwork*—teamwork is the practical application of collaboration. To be effective, teams must be trained in creative and analytical problem-solving techniques.

7. *Empowerment*—people should be empowered. That is, they should have real input and decision-making power in job design and organizational policies that affect them.

8. *Education and training*—education and training are essential. Indeed, according to another author, Ishikawa, TQM begins and ends with education.

9. *Shared vision*—a shared vision must be known and shared by all employees and managers. This is the key to any organization's unified direction, and avoids wasteful duplication of efforts, and infighting.

10. *Leadership*—organizational change is possible only through effective leadership by example. Empty promises and speeches only make existing problems worse.

Other authors prefer to express the core ideas of TQM in different terms, and the above list is certainly not presented as being the "last word" on the subject. However, the above list does give a good guide to the essential elements of TQM.

A perusal of the above 10 points reveals certain recurring themes. Whichever words are chosen by different authors, and whichever points are emphasized, there are certain recurring themes of the sort we note in the list suggested by Marchese (above). In terms of these *general recurring themes* of TQM we note that:

✳ TQM is customer-centered and customer-driven;

✳ TQM has a conscious philosophy of continual systemic improvement;

✳ TQM requires empowered employees involved in collaborative action; and

✳ TQM requires committed management showing inspiring leadership.

The special case of service quality

Lacking a philosophy of service quality

Most of the above discussion on the historical development of quality "control" has centered on goods-manufacturing industries. In virtually all industries, the combination of globalization, deregulation, and more demanding consumers has increased competition and pushed product quality to the forefront of management concerns. The services sector has certainly not been immune to these developments. Indeed, delivering high-quality services has been recognized as the most effective means by which a service company's offerings can be made to stand out from a crowd of look-alike competitive offerings (Parasuraman, Berry, & Zeithaml, 1991). Research studies have repeatedly demonstrated the strategic advantage of superior quality in contributing to market share and profits (see, e.g., Buzzell & Gale, 1987; Jacobson & Aaker, 1987; Peters & Waterman, 1982).

As we have seen, the "quality movement" in goods manufacturing gained enormous impetus in the decades immediately after World War II. But the services sector lagged behind in coming to grips with these ideas, and "quality" was not really introduced into the services literature until the beginning of the 1980s.

When service quality did start to become an issue, it was, to a large degree, influenced by traditional goods marketing, and it tended to follow a similar historical pattern. That is, initially, there was minimal reference to an overall *philosophy* of quality; little was said about *concepts* of quality, or *management models* of quality. Rather, as had occurred in the very early days with manufactured goods—when quality had been traditionally equated with "quality checking" of completed goods at the end of an assembly line—service quality was more or less treated as a given variable (Grönroos, 1992). Variations in quality were seen as an unavoidable fact of life. Indeed, this is a situation that still unfortunately applies in many areas of service marketing.

But services are different

As they attempted to develop an appropriate philosophy of services quality, service marketers recognized that the characteristics of services did not fit the characteristics of physical goods. Although the rendering of a given service might involve some physical goods, the service "products" themselves were clearly different (Shostack, 1977a, 1977b; Grönroos, 1980). Whereas goods quality could be measured objectively by such indicators as durability and the number of defects (Crosby, 1979; Garvin, 1983), there were no objective measures to assess the quality of intangible services (Parasuraman, Zeithaml, & Berry, 1988).

Because most published works on quality focused on manufactured goods, the clear differentiation of products from services (see Chapter 2) became an important issue. It was clear that many of the "quality strategies" available to manufacturers were inappropriate for service firms (Berry, Zeithaml, & Parasuraman, 1985). Researchers and practitioners alike realized that available knowledge about goods quality was insufficient for a proper understanding of service quality.

Looking to the consumer

Because of these historical and conceptual factors, ideas of service quality had to be developed very much "from scratch." Instead of using quality concepts from the manufactured-goods industry, services marketing researches developed their own concepts of service quality. In drawing up these "service-specific" models, they turned from an emphasis on manufacturing design to an emphasis on *consumer behavior* (Grönroos, 1992). The consumers' ideas of quality became the benchmark.

The consumer became central in these deliberations because, as many authors have noted, people evaluate services in a fundamentally different way from that in which they evaluate goods (Fisk, 1981; Zeithaml, 1981; Grönroos, 1981; Parasuraman et al., 1985). Services are *performances,* usually conducted in the presence of the customer, and service quality is therefore very much a function of subjective perception of an experience, rather than objective examination of a physical object (Berry, Zeithaml, & Parasuraman, 1985).

Service quality literature has thus been firmly based on the notion that service quality is defined by the *customer*—as opposed to the situation in manufactured goods where quality tends to be defined by *designers* or *operations managers.*

Understanding service quality theory

Intangible and personal

Service quality has become a great differentiator among service providers. Indeed, it is the most powerful competitive weapon that many leading service organizations possess. Business survival and success are dependent on the delivery of superior service quality (Berry, 1995, 1999; Berry & Parasuraman, 1991; Zeithaml & Bitner, 2000). However, even though it is well accepted that service quality is a crucial element in the success of any service organization, there are no clearcut definitions of service quality.

According to Parasuraman and colleagues (1985), service quality is an abstract and elusive concept because of the well-known distinctive features of services—intangibility, perishability, heterogeneity, and inseparability of production and consumption (see Chapter 2). Because of these features, definitions of quality can vary from person to person, and from situation to situation. Furthermore, experiences are incidents in time, and the critical time to be considered is difficult to define and control—it falls in the variable one-to-one personal interactions that occur between the consumer and the provider.

In developing an understanding of service quality, it is therefore important to understand what *customers* are looking for, and what *they* deem to be quality in services. According to Grönroos (1982b), such an understanding requires two distinct elements:

* a clear conception of service quality—a conception that describes how customers perceive the quality of a service; and

* an understanding of how such service quality is influenced, and which resources and activities affect service quality—that is, how service quality can be managed.

Comparing expectations and performance

How do consumers choose among various service offerings, and how do they evaluate the quality of the service offerings they receive?

Choosing a service

When purchasing physical goods, consumers employ various tangible cues to ascertain quality. These include style, color, hardness, feel, packaging, brand name, price, and so on. In contrast, when purchasing services, consumers are forced to rely on a smaller number of available cues. In many cases, tangible evidence is limited to the service provider's physical facilities, equipment, and personnel (Hartline & Jones, 1996; Parasuraman et al., 1985). In services in which personal experience of quality is a high priority (e.g., tourism and hospitality services), consumers who are attempting to evaluate services before purchase seek and rely on information from personal (word-of-mouth) sources rather than from nonpersonal sources (such as advertisements) (Zeithaml, 1981).

Confirmation and disconfirmation of expectations

Having made a choice, how do consumers assess the quality of the service they have received? According to theories of consumer behavior, the subjective evaluation of various experiences associated with consumption is based on what is technically called a "confirmation/disconfirmation paradigm"—that is, consumers compare their *prior expectations* of product performance with the *actual performance* of the product (Swan & Comb, 1976).

Several studies have been conducted in an effort to clarify how customers' expectations and preconceptions of product performance affect the subsequent level of customer satisfaction or dissatisfaction with actual performance. In these studies, after using the product or service, the consumer compares the perceived or actual performance of the product with the expected performance (see, e.g., Woodruff, Cadotte, & Jenkins, 1983). In the jargon of the "confirmation/disconfirmation paradigm," we can say that:

* *confirmation* results when the two performances match; but

* *disconfirmation* results when the two performances do not match; this can be of two types—*positive disconfirmation* when the perceived performance exceeds expectations, and *negative disconfirmation* when the perceived performance falls below expectations.

Because service experiences are inherently *personal* experiences, this confirmation or disconfirmation (as defined above) leads to an emotional reaction—referred to as "arousal." That is, if a product or service appears to be performing above or below expectations, the customer experiences an emotional reaction of significance (a sense of growing pleasure or a sense of growing concern). This arousal is then followed by a final assessment of satisfaction or dissatisfaction. In experiencing these changing emotions, the consumer is comparing prior expectations with actual experience.

Expectations—what will happen or what should happen?

As we have seen, the *perceived quality* of a given service is the outcome of an evaluation process during which consumers compare their prior expectations of the service with what they have actually received. That is, having received the service, they put the *perceived* service against the *expected* service (Grönroos, 1984b).

But what did they expect? What is an "expectation"?

The term "expectations," as used in the literature on consumer satisfaction, differs from the term as used in the literature on service quality. In the consumer-satisfaction literature, expectations are viewed as predictions made by the customer about what is likely to happen during an impending transaction (Lewis & Michell, 1990). In contrast, in the service quality literature, expectations are viewed as what the customer desires, or wants, or thinks should happen (Grönroos, 1984a; Parasuraman et al., 1985; Berry, Zeithaml & Parasuraman 1990; Berry, Parasuraman, Zeithaml, & Adsit, 1994). The crucial difference is between what consumers expect a service provider *will* offer and what they think the provider *should* offer.

This subject will be discussed in more detail below (see "Service Quality Gap," this chapter).

Expectations—what causes them?

This difference (between an expectation of what is *likely* to happen as opposed to what *should* happen) raises the question of what factors influence expectations—that is, the identification of variables that *contribute* to customer expectations. These include previous experiences of the service or a similar service, word-of-mouth advice from other consumers, and conclusions drawn from various cues surrounding the service—including tangible cues such as furniture, fittings, and equipment associated with the service (Zeithaml, Berry, & Parasuraman, 1993, 1996).

Meeting or exceeding expectations

Service organizations can achieve a strong reputation for quality service only when they consistently meet or exceed customer service expectations. As we have seen, service quality is a measure of how well the services (as received) match with expectations (as preconceived). And, as we have seen, these expectations might be expressed in terms of what is *likely* to happen or in terms of what *should* happen. Firms that satisfy what is *likely* to happen will do well. Firms that satisfy what *should* happen will do even better. Truly successful firms are those that consistently exceed these customer expectations.

Above expectations and below expectations

At Mahon airport, Menorca, a member of the airport staff drove across the tarmac to the terminal, and back again to the aircraft—not just once, but twice. On the first trip the staff member had kindly located and retrieved a jacket that a boarded passenger had left behind in the terminal. On the second trip, the same staff member retrieved a bottle of gin that the same boarded passenger had left behind in the airport shop! Service beyond what any customer could reasonably expect.

Compare this with a well-known hotel that refused to provide a late arrival with a room-service cheese sandwich after 9:30 PM because the staff were "too busy." No alternative food or service was offered, no concern was shown for the welfare of the guest, and no apology was given. Service well below what any customer would expect.

Expectations of what is *likely* to happen and what *should* happen are at the heart of understanding customer satisfaction.

Gillian Lyons

Service-quality concepts

No easy task

So, how do customers assess service quality? What parameters matter in their assessment? How can service quality be analyzed in conceptual terms?

There have been various models proposed by different researchers in the field. Some of these proposed models have certain similarities to one another. Others are quite different in their ideas and arrangements of factors. The variety of conceptions in the services, literature demonstrates the difficulty in developing a single acceptable model that adequately describes all aspects of service quality. This is to be expected. After all, it is not easy to find a single model that takes into account every aspect of something as complex as how human beings make a subjective assessment of a personal experience. And this is what service quality is essentially all about—the subjective assessment of a complex human experience. This is certainly not an easy concept to analyze and model in simple terms!

Exceeding expectations

The customer in the supermarket was not surprised at his sense of frustration. It happened often in this supermarket. How many times had he gone looking for an item, only to find that the stock had run out? The explanation was always the same—he was always told that the warehouse that supplied the supermarket must have run short of that item this week. It was always someone else's fault! This had happened so many times that the customer had stopped shopping in this supermarket. He was back again on this particular day only because he was looking for "last-minute" Christmas purchases and this supermarket was conveniently close to home. But, as expected, he couldn't find what he wanted.

Although he did not expect any worthwhile assistance, the frustrated customer asked a young assistant if the supermarket stocked Christmas puddings at this time of the year. The young assistant looked vaguely at the shelves where the Christmas puddings should have been displayed and replied that it didn't look as though they had any. The customer groaned. He already knew that! Shaking his head in disbelief at the apparent lack of any interest in his problem, the customer walked off in search of another item he required.

A little later, becoming more frustrated by the minute, the customer reluctantly asked another young assistant if the supermarket stocked cranberry sauce for the Christmas turkey. Like his colleague, the young assistant looked vaguely at the shelves where cranberry sauce should have been displayed and replied that it didn't look as though they had any! He added that he had been hired as a temporary member of staff for the Christmas "rush" and really didn't know much about the stock in the supermarket.

Utterly frustrated by now, the customer completed his shopping as quickly as possible and proceeded to the checkout, muttering to himself about the need for this supermarket to improve the customer-service skills of its young employees—even if they were only temporary.

Imagine his surprise and delight when he was unexpectedly tapped on the shoulder and turned to find both the young assistants standing behind him—one clutching a Christmas pudding and the other holding a jar of cranberry sauce!

"We found these out in the storeroom," said one young man with a smile.

"Hope they're OK," added the other.

As it turned out, the items were not all that good, but they were adequate. However, the customer didn't really mind at all. The items themselves were less important than the service supplied. And the fact that the young assistants had exceeded expectations so unexpectedly was especially delightful.

Three important lessons come out of this story.

1. Those young temporary assistants have a future in the service industry—as have any staff members who go out of their way to satisfy customer expectations.

2. Service firms should strive to go beyond the service that customers expect they will get. Truly successful firms supply (or even exceed) the service that customers think they should get.

3. The manner in which the service was delivered was more important to the customer than the goods purchased. See the difference between "functional quality" and "technical quality" (this chapter).

One of the earliest models was that proposed by Sasser, Olsen, and Wyckoff (1978) who identified three different dimensions of service performance—*materials, facilities,* and *personnel*. Thus, service performance (or service quality) was conceived to be affected by:

* the quality of the *materials* that form part of the service offering (e.g. food in a restaurant);

* the quality of the *facilities* that complement the core offering (e.g. comfortable seating in an aircraft); and

* the quality of the *personnel* (e.g., a friendly and pleasant hotel receptionist).

All have the potential to influence service quality. The important point to appreciate in this trichotomy is the notion that service quality involves more than the outcome quality—that is, the methods and manner by which the service is delivered are of vital importance.

Developments and variations of this view of service quality have been offered by Grönroos (1982a); Lehtinen and Lehtinen (1983); Parasuraman, Zeithaml, and Berry (1985, 1988); Rust and Oliver (1994); Dabholkar, Thorpe, and Rentz (1996); and Brady and Cronin (2001), among others. They differ in their approaches, but what they have in common is a recognition that service quality is multifactorial in origin.

Space does not permit a full exploration of each of them here, but all have important contributions to make. The rest of this chapter provides a summarizing overview of these various models. Readers who are interested in particular models are invited to review the various contributions of researchers by noting the reference citations given in this text.

Grönroos: technical quality and functional quality

Grönroos (1982a) identified two dimensions in service quality. He argued that service quality is a combination of *technical* quality and *functional* quality (see Figure 3.2).

Figure 3.2 *Technical quality and functional quality in service quality*

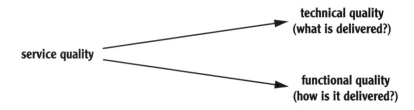

Author's presentation

In discussing *technical* quality, Grönroos (1982a) argued that, although services are basically intangible, and although production and consumption are virtually simultaneous, the material content in the buyer–seller interaction is still important in the customer's assessment of perceived service quality. Examples of this technical quality include:

* food in the restaurant service;

* the room and bed in a hotel;

* computerized systems in a bank;

* machines used in a car-repair service center;

* an employee's technical ability in serving a firm's customers;

* and so on.

In short, *technical quality* relates to *what* the customer receives in material terms.

In discussing *functional* quality, Grönroos (1982a) pointed out that, because many services are subjective experiences of the customer (e.g., the experience of a meal in a restaurant), and because these experiences are produced through close interaction with the employees of the service firm, the technical quality dimension alone cannot account for customers' perception of the total quality they have received. Customers will be influenced by *the way in which the technical quality is transferred to them.* Examples of this functional quality include:

* the appearance of a hotel receptionist;

* the behavior of a restaurant waiter;

* the helpfulness of a train conductor;

* the attitude of a consultant;

* the accessibility of a teller machine;

* and so on.

In short, *functional quality* relates to *how* the customer receives a service.

Of these two elements—technical quality ("what") and functional quality ("how")— the former can often be quantitatively measured (as an objective phenomenon), whereas the latter is difficult to evaluate (because it constitutes a subjective perception). Despite the fact that technical quality is easier to measure, it is of lesser importance in the perception of service quality by the customer. How the service is rendered (i.e., the functional quality of a service) is, in most cases, much more important than the material means by which it is rendered (i.e., the technical quality of the service). Functional quality commonly constitutes the key to an organization's success. (See the story of "Exceeding Expectations." This story was essentially about a customer's expectations of the service, but it is also a good example of how functional quality is more important than technical quality—the goods were not all that impressive, but the delivery of the service exceeded all expectations.)

In addition to this basic idea (that service quality involves both technical quality and functional quality), Grönroos (1984a) incorporated the concept of "corporate image," first proposed by Bessom (1973) and by Bessom and Jackson (1975), who were of the view that corporate image is of the utmost importance to most service organizations, since this determines the way in which consumers perceive the firm. The most important part of a firm, as seen and perceived by its customers, is its service. Combining this with his idea of technical and functional quality (see Figure 3.3), Grönroos argued that corporate image is derived mainly from a combination of a firm's technical quality and its functional quality. He went on to suggest that corporate image often influences customer expectation, and helps to reinforce the organization's advertising, marketing, and public relations activities.

Figure 3.3 *Perceived service quality involves corporate image*

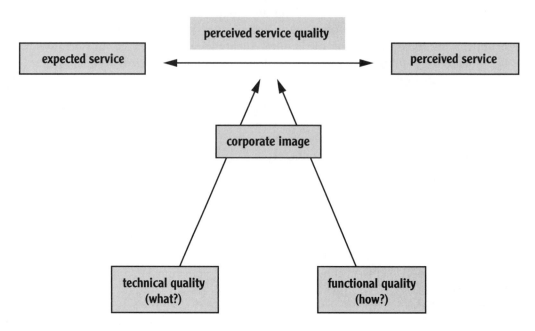

Source: Adapted from Brady & Cronin (2001)

The effect of multiple consumption

Grönroos also pointed out that in many service situations, other customers can affect the functional quality perceived by any given individual. Examples include eating in a restaurant, being on vacation, being transported somewhere, and enjoying entertainment. The effect of other customers on the perception of service quality has been well explained by Grove and Fisk through a series of research projects involving real-life "dramatic" events (see Grove & Fisk, 1982; Grove, Fisk, & John, 2000). In their framework, using the idea of a drama being enacted in a theater, they considered that a number of people being served simultaneously was an "audience," and that the service personnel were like "actors" performing roles in a drama. In such situations, the audience influences the performance, and some members of the audience affect other members of the audience. The audience component clearly becomes important in an environment in which consumers are required to share the same service facility.

The concept of *multiple consumption* is an important related idea. Unlike tangible goods, many service products can be enjoyed by more than one consumer simultaneously—but without having to share the product. Musical concerts, educational lectures, and cinema screenings are good examples. However, although the consumers do not share the actual product, the intimacy that links production and consumption of these services means that consumers are influenced by their co-consumers.

Furthermore, the size of the "audience" can have an effect (positive or negative) on the service experience. In the case of a crowded dance floor in a nightclub, a large group adds to the atmosphere of the experience. However, in a crowded grocery shop, a large group can have a negative effect on the service experience.

In many service situations, the presence of other customers can affect the functional quality perceived by any given individual. This effect can be positive or negative. In the case of a crowded dance floor in a nightclub, a large group adds to the atmosphere of the experience.

With kind permission of Long Street Entertainment, Columbus, Ohio

Baker (1986) thus proposed audience behavior to be a third factor or dimension in this interaction between the provider (the first dimension) and the immediate consumer (the second dimension). Baker gave the example of a crowd at a football game as being a third dimension in this interaction. Being surrounded by an enthusiastic, involved crowd provides a different experience from that provided by a quiet, uninterested crowd. For these sorts of reasons, Grönroos (1982a) was another to argue that, in many service situations, customers themselves create a positive or negative atmosphere.

Service managers have difficulty controlling such customer-generated effects. However, being aware of what cannot be controlled at operational stages encourages managers to assess overall design modification. Assessment of these variables when designing (or redesigning) the service process is an important aspect of quality management.

Instrumental performance and expressive performance

Another important development in the theory of consumer behavior came from Swan and Comb (1976). They examined expectations, performance, and satisfaction using clothing as the consumer product for testing. Employing "critical-incident" methodology, Swan and Comb identified two qualitatively different sets of dimension, which they termed "instrumental performance" and "expressive performance."

* *Instrumental performance* refers to the performance of the physical product, and whether this meets expectations. In the clothing industry, for example, instrumental performance is reflected in the durability of the product.

* *Expressive performance* refers to the "psychological" level of performance. In the case of clothing, this relates to the style of the clothing or to some other special attractive features.

Because clothing in such an indication or extension of "self," Swan and Comb (1976) argued that most of the functions of clothing that are important to consumers involve performance at a "psychological" level.

Empirical tests such as these in the study of consumer behavior—including the results of Swan and Comb (1976), and of others such as Maddox (1981)—have proved to be of considerable theoretical relevance to services. Relating Swan and Comb's theory to the service context, Grönroos (1984b) suggested that "instrumental performance" corresponded to his idea of the *technical* quality of services (i.e., *what* the customer is left with), whereas "expressive performance" can be equated with his dimension of *functional* quality (i.e., *how* the service is rendered) to the consumer during buyer–seller interaction.

As noted above, Swan and Comb (1976) argued that a satisfied consumer is more likely to mention "expressive" attributes rather than "instrumental" attributes as a reason for satisfaction with a product. This was tested in a service context, and it was found that more than one-third of the respondents agreed with the view that the performance of the employees compensates for a lower level of technical quality (Grönroos, 1984b).

Lehtinen's process quality and output quality

Another way of conceptualizing service quality was proposed by Lehtinen (1983) who also identified two sets of quality dimensions. He called his dimensions "process quality" and "output quality." These, he said, are inherent in all services, and combine to form service quality (see Figure 3.4).

Process quality

Lehtinen (1983) argued that customer participation is integral to the experience of process quality. The intimacy of the service-production process means that the customer experiences the production process through interaction and participation. The customer therefore judges "process quality" during the service. This judgment is based on the customer's subjective judgment—how the customer sees and assesses the production process. For example, in delivering hairdressing services, the stylist's conversation with the customer while cutting the customer's hair contributes to process quality. Of course, the stylist's demonstration of technical skill in cutting the hair is important, but process quality is more than technical skill. Process quality is about the customer's perception of how those technical services are delivered.

Figure 3.4 *Service quality—process and output*

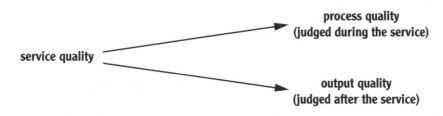

process quality
(judged during the service)

service quality

output quality
(judged after the service)

Author's presentation

Customer participation is present in almost every consumer and professional service production, and is thus integral to the assessment of process quality. In some services in which customer participation is especially direct and active—such as in the case of the entertainment business, including music concerts, magic shows, comedy shows, and so on—customer participation positively influences the customers' perception of process quality, and simultaneously positively influences the producer of the service, bringing out the best in the performance.

Output quality

According to Lehtinen (1983), output quality is the consumer's evaluation of the service following completion of the service-production process. For example, output quality depends on evaluation of the appearance of a finished haircut. In addition, in some service situations, output quality is not always evaluated by the customer alone, but is also evaluated by others. For example, a haircut is often evaluated by friends and colleagues of the customer. When customers value the judgment of friends and colleagues, this aspect of output quality becomes crucially important.

However, Lehtinen (1983) asserted that the customer is the only one to judge the *process* quality (as opposed to *output* quality). A classic example of this can be found in educational services. If a degree obtained by a student from a famous university is considered by the student's friends and family to be of a high quality (an assessment of output quality), the student's personal sense of status and prestige is enhanced. However, the educational services that he or she received throughout the period of academic study at the university were experienced only by the student, and thus only the student is capable of judging the *process quality* of the educational services.

Two types of output

Lehtinen, (1983) also drew attention to two types of output in service production, which he termed "tangible" (or physical) and "intangible." Both a car wash and a haircut constitute typical tangible outputs, since both can be evaluated by outsiders who have not participated in the production process. In contrast, the output in tourism services is intangible—because it reflects a feeling or an experience, and can thus be judged only by the customer. Thus, according to Lehtinen, the output of any service-production process is created during the entire period of the transaction. As a result, by controlling the process and process quality, output quality can also be controlled.

Service production process

Finally, in considering Lehtinen's useful contribution to an understanding of these concepts, we come to the idea of a service production process (SPP). Lehtinen (1988) identified three resources for an SPP—customer resources, contact resources, and physical resources. Both customers and contact persons (representatives of the service provider) participate in the SPP. The interactive quality is judged by the customer according to how his or her expectations are met during the SPP and, more pertinently, how the customer's participation style is understood by the contact persons and the degree to which these persons can adapt their service styles accordingly.

Service quality gap

As noted previously, according to Parasuraman and colleagues (1985), the quality perceived in a service is a function of the gap between consumers' expectations of a service and their perception of the actual service delivered. In other words, customers assess service quality by comparing the service they receive (perceptions of "what I get") with the service they *desire* (expectations of "what I want"). See Figure 3.5.

Figure 3.5 *Perceived service quality gap*

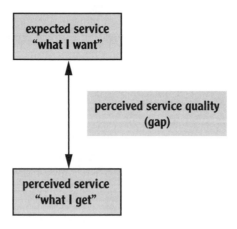

Author's presentation

This gap is actually made up of several other gaps—all of which are potential breaks in the links of the relationship. Research has identified four intermediate gaps that, taken together, lead to the overall gap between expected quality and the overall perceived quality of service as received (Zeithaml, et al., 1988).

In developing this idea of four intermediate gaps (and a resulting overall fifth gap, being the total of the other gaps), the researchers looked beyond a single transaction and developed a model of service quality representing customer judgments across multiple intermediate encounters involving service design, communication, management, and delivery.

Gap 1

Gap 1 is the difference between consumer expectations and management perceptions of consumer expectations.

According to Parasuraman and colleagues (1985), management might not always understand what features connote high quality to consumers, what attributes a service must have in order to meet consumer needs, and what levels of performance of these particular features are necessary to deliver high-quality service.

Furthermore, the gap between what consumers expect and what managers *think* they expect might be considerably larger in service industries than is the case in goods manufacturing.

Gap 2

Gap 2 is the difference between management perceptions of consumer expectations and the means by which these expectations might be met.

Even if knowledge of customer expectations *does* exist, the means to deliver services that match or exceed customer expectations might not exist. Executives frequently cite various constraints to explain the fact that services have not been designed effectively to meet customer needs. These constraints are often expressed in terms of difficulties with resources and/or markets.

However, many managers go further than this and believe that it is actually *impossible* to meet customer needs. They therefore find it impossible to establish specifications to meet those needs. In these cases, the gap between customer expectations and means by which these expectations might be met can be attributed to the absence of meaningful management commitment to service quality.

Therefore, a variety of factors—resource constraints, market conditions, and/or management indifference—can result in a discrepancy between management's perception of consumer expectations and the actual specifications established for a service.

Gap 3

Gap 3 is the difference between the specifications for the service and the actual delivery of the service. It can be referred to as the "service-performance gap"—that is, the extent to which service providers do not perform at the level expected by management. The service-performance gap occurs when employees are unable or unwilling to perform the service at the desired level.

Gap 4

Gap 4 is the difference between service delivery and external communications. Media advertising and other communications by a firm can affect consumer expectations. Such media advertising might contain exaggerated promises or might not contain certain vital information about aspects of the service delivery. This can create discrepancies between external communications and actual service delivery.

Gap 5

Gap 5 is the overall difference between expected service and perceived service. It is made up of the sum total of the preceding four gaps, and is thus determined by the nature of the gaps associated with the overall design, marketing, and delivery of services.

In comparing expectations and final perceptions across this overall gap, Berry and colleagues (1990) suggested that:

* if expectations are met, service quality is perceived to be satisfactory; if expectations are not met, service quality is perceived to be less than satisfactory; and if expectations are exceeded, service quality is perceived to be more than satisfactory;

* quality evaluations derive from both the service process and the service outcome (see "Lehtinen's Process Quality and Output Quality"); the manner in which the service is performed (politeness, willingness to help, trustworthiness, and so on) can be a crucial component of the service from the consumer's point of view;

* service quality is judged against (1) expectations of regular service and (2) expectations of exceptional services; the first refers to the quality level at which the regular service is delivered (such as a bank teller's typical handling of a transaction), and the second refers to exceptions or problems (such as a monthly credit card statement being incorrect, and how the service provider responds).

The five-factor American model

In developing their SERVQUAL model of measuring customer satisfaction (discussed in more detail in Chapter 4), Parasuraman and colleagues (1988) identified five service dimensions as factors that are considered highly by customers when assessing the quality of service (see Figure 3.6).

These five dimensions were reliability, responsiveness, empathy, assurances, and tangibles.

* *Reliability* represents the service provider's ability to perform service dependably and accurately; this includes such qualities as dependability, consistency, accuracy, "right first time," and so on.

* *Responsiveness* represents the willingness to help customers and provide prompt service in a timely manner; this includes helpfulness, friendliness, warmth, willingness, openness, and so on.

* *Empathy* involves the caring personal attention that the firm offers its customers; this includes ease of approach and contact; jargon-free, understandable communication; an understanding of the customer's needs; and so on;

* *Assurances* reflect the knowledge and courtesy of employees and their ability to inspire trust and confidence in the customer; this includes competence, experience, qualifications, skills, courtesy, politeness, credibility, trustworthiness, honesty, and security of all types (physical, financial, confidentiality, etc.).

* *Tangibles* consist of the appearance of physical facilities, equipment, personnel, and communication materials used.

Figure 3.6 *Five service dimensions in the SERVQUAL model*

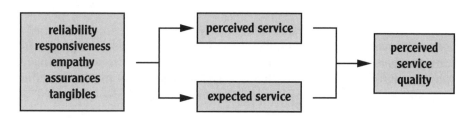

Source: Adapted from Brady & Cronin (2001)

Rust and Oliver's three-dimensional model

As previously noted, various scholars have produced different models of how service quality concepts can be understood. We have noted the seminal conceptualization of service quality proposed by Parasuraman and colleagues (1988) in their idea of the quality gap and their five-factor American model. We have also noted the two-dimensional idea of functional quality and technical quality as outlined by Grönroos (1984a), and Lehtinen's (1983) "Nordic conceptualization" of process quality and output quality (another two-dimensional model). These various conceptions demonstrate the difficulty in developing a single acceptable model that adequately describes all aspects of service quality. This is to be expected. It is not easy to find a single model that takes account of every aspect of something as complex as how human beings make a subjective assessment of a personal experience.

Rust and Oliver (1994) suggested a simple three-dimensional model. They said that the overall perception of service quality is based on the customer's evaluation of three dimensions of the service interface:

* service product;

* service delivery; and

* service environment.

See Figure 3.7.

Figure 3.7 *The three-component model of service quality*

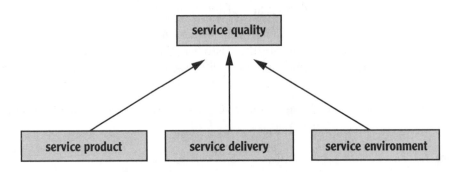

Source: Adapted from Brady & Cronin (2001)

Numerous studies have clearly indicated that the service environment affects perceptions of service quality. This model is of particular interest to the hospitality and tourism industry in view of the fact that the service environment (buildings, tourist attractions, decor, and so on) plays such an important part in the delivery of service products in this industry.

Multilevel models

The complexity of human reactions to a service experience has led some researchers to propose that perceptions of service quality are not only multidimensional (as noted above), but also occur at various levels.

Dabholkar and various colleagues (1996, 2000) thus developed a multilevel model of retail service quality involving primary dimensions and subdimensions (Figure 3.8, page 91). According to them, the primary dimensions include physical aspects, reliability, and personal interaction, whereas the subdimensions encompass appearance, convenience, promise, "doing it right," inspiring confidence, and being courteous and helpful.

Similarly, Brady and Cronin (2001) proposed a hierarchical model to conceptualize perceived service quality. Their model suggested three primary levels of service quality—interaction quality, physical environment quality, and outcome quality. In turn, each of these were conceived to have three subdimensions (see Figure 3.9). Thus:

* ✱ *interaction quality* was understood to be made up of the three subdimensions of attitude, behavior, and experience;

* ✱ *physical environment quality* was made up of the subdimensions of ambient conditions, design, and social factors; and

* ✱ *outcome quality* was conceived as being made up of the subdimensions of waiting time, tangibles, and valence (variable personal factors that affect experience).

Figure 3.8 *A multilevel model*

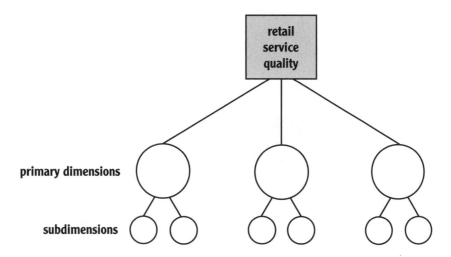

Source: Adapted from Brady & Cronin (2001)

Their studies found that customers aggregate their evaluations of the subdimensions to form their overall perceptions of an organization's performance in each of the three primary dimensions. These perceptions, it was argued, lead to customer's overall service quality perception.

Figure 3.9 *A hierarchical model of perceived service quality*

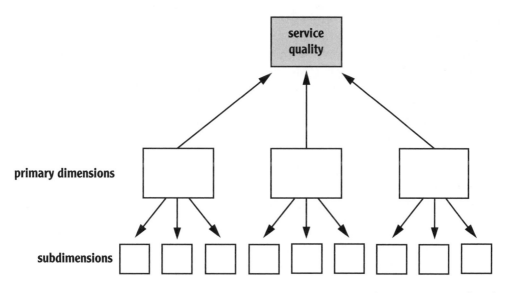

Adapted from Brady & Cronin (2001)

Summary of chapter

To remain in business, sellers in the modern marketplace must be able to offer quality to increasingly demanding customers. This applies equally to those offering manufactured goods and those offering services. Failure to maintain consistent quality standards jeopardizes a firm's reputation and its ultimate profitability.

Quality has thus become essential to business performance. Although the importance of product quality has long been recognized in the manufacturing industry—in which various quality management concepts and strategies have been developed and implemented over the years—the services sector has been less aware of the importance of these matters. However, the increasing economic importance of the service sector and the emergence of services marketing in recent years have highlighted the need for management to gain an understanding of quality strategies that are specifically appropriate for service firms.

In today's economy, service is crucial to customer satisfaction and business success in every industry. For a service firm, the ability to provide quality service is, in fact, the most effective means of differentiating itself from competitors. But the distinctive nature of services means that quality of service products is different from that of manufactured goods. Quality in services is not only different, but also more difficult to define, measure, and control. In addition, a firm's service quality is significantly affected by the subjective judgment of the customers.

From a marketing perspective, service quality is the most important determinant of hospitality satisfaction. Thus, the focus of hospitality management should be placed on providing quality service to enhance customer satisfaction. It is therefore imperative that hospitality managers understand the factors that influence a customer's perceptions, expectations, and satisfaction with services—and design their strategies accordingly.

This chapter has offered an overall understanding of quality concepts in general, as well as specific information pertaining to quality management in a service context. It should thus prove of assistance to hotel managers, as service providers, to focus their efforts and resources effectively on improving their firms' market position through quality services and customer satisfaction.

Review questions

1. Analyze the importance of quality in terms of costs and benefits.

2. Briefly describe the various quality principles proposed by Deming, Juran, and Crosby.

3. Briefly describe the concept of "total quality management" (TQM).

4. What is your understanding of service quality? How is service quality different from product quality?

5. Briefly describe the service quality concepts and theories presented in this chapter.

6. Choose any service quality model as described in this chapter and analyze and apply the model in the context of a hospitality operation.

Suggested reading for this chapter

This is a list of suggested further reading on topics covered in this chapter. For a separate list of full reference citations quoted in the chapter, see "References," Chapter 3, at the end of the book.

Bank, J. 2001. *The Essence of Total Quality Management*, Prentice Hall, New York.

Berry, L. L., Zeithaml, V. A., & Parasuraman, A. 1990. "Five Imperatives for Improving Service Quality," *Sloan Management Review*, September.

Brown, W. S., Gummesson, E., Edvardson, B., & Gustavson, B. 1991. *Service Quality: Multidisciplinary and Multinational Perspectives*, Lexington Books, New York.

Grönroos, C. 1991. "The Marketing Strategy Continuum: Towards a Marketing Concept for the 1990s," *Management Decision*, vol. 29, no. 1, pp. 7–13.

Kandampully, J., Mok, C., & Sparks, B. 2001. *Service Quality Management in Hospitality, Tourism and Leisure*, Flaworth Hospitality Press, New York.

Kimes S. E. 2001. "How Product Quality Drives Profitability: The Experience at Holiday Inn," *Cornell Hotel and Restaurant Administration Quarterly*, June, pp. 25–28.

Parasuraman, A., Berry, L. L., & Zeithaml, V. A. 1991. "Understanding Customer Expectations of Service," *Sloan Management Review*, Spring, pp. 39–48.

chapter four
Understanding
Customer Needs

Study objectives

Having completed this chapter, readers should be able to:

* understand the notion of the "customer" from a managerial perspective;

* understand the cross-functional relationships among service employees and the importance of internal marketing for successful external marketing;

* appreciate the importance of understanding customer expectations and perceptions of quality in a service context, and be familiar with the major techniques of gathering customer information; and

* understand the various methods of measuring service quality.

The framework of this chapter

This chapter is set out as follows:

* Introduction
* Customers of a service organization
  - The importance of understanding customers
  - Categories of customers
* Internal customers
  - Customers of first priority
  - Internal services to one another
  - A service blueprint of internal services
  - Implications for quality
  - Internal marketing makes external marketing
* External customers
  - The importance of customer information
  - Customer-perception research
    In-depth interviews with individual customers
    Focus-group interviews
    Customer surveys
    Critical-incident technique
    Transaction analysis
    Mystery shoppers
    Complaint analysis
* Measurement of service quality
  - Operations perspective
  - Performance perspective
    The SERVQUAL approach
    The SERVPERF approach
    Customer-satisfaction measurement (CSM)
* Employee research
  - Employees as "listening posts"
  - Inseparability makes employees important
  - Management involvement
  - Employees as customer "advocates"
  - Making it work effectively
* Summary of chapter

Introduction

If a commercial organization is to remain in business, it must understand and satisfy the needs of its consumers. Meeting or exceeding the expectations of customers is the essence of service quality (see Chapter 3). Having explored the concept of *quality* in Chapter 3, we now move on in the present chapter to explore the idea of *customers* and *customer satisfaction* in greater detail.

From a managerial perspective, the term "customers" encompasses more than those from whom an organization earns revenue. This chapter explores the idea that a service firm really has *two* groups of customers—"internal customers" and "external customers."

The very nature of services emphasizes the role of human beings in producing service products and delivering service experiences to other human beings. To offer quality service to *external* customers (those who ultimately pay for the final service offering), service firms must first realize the importance of the *internal* customers (the staff personnel who render the various services that make up the final service offering to the external customer). It might seem strange to describe staff personnel as "internal customers," but these people actually give and receive services from one another as part of an internal chain of staff interactions preceding the final delivery of service to the external customer. These internal customers must give and receive satisfactory service to and from one another if the final external customer is also to receive satisfactory service. This concept is explored in greater detail later in this chapter.

To fulfill customers' expectations and perceptions of *service quality,* service firms must continuously collect customer information and measure customer satisfaction as a basis on which to assess performance. This chapter presents various methods of acquiring and using customer information, and explores the role of service employees in gathering and providing management with customer feedback. Various techniques of measuring different aspects of a firm's performance are also introduced.

This chapter therefore examines two very important themes—the idea of internal and external customers, and the importance of customer feedback. In so doing, the chapter focuses on the ultimate measure of service quality—customer satisfaction.

Customers of a service organization

The importance of understanding customers

Service quality is defined as the extent to which a service meets the expectations of customers (see Chapter 3). The first challenge of management is to identify just what those expectations are.

Firms typically invest considerable resources (time, talent, and money) in attempting to understand the needs, wants, and expectations of buyers. However, in the case of services (as opposed to physical goods), there are few easily understood criteria by which the subjective expectations of service quality can be assessed and communicated.

Much research remains to be undertaken to understand the process by which expectations of service quality are formed. Zeithaml, Berry and Parasuraman (1993) suggested that three levels of expectations can be defined against which quality is assessed:

* the *desired* level of service (what the customer wants);

* the *adequate* level of service (what the customers are willing to accept); and

* the *predicted* level of service (what the customers believe is most likely to occur).

The benefits of understanding and measuring service quality are now widely recognized (Heskett, Sasser, & Schlesinger, 1997). One of the major causes of poor performance by service organizations is not knowing what customers expect (Klose & Finkle, 1995). Organizations are eager to provide good service, but fall short simply because they do not understand exactly what customers expect from the service offer (Palmer & Cole, 1995).

Categories of customers

Customers can be categorized into four broad groups:

* *external customers*—a firm's end-consumers;

* *internal customers*—employees and managers of the firm;

* *competitor's customers*—those whom the firm would like to attract and make its own; and

* *ex-customers*—customers who have chosen to leave, and now use a competing firm's services.

Although all of the above are vital for a full understanding of customers, this chapter focuses predominantly on the first two categories—internal and external customers.

Internal customers

Customers of first priority

The customers of first concern to a firm should be its internal customers—its own service personnel. Management's primary task is to "sell" its service concept to the firm's employees, before attempting to sell it to external customers. And the most important of these employees in this context are those who actually deliver the service to the external customers. Management thus needs to develop a philosophy of first "selling" its service concept to its own internal customers—a philosophy of "internal marketing."

The concept of internal marketing is relevant to virtually all organizations. It is particularly important, however, for labor-intensive service organizations (Berry, 1992). The concept of the internal customer should be viewed as a managerial philosophy that has strategic and tactical implications throughout the company and its various business functions (Grönroos, 1984; Hartline & Ferrell, 1996).

In any service organization, employees are both receivers and providers of some services. Hence, services offered and received by internal customers inside the organization invariably affect the services offered by the firm to its external customers. Given the relationship between employee performance and the delivery of service quality (Bowen, 1996), service-oriented organizations should treat front-line employees as "partial customers"—that is, as individuals deserving treatment similar to that which management wants its customers to receive. This concept is discussed further in Chapter 7 under "Internal Marketing."

Internal services to one another

Because a single isolated service is of limited use to the customer in the absence of various supporting services, customer demands on most service organizations are "cross-functional" in nature. Services are *interdependent* in nature, and cannot exist or function independently. It is therefore essential that the various departments and personnel work collaboratively to offer services commensurate with the customer's requirements.

Within every service organization, there are numerous departments and personnel performing various tasks, functions, and services. These can be fundamentally different—for example, in a hotel, an accountant might be preparing a guest's account folio while a chef is preparing the guest's meals. In other cases, the different functions are more closely linked—for example, a chef preparing a meal, and a waiter serving it. However, whether the functions are closely allied or not, the provision of a full hotel service requires all functions to be interlinked and coordinated.

Against that background, it can be argued that all personnel in a service organization receive or offer services from other members of the organization. In this sense, everyone in a service firm *is* a customer, and *has* customers. For example, the waiter receives a service from the chef (the provision of a meal), and provides a service to the guest (the serving of that meal). Essentially, this is the idea expressed by the concept of the "internal customer"—it indicates the interdependency of every function within the organization.

The success of every service organization is dependent on collaboration between the internal customers (the employees) of every department. No service firm can give its external customers the quality they want and expect without the active participation of all of its employees. J. W. Marriott, Jr., president of the Marriott Corporation, summed up the idea in these words. "We must do all we can to ensure that our organization's systems, methods, and policies serve the people who serve the customers" (Marriott, 1988).

Unless employees receive good service from the other employees with whom they interact, they will be unable to serve their customers well. For example, it is difficult for a hotel receptionist to settle the accounts of a guest quickly if the accounting personnel have not entered charges in the customer's account in an appropriate fashion. It is equally difficult for a waiter to "sell" the service quality of a meal to a diner if the waiter is dissatisfied with the service that he or she has received from the chef.

Quality internal service and satisfied internal customers are essential if an organization is to establish an effective customer-oriented service culture.

A service blueprint of internal services

The concept of internal customers can be better understood by mapping out the service-delivery process. Such a service-delivery map is called a "service blueprint," and constitutes a very effective management tool. Blueprinting assists management to identify the service relationships that exist among its employees and its customers during the various stages of service delivery.

Consider, for example, the relationships among kitchen and restaurant employees in the production of a meal service (Kingman-Brundage, 1989; Shostack, 1983). In a typical restaurant service, the external customer is the person who comes in to have a meal. The waiter who takes the orders represents the external customer's service supplier. However, the waiter has received the cooked food from the chef. In this sense, the chef has become the "internal supplier" and the waiter has become the "internal customer." If the service chain is followed further back, the chef has received raw ingredients from the restaurant's storekeeper. Thus, the storekeeper was the internal supplier of raw materials and the chef was the internal customer of this supplier. If the storekeeper had been unable to supply the appropriate ingredients, the chef would have been unable to produce the right food, and would therefore have been incapable of meeting the waiter's request. In turn, the waiter would have been unable to satisfy the external customer.

Setting this out in a visually accessible form (on paper or on a computer screen) produces a "service blueprint." Examination of the blueprint clarifies relationships, and often reveals unexpected or previously unrecognized service relationships. (The concept of "blueprinting" of this type is discussed further in Chapter 5.)

Implications for quality

Tracing these internal links from contact with the firm's external customer, and then backward through the chain of internal customers, is a useful method of assessing quality. It is apparent that it is just as important to deliver high-quality products and services to the internal customers as it is to deliver high-quality products and services to the external customers. Ultimately, quality is a satisfied external customer—the road to which is paved by satisfied internal customers (Heskett et al., 1997).

One of the first steps toward enhancing the quality of a service organization's daily work is by implementing the concept of *internal service improvement.* It can be conducted by all members of the organization, each of whom should ask the following sorts of questions:

* Who uses my internal and external services, and how?

* Who are my internal customers?

* What do I do for my internal customers?

* What is the most important thing I do, and what is the order of importance of the things that I do?

* What measurements do I use to gauge how I am doing?

* Which aspects of my service are beyond my immediate control? Of these, which are the most important?

Having completed such an analysis, each person should inform colleagues (internal customers and suppliers) of the most important thing that is outside his or her immediate control—and subsequently negotiate a quality standard of performance.

In the example of a restaurant, the chef might feel that the most important thing outside his control is the waiter's clear communication of the external customer's special requests. Once the chef and waiter agree on a standard, the next step is to draw up a flowchart of the process to ascertain whether modifying the process will assist in meeting their immediate needs, and hence ultimately meeting the external customers' needs. This will also allow the two parties to recognize other aspects of their internal service relationship, and help them to establish targets and measure the effectiveness of their parts in the overall process.

Internal service teamwork and efficiency thus dictates external service quality. See the box "Internal teamwork makes for external quality" for an example of how empathy and efficiency in the internal market can improve teamwork, and thus improve service to the external customer.

Internal marketing makes external marketing

Such an assessment of internal service functions has maximum effectiveness when personnel are empowered to make quick adjustments to meet the changing demands of external customers. In marketing terms, the successful reshaping of "external markets" requires the reshaping of "internal markets." Internal marketing is any form of marketing within an organization that focuses staff attention on the internal activities that need to be changed to implement changing external marketing plans.

This concept of internal marketing can be extended to include the development of an organizational climate in which cross-functional quality improvement is undertaken by *all* members of the organization—from the chief executive officer who directs the process to the service staff members who actually offer the service to the customer.

Internal teamwork makes for external quality

Teamwork is an essential ingredient in the delivery of quality service. For a seamless quality guest experience in a hotel, all departments must work efficiently together.

For example, one of the recurring challenges in hotel operations is how to manage the relocation of guests following overbooking. When this situation occurs, the front-desk employees are in the "firing line." They are the ones who have the awkward responsibility of explaining to guests that rooms are not available and that other accommodations have been arranged, perhaps across town. Front-desk employees resent being put in this situation, and they can feel quite angry with the sales and reservations departments for having allowed this to happen. Resentful and angry front-desk staff are unlikely to discharge these difficult duties with care and sensitivity toward customers.

Similarly, housekeepers can become angry with front-desk staff if they have shown too much leniency in allowing late check-out times to guests at a time when there are numerous incoming early arrivals expected. A shortened time period for cleaning guestrooms puts the housekeepers under pressure and can result in new guests having to wait impatiently for their rooms to become available. Harassed housekeepers are unlikely to offer a quality service to the guests, to their colleagues, or to management.

To overcome these sorts of difficulties, one hotel regularly gets together employees from different departments, such as those indicated above, for a half-day training session. This training session is devoted to helping employees from one department gain an understanding of the challenges and viewpoints of those in other departments. The training involves experiential and interactive teaching techniques in which employees gain cross-functional perspectives by role-playing the jobs of others in simulated operational challenges. For example, a front-desk employee enacts the role of a sales manager—explaining why and how the hotel came to be overbooked. Conversely, a sales manager is asked to play the role of a front-desk staff member—explaining to guests why and how they are to be relocated. Afterward, in discussion following the role-plays, employees openly discuss their concerns, and propose solutions for better teamwork.

The hotel's policy of providing consistent quality service—to both external customers (guests) and internal customers (employees)—is thus reinforced by improving empathy and cooperation between staff members in different departments.

Debby Cannon

J. W. Marriott, Jr., president of the Marriott Corporation, said to his managers: "Take care of your employees and they'll take care of your customers" (Marriott, 1988). This, of course, does not necessarily mean increased pay or other material gifts. Rather, it means attentive, caring leadership that treats its employees in the same way that it expects its customers to be treated.

The concept of "internal customer" is thus all-encompassing. Anyone who assists the organization to service its external customers constitutes an internal customer. According to this broad definition, the firm's leaders, employees, external intermediaries, representatives, and suppliers are *all* internal customers. Everyone in the service production process chain is either directly serving the external customer, or is serving someone else—if not an external customer, then an internal customer.

"Take care of your employees and . . ."

The Marriott group of hotels is renowned for its customer-centric service philosophy. But such a philosophy cannot be put into effect through wishful thinking. It must involve everyone—including the top person in the organization, all levels of management, and every member of staff.

The necessary philosophy and its implementation is neatly summed in two quotes from J. W. Marriott, Jr., president of the Marriott Corporation (Marriott, 1988).

First this:

We must do all we can to ensure that our organization's systems, methods, and policies serve the people who serve the customers.

And then this:

Take care of your employees and they'll take care of your customers.

External customers

The importance of customer information

The most important component of any business endeavor is the customer. Organizations conduct various forms of research to obtain information about the needs, expectations, and perceptions of their present and prospective customers. These expectations and perceptions are constantly changing, as is the nature of the service offered by competing organizations. It is therefore important that research into these matters is administered on a continuous basis—so that any changes can be picked up quickly, and acted upon as appropriate.

Research might establish answers to the following sorts of questions:

* Why did a customer buy (or not buy) a particular product or service?

* Is the customer satisfied or not with the product or service?

* What were the customer's expectations about the product or service before purchase and consumption?

* How do customers experience the different components of a given service?

* What are the trends in customer preferences over time?

All of this information (and much else besides) is useful. But, from the organization's perspective, the two "bottom-line" questions to be answered are:

* Is the customer satisfied or dissatisfied with the services offered?

* Will the customer return?

The way in which the information is utilized is of the utmost importance. It is the responsibility of management to collect, analyze, and interpret information accurately, and to communicate the findings to employees. Such information—gathered from the customers and fed back to the employees—is a powerful tool in effecting changes in both the "controllable" aspects of services (service systems, methods, and processes) and the "uncontrollable" aspects of services (the quality of the service encounter as perceived by the customer).

Customer-perception research

Customer-perception research usually employs a combination of qualitative and quantitative methods. Many hospitality establishments employ such studies to develop future marketing strategies. The aim is to gain a better understanding of how customers view the establishment to help management see its establishment as guests see it.

* *Quantitative* study involves the collection of statistical data on various *measurable aspects* of customer behavior.

* *Qualitative* study involves researchers identifying *attitudes* of current (and potential) clients, as well as those of the wider community. This might involve eliciting information from journalists, intermediaries, and even competitors.

The objective of customer-perception research is the identification of the characteristics of the service product that are most critical to the customer, and thus to isolate characteristics that can form the basis for successful differentiation of the organization's service product from others in a competitive market. The most commonly used methods for learning about customers' perceptions are:

* in-depth interviews with individual customers;

* focus-group interviews with selected groups of customers;

* statistical customer surveys of representative customer populations;

* critical-incident analysis;

* transaction analysis;

* mystery shoppers; and

* complaint analysis.

Some comments on each of these techniques for assessing customers' perceptions follow below; but first some general observations.

With all these methods, it is important to select carefully the people from whom the information is to be collected. They should constitute a reasonably representative sample of the customer population being studied. Ideally, the sample should include people who have never bought the service, as well as those who have. It is also helpful to collect information from people who prefer the services of a competitor—because disgruntled customers can provide information that is as valuable as that from happy customers (Reichheld & Sasser, 1990). Perception studies also frequently include an analysis of the perceptions of a firm's employees.

It is also good practice to offer external respondents a small honorarium or gift as an incentive to participate.

Customer-perception research

The most commonly used methods for learning about customers' perceptions are:

* in-depth interviews with individual customers;

* focus-group interviews with selected groups of customers;

* statistical customer surveys of representative customer populations;

* critical-incident analysis;

* transaction analysis;

* mystery shoppers; and

* complaint analysis.

In-depth interviews with individual customers

In an in-depth interview, the interviewer asks numerous questions about all aspects of the service product. This might involve a half-hour or more (perhaps extending to several hours) with a single customer. Because of the time and expense involved, this type of interview is the least frequently used. However, it often proves to be the most effective because it provides the most pertinent and current information. The aim of the interviewer is to uncover the key attributes of the service that customers deem to be important and desirable, and the attitudes of customers toward these attributes.

For example, in researching the service offered by a restaurant, the interviewer first wants to know why customers choose to go to a restaurant at all—rather than eating at home, or having a meal in some other way. What attributes of a restaurant meal induce a decision to go to a restaurant in the first place? Then enquiries can be made about price, meal times, preferred locations, favorite restaurants, favorite types of food, whether customers usually go out for a meal with friends, whether they ever go alone, and so on.

In-depth interviewers "actively listen"—to detect "cues" that reveal aspects of the experience about which customers seem to feel strongly. The effectiveness of the interview lies in discovering more about customers' feelings, needs, and expectations regarding particular aspects of the service, and knowing which aspects to explore in greater detail. The interviewer needs skill in knowing which "cues" to follow.

Following a series of interviews, the interviewer will frequently detect that a certain pattern of response is developing. At this point, nothing new seems to be forthcoming, and the interviewer can assume that it is reasonably safe to stop interviewing and compile the results. An analysis usually identifies recurring themes in the customers' statements regarding aspects of the service and its delivery. From this, the researcher might be able to draw up a list of attributes that defines the total service experience, as perceived by this customer.

(For a more detailed discussion on interviews and other qualitative research methods, readers are referred to Denzin & Lincoln, 1998.)

Focus-group interviews

Customer focus groups can provide a continuous source of information on customer expectations. The purpose of focus-group interviews is similar to that of individual interviews, but the discussion techniques are somewhat different.

Groups of customers, usually frequent users, are regularly brought together to allow a study of their opinions about the quality of service provided. The interviewer tries to involve everyone in the group, and attempts to draw out as many various opinions as possible. If one person states a strong opinion and there appears to be a general consensus, the interviewer probes to ascertain whether there are opposing views that are not being stated.

These groups can be usefully employed to monitor the introduction of a new or revised service. For example, following the experimental introduction of a new business center in a hotel, a panel of business travellers could be brought together to assess responses.

For established and ongoing services, the use of continuous groups can be a means of anticipating problems. Discussion in the group might reveal emerging issues of importance that can be addressed before they become real problems.

The validity of this research is dependent on how accurately the views of the group represent those of consumers as a whole. Careful selection should therefore be undertaken to ensure that the group possesses the same characteristics as the population of customers being analyzed—in terms of social, economic, and demographic factors, and in terms of frequency of use of the service. Having chosen such a group, the accuracy of focus-group information is then dependent on the skill of the researcher in ensuring that all views are heard, and in ensuring that an apparent consensus is a true consensus—representative of the group as a whole, and therefore likely to be representative of consumers as a whole.

Customer surveys

Statistical questionnaire surveys are often used if customer-perception information is required from a relatively large number of people. Individual interviews and focus-group interviews (as described above) might not involve a large enough sample to make statistically valid judgments about the customer base. Wider surveys are required for such statistically valid judgments. However, in-depth interviews and focus-group interviews are relevant to surveys. Such interviews serve a crucial role in determining the questions to be asked in surveys. In other words, the interview process involving a small number of people provides the basis of a research model for questionnaires aimed at a bigger population.

A research model involves the selection of the desired demographic group to be surveyed, and a list of key topics about which information is desired—opinions or preferences about the key attributes of the service being offered. This information can be processed statistically to develop a profile of the service preferences of the customers and their attitudes toward the organization and competing organizations. All of this information can be expressed as a demographic breakdown of preferences in terms of age, gender, educational level, and income level.

The use of customer-satisfaction surveys has become increasingly common in service industries (Pizam & Ellis, 1999). Hotels, for example, frequently leave guest questionnaires or comment cards in bedrooms, lobbies, and restaurants. Such surveys usually ask customers to relate positive and negative features of the service experience, as well as suggestions for improving the services. Customers believe that their feedback will be considered and acted upon by management immediately. However, this is often far from the truth in the vast majority of organizations.

If such surveys are to be beneficial to management, customers, and employees, planning and management of the questionnaire feedback system is essential. Questionnaires should have a definite purpose, and the survey should deal with a limited number of issues at any one time. Moreover, a definite time period should be designated for the gathering of information, and for subsequent action on any identified issue.

Critical-incident technique

Incident-based measurement or critical-incident technique (CIT) is based on the principle that long-term total customer satisfaction can be achieved only by identifying a list of all the problems that customers experience when using a service. Management needs to know what worries customers. A related phenomenon is that observed in many surveys—when it is often the case that the "additional comments" made by customers at the end of the survey prove to be the most valuable of all the information elicited from surveys. A survey might be carefully constructed and might seem to ask all the right questions. But then researchers discover that the most important information is contained in an "additional comment" about a subject that had not even occurred to researchers!

The fundamental idea of all incident-oriented measurement thus hinges around efforts to express the quality experiences of customers as precisely as possible through evaluation of *their own accounts* of these experiences. CIT focuses on the active and systematic investigation of customer experiences of critical incidents. In general terms, for an incident to be defined as "critical," it must deviate significantly from what is expected—either positively or negatively—and it must be possible to describe it in detail.

In formal terms, the CIT process has been defined in the following words: "a systematic and sequential effort to gather and analyze specific incidents of effective or ineffective behavior with respect to a designed activity" (Bitner, Nyquist, & Booms, 1984). The aim of this method is therefore to compile and evaluate "critical incidents" in a systematic and planned manner (Stauss, 1992, 1993).

> ## As perceived in practice by the customers
>
> The great value of critical-incident technique (CIT) is that it is firmly based on understanding the most important quality attributes *as perceived in practice by the customers*—not as perceived in theory by the management (Hope & Muhlemann, 1997).

CIT can assist management to identify problems in service delivery, and can also help management to redesign the service-delivery system. The important point is that any such redesigned system is firmly based on the most important quality attributes *as perceived in practice by the customers*—not as perceived in theory by the management (Hope & Muhlemann, 1997).

Capturing guests' feelings through comment logs

To assess customers' evaluation of their hospitality experience, hotel and resort managers often provide customer comment cards or use interactive computer systems with the television monitor in guest rooms. These quick surveys typically include a few dichotomous or forced-choice questions, and perhaps some scales to rate service quality. Despite the convenience of such surveys, response rates are usually low and the data generated from these surveys have somewhat limited use.

An alternative approach is to use customer comment logs as a "free-elicitation" device in assessing what is on the minds of guests during the service experience. The emotive content of these entries complements the more formal information gained from quantitative data-gathering methods. Instead of just perusing the comments, managers can (and should) conduct a systematic content analysis of the data. Content analysis uses an analytical framework to organize data by the frequency of occurrence.

At a beach resort in the British Virgin Islands, the comment logs used in eight cabanas over a two-year period were analyzed in this way. Some of the more interesting findings were as follows.

* Of the 550 entries, 86% of guests filled one whole page (and adjusted the size of their handwriting to do so), and the rest used two or more pages.

* Male and female guests were equally likely to write in the guest book.

* In two-thirds of the log entries, two individuals (presumably both parties occupying the room) signed the note.

* Many guests mentioned the activities of snorkeling, scuba diving, and sailing (158 all together).

* Of all the interior and exterior physical features of the resort, the bedroom area of the beach house was mentioned at least five times more often than any other feature.

* The physical attribute mentioned most often was the view.

* Although very few guests mentioned a specific food item, the quality of the food was acknowledged by nearly a third. Because the owners heavily promoted one food item, the information regarding food, although nonspecific, was able to be used to prompt some changes in promotional material.

* The resort management team was most interested in the words its customers used to describe the resort so they could use them in their brochures to help position the resort. The most common descriptors were "wonderful," "beautiful," "relaxing," "peaceful," and "tranquil." The emphasis was on restfulness as opposed to physical activity.

* Without solicitation, 44% of writers mentioned their intention to return.

* One famous U.S. senator wrote: "We must never let the Republicans know about this [resort]!"

Linda Shea

Transaction analysis

Although a relatively new concept within the hospitality industry, *transaction analysis* is an increasingly popular research method. It is used by many organizations to "track" the satisfaction of customers regarding particular transactions with which they have recently been involved. This type of research enables management to assess *current* performance as it affects customers' satisfaction with the immediate contact personnel, and customers' overall satisfaction with the service.

Hosting seminars and conferences requires excellent facilities including comfortable auditoriums and modern audiovisual technology. But the service can be maintained at the highest level only by careful transaction analysis after the event in which participants are asked to review, analyze, and assess the service received. Customer feedback is essential for service quality.

With kind permission of Hyatt Hotels Corporation

Such research is often conducted via postal questionnaires or telephone surveys of individual customers immediately after a transaction has been completed. For example, following a function or conference, many hotels contact customers and organizers and perform a "debriefing" in which the function is reviewed, analyzed, and assessed.

Apart from assessing the function as a whole, the immediate nature of transaction analysis allows the hotel to associate the quality of its service (as perceived by the customer) with individual contact personnel. This information can then be used as a basis for appropriate reward systems for deserving members of staff, or for appropriate corrective action for those whose service has been unsatisfactory.

Mystery shoppers

Mystery shopping is a means of auditing the standard of service offered. In this case, the main focus is to assess the capacity of service personnel to offer services at the established standards.

Regular checks on the levels of service performance are essential for any service organization if it is to maintain a consistent quality of service. Indeed, eliminating or reducing variability is one of the major tasks of service managers. The service performance "gap" (the variation from the established standard of service) might be due to a number of causes—defective systems or procedures, inability of the employee, unwillingness of the employee, and so on (see "Service quality gap," Chapter 3). The function of mystery shopper surveys is to monitor the extent to which specified quality standards are actually being met.

This method of research is frequently used by hotels and restaurants. It involves trained assessors who visit service organizations, observe service levels, and report back. Audits are often tailored to issues that the company wishes to evaluate. For example, in an effort to increase value for stakeholders, Hilton Hotels once implemented what they referred to as a "balanced scorecard"—which consisted of guest surveys, employee surveys, *and* reports from mystery shoppers (Huckestein & Duboff, 1999). In this case, the mystery shopper audit was seen as part of a wider program of assessment. Other firms might organize other combinations of audit. The actual form of enquiry to be used is determined by the organization, the researcher, and the specific local issues at hand.

When correctly implemented, mystery shopping can provide service managers with detailed information about what is being routinely experienced by customers at the front line of the business. To be effective, mystery-shopping surveys must be:

* independent;

* objective; and

* consistent.

The researcher must have a comprehensive knowledge of the industry, job tasks, and procedures—combined with good observation techniques. This can entail the ability to differentiate quite subtle nuances—for example, there is a difference between an initial greeting of a guest (which is crucial and must be done in a way that makes the guest feel special) and a passing acknowledgment later on (which is of lesser significance, and can be more casual and less "intense"). As another example, there is a subtle difference between a receptionist's efficient and business-like tone of voice (which might be perfectly acceptable) and an unduly cool or impersonal attitude (which is unacceptable). Such differences can be subtle and subjective. Mystery shopper data are therefore *qualitative,* and must be conducted by people who know what they are doing. Even so, the qualitative subjective data must be validated by a carefully designed and tested measurement process.

Making the most of mystery shopping

As a hospitality professor, a part-time hospitality industry employee, and a customer, I have seen mystery shopping used in a variety of contexts. One personal experience sticks in my mind.

Several years ago, a chain of casual restaurants retained me to conduct service evaluations for them. At first, it seemed strange that this particular company even bothered to employ mystery shoppers. The company was already a market leader in its segment, and everything that it did seemed to be of the highest quality. It was not until I began my visits that I realized the secret of its success.

This was no ordinary company. The way in which the company handled the details of my mystery shopping activities was nothing short of remarkable—from the detailed information they asked for in my reports, to the way in which this information was presented to the restaurant managers, to the speed with which the information was disseminated to individual restaurants. Furthermore, everything was done in a constructive fashion. Managers and employees actually looked forward to receiving the evaluations from corporate headquarters. And, in some cases, they wanted even more information than was provided—all in the interests of improving the service to their customers.

Here was a company with the right corporate culture. Here was an organization that welcomed reliable and immediate feedback to managers and employees as part of its customer-centric attitude to quality service.

Clayton W. Barrows

Complaint analysis

Why complaints should be encouraged

Many companies undertake no formal research of customer attitudes, and therefore depend entirely on customer complaints to stay in touch with market perception. For these companies, complaints are generally a tiresome business with the minor redeeming feature of providing some vaguely useful information on customer opinion.

In contrast to this very narrow view of complaint feedback, research has provided convincing evidence that significant rewards are available to organizations that handle complaints creatively and appropriately. Appropriate management of complaints goes beyond merely "handling" dissatisfied customers. Rather, it involves the active *encouragement* of complaints, followed by appropriate *remedies*.

The idea of actively encouraging complaints might seem strange. However, the idea is firmly based on some interesting and insightful research (see box "Interesting research on complaints," below). In essence, this research suggests that, far from being discouraged, ignored, or disposed of, complaints should actually be encouraged, facilitated, and acted upon.

Interesting research on complaints

Research conducted by a U.S.-based research organization, Technical Assistance Research Programs Inc. (TARP 1979, 1986), has provided convincing evidence that significant rewards are available to organizations that handle complaints creatively and appropriately. For example, among TARP's key findings were the following.

* The average business never hears from 96% of its unhappy customers. For every complaint received, the average company has actually had 26 customers with problems, 6 of which were "serious" problems.

* Complainers are more likely than noncomplainers to do business again with the company that upset them, even if the problem is not satisfactorily resolved.

* Of the customers who register a complaint, 54–70% will do business with the organization again if their complaint is resolved. This percentage goes up to a staggering 95% if the customer feels that the complaint was resolved quickly.

* The average customer who has had a problem with a firm tells 9–10 people about it. Of people who have a problem with an organization, 13% recount the incident to more than 20 people.

* Customers who have complained to an organization and had their complaints satisfactorily resolved tell an average of five people about the treatment they received.

More than listening

Merely listening to complaints is insufficient if service providers wish to understand customers (Zeithaml, Parasuraman, & Berry, 1990). The reason for this is that complaints provide information only about the *problems* experienced by customers, not about their *expectations*. It is necessary to have a system in place that gathers and analyzes information about expectations, as well as about immediate complaints, so that changes can be made to reduce or eliminate future mistakes.

Complaints can become part of a larger process of staying in touch with customers. In particular, complaints can provide important information about the failures or breakdowns in the *overall service system,* and not just about isolated incidents. If compiled, analyzed, and fed back to employees who are empowered to correct the problems, complaints can become an inexpensive and continuous source of adjustment for the overall service process.

But this must be part of a conscious and deliberate system of *wanting* to institute remedial action. It is insufficient to set up systems that purport to "learn" from complaints. This is insufficient because it is essentially reactive in nature, and basically allows the firm to tolerate failure. In such a culture of tolerating failure, management is effectively saying: "We're learning; we don't actually do anything, but we're learning!" Such reactive practices represent a fundamental flaw in much of the current theory and practice of firms that *profess* to be pursuing superior service. In fact, what the customer expects, and what the customer is entitled to receive, is *good service first time, every time.* And an active policy of responding to complaints quickly and effectively is essential if this objective—good service first time, every time—is to be achieved.

"Silent" complaints

Although it is important to take note of complaints, and act upon them, neither the incidence of customer problems nor the extent of customer satisfaction can be assessed adequately on the basis of complaint information alone. Part of the problem is that most consumers do not complain—they simply remain dissatisfied, and tell others about their dissatisfaction. Dissatisfied customers do not complain because they do not think it will do any good, or because they want to avoid hassle (Berry & Parasuraman, 1992). Instead, they take their business elsewhere (TARP, 1986; Thomas, 1988), while spreading negative comments by word of mouth.

The TARP studies described in the box provide strong evidence to support the relationship between complaint response on the one hand, and the final state of satisfaction and future repurchase intentions on the other. Consistent with these research findings, Gilly (1987) and Bitner, Booms, and Tetreault (1990) provide empirical evidence that supports the view that the way complaints are handled by customer contact staff is a major factor in determining the future attitudes and repurchase intentions of customers.

It is therefore apparent that steps must be taken to ensure that "silent" complaints do not remain silent. Firms must actively seek out complaints, prevent "silent complainers" from privately nursing a perceived grievance, and thus enhance overall satisfaction and repeat business.

Proactive rather than reactive

In this competitive marketplace, a proactive approach is thus essential. Service providers should take the lead in gathering information about customers' expectations, needs, and views such that management can set priorities and take strategic action. Organizations should therefore have systems that are easily accessible for customers to voice their views. To ensure effectiveness, such easily accessible systems should be complemented by rewards that actively encourage customer feedback.

Analysis of a hotel complaint log

It has become increasingly common for hoteliers to document customer complaints. What is less common is for these logbooks to be recognized as treasure troves of valuable data.

One four-plus star property in New York City maintained such a log. It had been useful on a case-by-case basis—mostly as a follow-up of individual complaints as required. It was not until log entries were *content analyzed* that the general manager realized the full value of the data. Instead of reviewing one case at a time, content analysis allowed an *overall view* of the types of complaints, the characteristics of complainers, the complaint-resolution process offered, and the customers' satisfaction with each resolution.

Some of the interesting findings regarding 220 complaints logged over a one-year period were as follows.

* Most complaints involved equipment failures (42%) or service failures (38%).

* The majority of complaints (70%) were lodged by male guests—that is, more than twice the complaints logged by females (although slightly more males than females did visit the hotel).

* The most common resolution was simply to correct the problem (27%), followed by room upgrade or change (23%).

* More than 85% of guests were satisfied with the complaint-resolution process. However, they were more likely to be satisfied with a solution to an equipment failure than with a solution to a service failure. Guests were least likely to be satisfied with a follow-up letter or a statement of hotel policies.

Linda Shea

The existence of systems for receiving and processing complaints must be made known to customers. This acts effectively as a service guarantee ("If you are not happy we want to know"), and creates a positive image of the firm. British Airways, for example, installed customer-complaint booths at Heathrow Airport where disgruntled passengers could record their grievances on videotape. In addition to providing customers with immediate relief from their annoyances, British Airways found that the complaint videotapes gave vivid information to management and employees about customers' problems and expectations. In a similar way, companies such as American Motors have effectively used consumer concerns as a central element in their marketing strategy by providing incentives for making complaints.

The making of complaints should therefore be encouraged and facilitated. Because customer complaints are opportunities whereby firms are given the chance to correct problems that would otherwise have gone unnoticed and been left to alienate large numbers of customers for months or years, barriers should be broken down to make complaining easy. The function of a complaint service is, in effect, to discover wounds in the body corporate and to dress them before infection sets in, with the potential loss of an entire market (Tschohl, 1991).

Measurement of service quality

Apart from gathering (largely qualitative) data from the methods described above, various attempts have been made to assess service quality by objective measurement. The methods for measuring service quality are essentially of two types:

* monitoring operations to ensure conformance to specifications (an operations perspective); and

* measuring customer satisfaction (a performance or marketing perspective).

Operations perspective

Many goods-manufacturing companies routinely conduct surveys to study their own operational systems. From a methodological perspective, these studies belong to what are technically called *multi-attribute measurement tools* (Stauss, 1992).

Numerous authors (see, e.g., Rosander, 1985, 1991) have extended these traditional statistical quality-control tools from the goods sector to the service environment. However, there are two inherent problems with applying statistical quality-control tools to service operations:

* the intangibility of services makes objective measurement of the operation difficult in many cases; that is, there is no distinct physical "assembly line" to measure; and

* such tools all aim to keep operational variation within specific conformance standards; however, in delivering services, variation is not always undesirable (indeed, in the case of services that are "customized," variation is often positively desirable) (Armstrong, 1992).

Performance perspective

It is therefore apparent that, for services, quality is best assessed by measuring customer satisfaction—rather than by measuring operations efficiency. As noted above, the very nature of services (as opposed to goods manufacturing) means that there is no "assembly line" that can be easily looked at and objectively measured. Even if it were possible to do so, absolute conformity to some sort of set standard is not necessarily desirable in services—effective service delivery at its best is a dynamic and responsive process.

In the ultimate, therefore, services quality is best assessed by measuring customer satisfaction. A "performance perspective" is of more use than an "operations perspective."

In this section of the chapter, such performance measurement is considered under the following heads:

* the SERVQUAL approach;

* the SERVPERF approach;

* customer-satisfaction measurement (CSM); and

* service-attribute score.

The chapter then concludes with consideration of the important topic of employee feedback in assessing customer satisfaction.

The SERVQUAL approach

Measurement of perceived quality of service has been extensively studied by Parasuraman, Zeithaml, and Berry (see "Service quality concepts," Chapter 3). They developed a tool called "SERVQUAL" for evaluating a consumer's assessment of service quality, and have used the instrument successfully in many sectors of the service industry. SERVQUAL consists of survey questions about a number of service-quality attributes or dimensions. As was noted in Figure 3.6, these attributes include:

* *tangibles*—physical facilities, equipment, and appearance of personnel;

* *reliability*—ability to perform the desired service dependably, accurately, and consistently;

* *responsiveness*—willingness to provide prompt service and help customers;

* *assurance*—knowledge, competence, ability to convey trust, confidence, and credibility; and

* *empathy*—provision of caring, individualized attention.

It is important to note that the service-delivery process itself is *not* evaluated using SERVQUAL (as was the case with the "operations perspective" noted above). Rather, with this "performance perspective," service quality is assessed solely on the consumer's feedback.

For each of the above attributes, SERVQUAL measures:

* the service *expectations* of the consumer; and

* his or her *perceptions* of the service received.

The difference between these two measurements is then assessed and used as an indication of service quality. In the SERVQUAL model, quality is defined as a weighted average of the quality determinants (Parasuraman et al., 1988). The weights used in the model are effectively defined by the consumer, according to the relative importance of each quality attribute.

There are some criticisms of the general applicability of the SERVQUAL model. Some customers have difficulty in differentiating among many of the scale items, and it is sometimes impractical to ask customers about their expectations before consumption and then again immediately after consumption. Despite these misgivings, this instrument is a concise multiple-item scale with good reliability, and it has been widely accepted as a valid instrument in the measurement of service quality (Fisk, Brown, & Bitner, 1993).

The SERVPERF approach

As noted above, there is some doubt as to whether the SERVQUAL instrument is reliable in all circumstances. Some researchers have indicated that a more direct approach to the measurement of service quality might be appropriate. Cronin and Taylor (1992) proposed "SERVPERF"–a measurement of service quality based only on performance (not on expectations *and* performance).

SERVPERF is thus similar to SERVQUAL in some respects, but differs in others. It is similar in that it requires customers to rate the performance of service providers, but it differs in not seeking to establish any difference between expectations and perceptions. Under the SERVPERF model, only the post-consumption perceptions of performance are assessed. Customers are asked to rate the perceived performance (but *not* their prior expectations) on a five-point Likert scale ranging from a score of "1" (strongly disagree that service is satisfactory) to "5" (strongly agree that service is satisfactory).

Cronin and Taylor (1992) claimed that the SERVPERF scale is superior in comparison with other measurements. They were supported in this view by McAlexander, Kaldenberg, and Koenig (1994) who used the performance-only SERVPERF scale in a study conducted in a health care setting. In this study, they showed that SERVPERF does overcome some of the technical problems associated with SERVQUAL—including the possibility of raised customer expectations altering later perceptions, difficulties in administering two parts of the questionnaire (before and after), and certain statistical problems in measuring and comparing different properties that were not strictly equivalent (Hope & Muhlemann, 1997). The use of a single measure of service performance (as opposed to a dual measure of expectation and performance) was found to circumvent all of the above problems.

However, although it is simpler, the SERVPERF model does ignore potentially valuable information. As we have seen, a customer's prior expectation is an important aspect of that customer's perception of service quality, and this information is necessarily lost if the assessment is based only on performance. Simplicity is gained, but detail is lost.

Customer-satisfaction measurement (CSM)

What is CSM?
Apart from the SERVQUAL and SERVPERF instruments, there are various other methods used to assess customer satisfaction. Whatever precise methods are used, companies need answers to the following sorts of questions:

* What are the key attributes of a product or service that customers use to make the purchase decision?

* How important is each of these attributes?

* What are the performance ratings of each attribute, as perceived by the customer?

The last of these is a measurable variable. Having obtained the performance ratings (the third question above), a customer-satisfaction score, or customer-satisfaction measurement (CSM), is calculated as a weighted average of the performance rating (Gale, 1990).

CSM is not simply a research activity. It provides key management information, and gives direction to a firm's ongoing quality-improvement activities. CSM is thus:

* a strategic tool for determining the allocation of company resources;

* an operations tool for determining improvement of the company processes; and

* a public relations tool for communicating the company's commitment to quality.

See the box for some examples of the wide variety of CSM methods that can be used.

Problems with CSM
The design of measurement instruments and systems for the regular collection of satisfaction data appears intuitively simple, but there remain many important questions. These include the following (Czepiel, 1980).

* When should the data be collected—immediately after consumption or after a period of time? What differences result from collecting the data at different times?

* What consumption experience should be evaluated? Should it be the one just completed, or an "average" experience, or the "average" over some recent period of time? Which of these methods is most valid, reliable, and useful?

Some examples of CSM activities

A variety of programs and methods can be used to measure customer satisfaction.

* Holiday Inn gives its customers questionnaires at reception, and these can be dropped into a specially designated box after completion.

* Dell Computers includes a questionnaire diskette with its computers.

* Volkswagen conducts a questionnaire survey of approximately 660,000 customers in Germany every two years.

* Panasonic attaches reply cards to each product sold.

* Domino Pizza has a total of 10,000 unidentified customers who receive US$60 every year to buy twelve pizzas and evaluate the quality and service they experience.

Some organizations provide attractive incentives in an attempt to increase customer feedback.

* Bang & Olufsen extends its guarantee for another year to customers who respond to their questionnaires.

* Dell Computers rewards its respondents with 10 diskettes.

---

* What methodology is best, and for what purpose? Does personal interviewing obtain the same data as self-completed questionnaires? Is telephone interviewing better than interviewing in person?

* How many of the numerous different service features can (or should) be evaluated? At what point do responses become more a function of a previous response rather than an evaluation of the specific service attribute? What degree of specificity is useful to management?

* What methods are available to validate measures of satisfaction with service quality? To what extent does the measurement of satisfaction itself affect satisfaction?

* To what extent should one try to "anchor" the satisfaction scale? Should this "anchor" represent the level of the competition? To what degree is satisfaction affected by the availability of alternatives? How stable is a measure of satisfaction across varying competitive sets of data? On any given scale, what is good performance or poor performance?

Although much work has been done in the area of CSM, important questions such as those above still seem to be inadequately answered.

Setting up CSM

The design of a CSM program is usually a joint decision, involving the company's managers and its consultants. Typically, the company engages a CSM consulting firm, which performs the role of prime contractor for the program. Working as a team, the internal managers and the external consultants make decisions about the research methodology—taking into account the objectives of the program and the special circumstances of the firm.

Irrespective of the scope of the program, a common core of methodological decisions must be made. Some of the basic methodological questions that need to be addressed include the following (Crosby, 1992).

* Will any exploratory research be conducted?

* Will the exploratory research involve focus groups or in-depth interviews?

* How will the main survey be conducted?

* What is the population, and how should it be sampled?

* Will the data be collected using telephone, mail, or personal interviews?

* What questions will be asked? What analyses will be performed?

* How will the data be presented?

An important data-collection issue in CSM concerns the frequency of measurement. A continuous monitoring program is better than an intermittent program. The specific design must also consider the potential for respondent "burnout" in finite customer populations, the ability of the organization to assimilate and respond to CSM results, and the length of time it takes for managerial actions to affect customers' perceptions of quality.

In many organizations, especially those dealing with physical goods, CSM programs usually involve quantitative survey research. However, in the case of services, satisfaction and quality are highly subjective matters. In these circumstances, quantitative methods might not be appropriate for assessing perceptions of quality. An effective CSM program should therefore use both qualitative and quantitative research methods. Moreover, exploratory work should be conducted both outside and inside the company.

Summing up CSM

CSM is thus an umbrella term used to describe various means of identifying customer requirements and assessing the company's performance in meeting those requirements.

CSM has the capacity to focus the entire organization on satisfying customers' needs (Crosby, 1991). To do this, organizations require information—both qualitative and quantitative, and from both external and internal customers—on a regular basis. A combined internal and external perspective is necessary to identify and solve quality problems.

Ultimately, the goal is to understand the links between the perceptions of customers regarding quality of service, and the variables that managers and employees control.

Service-attribute score

The service-attribute score is a structured presentation of critical service attributes. It indicates the priority given to certain attributes by customers as a relative score that can be compared with the scores given to competing organizations. This allows management and employees to identify those critical attributes in which they need to take action to maintain market leadership for superior service.

In a presentation chart of attribute scores, attributes are grouped under functional categories, and the relative importance of each is rated in terms of customer preference, and in terms of the potential benefit in maintaining market leadership. The attribute score of competing organizations can also be established by such customer research.

The attribute report thus correlates three kinds of information:

* the key quality attributes of the service;

* the relative desirability of each attribute to the customer; and

* the organization's score on these attributes, and its ability to compete in the marketplace on each activity level.

As can be seen in Figure 4.1, an attribute score report recorded in a hotel reception area might include assessments of various service tasks, including room/conference bookings, arrival/departure, concierge, meal service, and so on. Service, as referred to here, is the total service experience of the customer, and involves various tasks. Thus, a service attribute score report indicates the standard and level at which each service and its components should be offered. For example, if an attribute's customer priority score is 8 and the score of the competition is 8, this indicates that a score of 8 is the minimum operating level. The aim is to improve to score 9 or 10 to lead the market. In contrast, a score of 7 would be an unacceptable level (compared with an opposition score of 8). An attribute score report can thus be used as a unique tool to assist service personnel.

Employee research

Employees as "listening posts"

In a service business, *everyone* is responsible for managing service, and front-line customer-contact employees represent one of the most valuable means for gathering information about customers. By eliciting information about customers, these employees are ideally placed to help senior management know their customers better. They are, in effect, "listening posts" (Heskett et al., 1997). And a service firm probably has more such "listening posts" than management commonly believes—virtually every employee can function as a valuable "data-collection center" and on-the-spot "market researcher" (Albrecht & Bradford, 1990). Service personnel are, in fact, in a better position to evaluate the customer's experience than anyone else in the organization.

Figure 4.1 *A presentation of service-attribute scores as collected in a hotel reception area*

Service attribute	Customer score	Competitor's score
Room/conference booking		
Product selection	7	8
Special packages	8	4
Value for money	8	6
Confirmation follow-up	8	3
Arrival/departure		
Ease and speed	8	5
Efficient handling of requests	7	6
Friendliness	8	7
Willingness to help	8	6
Concierge		
(various attributes listed)	(scores listed)	(scores listed)
(various attributes listed)	(scores listed)	(scores listed)
Meal service		
(various attributes listed)	(scores listed)	(scores listed)
(various attributes listed)	(scores listed)	(scores listed)
Other services to be studied (as appropriate)		
(various attributes listed)	(scores listed)	(scores listed)
(various attributes listed)	(scores listed)	(scores listed)

Author's presentation

Inseparability makes employees important

As previously noted on several occasions, one of the distinctive features of services is "inseparability"—that is, services are produced and consumed simultaneously, and services therefore differ from physical goods in that there are no channels of distribution to isolate the producer from the consumer. Service personnel meet and communicate personally with the customer each time a service is rendered. Service personnel are thus the direct "face" (or "marketer") of the organization, and are the most important link in a service organization's communication with its customers.

Management involvement

Such communication is one of the critical factors in the success of any service organization. In the words of Deming (1982), effective two-way communication can "drive out fear." But the emphasis must be on effective *two-way* communication. Unless management makes itself easily accessible and approachable, upward communication will not take place. Top management must emphasize a company philosophy in which the focus is on the customer, and must demonstrate its support of those employees who actively live this out by really serving customers.

Management must recognize the importance of feedback from employees, and actively encourage it. If information regarding customers' expectations and perceptions, as obtained by customer-contact employees, is passed onto top management, management's understanding of their customers *must* be enhanced. Indeed, in most companies, management's understanding of their customers largely depends on such communication as received from customer-contact personnel. However, large organizations often have an organizational structure consisting of many levels, and usually communicate through fixed and formal systems. Such formal communication systems can prevent the full benefit of feedback information—which might otherwise be more readily available from employees in less-formal arrangements.

Managers must encourage and support employees in their service endeavors, and senior managers must make themselves available to receive feedback. They must be active in personally seeking feedback from employees, and transparent in their willingness to act upon it.

Employees as customer "advocates"

Employees should be encouraged to become "advocates" for the customer. Indeed, many employees have a natural tendency to do so.

In many service-interface situations, employees take customers "under their wings" to see that their needs and wants are met and that their problems are solved. By so doing, a door is opened to much important information about the buyer of the service. If employees begin to function as customer advocates, a new sense of responsibility for knowing those customers "inside-out" will develop.

A customer advocate goes beyond providing a service or product to the customer. In many service situations, a personal relationship with the customer becomes established (as is evident in the case of many professional services, such as educational services, medical services, and so on). The same sort of relationship can be encouraged in a service organization such as a hotel. Although the relationship is clearly not as intimate as, say, a medical consultation, the same general principles apply. As customers become known on a more intimate basis, their trust grows, and their willingness to express their concerns, wishes, and preferences increases.

Indeed, relationships can develop such that front-line employees sometimes prove to be more loyal to their customers than to management. This is consistent with the Japanese management approach, whereby employees are constantly informed that their loyalty *should* be with the customers because, ultimately, the customers are paying their wages. This sort of strong commitment to customer orientation is to be encouraged. It can ensure a service firm's survival in even the most turbulent market conditions.

Employees as "listening posts"

A family dairy business located in the rural United States is a classic success story. Its success comes from providing customers with exactly what they want. And how does the business find out exactly what they want? By listening!

It is hard to believe, but what started out as a small family dairy farm selling milk turned into a multimillion dollar and multifaceted tourist attraction in a matter of years. It all started when a customer suggested that homemade ice cream might be a good idea to sell alongside the milk. The owner listened and decided to diversify his product line from plain milk to include ice cream and baked goods. This was followed by the opening of a small store on the property selling a variety of fresh and processed foods. The ice cream in particular proved to be a "hit." In fact, the quality of the ice cream was so good that some customers were driving more than 25 miles to purchase it. In turn, this led to a few regulars suggesting to employees that a restaurant on the premises might be a success. The alert employees mentioned this to the proprietor who picked up on this opportunity and soon opened a restaurant offering breakfast, lunch, and dinner. Weekends were always packed and the restaurant soon became a routine stop for tour bus operators. Locally, the dairy became known as the breakfast meeting place for the "who's who" of the town and district.

But more was to follow! The farm also became a regular outing for grandparents taking their grandchildren for ice cream treats—a trend that provided another opportunity. Some grandparents suggested to employees the desirability of some form of activity for their grandchildren on site. Again, the employees, who saw themselves as friends and confidants of their customers, took this suggestion to the proprietor. Again, the proprietor listened to his trusted employees. Soon the dairy had a small zoo—a "petting zoo" consisting of goats, pigs, sheep, and calves where small children could safely interact with farm animals.

More suggestions followed. Again they were faithfully passed on from guests to employees to the proprietor, and again they were acted upon. In conjunction with the "petting zoo," the dairy introduced a feed-vending machine that dispensed a handful of feed in exchange for a coin. These vending machines eventually reaped thousands of dollars in revenue.

Following the success of the "petting zoo," and again acting upon employee feedback from customers—this time a request for something for older children and teenagers—the proprietor installed some baseball "batting cages," which provided youngsters with the opportunity to practice their favorite sport. This turned out to be an instant success with the youth. Later, acting on further suggestions, he added a pumpkin patch where customers could pick their own pumpkins for Halloween. Then someone suggested a maze. The family who owned the farm also had cornfields next door. So they built a huge corn maze to entertain their visitors. A small "mini-golf" course followed.

Soon people of all ages were having lots of fun at the erstwhile "dairy farm." Accompanying the growth of the farm and its attractions was a web-page announcing family fun activities at the farm.

In addition to all of this, the farm has involved itself extensively in a wide range of humanitarian and environmental community projects in partnership with local people and organizations.

So, what is the secret of the stunning success of this venture? The vision and initiative of the proprietor should not be underestimated. But, most of all, the farm succeeded brilliantly because it responded promptly and pre-cisely to what its customers told it they wanted. And how did these cus-tomers pass on their desires and ideas? Through the loyal and hardworking staff members who saw themselves simultaneously as service providers and as "customer advocates." They formed close working and personal relation-ships with their guests. They wanted to serve them. They wanted to hear from them. And they really listened to them!

Employees can be excellent "listening posts." They are "out there" in touch with the guests. Empowered employees who care for their customers and their organizations are a service provider's greatest asset. Proprietors who lis-ten to them have a veritable goldmine of ready-made market research!

H. G. Parsa

Making it work effectively

Shapiro (1992) recommended that employees become directly involved in the process of collecting customer feedback for the following reasons:

* to create an opportunity to extend appreciation to customers for their business; and

* to establish communication back to customers, to reassure them that they are being listened to.

It might be desirable to implement service quality "circles" as a deliberate, formal mechanism for gathering customer feedback. Many service settings provide the oppor-tunity for joint problem-solving activity, involving both the customer and the contact person. Through such active communication, employees who provide services can identify the customer's needs and find a configuration of the service that best satisfies those needs.

This encourages employees to participate actively in problem solving and decision making. This improves morale in the workplace, and fosters a positive, customer-oriented culture.

Regular feedback communication systems ensure a continuous flow of information from employees to management, and back again. This communication system should have formal and informal channels to capture the full spectrum of available knowledge, and thus to provide maximum benefit in tailoring effective quality service.

Summary of chapter

In the present competitive marketplace, business firms must adopt a customer-oriented managerial approach to attract and retain their customers. As discussed in previous chapters, the distinctive nature of service products forces service organizations to place even more emphasis on *customers* in the design, development, and delivery of their service offerings. It is thus imperative that the firms understand customer expectations and perceptions, as well as the factors that influence their evaluation and satisfaction with the services.

Market-oriented firms must be up to date with new market trends in customer needs, perceptions, and expectations. And service providers who are able to anticipate customer needs and desires before they become apparent in the marketplace will be advantaged in gaining a winning market position. To gather, analyze, and act on market information effectively is thus of paramount importance to service providers who wish to stay ahead in the marketplace.

Within the service sector, the hospitality industry offers services that entail prolonged and intensive customer contact. Quality interaction is therefore essential to quality service and guest satisfaction, and also presents an opportunity for hoteliers to solicit and gather customer information and feedback. To realize this potential advantage, however, management should not restrict its efforts and resources to traditional forms of market research. Hospitality management should also facilitate the understanding and participation of all employees in the organization in every form of guest contact. The contribution of service employees forms a foundation on which hospitality managers can obtain and collate information that provides valuable market insights. Appropriate strategies can then be designed in response to customer demands as well as competitive forces.

This chapter has emphasized the importance of understanding the needs and desires of service customers from different perspectives—those of the customer, management, and employees. In addition, the chapter has discussed some of the most effective methods of customer research. These methods, which can be used independently or in conjunction, can assist hospitality managers in understanding the behavior and characteristics of hotel guests, and in improving their managerial effectiveness and business performance.

Review questions

1. Briefly explain the concept of internal marketing.

2. Explain how internal customer service can affect the quality of external customer service. Give examples of how a hotel manager might serve his or her internal customers.

3. Briefly describe the techniques for gathering customer information, as presented in this chapter.

4. Briefly describe the techniques for measuring organizational performance, as presented in this chapter.

Suggested reading for this chapter

This is a list of suggested further reading on topics covered in this chapter. For a separate list of full reference citations quoted in the chapter, see "References," Chapter 4, at the end of the book.

Bitner, M. J. 1990. "Evaluating Service Encounters: The Effect of Physical Surroundings and Employee Responses," *Journal of Marketing*, vol. 54, April.

Crosby, L. A. 1991. "Expanding the Role of CSM in Total Quality," *International Journal of Service Industry Management*, vol. 2, no. 2.

Lewis, B. R., & Mitchell, V. W. 1990. "Defining and Measuring the Quality of Customer Service," *Marketing Intelligence and Planning*, vol. 8, no. 6.

Parasuraman, A., Berry, L. L., & Zeithaml, V. A. 1991. "Understanding Customer Expectations of Service," *Sloan Management Review*, Spring.

Prokesch, S. E. 1995. "Competing on Customer Service: An interview with British Airways' Sir Colin Marshall," *Harvard Business Review*, Nov.–Dec.

Reichheld, F. F. 1996. "Learning from Customer Defections," *Harvard Business Review*, March–April.

Part III

Services that Serve

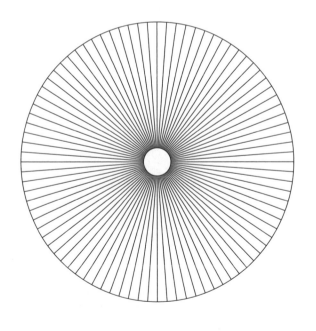

chapter five
The Service Vision

Study objectives

Having completed this chapter, readers should be able to:

* appreciate the importance of a service vision and service strategy to an organization's long-term success;

* understand the importance of a well-designed service system;

* understand the implications of service networks in building a firm's competitive advantage; and

* understand some of the most practical techniques for managing service operations.

The framework of this chapter

This chapter is set out as follows:

* Introduction

* Service vision or concept

    − Like an architect's drawing
    − Set apart from the rest
    − Ingrained into the fabric
    − Design and practice
    − Customer-centric
    − But still market-aware

* Service strategy

    − What is a service strategy?
    − Everyone is involved
    − Marketing implications
    − Changing needs mean changing strategies
    − Some practical examples
    McDonald's
    Holiday Inn
    Hyatt
    Ritz-Carlton
    Marriott Fairfield

* Service processes

    − What is a service process?
    − Process as the "essence" of service
    − Quality at every stage
    − Analyzing the steps
    − Process quality and output quality
    − Ultimately a management responsibility

* Perfecting the service system

    − By design not by evolution
    − Designing a service to serve
    − Inbuilt flaws
    − Design is a dynamic process
    − Creative thinking

* Service design and blueprinting

    − Leading to a "moment of truth"
    − The nature of a service blueprint
    − A "snapshot" of a dynamic process
    − The "line of visibility"
    − "Fail points" and "encounter points"
    − Looking back and looking ahead
    − Blueprints within blueprints
    − Dreams and reality
    − Flowcharts
    − Moments of truth remain crucial

* Managing the "critical encounters"

    − This is what it's all about
    − Pareto analysis
    − Fishbone analysis

* Designing and managing service networks

    − Advantages of networks
    − Again, a customer focus
    − Big is beautiful

* Summary of chapter

Introduction

Having discussed the needs of customers in Chapter 4, we now proceed in the present chapter to discuss how a service firm might organize its internal arrangements to ensure that these needs are met.

Successful service organizations pursue visions of service excellence that clearly indicate to customers and employees the objectives of the firm and its position in the marketplace. This *vision of service* (or *service concept*) provides the foundation upon which the firm designs its service offerings such that they are always consistent with the overall image that the organization has attempted to create in the minds of customers.

The nature of service products makes the service-delivery process especially important. It is imperative that firms design service systems that effectively organize the firm's processes to produce the desired outcome. To this end, various techniques, such as "blueprinting," have been developed to visualize interrelationships of service processes, to identify common pitfalls, and to enable firms to channel their efforts efficiently to achieve maximum benefits.

Because every organization has a limited number of core competencies, different service firms can combine their resources by forming collaborations with other firms to offer additional values and benefits to their customers, and to create a competitive advantage.

Service concept, service strategy, and service process

This chapter talks about (1) service concept, (2) service strategy, and (3) service process. These terms are obviously interrelated, but they do have distinct meanings and applications.

* A *service concept* is an overall vision of a firm's service orientation and position—a sense of self-awareness (perhaps even a sense of "self-destiny") that explains to staff and customers what the organization stands for and what it aims to offer.

* A *service strategy* is a distinctive formula for delivering the above service vision—a plan of action that energizes an organization and effectively defines the practical meaning of the word "service" for that firm (Berry, 1995).

* A *service process* is the actual delivery of the service—a series of acts or performances that make up the very *essence* of a service (Shostack, 1981).

This chapter addresses the above issues from a managerial perspective to provide readers with a broader *vision* of strategic service management, and to provide readers with an understanding of the more important *techniques* in service operations management.

Service vision or concept

Like an architect's drawing

The service vision represents all that a service organization stands for—the image of the organization as the customers see it. From a theoretical point of view, it is the service concept that explains to both employees and customers what the organization stands for and what it aims to offer. An analogy is an architect's drawing of a building—indicating how a building will look when its construction is complete. In designing a building, an architect's task is to visualize the final product, and then to fulfill that vision with a detailed plan that indicates all the components to be put together to bring the plan to fruition. In the same way that a good design from an architect is necessary for a builder to deliver the final desired construction, the service vision or service concept is necessary as a statement of the final service benefits that a service organization proposes to deliver. The service concept is the expression of the planned service offer, including the delivery systems and procedures required to achieve this objective.

Set apart from the rest

All outstanding service companies have a compelling vision of their own position of leadership in the marketplace. This sense of self-awareness (perhaps even a sense of "self-destiny") provides outstanding firms with a direction that differentiates them from other companies. In a sense, firms with such a vision of superior service do not have to compete—because they always stand apart from other firms. Their vision represents quality, superiority, and value to the customer, and this vision nurtures, motivates, and binds every member of the organization in pursuit of a common goal.

As it works toward this compelling vision of superior service, successful service organizations meticulously orchestrate every employee, every individual process, and every system. In turn, this uncompromising vision of superior service captures the attention of customers, provides value to those customers, and gains the loyalty of those customers.

Ingrained into the fabric

Because the service outcome is intangible in nature, it is imperative that all service personnel from the boardroom to the shopfloor know and understand the service vision. The vision must be nurtured, promoted, and "sold" to all personnel in the organization until it becomes ingrained in the fabric and thinking of the organization. The vision should communicate what the organization is, what the organization does, and what the organization believes in (Rust, Zahorik, & Keiningham, 1996; Rust, Zeithaml, & Lemon, 2000).

The service vision of an organization should provide employees with clear information as to:

* the offerings of the organization; and

* the specific needs and wants of the customer that the organization is offering to fulfill.

That is, every person in the organization needs to have a clear vision of *what* the firm is trying to do for its customers, and *why* it is trying to do these things. Once these basic goals are established, the service vision moves on to the more practical questions of designing a structure and putting that structure into effect.

Design and practice

As Fitzsimmons and Fitzsimmons (1994, 1998) pointed out, a service concept provides clear direction for two distinct functions:

* the structural design of the service in theory; and

* the management and execution of that design in practice.

The first of these, the structural design of a service, involves careful consideration and detailed advice on such factors as:

* *delivery systems*—front office, back office, automation, customer participation;

* *facility design*—size, aesthetics, layout;

* *location*—customer demographics, single or multiple sites, competition, site characteristics; and

* *capacity planning*—managing queues, number of servers, accommodating average demand or peak.

The second of these, the management and execution of that design in practice, involves careful consideration and detailed advice on such factors as:

* *the service encounter*—service culture, motivation, selection, training, and empowerment;

* *service quality*—measurement, monitoring, methods, expectations vs. perceptions, service guarantee;

* *managing capacity and demand*—strategies for altering demand and controlling supply, queue management; and

* *information*—competitive resources, data collection.

Customer-centric

The service concept is thus an umbrella concept covering the whole service offering of a firm (Grönroos, 1987). But, in talking of how a firm proposes to operate, the service vision should never lose sight of the fact that the *customer* is the focus and purpose of the whole concept. In discussing the *firm* in detail, and how the firm proposes to behave, it is easy to lose sight of the fact that the whole purpose of the service vision is to serve the *customer*—not the firm.

The service vision should therefore state the core service (or services) that the firm proposes to offer to the customer, the facilitating and supporting services it proposes to offer to the customer, how the basic package is to be made accessible to the customer, how customer interactions are to be developed, and how customers are to participate in the process.

The service concept is thus not ultimately defined in terms of products or service. Rather, it is defined in terms of *the results produced for customers.*

The components of a service vision

The service vision is defined in terms of the *results produced for customers.* The service vision of a firm should therefore state:

1. the core service (or services) it proposes to offer to the customer;
2. the facilitating and supporting services it proposes to offer to the customer;
3. how the basic package is to be made accessible to the customer;
4. how customer interactions are to be developed; and
5. how customers are to participate in the process.

Although the focus of a service vision is on the *customer* and hence on the service attributes that best express benefit to the customer (Eiglier & Langeard, 1981), an effective service vision must nevertheless be mindful of the realities of the marketplace in which the organization wishes to operate. The service concept must take into account a realistic assessment of the organization's position in that marketplace, and must develop a clear idea of a service offer that matches this position.

In making such a market assessment and the appropriate service offer to match that assessment, the service vision must therefore provide direction for:

* *market segments*—the specific market segments that have been identified;

* *service processes*—how the proposed service is produced, distributed, and consumed in the marketplace;

* *organization of the service offer*—how the interface with the customer is to be organized in the marketplace; and

* *service image*—how to maintain the desired marketplace image to present to potential customers.

Service strategy

What is a service strategy?

If a *service concept* is an overall vision of a firm's service orientation and position, a *service strategy* can be defined as a distinctive formula for delivering that service vision.

An overall strategy can be made up of smaller strategies related to specific benefits or promises that are valuable to customers. By developing specific strategies rather than vague "wishes," management has an opportunity to reassess and reorganize its options in its attempts to establish and maintain an effective competitive position.

Such service-focused strategies are incorporated into the overall service vision that delivers a powerful corporate statement to the internal and external markets. An effective service strategy energizes the organization—effectively defining the practical meaning of the word "service" for that firm (Berry, 1995).

Everyone is involved

A service strategy is thus an organizing principle that allows everyone in a service organization to focus his or her efforts within the an overall plan of action. The value of each individual employee's offerings is enhanced if conducted in such an integrated service system.

A service-oriented strategy that percolates effectively through the entire organization strengthens the service culture from the inside and thereby strengthens the image of the organization as perceived from the outside. It clearly communicates to every member of the organization what the business is all about, the key operational priorities, and the things that they should all try to accomplish. If comprehensively explained to all employees, it establishes itself as the firm's corporate strategy, and as the personal strategy of every individual employee.

What a service strategy does

A service strategy determines every aspect of a service offering—including its development, its distribution, and its promotion.

To be effective, a good service strategy should thus provide detailed guidance for:

1. the conception of the service offering;
2. the delivery of that service offering; and
3. the marketing, advertising, and promotion of that service offering.

Marketing implications

A service strategy ultimately promotes the development and maintenance of an organization's market position. It assists the advertising people to use their most creative and effective techniques to communicate their positioning message in the marketplace. If the service strategy has been effectively communicated to all staff members, including the marketing people, the basis of the firm's marketing strategy should already be apparent to all. Instead of casting about for inspiration for advertising copy, advertising staff should already have a definite strategy on which to base their creative efforts and their marketing campaigns.

The service strategy thus not only determines the conception and delivery of the service offering, but also dictates its marketing, advertising, and promotion.

Taco Bell's comprehensive service strategy

The service strategy adopted by the fast-food restaurant company Taco Bell is to offer "the best-value fast meal whenever and wherever customers are hungry."

In accordance with this strategy, Taco Bell management not only designed appropriate food at good-value prices, but also methods of taking its service to customers via carts, kiosks, vending machines, and distribution points at stadiums, schools, offices, airports, and so on.

The service strategy is carried through every aspect of development, distribution, and promotion.

Marketers and advertisers should therefore have a comprehensive understanding of an organization's strategic orientation if the advertising and marketing campaign is to match the overall strategy and prove effective. Advertisements in the hotel industry often appear to show little regard for this principle of adherence to a coherent strategy. Advertisements frequently provide very little relevant information for the specific customers to whom they are directed. A colorful brochure of the hotel lobby, golf course, swimming pool, and restaurant might be aesthetically and creatively pleasing to the advertiser who created the brochure, but of limited significance to the customer. For example, conference customers spend two or three days in a conference room, hammering out important business decisions. Of course, they do enjoy the pool and the golf course in passing, but they choose the hotel predominantly for its ability to support their primary needs—that is, their conference needs. If a hotel's strategy involves attracting such conference customers, it would be more appropriate to promote the hotel's personalized support services, secretarial assistance, and office infrastructure. These are the things that ensure the smooth running of such a meeting, and these are the things that should be promoted if the overall service strategy is to have any meaning in promoting the hotel as an integrated service.

Changing needs mean changing strategies

Service organizations have an ongoing need to make themselves aware of important changes in customer needs, preferences, and buying motivations. Customer-focused strategies must therefore continuously anticipate changes in such needs and motivations, and must adjust accordingly.

Ideally, readjustment of the service strategy should take place before the trend in the marketplace has become apparent. Systematic market research and other methods of feedback information concerning current and changing customer behavior can provide appropriate information (see "Customer-perception research," Chapter 4).

Some practical examples

All successful hospitality service firms have developed and implemented effective service strategies. Indeed, they are successful precisely because they have gone to the trouble of thinking through their strategies and ensuring that all aspects of the organization work in conformity with an overall agreed strategy. Some well-known successful strategies are briefly considered below.

McDonald's

McDonald's has been the world leader in the fast-food market for more than 30 years. McDonald's service strategy is to offer *speed, efficiency, low price,* and, most importantly, *convenience*. The target market is customers who have little time to spend on a meal.

Every feature of McDonald's is aligned with this service strategy, including the decor, systems, machinery, and management style. The company spends a great deal of its resources in testing new food products before introducing them, and in improving the already efficient service-delivery system.

McDonald's goes beyond a minimal interpretation of a franchise contractual role to ensure full adherence to its strategy among all franchisees. All of McDonald's franchisees worldwide maintain the same corporate strategy (the so-called "McDonald's promise"). The food is prepared in the same high-quality manner worldwide, and is tasty and reasonably priced. The service level rarely varies from one outlet to another, or from one country to another. The low-key decor and friendly atmosphere of all outlets remain constant.

Holiday Inn

The Holiday Inn chain of hotels offers *convenience at a moderate price* for business and middle-class travellers. The hotels are usually located near a city center or airport. The accommodation is clean and comfortable, with special facilities for businesswomen, nonsmokers, and others. Their focus on service makes Holiday Inn hotels an exceptional value for travellers. The service strategy is consistently and rigorously applied.

Hyatt

Hyatt hotels are *luxury* hotels that pride themselves on providing the best amenities to their guests. Hyatt's service strategy is to provide a luxury environment for business travellers. Hyatt's management strives to offer superior service to attract repeat business and to promote customer loyalty to their brand name. Hyatt believes that corporate customers are willing to spend additional money, confident in the knowledge that they will receive extra luxury service. The service strategy reflects this in every aspect of the service offering.

Ritz-Carlton

"We are Ladies and Gentlemen Serving Ladies and Gentlemen," proclaims the slogan for Ritz-Carlton hotels (see Figure 5.1). This saying neatly conveys the dignity of the service received by guests, and the style in which it is delivered. This motto is printed on a small card (known as Ritz-Carlton's "Golden Standards and Credo"), a copy of which is given to every employee of Ritz-Carlton hotels, to be kept in his or her pocket at all times.

The superior service with which the company's name has become synonymous is reflected in its strategy. This strategy is communicated to the whole organization and every person in it, and therefore percolates through every single aspect of its service offering.

Figure 5.1 *The service strategy of Ritz-Carlton hotels is carried by every employee at all times*

The Ritz-Carlton

"We are Ladies and Gentlemen, serving Ladies and Gentlemen."

We pledge to provide the finest personal service and facilities
for our guests who will always enjoy a warm, relaxed, yet
refined ambience.

Author's presentation

Marriott Fairfield

The Marriott Corporation's service strategy at its Fairfield Inns is to offer "clean rooms, a friendly atmosphere, and budget prices" to its target market of frequent business travellers. The simplicity of this service strategy requires Fairfield Inns to focus the bulk of its energies on two functions only—front-desk and housekeeping. The adoption of a conscious service strategy thus gives focus and direction to Fairfield's efforts, and helps it to excel in what it does best—attractive, "no-frills" accommodations.

Service processes

What is a service process?

Having described the *service vision* (the overall service philosophy of a firm), and the *service strategy* (the distinctive formula for delivering that service vision), we now turn to the actual *service process* itself.

Services are acts or performances—often carried out in a series of steps. Such a series of steps makes up a service process. As previously noted, such service processes have certain features that distinguish them from physical goods (see "How services differ," Chapter 2). These include the fact that services are produced and consumed almost simultaneously, and that customers participate with the service organization in the process of production and consumption.

Analyzing a service process

Compared with the theory involved in analyzing a "service concept" and a "service strategy," the idea of a "service process" sounds simple enough—the actual practical delivery of a service. But a service process is more complex than it seems. It really involves three distinct parts, and all three must be analyzed and assessed if the service process is to be effective (Shostack, 1990b).

1. First, there are the steps, tasks, and activities necessary for the rendering of the service—the list of activities involved in the actual service process itself;

2. Second there are the means by which the tasks are executed—the combination of people and goods that make up the surrounding "infrastructure" of the service-delivery process.

3. Finally, there is the role and personal experience of the consumer—what Shostack calls the "evidence" presented to the consumer.

In summary, to understand a service process properly, we have to: (1) analyze what has to be done; (2) work out how it is to be done (and by whom); and (3) assess how the customer responds to it.

Process as the "essence" of service

Production and consumption of services, and consumer involvement in these, all occur at about the same time. Simultaneously, the quality of service is judged by the consumer. The design of a service process—the mapping out of how a service is to be rendered—is thus of vital importance in maintaining the quality of service. Process is so important that Lynn Shostack (1981) described process as being the very *essence* of a service.

According to Shostack (1990b), the actual delivery of a service is part of an overall integrated service system that can be broken down into three distinct parts. Each of these must be analyzed and assessed if service delivery is to effective.

* First, there are the steps, tasks, and activities necessary for the rendering of the service—this is the list of activities involved in the actual service process itself.

* Second there are the means by which the tasks are executed—the combination of people and goods that make up the surrounding "infrastructure" of the service-delivery process.

* Finally, there is the role and experience of the consumer—what Shostack calls the "evidence" presented to the consumer.

All service-delivery systems can be understood in their entirely by understanding the above three elements.

Quality at every stage

Quality advocates—such as Deming (1986), Juran (1989a), and Ishikawa (1985)—have been unanimous in their insistence that quality must be built into *every component* of a product or service system if total quality is to be achieved. (See Chapter 3 for more on these quality advocates.)

Tangible manufactured goods are comprised of many physical component parts made of various materials (such as plastic, rubber, steel, and so on), and quality is necessary in every sort of component. Services, in contrast, are the end result of an intricate combination of steps and activities that make up an overall process (Shostack, 1981). Because, unlike physical goods, services cannot be "inspected" after they have been produced, improved quality in services comes from *improving the process,* not from *inspection* (Deming, 1986).

Just as Deming (1982) was of the view that workers are never to blame for flaws in a manufacturing process (because manufacturing process design is the responsibility of management), so it can be argued that service quality is also ultimately the responsibility of management (because service process design is similarly the responsibility of management).

Analyzing the steps

Let us take the example of a typical meal service offered in a restaurant, and examine the processes involved. A huge number of definable steps and activities is involved in the performance of this service. These are of various sorts.

* The consumer performs some of them—such as choosing the food and drinks from the menu selection.

* Some are performed through the collaborative effort of both the consumer and the restaurant. Consider a buffet service, during which the customers collect the food, but in which restaurant staff members often help the customers by carving meat, by serving the food onto plates, and so on.

* Some activities are invisible to the consumer—such as the preparation of the food in the kitchen, preparation of the buffet service furniture, and preparation of cutlery, crockery, napkins, salad dressings, and so on.

So there are different sorts of activities in various steps in the process.

Moreover, each of these basic steps can, in turn, be broken down into smaller steps—each forming a part of a complex system of processes designed to produce the overall service. For example, in the case of the meal service, the step of setting up the buffet furniture can be further analyzed. In setting up the furniture, various "subservices" were required. These were performed "internally" (from employee to employee) as people decided what furniture was required, where to get it, when and how it would be delivered, where it should be arranged, and so on. And each of these smaller steps had to be planned and executed flawlessly if the service was to meet its overall objec-

A buffet in readiness. Consider the huge number of individual "steps" required to prepare the room, the food, the tables, the decorations, and so on. And consider the "substeps" involved in each of these steps. Every one of these "steps" and "substeps" must be executed with precision.

With kind permission of Holiday Inn On The Lane, Columbus, Ohio

tive—which is to offer a food and meal experience commensurate with the expectation of the customers.

To take another step as an example within the overall process, the preparing of the food in the kitchen involves planning the menu, forecasting the food requirements, ordering and purchasing the food, arranging the staff work roster, and so on. Every one of these "substeps" must be executed with precision.

In addition, it must be recognized that analysis of the two steps mentioned above (the furniture and the food) represent only a small proportion of the huge number of individual processes that constitute the meal service under consideration. When looked at in this way, the intricacy and complexity of the process is impressive at every level.

Process quality and output quality

When considering service-quality concepts in Chapter 3, the service-quality dimensions proposed by Lehtinen were noted earlier. It will be recalled that Lehtinen identified two sets of quality dimensions—*process quality* and *output quality* (Lehtinen & Lehtinen, 1983).

In appreciating the significance of service quality, it is therefore important to recognize that most services are experienced by customers as both an *outcome* and as a *process*. Both are significant in the assessment of quality.

* The *outcome* is the culmination of having a service need met—a customer *does* wish to obtain a loan, *does* wish to have a car properly repaired, and *does* wish to enjoy a delicious meal.

* But the *process* is equally important. In obtaining these outcomes, the customer *does* wish to have simple paperwork at the bank, *does* wish to experience a short wait time at the car repairer, and *does* wish to be served by a courteous waiter.

According to this view, the output of any service "takes form" during the whole transaction, and is being judged by the customer during that transaction. By controlling the process (and the quality of that process), the output quality can also be controlled.

Ultimately a management responsibility

As noted above, one of Deming's great contributions is his insight into process design as being a management responsibility. In goods manufacturing, management alone has total control over the resources needed for goods production (Deming 1982). Similarly, in the services sector, only management can set up appropriate service processes.

The key to a comprehensive service-quality program is thus achieved through management taking responsibility for the philosophy, strategies, and processes involved in the delivery of service (Albrecht & Zemke, 1985). To achieve this, service managers need to analyze each of the processes in the overall service offering, and must ensure that they are coordinated and effective as an integrated system.

This chapter now proceeds to examine some of the principles and techniques that can be used to perfect such a service system.

Perfecting the service system

By design not by evolution

Deming pointed out that fiddling with the strategy, changing the personnel, and improving the general "know-how" of those involved will not improve the final result if the overall service system is defective.

In survey after survey of customer dissatisfaction, mediocre service consistently tops the list. Legendary service organizations—such as Marriott (in the hotel business), Disney (entertainment), Federal Express (transport), and Nordstrom (retail)—seldom feature in such surveys of dissatisfaction. Competing organizations find it difficult to duplicate the superior service of these firms in their various fields because the service systems of the opposition are inferior.

We often wonder why so many of the service systems that we encounter in our daily lives are so bad in meeting our needs as customers. This does not result from someone deliberately developing a system that is capable of providing only mediocre service. Rather than being deliberately designed, such a system is likely to have *evolved*. But if an organizational system is allowed to evolve on its own, it is certain to evolve in the direction of the self-convenience of the people inside the organization, rather than for the benefit of the people whom they are supposed to be serving (Albrecht & Zemke, 1985).

Allowing a service system to evolve is insufficient. It is imperative that services be systematically designed if the organization is to offer reliable superior service. The goal of systematic design is to eradicate or minimize any policies or "rules" that stand between the service and the customer.

The basis of a well-planned and executed service system in any line of business is:

∗ keep the service itself simple and uncomplicated;

∗ make the service truly customer-friendly; and

∗ add value for the customer.

How does a service organization design such a system?

Worth remembering

If an organizational system is allowed to evolve on its own, it is certain to evolve in the direction of the self-convenience of the people inside the organization, rather than for the benefit of the people whom they are supposed to be serving (Albrecht & Zemke, 1985).

Designing a service to serve

The term "service design" refers to making a service system tangible in the form of drawings, flowcharts, specifications, computer programs, instructions, and so on. There is a wide variety of forms in which the design can be visually presented. This sort of tangible representation clarifies what the service includes and how the service production is to be performed.

Those who design a service system need to hold two perspectives in mind at the same time:

∗ the *external aspects*—those factors that will directly affect customer satisfaction; and

∗ the *internal aspects*—the supporting systems and processes that are coordinated to fulfill customer needs.

There are four major steps involved in designing services and their delivery systems (Shostack, 1984a).

* First, identify the processes that constitute the service. It might be necessary to break the organization down into detailed parts to develop the appropriate flow throughout the entire organization. Project programming and computer-aided devices can assist in identifying the appropriate flows. These procedures allow managers to visualize the process, and to define and manipulate it at arm's length. However, what they miss is the consumer's interaction with the service— that is, they make no provision for people-rendered services that require judgment and a less mechanical approach.

* Second, anticipate problems with service delivery in the service encounter, consider contingency approaches, and incorporate plans for reaction to problems.

* Third, establish an overall timeframe for execution of the service plan through various stages—including paperwork and the various service-handling steps that will be required.

* Finally, analyze the proposed layout in terms of (a) the expected satisfaction to the customer and (b) the expected profitability of the firm as a consequence. In other words, the designer should develop an expected *customer-satisfaction cost* (the positive or negative cost of goodwill). It might be necessary to compare alternative plans to determine which blueprint offers the best trade-offs of satisfaction and dissatisfaction in terms of the expected sales and profits for each proposed plan.

Steps in service design

There are four major steps involved in designing services and their delivery systems (Shostack, 1984a).

1. Identify the processes that constitute the service.
2. Anticipate problems with service delivery in the service encounter.
3. Establish an overall timeframe for execution of the service plan through various stages.
4. Analyze the proposed layout in terms of: (a) satisfaction to the customer and (b) the profitability of the firm.

These are explained in greater detail in the text (above).

Inbuilt flaws

Many errors in services have their root cause in the design of systems—especially those dealing with internal service encounters. These service faults then crop up in one form or another at the service encounter with the customer—producing negative experiences at the crucial "moments of truth."

Since such errors are often caused by inappropriate design of systems, they tend to be repetitive. Once a fault is built into a system, its users are faced with quality problems on a daily basis (Gummesson, 1993). Indeed, Deming (1986) maintained that, in manufacturing companies, only 6% of errors are due to a "special factor" (or a special cause)—that is, errors that workers and front-line staff members commit through carelessness, lack of knowledge, bad temper, and so on. This means that 94% of errors have a shared cause that emanates from flaws built into the production design of the organization.

For example, in a hotel setting, there might be a recurrent problem in allocating the wrong room to guests. This might not be due to carelessness on the part of the receptionists. It might be due to a systemic flaw in the system—perhaps a failure to enter room allocations onto the computer system immediately such allocations are made. A hotel might have a system of first recording room allocations on individual hardcopy guest files, and then later entering this information into the hotel computer. Such a delay in entering data might allow a room to be inadvertently allocated to two guests. The fault is in the system, not the service personnel, and the fault causes recurrent lapses in service quality.

In a large, complex organization such as a hotel there are innumerable possibilities for systemic flaws of this sort.

Design is a dynamic process

Designing a service system is a logical step-by-step process. But this does not mean that it is a static process in which a step is taken and assumed to be firmly established for all time. Rather, designing a service system is an interactive process. The first concept of the service leads to an initial design sketch. The concept is then modified, and more detailed designs are made. The process is continued as the service concept alters and the service design changes with it.

The customer plays a crucial role in this interactive process. As previously noted, in all service situations the customer contributes part of the service. This contribution must be clarified, assessed, and acted upon throughout the design process.

Flexibility is required to receive such customer feedback and promote an effective interactive environment during service design. Designs cannot be inflexible and prescriptive. There must be a balance between programmed behavior and personal initiative. Within this framework, employees can act in accordance with their own judgment, note customer reaction, and thus provide valuable interactive feedback to the design process.

For example, the blueprint might state that a customer at check-in *must* receive the room previously allocated by the reservations department. At the time of designing the service blueprint, this might have seemed to be a sensible measure to avoid confusion and double-booking. But the on-duty receptionist might become aware of unexpected special requirements—such as adjoining rooms for two guests, or some other reasonable request. The receptionist must be able to show initiative and make changes to ensure customer satisfaction. And the overall design of the system must then be adjusted to allow for such sensible last-minute changes by receptionists. This might require a rethinking of the overall system to allow for reasonable flexibility.

Creative thinking

As has been noted above, designing a service system does not mean that the service design becomes prescriptive and inflexible. Experience and feedback can produce sensible and effective changes to the service design. In a similar spirit of flexibility, service designers should always be prepared to think creatively about services—especially services that seem to be so routine and mundane that they are taken for granted. Consider hotel cleaning services as an example.

Cleaning services are often one of the last matters to be considered in an integrated hotel service system. Consider the following sorts of questions.

Q: When is cleaning done?
A: When a room is not wanted for any other activity.

Q: What routine is used?
A: Whatever routine is needed for the cleaning of the particular room shape and size.

Q: What chemicals and processes are used?
A: Whatever chemicals and processes are required for the furnishings, fabrics, and materials already built into the room.

When we look at the answers to the above questions, we notice that cleaning "comes last." It is reactive. That is, cleaning tends to be relegated to certain times and certain methods that are largely beyond the control of those responsible for cleaning services. Cleaning is "added on" later. It is not built into an integrated service system.

In contrast, in a property developed service system, this service could be taken into account from the very beginning when a room is being designed. Materials, furniture, room shape, and so on could be designed with a view to making cleaning efficient and effective. Everyone knows that it is inevitable that a cleaning service is going to be required. Rather than "adding it on" later, a creative service designer can plan ahead and make allowance for this essential service. After all, cleaning is really not an "added extra"—it is manifestly an essential service. It should be treated as such, and allowed for in designing an integrated service system.

As another example of creativity in designing a cleaning service, an insightful service designer will be aware that, in hotels, cleanliness is not just a matter of health and safety. Cleanliness is also a crucial marketing tool. This is obviously the case in guest rooms and public areas—cleanliness in these areas is essential if customers are to be attracted and retained. But what about "back-of-house" areas? Many successful restaurants have recognized the marketing potential of demonstrating the cleanliness of their kitchen areas by installing glass walls between the public areas of the restaurant and the kitchen. Customers can then see how the food is prepared and the cleanliness of the food-preparation environment. This effectively becomes a marketing tool. Firms can thus showcase that part of the organization that is not normally visible to the customer—in effect, the "service factory" becomes a showroom (Chase & Garvin, 1990).

Such creativity and lateral thinking is an essential feature of successful service designs. Those responsible for drawing up service systems must therefore be flexible, adaptable, and creative in their thinking. Customer satisfaction will never be achieved by systems that are rigid, prescriptive, and lacking in imagination.

Service design and blueprinting

Leading to a "moment of truth"

The quality experienced by the customer is created at the "moment of truth," when the service provider and the client meet in a face-to-face interaction (Carlzon, 1987; Normann, 1984, 2000; Schuler, 1996). The most perfectly designed and engineered service-delivery system will fail if the customer's needs are not fulfilled during this "moment of truth" at the service encounter. One of the most promising tools in designing an effective service system that meets the needs of the "moments of truth" is service "blueprinting" (Zeithaml, Parasuraman, & Berry, 1990).

What is a service blueprint?

A service blueprint is essentially a detailed planning and diagnostic document that depicts the service events and processes as a flowchart—a "map" of intersecting paths.

In essence, a blueprint represents, in diagrammatic form, the various processes that constitute the entire service system, and the interrelationships among these individual processes.

The service blueprint thus allows management and employees to visualize, organize, and manipulate the entire service system.

The nature of a service blueprint

Lynn Shostack was an early advocate for systematic service design, and she pioneered the concept of service blueprinting. In a series of articles (1981, 1982, 1983, 1984a, 1984b, 1985, 1987, 1990b), she convincingly argued the case for the undoubted benefits to be obtained from using a service blueprint as a tool for depicting and analyzing all the processes involved in the production and delivery of services. Such a service blueprint is essentially a detailed planning and diagnostic document that depicts the service events and processes as a flowchart—a "map" of intersecting paths.

Blueprinting rests on the notion that the "moment of truth" in rendering a service is the final act in a series of service processes. Blueprinting can be used to represent, in diagrammatic form, the various processes that constitute the entire service system and the interrelationships among these individual processes. The service blueprint thus allows management and employees to visualize, organize, and manipulate the entire service system.

A "snapshot" of a dynamic process

A service blueprint thus serves as a unique management tool that provides a "snapshot" view of what is actually a dynamic, living phenomenon.

Because it is reflecting a dynamic process, a blueprint is not frozen in time. A service blueprint also depicts the chronology and pattern of performances that make up a service (Kingman-Brundage, 1989). Thus a service system blueprint provides explicit answers to both the *structural* question (What are the various components of the service?) and the *functional* question (How is it offered?). It can therefore be used effectively to identify "encounter points" and "fail points" (or failure-prone areas) in any service system. This assists management to install preventive measures, and also to organize backup support services.

A service blueprint of this type gives meaning and structure to an otherwise intangible abstraction. As a management tool, it provides an opportunity to view, in a graphical presentation, the full range of customer needs, and the way in which the organization is structured in time and place to respond to these needs.

The "line of visibility"

As has been noted previously, a service business can be understood as a system comprised of two parts—those parts responsible for the *production* of the service offer and those parts responsible for the actual *delivery* of the service offer (Lovelock, 1996; Lovelock, Patterson, & Walker, 2001). In a typical service business, only part of the system is apparent to customers. The majority of the production processes are invisible to the customer, with only the final outcome being experienced.

In the hospitality industry, these two parts of the organization are typically referred to as "back-of-house" functions and "front-of-house" functions. Customers commonly do not know, or do not want to know, of the activities in the back of the house.

Figure 5.2 *The line of visibility in a service blueprint*

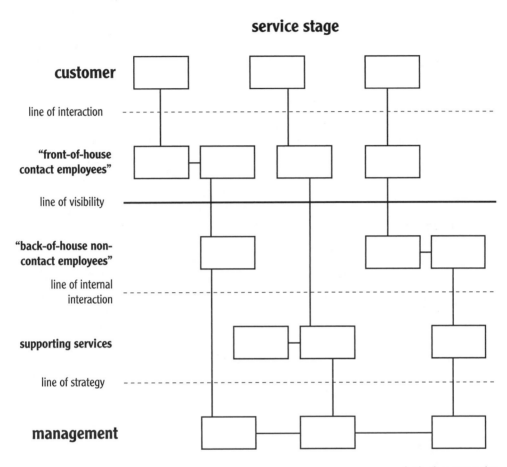

Author's presentation

In keeping with this division of functions, a service blueprint can be divided into two major parts–"front stage" ("front of house" in hotel operations) and "back-stage" ("back of house" in hotel operations). These are separated by a "line of visibility" (see Figure 5.2).

The visible front-of-house functions are supported by all the unseen back-of-house functions. These, in turn, are typically a combination of many cross-functional activities involving a whole range of people and skills. For example, the food served to a customer by a waiter in the visible service interaction has been first ordered, purchased, received, stored, prepared, cooked, arranged, and so forth.

Careful attention must be paid to designing quality into these service processes that are not visible to the customer. The proportion of the blueprint above the line of visibility varies according to each service, but the majority of the blueprint frequently remains hidden below the line of visibility. Shostack, who has done much of the pioneering work on blueprinting of services, likened what lies above the line of visibility to the tip of an iceberg. She believed that particular attention must be paid to the processes *below* the line, even though customers are often totally unaware of them. Activities below the line ultimately determine success or failure in the visible process, and therefore ultimately determine output quality.

"Fail points" and "encounter points"

It is apparent that the blueprint is a very useful tool for systematically evaluating a service. As such it can be used to identify potential problems that might ordinarily escape detection. Shostack described certain points in any service system as service "fail points." By this, she meant points in the service system where deficiencies are known to have occurred in similar systems in the past, or points in the system where it might reasonably be predicted that problems could occur in the future. These "fail points" are, therefore, the points in the system that require very close managerial attention (Senior & Akehurst, 1990).

Service blueprints also identify other places in the service process that are especially vulnerable to breakdown. We have already discussed the importance of the concept of the "moment of truth"—the interpersonal interaction when the service is actually delivered and experienced. In service blueprints, these are known as "encounter points." Where "fail points" and "encounter points" coexist, there is maximum potential for problems with service quality.

Identifying "fail points" and "encounter points" in a service blueprint can guide the attention of managers to the need for preventive action or remedial action—special training, additional support, the establishment of recovery processes, or even the re-designing of the whole system.

Looking back and looking ahead

A service blueprint can thus act as a "problem solver" in fixing problems quickly as they occur. More usefully, it can also act in a preventive fashion as a "change influencer" before problems actually become apparent (Hosick, 1989). Reducing vulnerability in a service system is one of the most important objectives of service managers. In effect, a service blueprint can assist managers to "pretest" the service concept on paper, and to identify the most effective methods to ensure failure-proof service delivery. It can be utilized in this way for various management tasks:

* the design of new services;

* the evaluation of existing services; and

* the identification of the cause of recurrent service problems.

Blueprints within blueprints

The very act of creating a service blueprint provides management with a rich insight into every aspect of the production, consumption, and quality of the overall service. Even if there are no apparent problems, managers gain a better perspective of their overall service system, and a useful insight into how various functions fit together (see Figure 5.3).

Moreover, any particular component of the blueprint can be further expanded into a detailed blueprint if needed. A "blueprint within a blueprint" gives management helpful guidance in the setting of standards for individual components within the system. It also enables particular problem areas to be examined in detail. For example, if it is learned that delay during check-out at reception is unacceptable to customers, that particular step can be blueprinted in detail to identify and rectify the problem.

Dreams and reality

A blueprint should represent reality—not dreams. That is, a blueprint examines how the system *really* works, as opposed to some ideal version of how it is *supposed* to work.

If it is to reflect the reality of the service, the blueprint must be developed in consultation with the people who are directly involved with the process in question. Managers might believe that they have an excellent overall strategic understanding of the system. But this is mere abstract theory unless it is informed by close consultation with the people who *actually know* how the system works.

Consider the blueprinting of serving breakfast to a hotel room. A blueprint could be drawn up in theory, but this might not reflect the reality of the service as it is actually practiced. For example, where does the breakfast service process actually begin? (see Figure 5.4). A guest might telephone through to room service in the morning. Another guest might leave an order card on the room door the night before. In this case, there are *two* process pathways that can be described in the blueprint. Should the blueprint start from the point at which room service receives a call from the guest, or from the point when the customer chooses the items on the card that the guest has discovered in the room? The two processes are clearly different, and they contain quite different potential "fail points" and different "encounter points."

In this case, *two* blueprints might well be necessary to ensure that the blueprinting exercise actually reflects the chain of service processes as they are conducted in reality. Input from those who actually conduct the service is required to assist management in understanding the two service pathways, and in sorting out answers to such questions as which service pathway is more frequently used, which service pathway fails more often, and which service pathway offers better quality outcomes for customers.

Figure 5.3 *Service blueprint of overnight hotel stay*

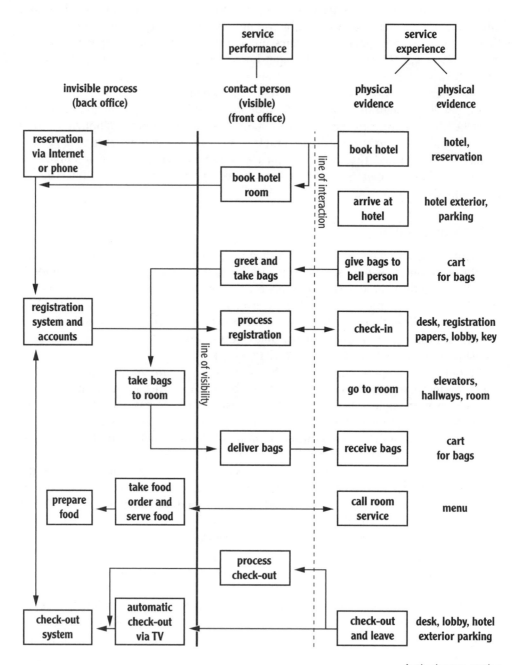

Author's presentation

Figure 5.4 *Service blueprint of room service breakfast*

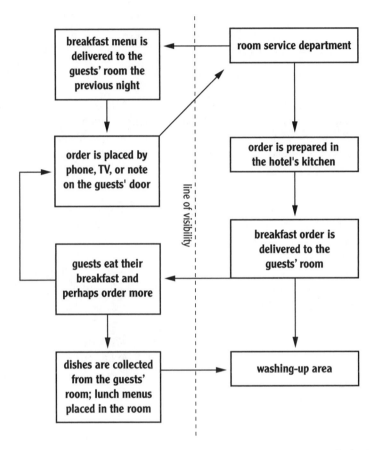

Author's presentation

Flowcharts

A blueprint sets out the overall arrangement of the service system. As part of the visual representation of such a system, various flowcharts might be developed.

Flowcharts indicate the chronology of events involved in delivering the service. As well as identifying the names of the various departments and service persons involved in the delivery of the service in question, flowcharts should also include the customers involved. The flowchart then lists, in chronological order, the steps involved in rendering the service, and links these with the departments, people, and support services involved.

Such flowcharts can be developed at various levels. They can first be developed as a chart for each service, then as a chart for each department, and, finally, they can be amalgamated to generate an overall service blueprint.

Moments of truth remain crucial

A "beautiful blueprint"—but does it work?

It is very important that designers of service blueprints never lose sight of the practical purpose of the blueprinting exercise.

The aim is not to produce a "beautiful" theoretical service system that satisfies management. The aim is to produce a quality practical service outcome that satisfies the customer.

A blueprint must always be customer-oriented.

In drawing up service blueprints, it is easy to become preoccupied with a comprehensive overall scheme, and consequently to lose sight of the vital importance of the "moments of truth" in service delivery. Designers must always be aware that the most important task in drawing up any blueprint is to identify the vital customer "encounter points" to ensure a positive outcome from each and every service interaction.

In this context, identifying possible service bottlenecks or failure-prone areas is crucial—for example, checking-in and checking-out procedures. Identified failure-prone points in the blueprints should then be complemented by support services—for example, assistance from food and beverage staff at reception during check-in and check-out times. Predesigned recovery mechanisms can also be included.

It is very important that designers of service blueprints never lose sight of the practical purpose of the blueprinting exercise. It is always customer-oriented. The aim is not to produce a "beautiful" theoretical service system that satisfies management. The aim is to produce a quality practical service outcome that satisfies the customer.

Managing the "critical encounters"

This is what it's all about

Earlier sections of this chapter have discussed management strategies for:

* service philosophies;

* service strategies;

* service processes; and

* service systems.

In a sense, all of this was a preliminary to the *real issue*–the management of the "critical encounters" or "moments of truth" when the customers personally experience the service. In many ways, this is the end-point of all management strategies for service industries. This is what it is all about!

Service managers can utilize various quality-management techniques to examine performance in these quality-sensitive areas (Wyckoff, 1988). Of these techniques, Pareto analysis and fishbone analysis are especially useful. These analytical techniques not only allow managers to identify service problems and solutions, but also assist managers to prioritize their responses to identified problems.

Pareto analysis

An Italian economist, Vilfredo Pareto (1848–1923), found that a large share of national wealth was owned by relatively few people. This idea has become generalized and formalized in the so-called "Pareto Principle"–that most effects come from relatively few causes. For example, it has been suggested by various authors that:

* 80% of national wealth is controlled by 20% of the people;

* 80% of the funds contributed to charity comes from only 20% of the possible sources;

* 80% of quality problems in goods manufacture comes from 20% of the possible causes; and

* 80% of most firms' sales are produced by 20% of its people.

For these and other interesting examples of the fascinating Pareto Principle, see Costin (1994) and Juran (1989b).

Pareto analysis is derived from this principle. Pareto analysis can be used for any identified problem. Management identifies the problem and then plots (on a graph) the relative contribution of various causes (see Figure 5.5). Any problem can be subjected to this sort of analysis. For example, in considering the problem of check-out delays at hotel reception, it has been discovered that 80% of such delays are due to three or four causes (Kandampully, n.d.).

By applying Pareto analysis, it is thus possible for management to identify the causes of virtually any problem in service delivery. According to the Pareto Principle, it is likely that management will not be faced with a huge number of causes of any given problem. Indeed, it is likely that the number of significant causes will be found to be rather small. Remedial action can then be assessed and prioritized.

This sort of analysis is especially valuable in investigating any problems encountered in the critical "moments of truth"–the actual moment of delivery of service, and the customer's simultaneous experience and assessment of that service.

Figure 5.5 *Pareto chart—causal factors arranged in order of importance*

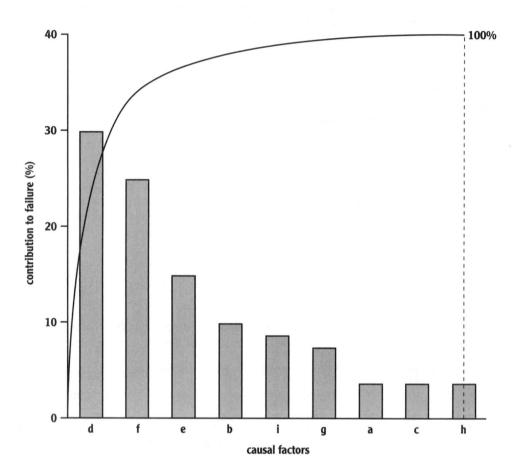

Author's presentation

Fishbone analysis

Professor Kaoru Ishikawa (1915–1989) of the University of Tokyo believed that any attempt to improve service delivery was doomed to failure unless management was prepared to engage in ongoing and continuous research—research designed to obtain more and more information about *exactly what constitutes the service-delivery process* (Ishikawa, 1985).

As a result of his studies, Ishikawa developed a diagram in the shape of a fishbone to explain how various factors could be related to cause and outcome (or cause and effect). This diagram is often referred to as the "Ishikawa diagram" or the "fishbone cause-and-effect diagram" (see Figure 5.6).

Figure 5.6 *Fishbone diagram*

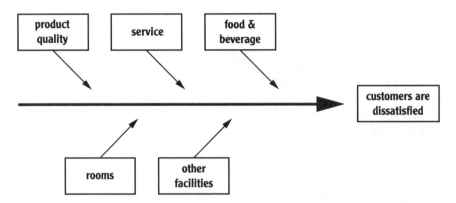

Author's presentation (based on Ishikawa, 1985)

The cause-and-effect diagram is used to represent the relationship between an effect and all the possible causes that influence failure or poor performance. Using fishbone analysis to study the airline industry. Lovelock (1994) organized all these possible causes under four categories—personnel, equipment, materials, and procedures. But various industries and various problems might require different categories. For example, when a customer makes a complaint about delay in room service of breakfast, the cause and its solution can be assessed under the five categories of personnel, equipment, materials, procedures, and others (miscellaneous other factors). See Figure 5.7 for a representation of this problem according to fishbone analysis.

Using such an analysis of this critical "moment of truth," the issues can be systematically addressed, and a solution identified. The first step is to identify the problem (delay in breakfast service), followed by an identification of the various resources that are required for breakfast services (personnel, equipment, material, procedure, and others). Problem causes associated with each resource are then identified and prioritized.

Finally, to prioritize the remedial action, Pareto analysis can be used.

This combination of fishbone analysis and Pareto analysis can be used by service management to assess and fix virtually any problem at the critical level of service delivery—the crucial "moment of truth."

Designing and managing service networks

Finally, in this chapter on service philosophies and strategies, we consider service networks. Networks are inherent in almost all service businesses, and service networks are often an important reservoir of resources for service organizations. When utilized efficiently, such networks can produce a significant competitive advantage.

Figure 5.7 *Fishbone analysis of delay in breakfast service*

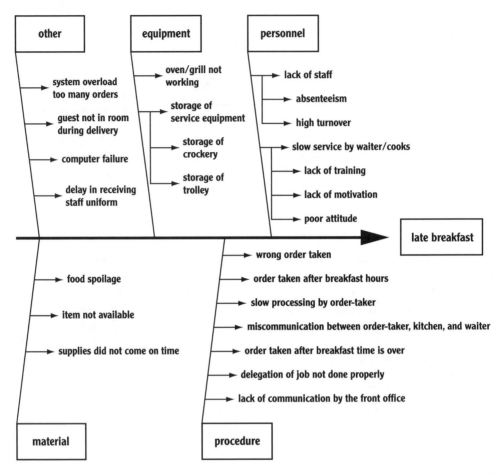

Author's presentation (based on Ishikawa, 1985)

As competitive pressures emerge, and as customer demands grow beyond the capability of an individual business, it becomes necessary for firms with different core competencies to collaborate and capitalize on the power of networking as a competitive advantage. This is critical if the firms are to achieve and maintain market leadership in their fields.

Advantages of networks

According to the type of service under consideration, networks assume a variety of forms. They can provide:

* specific physical facilities;

* specific information; or

* relationships that are generally useful (in miscellaneous ways) in rendering effective services.

The expenditure of money and time that is involved in developing such relationships is money well spent. The coordination of the service through a network frequently offers service firms a safeguard by effectively presenting a barrier for entry to their competitors. Moreover, firms with a substantial investment in networking enjoy a marked competitive advantage. For example, a hotel's collaboration with an airline, or with a local tourist attraction, gives it an advantage over other hotels that cannot provide customers with special package offers.

Designing a service network is also a means of minimizing the expenses of developing supply chains for delivering a particular service. For example, a firm that distributes prepared food to residential homes for the elderly three times daily might develop a network with a food service and a transport company. The network serves them all.

Again, a customer focus

As in all aspects of service delivery, service network design should focus on the customer rather than on the firms involved. In particular, maximizing the accessibility of service outlets for customers is an extremely important aspect of networks. The relative accessibility of one site to other sites in the network is important in this regard. For example:

* airline passengers should not have to spend a lot of time waiting to catch a connecting flight;

* transport for hot or frozen food should be arranged such that the food maintains its temperature while awaiting a connecting truck.

Big is beautiful

To a customer, the value of a service network is often directly proportional to the size of the network. A bigger service network often provides a greater benefit to customers. For example, a hotel chain that has a property in every city, and a central reservation system to coordinate them all, is very helpful for many customers. Similarly, a larger mobile telephone company, with more subscribers and a larger telephone network, is likely to provide greater reach, and hence greater value, to a mobile telephone owner.

Large networks also enhance the communication of information about the combined service to customers, suppliers, and intermediaries. One member of the network complements another. Consequently, the strength of the network relationship is greater than the strength of any one of the organizations comprising the network. Service networks are thus often perceived by customers as an indication of a more comprehensive and superior service offering. When considering networks, big is beautiful.

Summary of chapter

As discussed in Chapter 4, business organizations must adopt a customer-oriented managerial approach to compete successfully in today's marketplace. To satisfy the needs of customers, it is important for managers to improve the firm's internal efficiency on an ongoing basis—both in terms of strategic management and in terms of operational delivery of services.

Thus, at the macro level, the main task of management is to establish an organizational philosophy that drives the entire firm toward the achievement of its goals and objectives. Moreover, it is essential that this philosophy be communicated to employees at all levels, and be clearly understood by them. It must also be understood by the customers. Thereafter, the firm needs to design and implement service systems and processes that support, substantiate, and reinforce the organizational philosophy.

By establishing and communicating its service concept and service strategy, a firm positions itself in the marketplace and communicates its market position to its employees, customers, and competitors. This also assists managers to focus the firm's efforts and resources effectively on appropriate areas to improve its services and competitive position.

At the operational level, the ability to design, deliver, improve, and tailor services to meet the needs of customers is of paramount importance to success. Although the nature of service makes standardization and consistent delivery of quality service products difficult to achieve, service providers who can overcome such challenges will be able to improve customer satisfaction and enhance the firm's image and market position.

As competitive pressures emerge, and as customer demands grow beyond the capability of an individual business, it becomes necessary for firms with different core competencies to collaborate and capitalize on the power of *networking* as a competitive advantage. This is critical if the firms are to achieve and maintain market leadership in their fields.

A continuing theme of this book is that hospitality service providers in the present marketplace must adopt a managerial outlook that views hospitality services as service businesses—rather than maintaining a traditional narrow focus on the products of accommodation, food, and beverage. This chapter has provided hospitality managers with a holistic perspective that enables hotels to improve their competitive power at all levels of the organization. This approach creates a "win–win" situation in which customers benefit from improved services while the hotels enhance their operational efficiency and business performance.

Review questions

1. What is the relationship between service vision and service strategy?

2. Briefly describe the techniques for measuring organisational performance, as presented in this chapter.

3. Briefly describe the various techniques for managing a service operation, as presented in this chapter. Give illustrations in the hotel industry (for example, prepare a fishbone analysis for a breakfast buffet service).

4. Briefly explain the benefits of service networks. As the manager of a first-class business hotel, what kind of network would you choose to enter? Why?

Suggested reading for this chapter

This is a list of suggested further reading on topics covered in this chapter. For a separate list of full reference citations quoted in the chapter, see "References," Chapter 5, at the end of the book

Berry, L. L. 1995. *On Great Service: A Framework for Action*, The Free Press, New York.

Fitzsimmons, J. A. 1998. *Service Management for a Competitive Advantage*, McGraw-Hill, New York.

Heskett, J. L., Sasser, W. E., & Hart, C. W. 1990. *Service Breakthroughs: Changing the Rules of the Game*, The Free Press, New York.

Lovelock, C. 1991. *Services Marketing*, Prentice Hall, Upper Saddle River, New Jersey.

chapter six

Modern Marketing (1) — External Service Implications

Study objectives

Having completed this chapter, readers should be able to:

* perceive the limitations of the traditional "4Ps" model in modern services marketing;

* appreciate the practical implications of the "new Ps", and

* understand the significance of other marketing concepts especially applicable to services, and be able to use them in a hospitality context.

The framework of this chapter

This chapter is set out as follows:

* Introduction

* Toward a new marketing paradigm

- What does marketing do?
- How does marketing work?
- A new, integrated paradigm of marketing

* Integrating operations, marketing, and human resources

- Marketing "distance" in manufactured goods
- Marketing "distance" in services
- "Consumption marketing" becomes important
- "Preconsumption marketing" becomes less important
- Operations, marketing, and human resources

* An extended marketing mix for services

- A new formulation required
- Product
  What is a service product?
  A process, not a physical object
- Price
  Pinning a price tag on the intangible
  Price must reflect value
  Price discrimination important in services
  Putting a price on experience
- Promotion
  Traditional role of promotion
  Special role of word of mouth
  Promotion of production skills in services
  Promotion of image
- Place
  Accessibility important in services
  Timing and speed important in services

  - People
    People intrinsic to services
    Taking cues from employees
    Taking cues from other customers
  - Physical evidence
    No service is truly intangible
    Making the intangible somewhat tangible
    Other physical evidence
    Coordinating the physical evidence
  - Process
    The significance of process
    Customer-centric processes
    Customized service processes
    Planning ahead

* New marketing concepts for services

  - Four primary factors in new marketing concepts
  - Relationship is the key
  - Definition of a service encounter
  - What are "moments of truth"?
  - The "cascade" in "moments of truth"
  - At the "coalface"
  - Not to be left to chance

* Summary of chapter

Introduction

As we have seen, services have distinctive features that differentiate them from manufactured products, and the marketing of services is consequently different from that of product marketing. This chapter focuses on how the distinctive qualities of services affect the marketing of the service interface. The following chapter looks at the internal structures and strategies that are required to make this work.

Because they were primarily designed for goods marketing, the traditional "4Ps" of the marketing mix (*product, price, place,* and *promotion*) have proved inadequate for services marketing. They do not address the distinctive characteristics of services, nor do they take into account the importance of the human element in the production and consumption of service products. Additional "Ps" have thus been introduced as service marketers have attempted to create more appropriate marketing models for service industries. This chapter looks at these.

In a similar vein, new marketing concepts—such as the "service encounter" and the "moment of truth"—have been identified as being specifically related to customers' perceptions and satisfaction in a service situation, and these newer concepts are also discussed here.

It is obviously important that service managers understand and manage the challenges posed by the marketing of services at the interface with customers. This chapter addresses these challenges at the point of contact with the customer—the external service implications of services marketing. As noted above, the next chapter follows this up by examining the internal structures and strategies that are required to facilitate effective external services marketing.

Toward a new marketing paradigm

What does marketing do?

The primary function of marketing is to bring buyers and sellers together with the intention of exchanging products and services of mutual value. The exchange essentially involves the obtaining of a desired product or service from another party by giving something in return.

To effect successful exchanges (or transactions), the marketing department analyzes what each party can be expected to give and receive. A full understanding of marketing therefore requires product and service development to be planned in response to the changing needs and wants of customers. Marketing essentially constitutes a "knowledge bridge" between the customer and producer—effectively informing the producer of what must be offered if its products and services are to meet the expectations and demands of customers.

How does marketing work?

Marketing includes many interrelated and interdependent activities. In product marketing, the term "marketing mix" describes how management attempts to combine these activities creatively.

The marketing mix has many facets, but the four basic elements are known as the "4Ps":

* product;

* place;

* price; and

* promotion.

These are also described as the *controllable* variables of marketing because they are capable of being controlled and manipulated by the marketer. Some writers have incorporated other "Ps" into the services marketing mix. These other "Ps" have included *people, process,* and *physical evidence* (see, e.g., Booms & Bitner, 1981; Rust, Zahorik, & Keiningham, 1996).

A paradigm shift in thinking

The primary focus of successful service firms is now squarely on the customer first, and the profit of the firm second. Profit comes from customer satisfaction. This is a quantum shift in management focus.

Leading service organizations now concentrate their energies on improving the total experience of the customer through integrated strategies that satisfy, or exceed, customer expectations.

Such an integrated approach to operations and marketing develops exceptional service, and propels enlightened firms to the forefront of service leadership and success.

A new, integrated paradigm of marketing

Previous chapters have indicated the distinctive differences between manufactured goods and services (see especially "How services differ," Chapter 2). In a similar vein, the literature on services marketing insists that services marketing requires different approaches and strategies from that used in product marketing if the specific characteristics of services are to be addressed. In particular, the nature of services means that marketing is not an independent function of the service organization, but an *interrelated holistic concept encompassing every activity within the organization.*

From a basic business perspective, every business enterprise strives to achieve two basic objectives to stay in business:

＊ to satisfy the customer; and

＊ to make a return on investment (ROI).

See Figure 6.1. To achieve the second (a satisfactory ROI), the first is essential (the satisfaction of the customer). No organization will be able to achieve its ultimate objective in terms of ROI without first successfully attaining its primary goal of satisfying its customers. To create and expand an organization's customer base is the most important function of management.

Figure 6.1 *The two basic objectives of a business enterprise*

Author's presentation

ROI is thus totally dependent on customer satisfaction, but the reverse is not true. A focus on a high ROI will not guarantee customer satisfaction. In keeping with this, the primary focus of successful firms is now squarely on the customer first, rather than the profit of the firm. In turn, this change in focus has produced numerous changes in the way that businesses are managed and how they compete in the marketplace.

In the past 20 years or so, this quantum shift in management focus has caused leading service organizations to concentrate their energies on improving the total experience of the customer. Moving away from a departmentalized approach, successful service providers *unify* their efforts through cross-functional strategies that satisfy, indeed exceed, customer expectations. Such an integrated approach to operation and marketing has enabled some organizations to develop exceptional service, and propel themselves to the forefront of service leadership and success.

Integrating operations, marketing, and human resources

Because of the distinctive features of services (intangibility, inseparability of production and consumption, heterogeneity, and perishability), marketing in service organizations differs significantly from marketing in traditional goods manufacturing.

Marketing "distance" in manufactured goods

As practiced in the goods-manufacturing industry, marketing is distant, both physically and conceptually, from the production process. Marketing in manufactured goods can be said to exist primarily to connect production and consumption (see Figure 6.2). For example, a product might be manufactured in one country and used by customers in another country. In this case, production and consumption are physically distant, and the consumer has no direct interest or influence in the manufacture of the product. Marketing is often the only way in which the manufacturing firm communicates with its customer.

Figure 6.2 *Production, consumption, and marketing in manufactured goods*

Source: Adopted From Palmer & Cole (1995)

This separation of function not only separates the customer from manufacture, but also, within the firm itself, often separates production from marketing. This separation of production and marketing makes it more difficult for each of these vital functions to influence one another effectively and constructively. In contrast, in the case of services, the two are inextricably linked.

Marketing "distance" in services

In the case of services, as we have previously noted, production and consumption occur simultaneously. In addition, customers are often required to be physically present, and they therefore influence the production process itself (see Chapter 2). From the customer's point of view, production and marketing are inextricably intertwined, and the production and consumption process itself thus constitutes an important marketing instrument (see Figure 6.3).

Figure 6.3 *Production, consumption, and marketing in services*

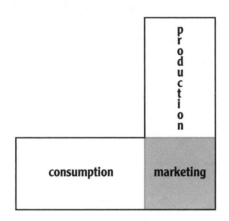

Adapted from Palmer & Cole (1995)

"Consumption marketing" becomes important

Because production and marketing are so closely interrelated in service industries, and because each has the capacity to influence the other, every employee within a service organization has to possess skills in both production and marketing. For example, a restaurant waiter not only serves food and beverages to customers but also, in the process, markets his or her personal waiting skills and the restaurant's overall service capability. The waiter is thus a "part-time marketer" on behalf of the restaurant. As another example, a receptionist providing advice and assistance to a guest is simultaneously *producing* a service and *marketing* that service. Since the service "factory" is at the "front of house," where services are both produced and consumed, it is imperative that service employees receive appropriate encouragement and incentives to market their own services and, through this, the services of the organization. Effective employees must demonstrate a real willingness to see marketing as part of their basic service role.

"Preconsumption marketing" becomes less important

The intangible nature of services makes it difficult for customers to assess the benefit of a service before consumption. For example, an airline customer cannot assess an in-flight experience until the service is actually being consumed. Most traditional approaches to marketing and advertising are therefore ineffective in services. Customers depend heavily on "word-of-mouth" information from others who have already experienced the service (Bone, 1995; Swan & Oliver, 1989). Apart from such word-of-mouth advice, customers seek cues (such as the cleanliness of a restaurant) to gain an indication of the likely quality of the service outcome.

Because services cannot be pretested before consumption, and because customers therefore rely on word of mouth and various cues, marketing of services is more effective if directed toward the consumption and postconsumption phases of service delivery. This is in contrast to the situation in the goods-manufacturing industry in which customers are able to assess products *before* purchase, and in which the marketing process therefore predominantly focuses on the preconsumption stage. This difference between services and manufactured goods can be expressed graphically (Figure 6.4).

Figure 6.4 *Marketing effectiveness before, during, and after consumption*

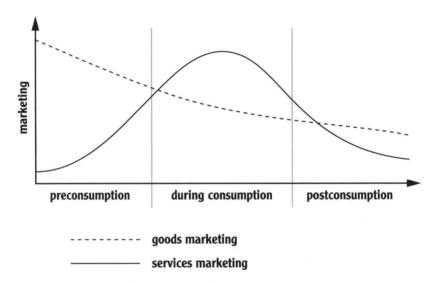

Author's presentation

The focus and effectiveness of services and goods marketing, when charted on such a graph, have markedly different patterns. As can be seen from the graphs, marketing techniques for services prove least effective at the preconsumption stage. The best that can be done at this stage is to enhance word-of-mouth communication. Not only is this the most effective means of marketing services before consumption, but it also happens to be the least expensive!

Operations, marketing, and human resources

In goods manufacturing, the departments of operations, marketing, and human resources are separate entities with separate functions. In contrast, in the services sector, these functions can never be separated.

The human element plays such a significant role in *every* aspect of services that it is impossible to separate out these traditionally distinct functions in any meaningful way. Production, consumption, and marketing are all dependent on the personality of employees, and the way in which they interact with customers.

The human resources department in most organizations is traditionally responsible for such personnel matters as selection, training, empowerment, discipline, and so on. In the case of services, these matters become intertwined with production, consumption, and marketing in a way that simply does not occur in goods manufacturing. Although it is true the functions of production, marketing, and human resources can be conceived and examined independently *as a matter of theory,* effective service delivery *in practice* requires an ongoing coordination and integration of all three departments (Lovelock, 1992).

In the hospitality sector, if a hotel or other service sees itself as a truly integrated service, all employees must be selected, trained, and empowered with a view to their aptitude in both production *and* marketing. The apparently separate functions of production, marketing, and human resources must thus become integrated and coordinated in effective service organizations. (See box, "Keeping up with service enhancements".)

Impossible to separate

The human element plays such a significant role in *every* aspect of services that it is impossible to separate out the traditionally distinct functions of *production, marketing,* and *consumption* in any meaningful way. These are all dependent on the personality of employees, and the way in which they interact with customers.

An extended marketing mix for services

A new formulation required

From the above discussion, it will be apparent that the traditional "4Ps" of the marketing mix in goods marketing—product, place, price, and promotion—are insufficient for the needs of modern integrated service organizations. There are two major reasons for this:

* the unique characteristics of services; and

* the interrelationship of marketing, operations, and human resources in services (this chapter).

The combination of these two factors means that a new formulation is required. As a result, an extended marketing mix of "7Ps" has been proposed for service products (Bitner & Zeithaml, 1987; Booms & Bitner, 1981). This extended services marketing mix consists of the traditional four "Ps," together with three new "Ps." It therefore consists of "7Ps," as follows:

* product;

* place;

* price;

* promotion;

* people;

* physical evidence; and

* process.

See Figure 6.5 for a pictorial representation of this extended services marketing mix. Each of these seven elements is examined in more detail below.

Figure 6.5 *Extended marketing mix in services*

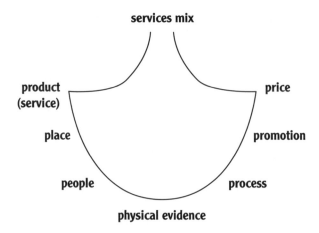

Author's presentation

Keeping up with service enhancements

A recent service-enhancement initiative at a major airline, marketed via a targeted email campaign, permitted certain customers to check in "virtually" using either the Internet or a toll-free number. The customers had to be frequent-flyer members, had to have an electronic ticket, and were required to be carrying only hand luggage.

Upon arrival at the airport, the customer was to report directly to the boarding gate, bypassing the front ticket counter and boarding area check-in counter. At the boarding gate, the customer was supposed to be asked only for his or her frequent-flyer membership card and personal identification. Convenience and speed were promised.

Attempting to use this service more than a week after the announcement, I found that the boarding attendant had no idea what I was doing. Indeed, he had never heard of this new process! As a result, I had to get back in the queue at the check-in counter, go through the full routine, and get a standard hardcopy paper boarding pass.

This experience was repeated at three other airports across the United States. Clearly, a highly trumpeted new service enhancement had became an embarrassment.

I contacted the airline and described my experience. The airline replied that its biggest problem with the new system was in properly educating the thousands of gate employees.

When I asked the gate employees about this, they indicated that they were overwhelmed with information and had missed the enhancement training.

So much for improving service . . .

This case indicates the importance of integrating production, marketing, and human resources in services industries. The people who deliver the service are also "selling" the service. These people must be trained, encouraged, and empowered to see their role as an integrated function aimed at serving the customer, and thus marketing themselves and their firm effectively.

Chris Roberts

Product

What is service product?

A service product, as defined here, is anything—either in isolation or in combination—that an organization offers to potential customers to satisfy their needs. The service product constitutes the foundation of an organization's existence. Accommodations in a hotel room, food in a restaurant, a conference function, a sightseeing trip, a taxi ride, an airline flight, secretarial assistance, and an insurance policy are all examples of service products.

A process, not a physical object

In services, the product is a process. The decisions on product mix faced by a service manager are therefore very different from those faced by managers who deal in goods. Most fundamentally, pure services can be defined only in terms of *process descriptions,* not as tangible descriptions or outcomes.

In addition, quality represents an especially key element in defining the service product. Other elements of the traditional product description—such as design, reliability, brand image, and product range—are less important in services. The key issue is *the customer's personal experience* of service delivery.

Price

Pinning a price tag on the intangible

The intangible character of services causes difficulties in pricing. Because the "product" is intangible, customers can have difficulty in assessing exactly what they are paying for. They cannot see it, or examine it, or assess it in the way that they can with physical goods. It is difficult to pin a price tag on something that does not "exist"!

In the absence of available cues, customers often use price as an indicator of the quality of service they might reasonably expect. Thus the price of a service offering can influence, in advance, perceptions of quality, satisfaction, and value. Customers often relate high-priced services to high quality and, consequently, *expect* high quality. On the other hand, if the service is priced too low, customers might doubt whether this organization is likely to deliver quality.

Pricing in service organizations is thus less influenced by cost than it is by the *customer's perception of value or worth*. The actual pricing of a service is often determined by matching the customer's perception of value.

Price must reflect value

Matching the customer's perception of value and achieving the right price mix involves a host of strategic and tactical decisions regarding such matters as:

* the average price to be charged;

* discount structures to be offered;

* terms of payment to be made available; and

* the degree of price discrimination to be allowed among different groups of customers.

In short, successful proactive pricing depends on recognizing the value that a customer places on a service, and pricing it accordingly (Berry & Yadav, 1996).

Price discrimination important in services

The personal and nontransferable nature of many services presents opportunities and challenges for *price discrimination* within service markets—opportunities and challenges that are less apparent in most goods markets. That is, in pricing services, there is much greater scope for significant price cutting in certain circumstances (and for price rises in other circumstances).

Price discrimination can be more readily used in services than in goods because the purchaser does not actually end up "possessing" the service in the way that a purchaser of goods takes possession of the product. Because the vendor is not actually "losing" the service to the ownership of the buyer, price cutting can be practiced more readily. The vendor does "lose" time and effort, but these can be offered again. In contrast, a goods manufacturer actually "loses" a physical object that might be difficult to replace. For these reasons, a services vendor might feel more comfortable about selling its product at a lower price. Indeed, this is often the only way for a firm to convince customers to use its service.

And the lack of transferability of ownership is not the only factor to be considered in price discrimination involving services. Perishability of services is also an important factor. Because services are characterized by variable capacity over time, such factors as operational efficiency, productivity, resource utilization, and profitability depend on astute management of demand—that is, by shifting the peaks to accommodate the troughs.

Extremely cheap hotel rooms or airline seats are examples of this sort of cut-price offering. Prices can be extremely low at certain times—not only because the room or the seat are not actually "lost" by the vendor in any physical or permanent sense (as previously noted), but also because the product will "perish" immediately if it is not sold. Vendors of services often cannot afford *not to* sell. In certain circumstances, it suits the vendor to "give it away for a song" (as the saying goes). Goods retailers can rarely do this.

Conversely, service firms can actively discourage demand at peak periods by putting prices up—thus diminishing the strain on limited resources. In a sense, a service firm sometimes does not want to sell more product. Goods suppliers are not often in this situation.

This issue of controlling demand and supply in services is further discussed in Chapter 7.

Giving it away "for a song"

Service prices can be extremely low at certain times. This occurs for a variety of reasons including, of course, overall supply and demand. But two distinctive characteristics of services are especially important in understanding the pricing of services.

1. The service product is not actually "lost" by the vendor in any physical or permanent sense. For example, an airline offering a cut-price seat does not physically "lose" its furniture for this low price. The buyer does not take the seat home!

2. The service product will often "perish" immediately if it is not sold, and vendors of services often cannot afford *not to* sell. For example, if a plane takes off with empty seats, that potential service sale has flown away forever!

In certain circumstances, it therefore suits service vendors to "give it away for a song" (as the saying goes). Goods retailers can rarely do this.

Putting a price on experience

Another difference in pricing policy between goods and services is the problem faced by service vendors in putting a price on experience, accumulated knowledge, and practiced skills. Some service products, such as a consultant's knowledge, might not involve any obvious additional cost at the point of production of the service. However, the extra cost is determined by the days, months, or years already spent in acquiring that knowledge.

The pricing of the intellectual component of a consulting service, and/or the pricing of practiced skills acquired over many years, is a very difficult problem for service vendors—a problem not faced by most goods vendors.

Promotion

Traditional role of promotion

Traditional promotion employs a variety of methods—including advertising, sales promotion, public relations, and personal selling—to attract the attention of existing and potential customers, and to inform them of the products, services, and special offers made available by the firm (Peattie & Peattie, 1995). Market communication performs three basic roles in marketing—to inform, to persuade, and to remind. However, due to the intangible nature of services, some of the traditional methods can prove to be inappropriate if applied to services. Nevertheless, with certain modifications, most of these traditional methods can be utilized to promote services effectively.

Special role of word of mouth

Studies of consumer behavior indicate that word-of-mouth communication is of special significance in the marketing of service industries. This is due primarily to the "high risk" of many service purchases—in that services cannot be pretested, returned, or reworked if they do not meet the expectations of customers. In an effort to minimize this perceived risk, customers seek out recommendations from others before deciding to purchase a service. In this way, satisfied customers often serve as "ambassadors" of service organizations, providing service firms with an inexpensive, but very effective, form of advertising. Conversely, dissatisfied customers can ruin even the best attempts at promotion.

Promotion of production skills in services

The fact that production and consumption are simultaneous affords an organization an opportunity to showcase their services, their personnel, and their skills to customers. This is particularly evident within the hotel and restaurant industry. For example, the flambé presentation of food or the guéridon carving of meat at the table are commonly utilized as marketing tools.

As a development from this, it has become increasingly common in restaurants for the presentation of personnel and skills to be extended to a visually exposed kitchen and cooking process. Many restaurants are setting up transparent glass walls that allow customers to observe the food-preparation process in action. There are few goods-manufacturing factories where the production process is actually promoted as a selling point! Such is the distinctive nature of services marketing.

Promotion of image

Image is crucially important for any organization—both goods providers and services providers—because it markedly influences customers' perceptions of the goods and services offered. The intangible nature of services poses special challenges for services marketers in developing and maintaining a desirable corporate image; but it also presents significant opportunities.

The image of an organization is built up in the customer's mind through advertising, public relations, physical image, and word-of-mouth comments, as well as through actual service experience. Some images are "corporate" in the sense of being uniform throughout the organization. In other cases, service organizations with multiple outlets might maintain a corporate image, but complement this with local branches that project a local image closely associated with a specific location. For example, McDonald's maintains a definite international image but, within individual countries, it operates with effective local images as well.

Image can be an extraordinarily powerful weapon. A positive corporate image often serves as an unwritten service "guarantee" in the minds of first-time customers, providing comfort and reassurance even when there is no explicit written guarantee. This extends to the engendering of customer "loyalty." Indeed, a positive image that is sincerely believed by customers has been shown to engender a sense of "loyalty"—even among customers who have not personally tried the service (Andreassen & Lindestad, 1998). The customer is loyal to the image!

In contrast, if the image of a service firm is unattractive, customers might not avail themselves of the services on offer, or might not form a positive view of those that they do try. Even if a firm has superior technical and functional quality, this might well be ineffective if customers are negatively disposed to a company before they even partake of the services on offer.

A positive image can, in certain circumstances, serve as a buffer when unexpected service failure occurs. On the other hand, it must also be noted that high expectations of a service firm can cause a minor service failure to be viewed less tolerably by some customers. That is, a very positive image "can lift the bar" for the organization, provoke high expectations among customers, and make minor errors seem important. However, in general, this is not a significant problem, and a favorable image is better than a negative one! Certainly, if consumers have an unfavorable image of an organization, they are more likely to become extremely challenging and unhappy when things do go wrong. They are, in a sense, "looking for trouble."

An often overlooked aspect of image in a service organization is its effect on the firm's internal customers (see Chapter 4). It is important to recognize that the image of an organization reflects on internal relationships, as well as external relationships. A favorable image will attract desirable employees, suppliers, and distributors to the organization because these employees, suppliers, and distributors prefer to deal with firms that appeal to them personally and that appear to have a better chance of success in the marketplace. In turn, having superior employees and products assists in gaining customer satisfaction. In this way, a good image leads to satisfied customers who, in turn, reinforce an organization's image and elevate it to a still higher level.

Moreover, a good image might even induce customers, employees, and suppliers to become shareholders in the firm, thus developing a vested interest in the success of the organization.

Image thus reinforces itself. Once it has become established within the internal and external community of the organization it becomes self-fulfilling (see Figure 6.6).

Figure 6.6 *Service interrelationships*

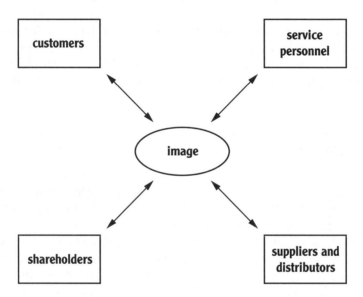

Author's presentation

Image is thus a management tool of great potential. Its ability to be self-reinforcing can exert a considerable "snowball effect." The image that a service company creates in the minds of its own staff and in its wider environment will be largely determined by the nature of its service, its organization, its culture, and the market segment it serves (Normann, 1991, 2000).

Place

Accessibility important in services

Place constitutes an important factor in the marketing of services (Bitner, 1990). In services, the "service factory" is at the front line (where the employee serves the customer). It is thus imperative that the physical location where the service is being offered is accessible to the customers. If customers are obliged to travel to avail themselves of the services on offer, as is the case with a restaurant or a retail shop, the accessibility of the location to the customer is clearly important. For example, the availability of car parking at a restaurant or retail shop might make the difference between a customer using or not using the service. In the case of a hotel service, the location and accessibility of the hotel is obviously a very important marketing factor.

Timing and speed important in services

In certain other services—such as fire services, plumbing services, pizza home delivery, and so on—the service center takes the service to the customer. In these cases, it is the speed with which these services reach the customer that determines their value. The arrival of an ambulance an hour after it is needed constitutes no service at all. In this and many other service situations, the proximity of the service to the community it serves becomes an extremely important consideration for the service provider.

People

People intrinsic to services

Customers of service organizations are very much aware of the emotions and attitudes of contact employees. From a customer's perspective, the behavior of contact employees represents more than the service product; in a very real sense the behavior of contact employees represents the organization itself.

This obviously affects the marketing of service products. People are more than usually important when it comes to consideration of a marketing mix for services. For example, a friendly barman might well prove to be more of an attraction to a customer than the drinks that he serves. Indeed, for many services—such as consulting services, medical services, educational services, and other professional services—the provider *is* the service. Although this one-to-one correspondence (between provider and service) is not as marked in hospitality services, it is still true to say that the quality of personnel is absolutely crucial to the perception of service quality.

Taking cues from employees

The employees of a service firm involved in service delivery provide cues to the customer regarding the nature of the service itself. The grooming, personal attitudes, and behavior of employees all influence customers' perceptions of the service (Bitner, 1992a; Rafaeli, 1993). A waiter who appears dirty or unkempt in an otherwise attractive environment might cause customers to avoid that restaurant.

Product, place, price . . . but especially people (1)

Two pleasures in life in which I frequently indulge are eating out and eating fish. My expectations of quality relate to all aspects of the experience. I consider all the traditional "Ps"—product, place, price, and so on . . . but especially *people*. In this box and the next are two contrasting service experiences in the restaurant industry.

On a recent visit to Florida, we chose a pleasant restaurant that presented itself as being lively rather than rushed. The tables were clean, the cutlery and glassware were sparkling, and the staff members were neat, cheerful, and competent. One of my companions is allergic to wheat and dairy products, and asked the waiter which dishes might contain, or be cooked in, the offending ingredients. Her disappointment grew as it became apparent that most of the dishes that whetted her appetite had to be eliminated. The waiter excused himself and returned to advise that the head chef would especially create the dish of her choice by substituting soy and gluten-free ingredients, at no extra charge. My friend was delighted—but more was to follow.

I chose fresh tuna—a first for me. Although the fish was fresh and perfectly presented, it was rather strong in taste for my palate. When the waiter appeared and asked us if everything was to our satisfaction, he immediately perceived that, for me, it was not—despite my polite assurances that everything was "fine." This time, the restaurant manager made an appearance. My disappointment was shared by him—despite my protests that there was nothing intrinsically wrong with the food. He removed the offending meal with one hand, produced a menu with the other, and invited me to choose another dish—politely recommending the Mahi Mahi (dolphin fish). I accepted his recommendation and was duly presented with one of the most delicious fish meals I have ever enjoyed. This was followed by the return of the rejected tuna fish, which was re-presented on a clean dish and placed centrally "for everyone to try if they wish." In addition, two extra (unordered) side salads and more hot vegetables were provided as compensation, together with an offer to replace all the other main courses, which were becoming cold as a result of the delay.

And it didn't stop there! Dessert orders were enhanced by a complimentary bowl of fruit salad, and the coffees with brandy chasers. When the bill was presented, we were advised that there was to be no charge for my main course.

Product, price, place . . . all important. But the most important ingredient in any service marketing mix is *people*.

Compare this superb service with our experience in another establishment (see box, "Product, place, price . . . but especially people (2)").

Gillian Lyons

Taking cues from other customers

Other customers in the service environment also provide such cues. The way in which a receptionist interacts with other customers influences a customer's perception of the receptionist's service, and the customer's perception of the organization as a whole (Rafaeli, 1993). Customers thus observe interactions between service personnel and other customers, and draw certain conclusions about the nature of the service.

However, interaction occurs not only between customers and the firm's personnel, but also among customers who are in the service environment at the same time. These customer-to-customer interactions also affect perceptions of the service. Before purchase, a person might make use of other customers as a cue to the type of service being offered and the market segment being targeted. For example, before entering a restaurant a potential customer might peer through the window to ascertain whether he or she "fits in" with the customers already in the restaurant. The decision to enter is then partially determined by other customers and the evidence they provide regarding the type of restaurant and the market segment being serviced.

Other customers also affect the actual service experience as it is being consumed. When purchasing services, as opposed to purchasing products, customers frequently have to share services and experiences. In classrooms, hospitals, retail stores, airlines, restaurants, and hotels, customers experience the service in the company of others. In these circumstances, the behavior of one customer influences the experience of others. Sometimes the needs of one customer might conflict with the needs of another—for example, smokers and nonsmokers in a restaurant, or a long queue for a restaurant or airline service. In other cases, the simultaneous consumption of services might be made more enjoyable by a crowd—as for example in the case of a busy dance floor in a nightclub (adding to the excitement of the experience) or the case of a crowded bar (providing a sociable, cheerful ambience).

Physical evidence

No service is truly intangible

It can be argued that no service is truly intangible because services are almost always accompanied by products. For example, the seats of an auditorium are part of the service of a music concert; the computer or books of an accountant are part of the accountancy service; the operating instruments of a surgeon are essential to the surgical service; and the aircraft is certainly essential for an airline flight! Although these physical objects cannot be categorized as true product elements (in that they are not "sold" to the customer in any meaningful sense), they play a vital role in the service-delivery process. In most cases, these product elements serve as cues to the customers during their assessment process.

Making the intangible somewhat tangible

These objects, as cues or pieces of evidence, play a critical role in making an intangible service somewhat tangible to the customer. For example, a theater ticket or a flight ticket provides confirmation of the services requested and expected; this is something that the customer can actually hold in his or her hand as tangible "evidence" of the promised service.

Customers desire the security of evaluating something tangible in this way, and do so by analyzing the physical evidence available to them. For example, patients evaluate the attractiveness of a physician's waiting room, passengers consider the comfort of a tour bus, and hotel guests assess the grandeur of a hotel foyer. This service setting (or "servicescape") defines the "built environment or man-made, physical surroundings of the service" (Bitner, 1992b). This provides a setting for the service, and conveys the values of the organization and the ideals it aspires to achieve.

Such tangible cues are an indication of the quality and nature of the service to be performed, especially in those cases in which consumers have little or no previous experience of the service offering. When consumers have little on which to judge the actual quality of service, they rely on the tangible physical cues, just as they rely on the cues provided by other people.

Other physical evidence

As noted above, a simple piece of physical evidence, such as a flight ticket, can be very important in services because it might be one of the few pieces of tangible evidence that a customer can actually "possess." Other tangible representations of the service might include items such as advertising brochures, billing statements, letters, business cards, and written service guarantees.

This sort of physical evidence provides excellent opportunities for a service firm to send clear and consistent marketing messages regarding the firm's purpose, the intended market segments, and the nature of the service (Bitner, 1992b, 1996).

Coordinating the physical evidence

Successful service firms are aware of the importance of coordinating these various pieces of physical evidence into a coherent marketing message. Airlines, for example, are careful to coordinate all tangible evidence—such as uniforms, aircraft decor, tickets, and all manner of advertising material. Although all airlines provide the same essential service, the differences that do exist are contrasting "packages" of evidence (Shostack, 1977).

In a similar way, an integrated hotel service ensures that its physical evidences are coordinated and coherent in sending the same marketing message. Staff uniforms, the hotel foyer, and all hotel literature and written material work together to produce the desired image in the mind of the customer. The hotel's ultimate product—its service

Product, place, price ... but especially people (2)

In the box, "Product, place, price ... but especially people (1)", I described the superb service received in a restaurant in Florida. Contrast that service experience with that of an English pub restaurant we visited some time later.

It was early lunchtime with relatively few diners present, and a single member of staff was on duty. This one person was attempting to serve at the bar, take food orders, deliver to tables, and clear up afterward. We were presented with uncovered tables (which felt "sticky"), and cutlery that appeared, at best, to have had a brief visit to the dishwasher!

Being a fish lover, and having noticed sea bass on the menu, I duly ordered one of my favorite dishes. After the waitress had been persuaded to clean the table (after which it still felt unpleasantly "sticky"), the fish arrived. What a disappointment! This fish was nothing like the large succulent specimens I had previously enjoyed. It resembled a small trout—except that the skin was gray and dry, toning nicely with the similarly gray and dehydrated flesh beneath. After cleaning my cutlery on the paper serviette, I speared a morsel of flesh and tasted the offering. My worst fears were realized. It was appalling! This time, when the waitress made her obligatory enquiry as to whether everything was "all right." I had to voice my thoughts and asked her to note how dry the fish looked. The waitress was unmoved.

"Oh, it always looks like that," was the indifferent response. "Nobody else has complained."

I did not consider this last comment to be especially significant—the English are noted for not complaining; they simply never go back! But I did feel somewhat intimidated. She had suggested that I was an unduly critical "problem" customer. I quickly passed a forkful of fish to my companion. He assured the waitress that, indeed, the sea bass tasted as dry as it looked.

The waitress responded with a dubious glance, asked if we had already paid for the meal, protested that she was the only one on duty, removed the plate perfunctorily, and headed for the kitchen.

Five minutes elapsed before she returned and asked if I would like to re-order. This time I chose chicken, which arrived about eight minutes later—my companion by then having almost finished his meal. Imagine my surprise when I noticed that the "new" meal was returned on the same plate, with the same vegetables!

There was no apology, no further enquiry as to whether we were now satisfied, and no offer of compensation.

Product, price, place ... all important. But the most important ingredient in any service marketing mix is *people*. And there is no doubt which restaurant I will patronage again!

Gillian Lyons

Changing the image and the physical evidence

A deluxe hotel was taken over by a hotel chain that wanted to project a different corporate image. The new owners wanted to offer a more homely atmosphere, and proceeded to make the physical evidence match the desired image.

Among other things, the marble and slate of the entrance foyer was covered in carpet to give a warm and inviting welcome. A real fireplace was installed in the foyer. Comfortable chairs were placed around the fireplace. Tables for card games, chess sets, draughts, and checkers were provided in the lounge. In short, the customers were treated like guests in a family home.

A hotel's ultimate product—its service experience—is intangible, but the physical evidence surrounding this intangible product is most certainly "real," and is very important in giving customers something definite on which to base a marketing impression.

experience—might be intangible, but the physical evidence surrounding this intangible product is most certainly "real," and is very important in giving customers something definite on which to base a marketing impression.

Physical evidence thus serves to reinforce customer perception of the firm's *image*—especially with respect to such qualities as capability, competence, trust, and safety. This can be quite subtle, and left "unsaid." Compare, for example, a 747 jumbo jet and a Concorde. A jumbo jet conveys an image of "solidity" and reliability. On the other hand, a Concorde suggests fast travel, social status, and so on. The service provider does not have to state this overtly for the customer to become aware of such an image. In a similar way, a hotel might convey its desired image of homeliness and relaxation simply by arranging comfortable chairs and an open fireplace in its lounge.

Such physical evidences are therefore important in contributing to the significant marketing concept of image. Visible evidence of a service must be designed as carefully as the service offering itself to ensure that it represents quality, value, and the desired image to the customer. (For more on image, see earlier in this chapter.)

Process

The significance of process

Unlike goods, services are *processes*. Services are the end result of deeds, acts, performances, and activities performed by the firms' employees alone or in conjunction with various equipment, machinery, facilities, and so on. These deeds are carried out in sequences that can be termed "service processes."

In almost all services, the customer participates in the production process. Some service operations (financial services, medical services, legal services, and so on) are very complex and require the customer to follow a complicated series of actions to complete the process. Others (e.g., hotel reservation and guest check-in) are less complex. From a customer's perspective, the service process provides vital evidence of the quality of service and the range of services offered.

Marketing of services must take this into account. Marketing of services involves marketing of processes.

Customer-centric processes

As noted above, the customers actively participate in most service processes. Indeed, they are often *essential* to the process—for example, in the reservation and checking-in processes customers provide essential information about the preferred kind of room, the time at which they are expected to arrive, special requirements, and so on. In a very real sense, the customer has no choice but to participate because the service simply cannot take place without his or her active involvement. This must be taken into account in marketing services. Because customers have no choice but to be involved, the ease and friendliness of the service process are crucial to their assessment of the quality of the service. If customers are, in a sense, "conscripted" into being involved, the least that a service company can do is to look after them during their forced labor!

Customers are thus impressed by a service process that is deliberately designed to make it easier for them to participate in the production process. Good service managers are aware of this, and consciously use this opportunity to arrange the process to appeal to the customer. This is the rationale behind such service processes as drive-through restaurants, drive-through banks, fondue food, and flambé food preparation in front of the customer. In all of these, the service is clearly designed to involve the customer in a very overt way. But the principle of designing customer-centric services to facilitate the involvement of the customer also applies to many other services in a more subtle way. For example, an astute reservations clerk can greet a customer by name, know the likes and dislikes of that customer, and generally facilitate the check-in process by being familiar with the guest's details *before* arrival—thus avoiding the need for a whole lot of unnecessary questions and filling-in of forms at the time of arrival. This reservations clerk is effectively marketing the hotel by facilitating the enforced involvement of the customer in the service process.

The importance of process in services

From the perspective of the customer, services are intrinsically *processes*. Customers do not perceive goods in this way. The service process is thus of the greatest importance in marketing services.

The following important points must be remembered.

* In almost all services, the customer participates in the production process.

* Often customers have no choice but to be involved in the production process. If customers are, in a sense, "conscripted" into being involved, the least that a service company can do is to look after them during their forced labor!

* Customers are thus impressed by a service process that is deliberately designed to make it easier for them to participate in the production process.

* In marketing services, management must be aware that efficiency is not everything. Personalized and customized service processes are crucial to services marketing.

* Successful marketing in any field of business demands foresight and planning. In the case of services, such planning must include careful assessment of process—in advance and in detail.

Process is thus an essential element of service marketing in a way that does not apply to goods marketing.

Customized service processes

In assessing process, customers evaluate whether the service follows a "production-line" approach or whether the process is a customized one in which the customer is given personalized attention (Bowen & Lawler, 1992).

For example, in the airline industry, it has been shown that flight delays are the single most important factor in producing customer dissatisfaction (Taylor & Claxton, 1994). The problem here is not so much the delay in itself—people will accept that delays occur in any complex transport service. What really irks them is an impression that they do not matter as individuals. Similar comments apply to checkout delays in hotels, when customers can easily feel like herded cattle rather than valued persons.

In marketing services, management must be aware that efficiency is not everything. Personalized and customized service processes are crucial to services marketing.

Planning ahead

Designing the service process in advance allows management to foresee the flow of interaction, and to anticipate the association of people and materials at various stages (see Chapter 5). This offers management the opportunity to prevent mistakes or to isolate the cause of recurrent problems, take corrective action, and influence the quality of the service outcome.

Successful marketing in any field of business demands foresight and planning. In the case of services, such planning must include careful assessment of *process*—in advance, and in detail.

In summary, the process characteristics of services are thus another important form of evidence used by customers to judge quality. Process characteristics are therefore of the greatest importance in the marketing of services.

New marketing concepts for services

The theme of this chapter has been that the distinctive qualities of services demand a reappraisal of the traditional marketing strategies, which were originally developed for the promotion and sale of manufactured goods. Such a reappraisal of marketing can be considered in two parts:

* the *modification of traditional marketing theories*—as in the expansion of the traditional "4Ps" to become a new set of "7Ps" (already discussed in this chapter); and

* the *introduction of new marketing concepts*—concepts specifically designed to respond to the distinctive ways in which customers perceive quality in services.

The rest of this chapter considers the second of these—new marketing concepts specifically for services.

Four primary factors in new marketing concepts

Zeithaml and Bitner (1996) turned their attention to the specific nature of services, and the question of customer perception. They identified four primary factors that influence customers' perception of service (and hence the marketing of services). They expressed them in these terms (see also Figure 6.7):

* service encounters (or "moments of truth");

* evidence of service;

Reappraising old strategies

The distinctive qualities of services mean that the traditional marketing strategies (which were originally developed for the promotion and sale of manufactured goods) are inadequate.

A reappraisal of marketing strategies for services involves:

* the *modification of traditional marketing theories*—as in the expansion of the traditional "4Ps" to become a new set of "7Ps," and

* the *introduction of new marketing concepts*—in particular, the concepts of the "service encounter" and the "moments of truth."

* image; and

* price (or value).

We have already made comment in this chapter on the last three items on this list—evidence of service (see "Coordinating the physical evidence"), image (see "Promotion of image"), and price (see "Price").

We now turn to the first item on the list—the service encounter and its "moments of truth." This is what marketing of services is really all about. This is where we need new marketing concepts and strategies specifically designed to respond to the distinctive nature of services.

Figure 6.7 *Factors influencing customer perceptions of service*

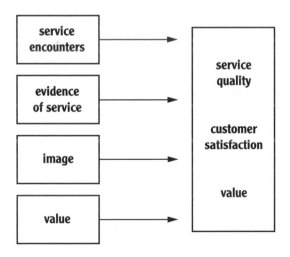

Author's presentation

Relationship is the key

Research into service quality management indicates that, in almost all circumstances, customers wish to develop relationships with their service providers. These relationships are important—whether interaction with the firm is frequent or intermittent. For example, a customer might visit a local retail outlet once a week, a hairdressing salon once a month, a dental clinic every six months, and a travel agent once a year. Whatever the frequency of visits, customers will choose to go back to the service provider with whom they have formed a good relationship.

Customers' perceptions of a firm are based on such factors as whether they had positive interaction with the employees, whether they believed the employees were friendly and helpful, whether they were satisfied with the services received, and whether they considered the goods and services to be of good value (Gould-Williams 1999). In almost all cases, staff interactions have a profound effect on customers' perception of the quality of service.

Personal relationship is the key to any new marketing strategies developed specifically for services.

Definition of a service encounter

The term "service encounter" has become part of the common vocabulary of marketing literature. Everyone seems to know what is meant by it, but how should it be defined?

A "service encounter" can be technically defined as "the dyadic interaction between a customer and service provider" (Surprenant & Solomon, 1987:87). This is a technical and precise definition—but it is rather narrow.

Shostack (1985:243) defined a service encounter somewhat more broadly as "a period of time during which a consumer directly interacts with a service." This somewhat broader definition encompasses *all* aspects of the service firm with which the consumer interacts—including its personnel, its physical facilities, and other visible elements. And note that Shostack's definition does not limit the encounter to the interpersonal interactions between the customer and the firm. In fact, taken literally, her definition suggests that service encounters can occur without any element of human interaction at all! Although such an idea is absurd in most services (in which human interaction is almost always central), this wider definition does present an important challenge to service marketers. It draws attention to the fact that apparently trivial external factors—such as insufficient parking at a hotel, or a key that does not open a guest room—can become negative "service encounters" at a hotel—whether or not personal interactions with staff members are otherwise satisfactory. The wider definition alerts managers to think "laterally" about the nature of "service encounters" and their implications for marketing.

But despite the usefulness of Shostack's wider definition of service encounters, the really important issue in service encounters is the handling of the face-to-face encounter at the critical time of service delivery—the so-called "moments of truth."

What are "moments of truth"?

The term "moments of truth" was introduced into the management literature by Normann (1984, 1991, 2000). It has subsequently been successfully used to illustrate service encounters in a variety of service organizations. The "moments of truth" are critical individual interactions that have the potential to determine a customer's attitude to the overall service offering. These are numerous such episodes that illustrate, to the customer, the *true value* of the organization—at least as the customer perceives it. Such "moments of truth" can "make or break" a service experience.

There can be no doubt as to the importance of these personal experiences. They are the single biggest determinant in customer perceptions of service quality (Berry, Parasuraman, & Zeithaml, 1988). These perceptions, in turn, influence the future purchasing intentions of consumers (Hartline & Jones, 1996).

"Moments of truth" in Japan

The best way to illustrate the nature of "moments of truth" is to give an example. Albrecht and Zemke (1985:31) narrated an incident that happened to one of their friends who was travelling alone in Japan on vacation.

> *At a train station in Japan he inquired in his limited Japanese which train he should take to go from Sapporo, where he was at the moment, to Tokyo. The man behind the counter wrote out all the information for him—times, train numbers, and track number. He even took the trouble to write it in both English and Japanese, in case our friend should lose his way and later need to show the note to some other Japanese person. This was a moment of truth, one of many that happened that day. At that instant our friend had an opportunity to form an impression of the train company, or at least of that one employee. He came away thinking, "that was a nice experience, there's somebody who really takes the trouble to help people." But the story goes even a bit further. Whilst waiting at the waiting area a few minutes later, he saw the information man come bustling through the crowded waiting hall looking for him. Locating him at last the man gestured for the return of the paper. He wrote something on it, gave it back, bowed quickly, and hurried back to his post. He had figured out a faster, more convenient sequence of trains, and came back to correct the note!*

Such "moments of truth" can "make or break" a service experience.

In services, the "human factor [is] the ultimate balance of quality" (Knisely, 1979). The human factor is therefore crucial to the marketing of services.

The "cascade" in "moments of truth"

Each of us has a personal storehouse of memories of the "moments of truth" in our own experience. As customers, we have experienced awful moments when it seemed that people or systems (or both) went out of their way to be difficult or unhelpful. And we have also had shining moments—when we felt appreciated, cared for, and genuinely valued as persons. As customers, as receivers of the service, each of us experiences the "moment of truth" as an intensely personal matter.

In this context, service interactions that occur in the first stages of an overall service experience are particularly critical. A failure at an early point in the relationship results in greater risk of dissatisfaction at each ensuing stage because we tend to take things personally, and interpret each successive failure as further evidence of the personal "insult" that we have initially received. Conversely, a cascade of goodwill can occur. If the first interactions are positive and affirming we tend to look positively on each ensuing interaction, anticipating goodwill and "looking for" satisfaction.

This phenomenon, both positive and negative, is known as the "cascade" in "moments of truth." See Figure 6.8.

This "cascade" has real, practical implications. For example, the Disney Corporation estimates that each of its amusement park customers experiences about 74 service encounters during each visit. This is a huge number, and the cascade phenomenon be-

Figure 6.8 *The "cascade" in "moments of truth"*

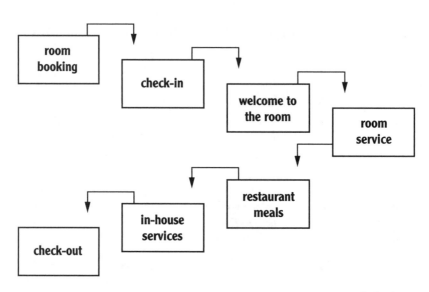

Author's presentation

comes very important when it is realized that a negative experience in any one of these 74 experiences, especially early ones, increases the risk of the next encounter being negatively interpreted. In turn, this substantially increases the risk of a negative evaluation of the overall service experience. Conversely, each positive experience reinforces the likelihood of the next encounter being viewed positively, and of the overall experience being perceived as enjoyable.

At the "coalface"

In assessing the importance of service encounters, it must be recognized that the service provider who is the "face" of the organization is typically the very last link in the chain of production, and is quite often the least-valued member of the service organization in terms of status and pay.

Jan Carlzon and SAS

As an example of the importance of "moments of truth," consider the case of Scandinavian Airline Systems (SAS).

Jan Carlzon, former president of SAS, used the phrase "moments of truth" to rally the employees of his airline at a time when the organization was in dire economic straits. Carlzon convinced his staff members that every contact between a customer and employee of the airline constituted a "moment of truth," and that these "moments of truth" had a cascading effect. In these brief encounters, Carlzon argued, the customer made up his or her mind about the overall quality of service offered by SAS.

Carlzon (1987) told his employees that "our business is not flying airplanes; it's serving the travel needs of our public." Carlzon estimated that, taken overall, the whole SAS workforce managed 50,000 "moments of truth" every hour of every day. This is a huge number of critical episodes—each one of them having the potential to wreak considerable damage on the overall organization.

Carlzon's success in turning SAS from near bankruptcy to profitability in less than two years is a case study in service management and marketing.

In goods manufacturing this might not be a critical matter. The last person in the production line of physical goods is important, but not nearly as important as the last person in the production line of a service. This is because production and delivery are virtually simultaneous in services. The last person in the production line of a service is also the customer-contact person, and this contact person is invested with enormous responsibility for conveying the "personality" of the service organization. In the eyes of the customer, at the point of service encounter, these contact employees *epitomize* the company (Cina, 1989).

In a very real sense, service quality is *created* by employees, but *judged* and *defined* by customers. The fact that customer-contact employees are often underpaid and undertrained can result in low levels of motivation, job dissatisfaction, high turnover—and, ultimately, in dissatisfied customers and unsuccessful marketing.

Effective management and marketing of the service encounter involves an empathic understanding of the motivation and behavior of such employees—behavior that can make the difference between a highly satisfactory service encounter and an unsatisfactory one. Effective management therefore involves training, motivating, and rewarding employees to exhibit the preferred behavior consistently (Bitner, Booms, & Tetreault, 1988). In short, effective marketing of services involves a real appreciation of the importance of the people at the "coalface," and a real commitment to their training and welfare.

As we have noted before, the management of truly integrated service operations cannot separate production, marketing, and human resources.

Not to be left to chance

The challenge of managing service encounters is thus vital for the successful marketing of any service organization. But, although it is generally recognized that the consistent quality of encounters is vital to the success of service operations, many organizations leave much of the process to chance (Deming, 1982; Shostack, 1985).

Every service interface can be broken down into its critical "moments of truth" (De Ruyter, Wetzels, Lemmink, & Mattson, 1997). To manage services effectively, it is imperative to identify, analyze, and manage these individual episodes of interpersonal interaction to ensure positive experiences, desirable customer reactions, and effective marketing of the entire service organization.

These critical "moments of truth" vary, depending upon the nature of the business, the nature of the product, and the nature of the service provided to the customer. But one thing is common in all cases—the critical "moments of truth," if left unmanaged, invariably lead to loss of customer confidence (Albrecht & Bradford, 1990). And once a firm loses the confidence of its customers, loss of loyalty and loss of repeat business follow soon after.

The ability to customize delivery, to diagnose needs, and to respond to these needs at each "moment of truth" thus makes the competitive difference for service firms (Davis, 1989). In any service organization, when the "moments of truth" go unmanaged, the quality of service drops to mediocrity (Albrecht & Zemke, 1985; Albrecht, 1988). Quality assurance in such interactions represents a major managerial and marketing challenge (Czepiel, Solomon, Surprenant, & Gutman, 1985).

The expansion of the traditional "4Ps" of marketing to "7Ps" is certainly useful in understanding services marketing—especially if the individual elements of the "7Ps" are understood and interpreted specifically *in services terms*. But the really significant development in understanding service marketing has come with the recognition of the need to develop specifically service-oriented marketing concepts—the central ideas of the service encounter and its "moments of truth."

Summary of chapter

Marketing has long been recognized as critical to the success of business organizations and, over the years, various marketing perspectives, theories, and practices have been developed. Although the traditional marketing mix of "4Ps" has long been useful to managers in planning and implementing their strategies, it is insufficient for many business firms, especially service firms, to compete successfully in today's marketplace.

As discussed in previous chapters, the increasing economic importance of the services sector, and the unique characteristics of service products, have highlighted the need for a different approach to marketing. This has led to the development of a new body of knowledge that aims to improve the competitive ability of service firms.

Various new concepts—such as the critical "moments of truth" and "service encounters"—are specific to the service context. These sorts of concepts, and the introduction of the "7Ps" marketing mix (an extension of the traditional "4Ps" model) as an extended services marketing mix, present marketers of service products with valuable insights into methods of improving their marketing effectiveness. On this basis, service marketers can design their service products and strategies in response to customer demands for quality service, and in response to pressures from competitors.

Review questions

1. Explain the differences between service products and manufactured goods that render the "4Ps" model inappropriate for services marketing.

2. Describe the "7Ps" model for services marketing. Give examples in the hotel industry.

3. Discuss the implications for hospitality managers of the various "new" marketing concepts designed especially for services. Give examples. (For example, identify the "moments of truth" in a hotel check-out situation.)

Suggested reading for this chapter

This is a list of suggested further reading on topics covered in this chapter. For a separate list of full reference citations quoted in the chapter, see "References," Chapter 6 at the end of the book.

Albrecht, K., & Bradford, L. J. 1990. *The Service Advantage: How to Identify and Fulfill Customer Needs,* Dow Jones Irwin, Homewood, Illinois.

Bitner, M. J., Booms, B. H., & Tetreault, M. 1990. "The Service Encounter: Diagnosing the Favorable and Unfavorable Incidents," *Journal of Marketing,* vol. 54, January.

Grönroos, C. 1990. *Service Management and Marketing: Managing the Moments of Truth in Service Competition,* Lexington Books, Lexington, Massachusetts.

Normann, R. 1991. *Service Management: Strategies and Leadership in Service Business,* John Wiley & Sons, Chichester, UK.

Zeithaml, V. A., & Bitner, M. J. 1996. *Services Marketing,* McGraw-Hill, New York.

chapter seven
Modern Marketing (2) — Internal Management Implications

Study objectives

Having completed this chapter, readers should be able to:

* appreciate, from a holistic perspective, the role of marketing in today's business environment;

* demonstrate an understanding of emerging trends in services marketing and the internal structures required to meet these challenges; and

* understand the importance of managing supply and demand, as well as the application of demand management strategies in the hospitality industry.

The framework of this chapter

This chapter is set out as follows:

* Introduction

* The shift in focus

    – Not merely a support function for sales
    – Complexity and alliances
    – Alliances within as well as outside

* Internal marketing

    – The basic idea of "internal customers"
    – Selling internal marketing to employees
    – The objectives of internal marketing
    – Promoting internal marketing in a service firm
    Compete for talent
    Offer a vision
    Prepare people to perform

* Relationship marketing

    – Why are relationships important in marketing?
    – History of relationship marketing
    – A strategy doomed to failure
    – Customers want to be loyal
    – Side-benefits of relationship marketing
    – Changing attitudes
    – Relationship as a customer guarantee
    – Fickle and loyal relationships
    – Reasons for growing popularity of relationship marketing
    – How relationship marketing changes firms
    – How relationship marketing assists customers
    – Networking and relationship marketing
    – Employees and relationship marketing
    – All relationships matter

* In-house marketing

    – What is "in-house marketing"?
    – Does it work?
    – Especially for services

✳ Managing and marketing service demand
  – Wanted, and wanted now!
  – Marketing is not just about sales
  – Services cannot be stored
  – Capacity management versus demand management
    Change capacity to fit demand?
    Change demand to fit capacity?
    Or both together?
    Key-features to be considered
  – Aspects of demand
    Variations in demand
    Effect of demand on quality
    Strategies for managing demand
  – Aspects of supply
    Capacity and quality
    Maximum capacity and optimum capacity
    Strategies for managing supply

✳ Summary of chapter

Introduction

The changing business environment and the increasing demands of customers have forced organizations to extend their business vision beyond short-term revenue-generating goals to encompass long-term sustainable objectives. Marketing today is no longer limited to external customer contact and no longer restricted to being a mere ancillary to the sales function. Rather, it has become the focus of the activities of the entire organization, integrating its competencies and resources to meet the competitive pressures that characterize today's marketplace.

Chapter 6 concentrated on the distinctive nature of services and how they affect the marketing of the service interface with customers. The present chapter concentrates on how modern concepts of marketing affect the *internal management* of service firms. In particular, this chapter considers the following important topics:

* internal marketing;

* relationship marketing;

* in-house marketing; and

* managing and marketing service demand.

In the services sector, because the employees create and render service products to the customers, a firm's most important resource and core competency is its people. This has prompted leading organizations to regard their employees as "internal customers" in the belief that, because the internal employees determine the firm's success in the external marketplace, internal customer satisfaction is ultimately reflected in external customer satisfaction. Successful external marketing therefore starts with effective internal marketing.

Faced with intense competition, services marketers have also realized the importance of customer retention to an organization's long-term survival. The focus of modern marketing has thus shifted from what might be called "transaction-seeking" to a model that can be described as "relationship-oriented." This extends to the relationships between service firms and other stakeholders, such as suppliers and retailers. We thus have seen the emergence of "relationship marketing" as firms strive to nurture long-term relationships with customers, suppliers, and retailers.

The chapter moves on to discuss the topic of "in-house marketing"—a form of marketing especially suited to service industries.

Finally, the chapter considers another problem for modern-day service marketers—management of demand and capacity.

This chapter presents some of the latest thinking in the services marketing realm, and outlines major strategies to overcome the fundamental challenges of managing human resources, as well as the problem of supply and demand in the modern marketplace.

The shift in focus

Not merely a support function for sales

The focus of marketing today extends beyond its traditional role—that is, beyond being merely a support function for sales. Marketing today assumes a guiding role—guiding the entire organization toward its corporate objectives. In this way, modern marketing management encompasses a combination of a marketing role (in the traditional sense) and a wider management role. It still performs a traditional *marketing role* by making predictions about the future, but it assumes a wider *management role* by establishing the most appropriate strategies required to guide the organization toward its objectives. Marketing is the only function that can undertake this dual task—because it is the arm that extends both *inside* and *outside* the organization.

A paradigm shift in marketing theory

Modern services theory has seen the transformation of marketing from a sales-oriented "task" to a philosophical concept that directs a whole organization toward its goals. Modern marketing is about focusing *all* the energies of the organization—including the energies of all the various functions and individuals of which the organization is comprised.

Modern marketing still performs a traditional *marketing role* by making predictions about the future, but it also assumes a wider *management role* by establishing the most appropriate strategies required to guide the organization toward its objectives. Marketing is the only function that can undertake this dual task—because it is the arm that extends both *inside* and *outside* the organization.

Modern marketing is thus about focusing all the energies of the organization—including all the various functions and individuals of which the organization is comprised. In focusing the energy of the organization in this way, modern marketing can be likened to a laser, in itself, is a weak source of energy. It takes a few kilowatts of energy and converges this into a coherent stream of light. It is the collective convergence of energy that provides a laser with the strength to outperform other (apparently stronger) sources of energy. In the same way, marketing harnesses and converges the energies of the organization to a specific goal. If a company has marketing focus of this sort, it possesses a powerful, laser-like ability to dominate a market (Ries, 1997). It is this guiding idea of *focus* that has marked the transformation of marketing from a *sales-oriented task* to a *philosophical concept* that directs a whole organization toward its goals.

Complexity and alliances

The products and services offered in the marketplace have become increasingly complex. Organisations these days offer not just one product or service, but a *collection* of products and services (Albrecht & Zemke 1985; Peters 1994). This collection of products and services (or "service package") represents the core competency of the firm.

Having a package of products and services augments the value of individual product and service offerings, and the specific configuration of the different components in the firm's service package (as determined by the marketing strategy) communicates added value to the customer.

For these reasons, a firm's competitive advantage is fundamentally determined by the firm's core competency (Prahalad & Hamel 1990; Stalk, Evans & Shulman 1992; Teece & Pisano 1994). This, in turn, is dependent on its capacity to combine core skills creatively both within and outside the organisation. As Prahalad (1993) put it: "what matters is the creative bundling" of a firm's core competency.

All of this needs a focus on the factors that signal value to the customer. To create superior value for buyers, a firm requires a comprehensive understanding of the buyer's holistic needs—not only as they are today, but also as they evolve over time (Slater & Narver 1994). The holistic requirements of customers frequently extend beyond the capacity of a single firm. Firms that understand this strive to "mix and match" various products and services from different sources to satisfy the needs of customers. This assorted mix might be comprised of services or products from one or more firms—a combination of offerings produced by the host firm and its partners.

Thus, products and services offered in the marketplace have become increasingly complex, and meeting the needs of customers can necessitate going outside the firm for a component, product, or service that the firm itself does not produce (Peppers & Rogers 1997). In the language of "core competencies", if customers require products or services that are not within the realm of a firm's core competency, the firm must find ways to procure these competencies by creating strategic alliances with other firms.

Alliances within as well as outside

This idea of alliances and relationships extends *within* the organization, as well as outside it. A firm that offers a collection of products and services is, in reality, a collection of services itself (Peters 1994). That is, there is an *internal network* of services.

The internal labor-intensive nature of service organisations, and the labor-intensive nature of the external networks that support them, require marketing to function both within and outside the organization (Grönroos 1991; Gummesson 1991). Modern marketing thus converges the energies of the internal and external networks with a definite focus on the customer. The value of the product or service on offer is enhanced by this convergence and the focus of the total energies of the organization (Chase & Garvin 1990).

Thinking like customers, and anticipating the future needs of customers, are concepts at the leading edge of modern marketing. From this, two activities that are fun-

---

Disney perfects packaging

The success of many leading organizations in the tourism industry can be attributed to the effective packaging of their products and services to meet and exceed customer expectations. What Walt Disney invented in 1955 was not just the concept of a theme park but a near-perfect package of product and service that produced a distinctive experience of sight, sound, and touch. Disney's advantage over other theme parks is not merely the number of attractions, but the unique mix of these attractions in a package that serves consumers at an exceptional standard of quality. The ability of Disney's management to bundle and unbundle products and services makes Disney's theme attractive to young and old at all hours of the day and night.

When Disney's managers design an attraction for their parks, they "imagineer" the entire experience. Their focus is not on how the ride operates mechanically, but on the entire sensory experience it creates for the customer—the things they see, hear, and interact with. Management could design the rides to run faster (and thus shorter) with a view to increasing productivity. But they do not do this. Rather, they allow sufficient time for their customers to look around, talk with fellow travellers, scream out with excitement, and become generally immersed in the surroundings. Every participant is given the time and opportunity to engage an imaginary world.

In the theme-park industry, Disney has redefined what can be done for the customer. It is this meticulous focus on customer experience that has made Disney consistently superior to its competition in the theme-park industry that it created.

---

damental to successful service organizations require further examination—internal marketing and relationship marketing.

Internal marketing

The basic idea of "internal customers"

The overall objective of services marketing is to plan, motivate, and manage the resources and activities of service organizations that affect the opinions and buying decisions of customers. In the manufacturing industry, marketing resources are devoted to developing effective product design, setting pricing, organizing promotion, and distributing goods (Kotler, 1980, 1984). In services, however, the focus of modern marketing is very much on the service employees. Employees constitute the most important marketing resource of services firms.

With this in mind, there has been a reevaluation of the word "customer" within service industries, and the intriguing concept of the "internal customer"—the firm's employees—has been proposed (Grönroos, 1981). Taking the same idea further, Berry (1981) suggested that, in service organizations, jobs constitute "internal products." The concept has been endorsed by other writers who have observed that the needs of internal customers reflect those of external customers (Heskett, Sasser, & Hart, 1990; Heskett, Sasser, & Schlesinger, 1997).

Employees, as internal customers, thus make or break most service organizations because employees create and maintain trusting relationships between a service firm and its external customers (Parasuraman, Berry, & Zeithaml, 1991). And these external relationships are ultimately dependent on satisfactory internal attitudes and relationships (Berry, 1995, 1997).

"If the staff won't buy it, why should the customer?"

All successful service organizations sell their service concept to their employees before they try to sell it to their customers. An employee who does not believe in the service that he or she produces is incapable of making customers believe in it (Hartline & Ferrell, 1996).

As Barnes (1989) observed: "If the staff won't buy it, why should the customer?"

Selling internal marketing to employees

Although service firms are dependent on personal relationships, both internal and external, this represents an *opportunity*, as well as a *challenge*. And service firms are inherently well placed to take this opportunity and to meet this challenge. After all, if service firms are good at anything, they should be good at *serving*, and the essence of serving is the development of positive personal relationships.

The very essence of the service encounter, in which the customer directly interacts with the firm's employees, is an ideal platform for the development of positive relationships with customers (Rosen & Surprenant, 1998). Service providers have the capacity, through their personal touch, to provide service excellence and to add value to the service offering (Antonacopoulou & Kandampully, 2000). For example, it is the human aspect of the service that truly differentiates one five-star hotel from another. Similar hotels might have comparable facilities and conveniences, but the human touch can make all the difference between these hotels. In the same way, similar shops might sell identical products, similar fitness centers might offer the same exercise equipment, and similar airlines might use the same types of aircraft on the same routes, but the personnel who serve in these organizations can, from the customers' perspective, make one of these organizations quite different from another, despite their superficial similarities.

This inherent capacity for personal "external" service is an enormous advantage to service firms in their efforts to develop personal "internal" marketing. Internal marketing is essentially "selling the firm to its employees." In service industries today, it is the attitude, knowledge, and skills of the workforce that provide a firm's competitive advantage, and progressive service organizations have to compete in the marketplace for appropriately talented employees. Attracting, developing, motivating, and retaining qualified employees is essentially achieved through the provision of jobs that satisfy their needs (Cahill, 1995; Foreman & Money, 1995). If employees perceive that there is insufficient enthusiasm, teamwork, communication, and training within the culture of the organization, this will be reflected in their own work, and will substantially reduce the quality of service offered to customers.

Internal marketing can thus be viewed as attracting, motivating, and retaining qualified personnel (internal customers) through jobs designed to satisfy their wants and needs (Berry, 1987), and through jobs that nurture and develop a customer-conscious attitude among employees (Grönroos, 1983).

Many of the marketing processes applied to external relationships (customers, suppliers, and wholesalers) can be equally applied to internal relationships (employees, different departments, and subcontractors). The main aim of internal marketing must therefore be to ensure that employees share an understanding of the overall objectives of the organization and the service position that it seeks to adopt with regard to its external customers (Unzicker, Clow, & Babakus, 2000).

The emphasis is thus on turning the well-honed communication techniques of marketing *inward*—such that they are directed toward the firms' employees (Figure 7.1). Use of internal staff newsletters, educational programs, training seminars, and formal and informal meetings are effective means of enhancing such internal marketing.

Figure 7.1 *Internal and external marketing*

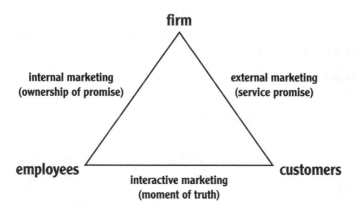

Adapted from Grönroos (2000)

Internal marketing ensures that all employees at all levels of the organization understand and experience the business activities that support a customer-oriented approach (Grönroos, 1990b), and ensures that all employees are motivated to act in a service-oriented manner. But these things do not happen without managerial planning and commitment. The concept of internal marketing redirects the focus of management to approach all activities in a strategic and systematic manner with a view to creating such a service culture within the organization. In traditional management, employees receive an abundance of information, but very little in the way of encouragement (Grönroos, 1990a). The simple provision of information, on its own, has limited impact on employees. Internal marketing aims for an *ongoing active process* of employee involvement.

The objectives of internal marketing

From the perspective of the organization, the overall objectives of internal marketing are thus twofold:

* to ensure that the employees are motivated toward customer-oriented and service-minded performance, and thus toward fulfilling their roles as "part-time marketers" during the service interface; and

* to attract and retain good employees to do this.

In pursuing these objectives, Christopher, Payne, & Ballantyne (1993) identified various factors that can contribute to the promotion of internal marketing.

* Internal marketing should be comprised of formal activities supported by various less formal *ad hoc* initiatives.

* Communication is critical to successful internal marketing.

* It should always be kept in mind that internal marketing performs a critical role in differentiating one competing firm from another.

* Internal marketing can play an important role in reducing conflict between functional areas of the organization.

* Internal marketing is an experiential process, leading employees to arrive at conclusions themselves.

* Internal marketing can facilitate an innovative spirit within an organization's workforce.

* Internal marketing is more successful when there is commitment at the highest level, the cooperation of all employees, and an open management style.

The objectives of internal marketing

From the organization's perspective, the overall objectives of internal marketing are twofold:

* to ensure that the employees are motivated toward customer-oriented and service-minded performance, and thus toward fulfilling their roles as "part-time marketers" during the service interface; and

* to attract and retain good employees to do this.

Promoting internal marketing in a service firm

To enhance internal marketing in an organization, Berry (1995) proposed various suggestions. In essence, he suggested that firms should:

* compete for talent;

* offer a vision; and

* prepare people to perform.

Each of these is considered below.

Compete for talent

Hiring the best possible people to perform the service is a key factor in services. One of the principal causes of poor service quality is hiring the wrong people to perform the service. Many firms fail to think and act like marketers when it comes to human resource issues.

Marketing is used by most firms to compete only for sales. That is, they compete for customer market share in seeking sales, but they do not compete for *talent* market share in seeking staff. The same firms that compete intensely and imaginatively for customers seem to be content to compete meekly and mundanely for employees. The service firms that turn their marketing powers to the labor market will fare best in the "talent wars" that lie ahead.

Offer a vision

A pay check might keep a person on the job physically, but it will not keep a person on the job emotionally. Great international marketing companies stand for something worthwhile, and they communicate this vision to employees with passion. The key is to add dignity to work. A good example is the motto of Ritz-Carlton Hotels—"Ladies and Gentlemen serving Ladies and Gentlemen" (see Chapter 5).

The contribution that each employee makes to the satisfaction of the end customer must be emphasized, and reemphasized. Employees work better when they understand the value of their contribution.

The personal involvement of senior managers in such a vision is essential to preserving the company's culture.

Prepare people to perform

Attract, develop, motivate, and retain superior employees. In doing this, remember that employees first require knowledge on "why" before they require knowledge on "how."

Learning should be an ongoing process, not a one-off event. Learning is a confidence-builder, a motivating force, and a source of self-esteem.

Better teachers should be promoted into middle management, and front-line service courses should first be offered to such middle managers, who can then pass this training on to front-line employees.

Relationship marketing

Why are relationships important in marketing?

Having discussed the importance of the modern marketing concept of *internal marketing,* we now move on to discuss another vitally important (and closely related) concept in modern marketing—the concept of *relationship marketing.*

Relationship marketing is all about securing and retaining trust and loyalty. The challenge for a service organization today is not merely to be successful, but to maintain its success. To achieve this, the primary focus of a successful service firm should go beyond merely attracting customers. It should seek to obtain their loyalty and their ongoing patronage for the long term.

Such loyalty is not easily obtained. It is the end result of ongoing relationships based on an organization's ability to maintain and extend its marketing contacts with customers (Gummesson, 1994). Buyer–seller interaction can be compared to a marriage in that the quality and duration of the union depends predominantly on the extent to which the partners work on the relationship (Levitt, 1983). A progressive, responsive relationship establishes service superiority and produces customer loyalty (Parasuraman et al., 1991).

This emphasis on relationships has been formalized in the academic literature with the coining of the term "relationship marketing." Since its introduction to academic literature (Berry, 1983; Jackson, 1985), relationship marketing has gained recognition and acceptance among academics and practitioners alike, and is widely cited as being "the future" of marketing. However, although relationship marketing is a relatively new theoretical concept, it has been practiced in various business contexts for many

Thinking like customers

Thinking like customers, and anticipating the future needs of customers, are strategies at the leading edge of modern marketing. There are two important modern marketing concepts that are at the "cutting edge" of learning to think and act like customers.

Internal marketing is one important modern marketing concept that facilitates this. It reflects the importance of a firm thinking like customers and "selling itself" to its own employees.

Relationship marketing is another important modern marketing concept that facilitates thinking and acting like customers. It reflects the mutual desire of customers and service firms for trusting, ongoing, loyal personal relationships. Relationship marketing is widely cited as being "the future" of marketing.

An understanding of internal marketing and relationship marketing is absolutely essential to any understanding of successful integrated service industries in the modern marketplace.

decades, perhaps even for many centuries—albeit without a comprehensive understanding of its true nature and its true potential.

History of relationship marketing

From a historical perspective, before the industrial revolution and the subsequent mass production of goods and services, business was characterized by personal service and direct contact with the providers of goods and services. A local store-owner, for example, was a true "relationship marketer" who nurtured customers as individuals and tried to fulfill their needs (Peppers & Rogers, 1995). In practice, merchants have had an interest in establishing close personal relationships with their customers for many centuries. This is well illustrated by an ancient Middle Eastern proverb: "As a merchant, you'd better have a friend in every town" (cited by Grönroos, 1994). The "friend" in this context refers to the customers and third parties associated with the merchant in his or her various transactions. In the context of modern trade, a firm's "friends" involve an even wider circle, and includes customers, employees, suppliers, retailers, and shareholders.

With the onset of the industrial revolution, firms were capable of increased production capacity, and large market shares emerged as a norm for some companies, thus distancing firms from their customers and other associates. This produced a substantial reduction in collaborative networks as they had traditionally been forged for mutual benefit among merchants, employees, suppliers, retailers, and customers. Rather, firms intensified their focus on the selling of their products and services.

However, an orientation on *present* sales does not necessarily produce *future* sales. A focus on present sales transactions essentially inhibits a firm's long-term orientation—because it does not provide for the laying of a foundation for future sales. It traps a firm in the present. Such a foundation for future sales is essential if a firm is to succeed in a changing global marketplace in which competition has produced a surplus of products, services, employees, suppliers, and retailers in so many different fields.

The advent of technology in every field of business has further exacerbated these problems. Modern technology plays a vital role in assisting firms with the development of innovative offerings—effectively rendering products and services obsolete in a short time (Achrol, 1991), and presenting customers with an abundance of products and services. It has thus become increasingly difficult for firms to maintain distinctive product and service differentiation over long periods, and to retain the ongoing patronage of customers over long periods. This reduction in customer base has a significant impact on the profitability of firms—because customer acquisition is substantially more expensive than customer retention (Hesket et al., 1990, 1997; Berry, 1995).

A strategy doomed to failure

Almost all business interactions can be understood as relationships between a firm and its customers, and maintaining these long-term relationships is the true indicator of a firm's success. However, in most business situations, it is not common to see truly longterm relationships between service providers and customers. Most of these relationships tend to be surprisingly short term in nature.

On the assumption that they will lose many of their customers, firms strive to attract more customers than those with whom they realistically expect to forge a relationship. The marketing emphasis is on outreach rather than retention. In a sense, firms thus consciously establish a system that ensures that only a proportion of their customers receive services commensurate with their expectations, while the remainder become dissatisfied. These subsequently leave, and the self-defeating cycle of attempting to attract new customers continues.

Customers want to be loyal

The distinctive qualities of services—intangibility, inseparability of production and consumption, heterogeneity, and perishability—ensure that customers have a greater need to maintain a relationship with service firms than is the case with goods manufacturers. This is because the distinctive qualities of services are heavily dependent on personal relationship if they are to fulfill the needs of customers—not only in the present, but also in the future. For example, because of the intangibility of services, customers cannot "try out" services; they purchase a service before experiencing it, and they must therefore trust the firm to deliver the perceived service promise (Berry & Parasuraman, 1992).

Although a firm attracts a customer's interest through its *promise* of service, the customer's considered decision to purchase is founded on the *trust* that the firm will, indeed, fulfill his or her needs. Promise and trust are at the heart of services marketing.

The human interaction that occurs during the service-delivery process should aim to re-inforce this initial seeking of trust (Evans & Crosby, 1988), and should aim to strengthen the developing relationship (McKenna, 1991). Customers want to trust. Customers want to be loyal.

Trust, however, can never be established from only one side of any partnership. Customers are loyal to service providers who trust them (Bell, 1993). Customers acknowledge and reward such trust by their allegiance, and transient sampling can then develop into a long-term relationship. Once customers receive confirmation that their trust is warranted, they *desire and seek* to maintain such relationships.

Customers seek a business interaction on the tacit understanding that they will receive the service they require. They neither desire nor expect mediocre service. Moreover, customers are really inherently loyal, and are actually *seeking* a loyal relationship. That is, when customers seek a service, they are essentially seeking to establish a relationship.

"You really do sound like someone I could trust"

A caller to talkback radio was telling her story. She spoke about how she had been "let down" by a lawyer who had apparently not fulfilled his service promise. The caller went on to explain how she had then gone to another lawyer. Again the lawyer had not fulfilled her expectations. Yet again she had sought another lawyer. Yet again she believed that the lawyer had failed her. Finally, she had rung the radio station to tell her story to a "talkback lawyer"— a lawyer who gives free legal advice on the radio to callers and listeners.

As the caller told her story, it was difficult to work out whether her complaints were justified or not. Perhaps she had unreasonable expectations? Or perhaps she really was the victim of poor service? The "talkback lawyer" listened sympathetically and gave some helpful advice, finally suggesting that the caller really did need another lawyer. He expressed his understanding that the woman had already been disappointed by three lawyers, but suggested that she might find a good lawyer through the Law Institute.

"Could I come and see you?" asked the woman.

There was a pause. The "talkback lawyer" was embarrassed. He was not supposed to get business through his radio work. He was there to offer free help, not to seek business for himself. He politely declined, and again referred the woman to the Law Institute.

"Oh dear," replied the woman. "You really do sound like someone I could trust."

The interesting thing about this story is that this woman was genuinely seeking loyal, trusting personal relationships in her service encounters. Despite her disappointments with previous lawyers, she was eager to try again. She was eager to trust.

Customers really do want to trust. Customers really do want to be loyal.

There are numerous examples in service industries of this inherent customer desire for trust and ongoing relationship. Consider, for example, the reluctance of customers to change their dentist, their hairdresser, their accountant, or their doctor. Their aim is to create an emotional connection with these service providers, and they transfer their allegiance only when providers fail to live up to their promises. They do not want to do so, but they will do so if their trust is abused.

Breaking the service promise is the single most significant way in which service companies fail their customers (Berry, Zeithaml, & Parasuraman, 1990). Although firms are ostensibly established on the premise of offering and delivering good service (and the subsequent creation of satisfied customers), they often fail to do so. Too often, the predominant concern of management is to "market" continuously—by which it means an increase in "awareness," and the subsequent attraction of more and more potential customers. In doing so, management "forgets" the customers it has, and fails to care for them. Aggressive expansive marketing strategies, supposedly implemented to ensure the firm's future survival, have precisely the opposite effect. Indeed, they ensure its demise.

The essence of relationship marketing

Management often fails to understand that the true purpose of marketing is to build and maintain strong relationships as a bridge between the producer and the customer. If it does this, marketing reinforces the customers' inherent desire for mutual loyalty.

This is the essence of the message of relationship marketing.

Side-benefits of relationship marketing

Apart from the importance of capitalizing on the customer's desire for relationship and trust, a marketing strategy that concentrates on relationships has another significant advantage—it facilitates a better appreciation of the changing needs and desires of customers. Companies that focus extensively on attracting new customers, and fail to pay sufficient attention to their existing customers, might fail to understand the changing needs and expectations of the market (Zeithaml & Bitner, 1996). In an ironic twist, companies that focus on expansion might thus fail to gather the information required for that expansion.

Changing attitudes

Having noted these failings in much modern marketing, it must be said that there has recently been something of a change in the focus of marketing from this sort of traditional *transactional marketing* (i.e., an emphasis on sales) to that of *relationship marketing* (i.e., an emphasis on long-term, ongoing relationships between a firm and its customers) (Christopher et al., 1993). It has become increasingly recognized that the development and maintenance of such long-term relationships is of paramount importance to a firm's competitiveness (Grönroos, 1990a). Relationship marketing encourages the *retention of customers* as a first priority, and reduces the attraction of new customers to the status of a second-order issue for marketing (Gummesson, 1996).

Relationship as a customer quarantee

From a customer's perspective, a strong relationship with the supplier constitutes something of a guarantee in the event of something going wrong. In professional services, such as medical and legal services, this emotional bond is frequently esteemed more highly than the service itself. Such an emotional bond is created through personal interaction with the principal service provider in a professional service, and/or by the employees in a larger firm, and constitutes a primary and effective marketing medium. Indeed, is often the case that a firm's customers exhibit more loyalty to the service providers than to the firm itself. In addition, as relationships develop, front-line employees are sometimes found to be more loyal to their customers than to their own management!

Fickle and loyal relationships

Service firms have many creative opportunities to utilize the relationships thus established between service personnel and their customers. However, many service firms fail to capitalize on this potential advantage, and continue to rely on traditional impersonal marketing techniques. A good example from the airline industry is the use of "frequent-flier" programs. Under such schemes, customers are essentially attracted by the potential material benefits rather than by personal relationship with the provider. This type of "forced" relationship does not constitute a loyal partnership, and tends to be fickle. It remains only until a better deal is offered by a competitor.

In contrast to the shallow and fickle nature of such arrangements, relationships based on trust are not likely to result in the abrupt departure of the customer if things go wrong. The true benefit of loyalty is not merely continued patronage, but a willingness to give an unsatisfactory service provider another chance. Loyalty induces a customer to voice dissatisfaction and to give a service provider time to improve the shortcomings of a service, as opposed to a quick exit by the customer (Hirchman, 1970).

It is often observed that a feature of true friendship is that it makes allowance for failure. True friends give and receive advice. They offer and accept constructive criticism in a way that would not be tolerated between two people who have no such underlying relationship of trust. In the same way, customers with considerable attachment to an organization will often seek ways to make themselves influential—particularly when the firm moves in what these customers perceive to the wrong direction. This seeking of a "voice" in the firm's affairs constitutes the true purpose of a firm's customer feedback system, its market research, and its other market communication channels. Such a yearning for "voice" should be encouraged and facilitated. Criticism should be encouraged and accepted with good grace. But this will occur constructively only if conducted within a relationship of attachment and loyalty.

Moreover, once in a bonded relationship, customers are less likely to be seduced by the offerings of competitors. Customers who have experienced service loyalty, and who have developed a close relationship with a company, are unlikely to see a competing firm's comparable offerings as being more attractive than those they already have. They want to stay.

Reasons for the growing popularity of relationship marketing

Proponents of relationship marketing (such as Buttle, 1996; Peppers & Rogers, 1995; Bitner, 1995) have identified various factors that have contributed to the growing importance of relationship marketing today. These include:

* the increasingly global nature of competition;

* the increasingly intense nature of competition;

* more demanding and more sophisticated customers;

* increased fragmentation of consumer markets;

* rapidly changing buying patterns of customers;

* increasing standards in quality;

* the inadequacy of quality in itself to create sustainable competitive advantages;

* the influence of technology in almost all products and services; and

* the unreliability of traditional marketing (as evidenced by a decline in overall advertising effectiveness).

This list of factors is consistent with the basic conceptual thinking that underpins relationship marketing. This conceptual thinking can be put in this way:

* Relationship marketing emphasizes that personal relationship is a first-order issue, and that sales will follow as a second-order issue.

* Relationship marketing emphasizes that the retention of existing customers is a first-order issue, and that the seeking of new customers is a second-order issue.

Taking these two points together, relationship marketing thus constitutes a new paradigm—a new theory of marketing management (Gummesson, 1994).

With respect to the first of these—that relationship marketing values personal relationship as a first priority—it needs to be stated again that the traditional goods-marketing approach, with its emphasis on sales as a first priority, has not provided the understanding, nor the tools, that are necessary for developing customer relationships as the basis of modern services management. (See Chapter 6 for more discussion on this point.) The traditional "4Ps"—which underpinned the "sales-first" paradigm of the

1950s and 1960s—have outlived their usefulness because they are not applicable to services marketing in the modern world. Personal relationship is at the heart of service interaction. Relationship marketing recognizes that personal relationship comes first and that sales follow.

Relationship marketing—a new paradigm

Relationship marketing rests on two essential concepts.

1. Relationship marketing emphasizes that personal relationship is a first-order issue, and that sales will follow as a second-order issue.
2. Relationship marketing emphasizes that the retention of existing customers is a first-order issue, and that the seeking of new customers is a second-order issue.

In many ways, these two ideas reverse the essential ideas of conventional marketing—with its traditional emphasis on the restless search for new sales to new customers.

Relationship marketing thus constitutes a new paradigm—a new theory of services marketing management (Gummesson, 1994).

With respect to the second of these—the benefits of retaining existing customers—researchers have highlighted the fact that it costs five times more to attract a new customer than it does to keep an existing one (Reichheld & Sasser, 1990; Holmund & Kock, 1996; Buttle, 1996). Furthermore, it has been noted that retained customers are especially profitable over time (Cram, 1994). For example, the lifetime revenue stream from a loyal pizza customer can be approximately US$8,000, and that from a Cadillac customer might be as high as US$332,000 (Heskett et al., 1990). Finally, as previously noted, the restless pursuit of new customers imperils relationships with existing customers (through neglect, poor service through inadequate resources, and so on). Indeed, the power of word-of-mouth recommendation in services marketing means that the best way to gain new customers is to satisfy and retain the old ones through meaningful personal relationships.

How relationship marketing changes firms

In changing the focus of marketing from that of a transaction-oriented approach to that of a relationship-oriented model, there has been an integration of customer service, quality, and marketing. Relationship marketing of this type will assist firms in many ways. According to Christopher and colleagues (1993), these benefits can be stated in this way:

* a focus on customer retention;

* an ability to offer superior product and service benefits;

* the pursuit of a long-term vision;

* an emphasis on exemplary customer service;

* the engendering of customer commitment; and

* an assurance that quality becomes the concern of all employees.

Similarly, Zeithaml and Bitner (1996) identified five important benefits gained by an organization that adopts the concept of relationship marketing:

* increased purchases;

* reduced costs;

* free advertising through word of mouth;

* employee retention; and

* lifetime value of retained customers.

Various writers have characterized the benefits in different terms. But the essential point is that, whatever words are used to enumerate and describe the benefits, modern marketing theory has identified a crucially important new concept in its development of the idea of relationship marketing—especially as it relates to the special attributes and requirements of service industries. For hospitality enterprises, this is obviously of central importance.

How relationship marketing assists customers

In any positive relationship, both partners benefit from their roles in maintaining the relationship. We have noted some of the benefits for service firms. There are also numerous benefits available to customers who engage in a long-term relationship with service firms. These include (Sheth & Parvatiyar, 1995):

* facilitating greater efficiency in their decision making and reducing the task of information processing (everyone desires to be spared unnecessary agonizing over multiple alternatives);

* achieving a sense of consistency in their decisions (everyone likes to believe that he or she is consistent, logical, and organized!); and

* reducing the perceived risks associated with future purchase choices (everyone desires a sense of security and wishes to minimize uncertainty).

We have already noted that customers inherently *want* to be loyal. But are there real benefits to customers in loyalty? The above-mentioned benefits of relationship marketing give customers good reasons for entering into long-term relationships with service providers. A customer can say to him- or herself that such a relationship with a single service provider removes the need to think about multiple alternatives, provides a sense of logical consistency in decision making, and reduces anxiety about risk-taking. These are, indeed, good reasons for responding to the inherent desire to be loyal.

Networking and relationship marketing

It is almost impossible for individual firms today to have the expertise and full range of skills needed to bring products and solutions to the market in a timely and cost-effective manner (McKenna, 1991). Rapid advances in technology, dynamic markets, and continuously changing customer needs have emphasized the importance of business relationships as an essential strategic tool. It has become imperative for firms to develop and maintain a network of relationships to offer products that are capable of satisfying market requirements.

As McKenna (1991, 102) observed: "to produce a personal computer, for instance, a company needs expertise in semiconductor technology, software applications, communications and systems integration, as well as other areas."

It is apparent that it is extremely difficult for any one firm to possess all of these skills and resources. This example is typical of the growing need for networking and relationship marketing in an increasingly complex and demanding marketplace.

Relationship marketing is thus not restricted to relationships between firms and customers. It also extends to relationships between firms in mutually beneficial networks.

Employees and relationship marketing

True relationship marketing involves a reciprocal relationship that helps both the firm and its stakeholders to reap the rewards of developing, nurturing, and maintaining the relationship. However, some firms appear to believe that relationship marketing is a one-way strategy that is adopted in a somewhat cynical fashion merely to gain customer patronage (Fournier, Dobscha, & Mick, 1998). Many firms have thus failed to understand the essential genesis of the loyal relationship. In their haste to improve the efficiency of the relationship, they have directed their attention toward measuring the effectiveness of the relationship as being defined by *customer satisfaction* and their perceptions of quality. However, the most successful service companies emphasize the skill and personal attention of the *employees* as being the preeminent factor in determining service delivery (Berry et al., 1990; Colgate & Danaher, 2000). Successful relationship marketing demands that the emphasis should first be on the *employees*.

A firm's relationship with its customers is instigated, established, and maintained by the service personnel who interact with the customers day in and day out. It is the service personnel's commitment to seamless, consistent, and superior service that enables a firm to create lasting, loyal relationships with customers in which personal interaction assumes center stage.

Direct personal contact with customers enables employees to develop an emotional connection through which they are able to appreciate the needs of their customers, and even anticipate the unexpressed desires of those customers.

The concept of relationship marketing therefore extends to internal relationships with employees. Indeed, it is difficult to see how a firm can hope to form meaningful relationships with its external customers if it is not prepared to first form such relationships with its internal customers—its own employees.

All relationships matter

The above discussion leads naturally to a consideration of the fact that *all* relationships matter. All service organizations have four major partners—customers, employees, suppliers, and shareholders. The growth and prosperity of a service organization is dependent on the harmonious growth of relationships among all of these partners.

The primary relationship is the firm's relationship with its customer—as facilitated through its employees or retailers. This primary relationship is the basic function and goal of the firm (see Figure 7.2).

Figure 7.2 *Primary service relationship*

firm ⟵——————————————⟶ customer
employee/retailer

Author's presentation

However, the effectiveness of the firm's primary relationship is also affected by the strength of its secondary relationships. These secondary relationships involve other stakeholders in the success of the firm—including suppliers and shareholders. These other stakeholders must be considered when a firm is assessing its attitude to relationship marketing. A firm needs to go beyond its "core relationship" to encompass a more "holistic" view of relationships in which *all* stakeholders are involved (see Figure 7.3).

The inclusion of these other stakeholders is important in developing a corporate sense of commitment to the concept of relationship marketing. It is this "holistic relationship" that makes a firm's offering distinctive in the marketplace. Although various other stakeholders could be included in the network of relationships, the above five partners (firm, customer, employee, supplier, shareholder) constitute those participants who are essential if a firm is truly to embrace relationship marketing.

Relationship marketing thus involves all stakeholders in the success of the firm. If proactive relationship marketing is not implemented and nurtured on an ongoing basis

Planning relationship marketing

The Hilton Group consists of 500 hotels across the world, employing more than 60,000 staff members in 50 countries.

In 1999, the Hilton Group purchased Stakis in an exchange worth £1.3 billion. The integration of the two organizations, each with its own organizational culture, structure, and history, led to an extensive market-research exercise to determine customers' expectations of the Hilton brand. This, in turn, led to the development of Hilton's new, worldwide quality initiative, "Equilibrium." This initiative centered on what was called "Hilton Moments"—in which Hilton sought to provide memorable experiences for individual guests. In essence, the "Hilton Moments" initiative aimed at providing a balance for guests between the external demands placed on them and their personal desires for comfort and relaxation—in the words of Hilton, this involved "putting in a little of what life takes out." With some adaptations for national cultures. "Equilibrium" (and its central idea of "Hilton Moments") has now been launched in all of Hilton's global regions.

In support of "Equilibrium," the company set up a human-resource strategy called "Esprit." This policy initiative was launched alongside "Equilibrium" because "Hilton Moments" (which are essentially quality service encounters) were to be delivered by the employees on their own initiative as "service performers." Esprit embraced the key principles of employee empowerment—recognition, respect, and reward—to encourage service quality in the "Equilibrium" program. (For more on employee empowerment, see Chapter 8.)

Relationship marketing is not just a "warm and fuzzy" idea. It can be planned and implemented by enlightened management using market research and a commitment to customer service and employee empowerment. The planning and implementation of "Equilibrium" and "Esprit"—with both having their focus on "Hilton Moments"—is an excellent example of such planning and implementation.

Gill Maxwell

Figure 7.3 *Secondary service relationships*

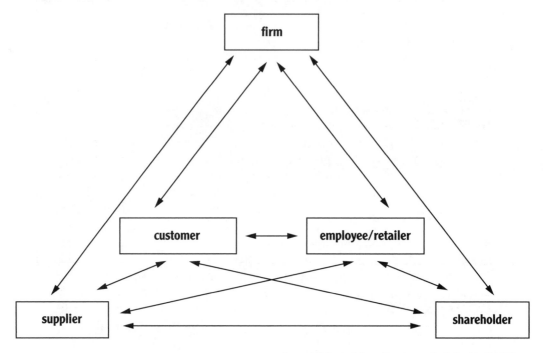

Source: Adapted from Kandampully & Duddy (1999)

among all such stakeholders, the value of the firm's service offer in the marketplace will inevitably fall away to mediocrity. This is particularly true of firms operating within industries in which service differentiation is difficult to achieve—such as professional services, high-tech industries, hospitality industries, and so on. The whole organization must be committed to relationships with one another, and to the overall concept of relationship marketing.

For integrated hospitality services, relationship marketing is the way of the future.

In-house marketing

Having considered *internal marketing* and the related concept of *relationship marketing,* we now examine another important aspect of modern marketing management in services—*in-house marketing.*

What is "in-house marketing"?

In-house marketing deals with the various marketing activities that a service organization undertakes to promote its products and services internally—that is, to already established customers. This is often done during the conception stage of new services. For example, a hotel might advertise to their house guests the coming availability of special buffets, musical evenings at the bar, Sunday poolside brunch, health club facilities, special menu selections, and so on.

Does it work?

In-house marketing often proves to be an effective marketing approach for services. Studies indicate that customers who have already experienced one service offering from an organization are inclined to avail themselves of additional services offered by the same organization. This is evident in financial services, for example, in which customers of a bank are likely to use various other available services—such as insurance, investment schemes, credit cards, and so on.

This tendency to make use of other services is in keeping with the relative effectiveness of marketing services before, during, and after consumption, as previously noted in Figure 6.4. It was noted there that marketing of services is less effective *before* consumption, but more effective *during* and *after* consumption. In-house marketing takes note of this distinctive characteristic of services, and attempts to exploit the fact that customers are more amenable to marketing of services during and after consumption. Additional services are therefore offered to customers who have already had an opportunity to gain an appreciation of the service offerings of the firm.

Especially for services

As compared with goods suppliers, service organizations are more likely to use in-house marketing (than traditional external advertising methods). The reasons for this are as follows.

* Service firms are more reliant on relationships than goods suppliers, and in-house marketing allows a service firm to enhance already established relationships. In addition, because the targeted customers essentially constitute a "captured" market, the marketing communication employed (advertising, brochures, message chosen, and so on) is likely to prove more effective because it is aimed at customers whose wants and needs are known to the firm.

* As noted above, it has been shown (Figure 6.4) that customers are less amenable to marketing of services before consumption, but more amenable during and after consumption.

Figure 7.4 *In-house marketing*

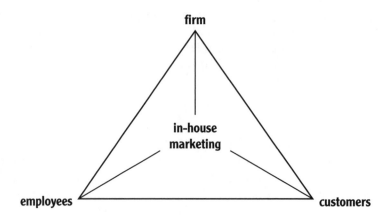

Author's presentation

"In-house marketing" thus naturally lends itself to service firms. Integrated hospitality services are aware of this and use it extensively. It is common practice for hotel chains to offer advance bookings, special deals, and other attractive services to induce customers who have sampled one hotel in the chain to try another in the group. A customer who is happy with one hotel in the chain is more likely to try another. Inside a given hotel, it is common practice to encourage a customer to use other facilities that he or she might not yet have sampled. A customer who is pleased with the dining room might also be induced to try the bistro.

In-house marketing is thus an extension of the philosophy of relationship marketing—building on experiences of trust and satisfaction (see Figure 7.4).

Managing and marketing service demand

Wanted, and wanted now!

Compared with consumers of manufactured goods, consumers of services are often relatively impatient and demanding. *Reliability* and *timing* are important issues for services consumers. This is understandable in many respects. Consider the importance of the reliability and timing of service delivery in the examples given in the box.

Reliability and timing are important in services

Reliability and timing are important issues for services consumers. Consider the following scenarios:

* An ambulance must arrive at the scene of an accident soon after an accident happens. A late ambulance service is a useless ambulance service.

* A hotel room must be available exactly when the traveller wants it. A vacant hotel room tomorrow is useless to a traveller who wants accommodation in a fully booked hotel tonight.

* A restaurant seat must be empty when the customer wants it, and the food must be served when the customer is hungry. It is no use telling a hungry customer that he or she might like to come back and eat in several hours' time.

* An airline seat on a suitable flight must be available when the customer wants to fly. An empty seat tomorrow is no use to a traveller who needs to be in a particular city tonight.

Goods consumption can often be delayed, but services are usually produced and consumed almost simultaneously, and delivery on time is crucially important to most consumers.

As noted in the box, goods consumption can often be delayed, but services are usually produced and consumed almost simultaneously. And more often than not, this must be when the customer requests the services, not before or after. These differences between manufactured goods and services mean that the delivery system used in the goods industry is inappropriate for services. Service managers are thus required to consider alternative systems for the efficient management of production and offer (i.e., demand and supply). Balancing supply and demand presents a real challenge; and success or otherwise in this area determines the overall fate of the organization. The crucial issue is the degree to which available capacity is effectively utilized.

Marketing is not just about sales

As noted several times previously, traditional marketing has always been associated with strategies for increasing sales volume. In other words, traditional marketing has targeted production. In services, however, marketing assumes a more holistic function by its involvement in the smooth running of production *and* consumption.

In services, marketing and operations are undertaken at *the same time* and by *the same employees* (see Chapter 6). The association of marketing and operations is thus conceptually and practically closer in services than is the case in the goods-producing industry. In services, marketing consequently assumes a different role in supply and demand.

Services cannot be stored

An imbalance between supply and demand in the manufacturing sector can be dealt with as an irregular and temporary phenomenon. A store (or inventory) of goods can usually be employed as a buffer until the imbalance is resolved. However, in the case of the services sector, the fact that a particular service cannot be stored for future use is a problem in dealing with significant variations in demand while operating with a certain capacity. When demand is low, productive capacity is wasted; but when demand is high, potential business is lost due to the inability to supply the services in accordance with that demand. This constitutes an irrecoverable revenue loss.

Capacity management versus demand management

Change capacity to fit demand?

Faced with the problems of supply and demand outlined above, one solution open to service managers is to attempt to tailor capacity to meet variations in demand.

An increase in capacity during periods of high demand (at peak periods) might be achieved by:

* employing part-time staff; and

* renting additional facilities.

Reduction in capacity during periods of low demand might be achieved by:

* laying off staff;

* scheduling employees' leave;

* renting out of surplus equipment and facilities; or

* removing surplus equipment and facilities for periodic maintenance and renovation.

However, service managers rarely find that these straightforward measures are sufficient to maintain high efficiency. The question then arises as to whether the opposite strategy might be tried—changing demand to fit capacity.

Change demand to fit capacity?

A more effective solution might be achieved by altering the demand for services. This is clearly a marketing question. That is, can strategic marketing techniques be used to manipulate demand to match available capacity?

In fact, this approach has proven to be very successful in many services. A simple example in the hotel industry is price manipulation to induce customers to come at particular times, and to stay away at other times. There are more sophisticated techniques available (see below), but the simple example of strategic price differentiation demonstrates that the manipulation of demand to suit capacity is certainly an option for service industries.

Or both together?

Despite the fact that capacity *can* be manipulated to suit demand, and despite the fact that demand *can* be manipulated to suit capacity, it is imperative that service organizations seek to manage *both* demand and capacity simultaneously—rather than working on either independently. Indeed, the fact that services are produced and consumed simultaneously means that marketing approaches to service capacity and service demand are inherently interrelated.

An integrated approach to marketing management requires a concerted attempt to coordinate capacity and demand. Modern marketing management demands such an approach.

Key features to be considered

Coordinating capacity and demand in services might be desirable, but it is not easy. In attempting to do this, the following key features of services must be taken into account.

Perishability

Service products are highly perishable and cannot be stored. The perishability of services does not allow management to have a buffer for periods of peak demand. This is clearly a very important feature of services that must always be kept in mind in any management strategy to coordinate demand and capacity. There can be no store of inventory upon which to rely.

Personal interaction

Because service delivery is very much dependent on personal interaction, there is a need for a high degree of close, one-on-one interaction between the producer of the service and the consumer of the service. In attempting to draw up a strategy to coordinate capacity and demand, marketers must be careful to avoid "imposing" a solution on their customers. If a strategy is to be successful, it will require a high level of consultation and coordination with consumers. Consumers might be encouraged to act in a certain way, but they cannot be forced to do so.

Transportation

Services cannot be transported. In assessing demand and capacity in services, management must always bear in mind that the consumer must be brought to the service-delivery system, or the system to the consumer.

Coordination of demand and capacity thus demands coordination of the transport requirements of provider and consumer. A simple example of the importance of this factor is the significance of transport arrangements during peak and off-peak tourist periods. An airline strike during peak holiday season is a disaster for hospitality service providers.

Transport considerations are crucial to services marketing because the services themselves cannot be transported. Either the provider must come to the consumer, or the consumer must come to the provider—a problem not faced by goods manufacturers in attempting to coordinate supply and demand.

Capacity difficult to assess

It is difficult to make an accurate assessment of the true capacity of any service organization. This is a result of many factors—especially the intangible nature of the service output, and the fact that customers play a significant role in the production process. Taken together, these factors make it extremely difficult to assess exactly how "much" service is possible, let alone how much is desirable.

A marketer cannot "count" services in the way that a goods manufacturer can count manufactured objects. Any plan to coordinate capacity and demand has to work with the fact that it is very difficult to know exactly how much capacity a service organization is capable of producing at any given time. Employees can work a little harder. Customers can cooperate a little more. These factors can make a significant difference to capacity, and therefore complicate any attempts to coordinate capacity with demand.

Aspects of demand

Although capacity and demand must be coordinated and considered in an integrated manner, it is conceptually useful to consider them separately in attempting to clarify the important issues involved. After the issues have been clarified in isolation, management is in a better position to consider integrated and coordinated marketing strategies.

In searching for strategies to coordinate demand and capacity in services, let us first consider the "demand side" of the equation. The following aspects of demand are worthy of note:

* variations in demand;

* effect of demand on quality; and

* strategies for managing demand.

Each of these is considered below.

Key features of services in supply and demand

As noted in the text, coordinating capacity and demand in services might be desirable, but it is not easy. In attempting to do this, the following key features of services must be taken into account.

* *Perishability*—service products are highly perishable and cannot be stored; the perishability of services does not allow management to have a buffer for periods of peak demand.

* *Personal interaction*—because service delivery is very much dependent on personal interaction, there is a need for a high degree of close, one-on-one interaction between the producer of the service and the consumer of the service; consumers might be encouraged to act in a certain way, but they cannot be forced to do so.

* *Transportation*—services cannot be transported; either the provider must come to the consumer, or the consumer must come to the provider—a problem not faced by goods manufacturers in attempting to coordinate supply and demand.

* *Capacity difficult to assess*—it is difficult to make an accurate assessment of the true capacity of any service organization; it is extremely difficult to assess exactly how "much" service is possible, let alone how much is desirable.

Variations in demand

The search for strategies to manage demand should start with an understanding of the factors that govern the demand for a specific service at a given point in time (Schemwell & Cronin, 1994). Some of the questions a service manager needs to ask to understand these governing factors are:

* Does the level of demand for the service follow a regular predictable cycle? If so, what are the underlying causes of these predictable variations?

* Or are changes in the level of demand largely random in nature? If so, what are the underlying causes of these random variations?

When demand for a service fluctuates widely in the short term, but follows a predictable pattern over a known cycle, it might be economically worthwhile to develop marketing strategies designed to smooth out major fluctuations over time. Regular fluctuations in demand—such as seasonal cycles—can be influenced, to a large extent, by creative marketing. However, no strategy is likely to succeed unless it is based on an understanding of why customers seek to use the service when they do.

In contrast, marketing efforts can do little to smooth out random fluctuations in demand over time—because these are usually the result of factors outside human control. Examples include natural calamities, political events, economic crises, personal illness, family disruptions, and so on.

Effect of demand on quality

Demand significantly affects quality in service organizations. Customers expect a firm's quality of service to be consistent—whatever the level of demand. To gain customer confidence, maintain image, and engender customer loyalty, quality must be delivered consistently. It is imperative that service managers design strategies that assist them to manage demand and quality simultaneously.

In general (but not invariably), increased demand tends to decrease quality. Personal service is less likely to be as attentive and comfortable if there is a crowd of people to be looked after. This can be likened to maintaining an appropriate balance on a "see-saw," as illustrated in Figure 7.5. (However, if a firm has adequate quality-improvement programs in place, the drop-off in quality in these circumstances can be minimized.)

There are circumstances in which increased demand actually improves quality as perceived by consumers. For example, a crowded dance floor in a nightclub might engen-

Figure 7.5 *Relationship between service demand and quality*

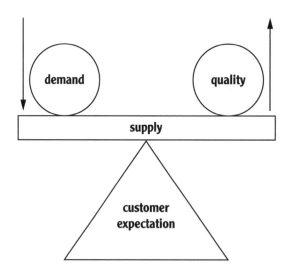

Adapted from Kandampully (2000)

der a desirable "party atmosphere", and a sporting event with a large crowd cheering enthusiastically might be experienced as a more exciting and stimulating event. Despite these exceptions, it is generally the case that increased demand threatens quality.

This question of demand and quality cannot, of course, be separated from capacity, and more will be said about this matter when capacity is discussed (see "Capacity and Quality").

Strategies for managing demand

The services literature contains many different strategies for managing demand. Some of these strategies include:

* the "chase-and-level" strategy whereby a firm actually "chases" demand by altering the marketing mix and going after a new target market (Sasser, 1976); this is usually accompanied by also manipulating capacity by employing part-time employees or offering flexible working hours;

* yield management, which is used to alter demand by careful forecasting, overbooking, choosing high-yield customers, and so on (Kimes, 1989);

* product variation, time-and-location variation, queuing theory, and pricing theory (Lovelock, 1992; Lovelock, Patterson, & Walker, 2001); and

* developing "coping" strategies that recognize dimensions within a total service delivery (Armistead & Clark, 1994).

Each of these is an enormous topic in itself, and readers are encouraged to consult the references given above for more detail on each of these various strategies. (See the full reference citations for the authors noted above; these can be found in "References," Chapter 7 at the end of the book.)

Apart from the above (often complex) strategies, the following "demand-leveling" options are especially useful in integrated hospitality services:

* marketing off-peak time;

* differential pricing schemes;

* product variation or packaging;

* developing nonpeak demand by promotions; and

* developing complementary services.

Each of these is considered below.

Marketing off-peak time

Various marketing approaches can be used to alter demand levels with a view to changing the time and place at which customers use services. This provides an opportunity to use and develop the available, but underutilized, resources. Marketing

Strategies for managing demand

There are many strategies for managing demand, including the following. See the text for further comment on these various strategies.

* "chase-and-level" strategy;

* yield management;

* product variation, time-and-location variation, queuing theory, and pricing theory;

* "coping" strategies that recognize dimensions within a total service delivery;

* marketing off-peak time;

* differential pricing schemes;

* product variation or packaging;

* developing nonpeak demand by promotions; and

* developing complementary services.

thus aims to alleviate a shortage of capacity through a process that might be termed "demarketing." In other words, the firm encourages customers *not* to use services at a certain time, but to avail themselves of the services outside periods of peak demand.

Differential pricing schemes

Differential pricing is the most common method employed to influence demand. Its effectiveness depends on customers' sensitivity to the price variations of the services that they consume. The incentive offered by the service organization needs to effect a change in the behavior of customers.

Managers of numerous service organizations use differential pricing schemes to encourage customers to shift demand from peak to nonpeak periods. Examples of such schemes include matinee prices for movies, "happy hours" at bars, "early bird" prices for meals, weekend and night rates for long-distance telephone calls, "two-for-one" coupons at restaurants on Tuesday nights, and so on. Hotels clearly have the same strategy in mind when they offer special room rates at particular times of the week or the year.

Product variation or packaging

Services can be packaged in such a way that they are presented to customers as a variety of product offerings. In technical terms, this is referred to as "service product variation." Such product variation commonly results in services being used by different customer groups during slack periods. A Sunday "brunch," as offered by many hotels and restaurants, is a good example of such a package. It attracts many customers who wish to sleep in late on a Sunday. Having skipped breakfast, these customers often welcome the option of an early lunch in late morning—a slack period of demand at most restaurants.

From a customer's perspective, service packaging constitutes the offer of a variety of service products to suit their various needs. Using the concept of the service package, and the effective alteration of the characteristics of the basic service product, service managers are thus able to influence demand levels.

Variations in the product offering can take place during a short time. For example, in a 24-hour period, many restaurants offer different menus at different times of the day. This might appeal to the varying needs of a given group of customers at different times of the day. Alternatively, the variety of menus might reach out to different customer segments according to the time of day.

Different versions of the same service can be offered simultaneously—in response to variations in customer preference and ability to pay. Examples include first-class, business-class, and tourist-class services on airlines, or the range of room and service categories in hotels, or different seating categories in theaters.

Developing nonpeak demand by promotions

Most service managers wrestle constantly with ideas to increase volume during periods of low demand—particularly in those facilities with a high, fixed cost structure. The impact of such extra revenue on the profitability of a business can be very significant.

However, it is important that caution be exercised when developing plans to increase demand for underused periods. Numerous companies have made costly mistakes by introducing such schemes without foreseeing the effect that they have on existing operations. For example, a hotel might introduce a special "one-off" promotion that is successful in its own right. But this same "one-off" promotion might adversely affect the experience of regular patrons to the extent that they cease to patronize the establishment, leaving the hotel with a "one-off" windfall, but the loss of its usual "baseline income" from regular off-peak patronage. The hotel might well discover that the net result is a decrease in off-peak income.

Developing complementary services

Another method adopted by managers to shift demand away from peak periods is the development of complementary services. These either attract consumers away from "bottleneck" operations at peak times or provide them with an alternative service while queuing for operations restricted by limited capacity.

For example, to reduce breakfast congestion in the restaurant during holiday periods, hotels might offer a poolside breakfast. Or they might offer a barbecue as an alternative to dinner. Restaurant owners have discovered that, on busy nights, most patrons complain less if they are sitting in a lounge with cocktails—effectively being pleasantly occupied while awaiting the clearing of a "bottleneck." Similar strategies are employed by banks in which automated tellers have reduced the waiting time of customers considerably.

Aspects of supply

In searching for strategies to coordinate demand and capacity in services, let us now consider the "supply side" of the equation. The following aspects of capacity are worthy of note:

* capacity and quality;

* maximum capacity and optimum capacity; and

* strategies for controlling supply.

Each of these is considered below.

Capacity and quality

Some comments on demand and quality were offered above (see "Effect of Demand on Quality"). This matter is obviously very much connected with the available capacity.

If the fluctuation of demand is rapid and unpredictable (e.g., as occurs on a stock exchange), it is extremely difficult for managers to forecast requirements, and to develop contingency plans in terms of altering capacity to meet demand.

However, simply increasing capacity can be a rather blunt response. Excess capacity not only results in a loss of profit, but also can actually decrease the quality of the service experience. For example, although many patrons might say that they like a *relatively* uncrowded restaurant, a restaurant that has only one table occupied has such an excess of capacity that it fails to offer the desired social ambience to its patrons.

Nevertheless, a chronic inability to meet service demand does constitute a serious quality and revenue problem for many service businesses. A demand far in excess of capacity usually leads to dissatisfaction regarding quality among those who are served, and no service at all for those who cannot be accommodated at all! Taken together this represents a significant loss (both potential and permanent) for the business—hotels and restaurants potentially lose the customers they do have, and can never recover the business missed completely during peak season.

Having said that, it must be noted that there is a subtle distinction between optimum capacity and maximum capacity. In assessing capacity and quality, a distinction must be made between these two concepts of capacity.

Maximum capacity and optimum capacity

There is a difference between maximum capacity and optimum capacity. At any given point in time, a service organization is faced with one of four conditions (Lovelock et al., 2001) (see Figure 7.6):

* demand exceeds maximum available capacity and potential business can be lost; or

* demand exceeds the optimum capacity level; no one is turned away, but all customers are likely to perceive deterioration in the quality of service delivered; or

* demand and supply are well balanced at the level of optimum capacity; or

* demand is below optimum capacity, productive resources are underutilized and, in some instances, customers might find the experience disappointing or have doubts about the viability of the service.

In this context, it is important to understand the distinction between maximum capacity and optimum capacity. Maximum capacity represents the upper limit that the organization can possibly achieve, whereas optimum capacity is the desirable level achievable. When demand exceeds maximum capacity, potential customers can be disappointed when they are turned away, and their business might be lost forever. When demand is operating between optimum and maximum capacity, there is a risk that all customers being served at that time might receive inferior service, and consequently decide not to return in the future. (However, if a firm has adequate quality-improvement programs in place, the drop-off in quality in these circumstances can be minimized.) The optimum level of capacity is likely to vary from one service business to another, and even from one market segment to another.

Occasionally optimum and maximum capacities are the same—for example, as previously noted, a crowded nightclub or bar is often regarded as both desirable and necessary to create the atmosphere of excitement and participation that enhances the service experience. In contrast, a restaurant's customers might feel that they receive a markedly superior service if the restaurant operates below full capacity. Similarly, airline passengers usually feel more comfortable if the seat adjacent to them is empty.

In most services, however, a full-capacity operation frequently results in a reduced service, and therefore represents a concern for service managers and customers alike.

Figure 7.6 *Variations in demand in relation to capacity*

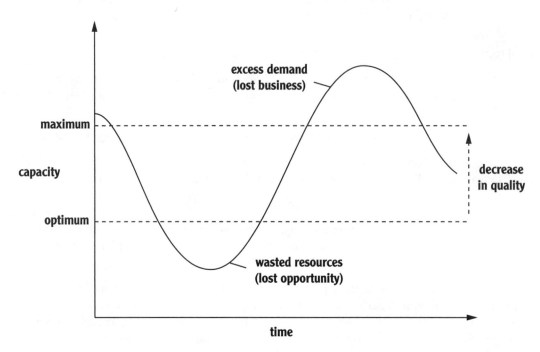

Author's presentation

Strategies for managing supply

Generally speaking, service managers are able to exert a more direct influence on the supply side of capacity planning than they are able to apply to the demand side. There are several measures that a service manager can adopt to adjust capacity to fluctuating demand.

> ### Strategies for managing supply
>
> There are several for managing supply, including the following. See the text for further comment on these various strategies.
>
> * using part-time employees;
> * maximizing efficiency; and
> * sharing capacity.

Using part-time employees

Many service companies have found it is more efficient to handle demand whenever it occurs rather than attempting to smooth out the peaks in demand. The peaks vary according to the type of business. Some peaks occur during the hours of the day (such as in restaurants), others vary across the days of the week (such as in city hotels, which are busy during weekdays, but not as busy on weekends), and still others differ according to the months of the year (such as in summer and winter resort hotels). These service businesses usually maintain a base of full-time employees who operate the facility during nonrush periods, and augment these staff members with part-time assistance during peak periods.

Maximizing efficiency

To maximize efficiency, managers examine peak-time tasks to discover if certain skills are lacking or are inefficiently used. If these skills can be made more productive, the effective capacity of the system can be increased. Even rearranging the layout of the service-delivery system can have a major impact on the productivity of the providers of the service. Many restaurants combine buffet service and table service during the peak periods of lunch and dinner. This helps management to enhance the efficiency of the supply system. Hotel check-out procedures during peak times can similarly be reviewed with a view to improving efficiency.

Sharing capacity

The delivery of a service commonly demands an investment in the expensive equipment and specialist labor skills that are necessary for the performance of the service. However, these resources might not be utilized at full capacity all the time. In such cases, the service manager might consider sharing capacity with another business. In this way, they jointly use the required (but expensive and underutilized) resources. For example, two or more hotels in close proximity often share complementary airport shuttle services. Despite representing competitors in the same market, the shuttle service provides the competitors with mutual benefits through shared expenses.

Summary of chapter

The competitive marketplace of today has forced service firms to revamp their management philosophies and practices to accommodate a shift in focus from profitability to customer orientation. In turn, this has caused a significant change in management's perception of the role of marketing.

Traditional marketing has focused on attracting potential customers to the organization to increase sales. This limits the role of marketing, effectively making it peripheral to the overall management of the firm, and causing a clear distinction between marketing and operation. In contrast, the emerging customer-oriented perspective of marketing has led to a redefinition of marketing as being central to management and inseparable from the overall operation of the firm. In today's marketplace, the role of marketing is to coordinate all of the firm's resources to improve its competitiveness.

Consequently, it is imperative that modern marketing management adopt a holistic perspective that encompasses strategic and operational levels. In addition, a firm's marketing efforts should target both its internal and external audiences. By developing and nurturing long-term relationships with the various constituencies inside and outside the organization (customers, employees, suppliers, and so on), a firm fosters a network of partnerships that is beneficial to all.

From a strategic management perspective, this assists the firm to achieve and maintain market leadership in the long run. At the operational level, the ability to manage and maintain the firm's service capability at its optimum level influences not only the firm's business efficiency and profitability, but also the other members of the network. Indeed, given the nature of service products, effective management of capacity is closely related to numerous other factors—such as employee productivity, customer perception, suppliers' performance, and so on. Effective management of capacity also enhances the satisfaction and loyalty of all these stakeholders. In a service context, therefore, capacity management possesses an indirect but significant impact on the firm's long-term marketing efforts.

Firms must identify and build upon various sources of potential competitive advantage, including tangible assets (e.g., facilities) and intangible assets (e.g., relationships with customers and employees). The advantages to be gained from such strategies as relationship marketing are both short term and long term. In the short term, a firm will obtain optimum yield from its service capacity, and thus ensure its financial viability in the immediate future. In the longer term, such an approach improves the overall marketing effectiveness of a service organization by bringing all assets together into a coordinated managerial process.

The hospitality industry is highly competitive, and the effectiveness of marketing is a major determinant of a hotel's immediate business success and long-term survival. Modern hotel managers must be very much involved with the planning and implementation of marketing efforts as an essential part of overall managerial responsibility. This chapter has aimed to enhance readers' awareness of the role and potential of modern marketing, and the importance of marketing for hospitality managers at all levels. In particular, the chapter has emphasized the importance and utility of:

* internal marketing;
* relationship marketing;
* in-house marketing; and
* managing and marketing service demand.

Review questions

1. Briefly describe the notion of "internal customers." How do internal customers affect a firm's marketing endeavors?

2. Relationship marketing has been described as a "paradigm shift" in marketing theory. What is your view of this statement? Do you think that relationship marketing differs markedly from traditional marketing approaches? Explain your answer.

3. Discuss the benefits of relationship marketing in a hospitality context. Give examples of how a hotel manager might apply relationship marketing to day-to-day operations.

4. Briefly explain the various strategies for managing demand, as presented in this chapter. Give examples from the hospitality industry.

Suggested reading for this chapter

This is a list of suggested further reading on topics covered in this chapter. For a separate list of full reference citations quoted in the chapter, see "References," Chapter 7, at the end of the book.

Berry, L. L., & Parasuraman, A. 1991. *Marketing Services: Competing Through Quality*, The Free Press, New York.

Christopher, M., Payne, A., & Ballantyne, D. 1993. *Relationship Marketing: Bringing Quality, Customer Service and Marketing Together*, Butterworth Heinemann, Oxford.

Gummesson, E. 1994. "Making Relationship Marketing Operational," *International Journal of Service Industry Management*, vol. 5, no. 5.

Heskett, J., Sasser, E., & Hart, C. 1990. *Service Breakthrough: Changing the Rules of the Game*. The Free Press, New York.

Part IV

Service Growth to Excellence

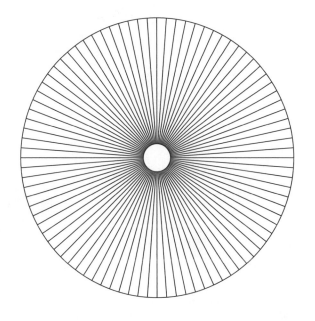

chapter eight

Empowerment, Guarantees, and Recovery

Study objectives

Having completed this chapter, readers should be able to:

* understand the challenges of marketing service quality to potential and existing customers;

* understand the benefits and challenges of service empowerment, service guarantees, and service recovery;

* appreciate the interrelationship of these strategies, and the link between a firm's marketing and operational functions; and

* apply the proposed service system in a hospitality context.

The framework of this chapter

This chapter is set out as follows:

* Introduction

* Service superiority

    — Perceptions of value

    — The problem of duplication

    — The two-way nature of "loyalty"

    — "Breaking the rules" to do the right thing

    — Strategies for a competitive advantage

* Empowerment

    — Tapping a huge resource

    — The guiding philosophy of empowerment

    — Empowerment and complaints-handling

    — Wider effects of empowerment

    — Two essential dimensions of empowerment
      The personal dimension
      The organizational dimension

    — Benefits to management, employees, and customers

    — Suitability of empowerment

* Service guarantees

    — Perceptions of risk

    — Assurance of reliable service

    — Guarantees and marketing

    — Guarantees and service delivery

    — Guarantees and mutual trust

    — Effective service guarantees

    — Benefits of service guarantees

    — The argument for a service guarantee

    — Guarantees, empowerment, and recovery

✳ Service recovery

    — Reliability as the core of service quality

    — Retaining old customers or gaining new ones?

    — "Doing it right the second time"

    — Combining the strategies

    — The forgiving customer

    — Learning from the experience

    — The importance of complementary strategies

✳ Coordinating empowerment, guarantee, and recovery

    — Two types of competitive advantage

    — Steps in establishing a service system

        Step 1: Identifying failure-prone areas

        Step 2: Obtaining feedback

        Step 3: Establishing service standards

        Step 4: Ensuring employee skills

        Step 5: Developing a service-failure strategy

    — The value of a service system in a nutshell

✳ Summary of chapter

Introduction

To maintain their position in today's competitive marketplace, leading organizations must continuously improve their service offerings and communicate the superiority of these offerings to various stakeholders. However, because services are intangible, their quality is difficult to quantify. And with nothing tangible to assure them of promised quality, service customers understandably perceive a risk in purchasing services.

In addressing this problem, many service organizations offer *service guarantees*—thus communicating their commitment to service superiority. However, from an operational perspective, the characteristics of service products present significant challenges to the control and standardization of service quality, and hence to the delivery of an effective service guarantee. The high level of human involvement in both the production and consumption of service products means that mistakes are unavoidable. Guarantees are therefore difficult to fulfill.

For these reasons, service companies attempt to *empower* service personnel, psychologically and practically, in support of the service guarantee. They also attempt to establish effective *service-recovery strategies* to back up the system in the event of failures occurring.

This chapter proposes a systematic approach to gaining a sustainable competitive advantage by combining these three service strategies—*empowerment, guarantees,* and *recovery*—to form a system that facilitates superior service quality and simultaneously reduces customer perceptions of risk and the chances of service duplication by competitors.

Why bother with empowerment, guarantees, and recovery?

The management strategies of empowerment, guarantees, and recovery can be combined to form a system that facilitates superior service quality, reduces customer perceptions of risk, and reduces the chances of service duplication by competitors.

Service superiority

Perceptions of value

The success of leading hospitality and tourism organizations can be attributed to their ability to increase the value of their service offering on a continuous basis (Vandermerwe, 1994). From a customer's perspective, it is the *service element*—that is, the service offered by employees at the time, together with the post-sales service—which effectively determines the value of an organization's product offering.

In addition, in the tourism and hospitality industries especially, value is delivered through "packages." Products and services are rarely sold in isolation. Commonly they are offered in combination as tour packages—comprised of travel, accommodations, food, sightseeing trips, entertainment, and so on. Such combinations significantly increase the customer's perceived value of the service product.

But the promise and delivery of quality service remains the most important aspect of value as perceived by customers.

The problem of duplication

Because hospitality and tourism services are intangible in nature, and because the customer does not receive product "ownership" at the time of purchase, such services cannot be patented (Lovelock, Patterson, & Walker, 2001). Hospitality services can always be duplicated.

In response to such competition, firms are choosing to differentiate themselves from the "copycats" by offering superior quality of service. Such superior service has become recognized as the most effective strategy for tourism and hospitality organizations to adopt if they are to maintain market leadership and customer loyalty (Zeithaml & Bitner, 1996). A hospitality and tourism organization's long-term market success is essentially determined by its ability to offer superior quality service while simultaneously expanding and maintaining a large and loyal customer base.

The two-way nature of "loyalty"

Loyalty is a key concept in services marketing. Service organizations aim to gain the loyalty of customers, and customers seek the loyalty of an organization through an assurance of a commitment to consistent and superior quality of service. Such a commitment on the part of a service provider can be termed "service loyalty."

In a competitive market, such *service loyalty* is a prerequisite if *customer loyalty* is to be achieved (Kandampully, 1998b). It is imperative that service organizations convince their customers of their commitment to superior quality of service—now, and in the future. Success in the hospitality and tourism industry is determined by an organization's ability to offer *loyalty*—a loyalty to quality that will fulfill their customers' present needs, anticipate their prospective needs, and facilitate and enhance ongoing relationships (Kandampully & Suhartanto, 2000).

"Breaking the rules" to do the right thing

Personal interaction between the customer and the service provider is at the heart of virtually all service experiences (Surprenant & Solomon, 1987; Czepiel, Solomon, Surprenant, & Gutman, 1985), and it is the responsibility of management to assist service personnel to offer exceptional service (Deming, 1982). Hospitality and tourism managers thus need to adopt innovative strategies and design procedures that facilitate service personnel to go beyond their immediate job descriptions and to cross functional boundaries (Kandampully, 2001). For customers, the most satisfying experiences are those that occur when employees "break the rules" to respond quickly and flexibly to a particular service need (Baron & Harris, 1995).

"Whatever it takes"

A porter of a New York hotel noticed that a customer, Mr. Schuster, had left his briefcase behind at the desk. He had just put Mr. Schuster into a taxi to La Guardia Airport so it was apparently too late to catch him. But the porter had been given freedom to depart from procedures if necessary to keep a satisfied customer.

The porter grabbed the briefcase, hailed a taxi, and followed Mr. Schuster to the airport. He arrived just as the Chicago plane left. The porter considered the situation for a moment, shrugged his shoulders, checked with his hotel to find out which hotel Mr. Schuster would be staying at in Chicago—and then followed on the next flight! Two hours later, as Mr. Schuster was booking into his Chicago hotel, he was amazed to have the New York porter arrive and hand him his briefcase!

"You left this behind, sir," said the porter.

He then turned and left, leaving Mr. Schuster with the impression that it was the type of service the New York hotel always provided!

When the porter returned to New York he wondered if he would still have a job. The story goes that he kept his job—and was thanked, congratulated, and promoted to duty manager. Today, so the story goes, that same porter is manager of a six-star hotel!

Wearne & Baker (2002)

Strategies for a competitive advantage

It is therefore apparent that hospitality and tourism organizations must utilize a variety of nontraditional strategies to gain and maintain a competitive advantage in the marketplace. Some of the strategies most commonly cited are:

* service empowerment;

* service guarantee;

* service recovery;

* service relationships;

* alliances; and

* technology.

Of these strategies, the first three are discussed in this chapter. Service relationships were discussed in Chapter 7 under "Relationship Marketing". Alliances are discussed in Chapter 9, and technology is covered in Chapter 10.

Before examining the strategies of *empowerment, guarantee,* and *recovery* in more detail in the present chapter, it is important to stress that these strategies should be seen as a cohesive service system of strategies. Strategies such as empowerment, guarantee, and recovery are inherently complementary, and a coordinated system of strategies will permeate the whole organizational culture—thus making it difficult for other organizations to emulate, and thus providing a sustainable competitive advantage for firms that coordinate their strategies effectively (Kandampully & Duddy, 2001).

Empowerment

Tapping a huge resource

In the past, service organizations have tended to neglect a huge potential resource—the individual abilities of their employees. The rigid policies, structures, and systems in many organizations have often presented barriers to individual talent and imagination. Moreover, they have prevented an organization from reaping the full potential of its human resources.

The traditional structures and work arrangements of many hospitality and tourism organizations can engender a feeling of disempowerment (Lashley, 1996). Organizations that wish to instill a culture of empowerment must evolve systems and procedures that do not restrict employees. For example, employees at Hampton Inn (a part of the Promus Hotel Corporation) are encouraged to break the "rules" of their traditional job descriptions if those rules inhibit the likelihood of customer satisfaction (Sowder, 1996). The concept of empowerment allows employees to utilize their personal resources in the workplace—to the benefit of employees, customers, and the organization.

The guiding philosophy of empowerment

The guiding philosophy of empowerment is nonbureaucratic and worker-oriented. Empowerment fosters an environment of commitment and ownership (Lashley, 1996), an environment in which employees utilize information that they glean from their daily interactions with customers to improve services and to contribute to management's understanding of customer requirements (Bitner, Booms, & Mohr, 1994). Empowerment also provides employees with a sense of control, which contributes to job satisfaction (Bateson, 2000).

Goal and strategy of empowerment

The goal of empowerment is the "best of all business worlds"—empowered employees confidently and capably addressing unique problems and opportunities as they occur.

This involves a company's commitment to:

* customizing and personalizing services;

* forming long-term relationships with customers;

* serving the unpredictable and nonroutine needs of customers;

* encouraging employees to make spontaneous decisions to assist customers; and

* seeking and retaining employees who have high aspirations, strong interpersonal skills, and a demonstrated ability to be self-motivated and self-managed.

Empowerment and complaints-handling

The empowerment of service employees is considered to be one of the best options available to hospitality and tourism managers when dealing with the problems of customer complaints and operational bottlenecks. Employees who perceive that they have the right and the responsibility to solve problems themselves are more effective in handling all manner of day-to-day service difficulties. For example, the outstanding service reputation of Marriott hotels was founded on a management philosophy of ensuring that employees possess high self-esteem (Bell & Zemke, 1998). Many other leading service organizations also utilize this philosophy successfully—seeking ways to encourage and reward their employees for exercising initiative in their day-to-day work. Such empowerment produces a state of mind (engendered by structures, practices, and policies) that assists employees to respond immediately and effectively to customers' difficulties (Bowen & Lawler, 1992, 1995).

Employees should consistently be treated as equals, and should receive the same sort of respect as they are expected to offer to their customers. As noted in Chapter 4, J. W. Marriott, Jr., president of the Marriott Corporation, when speaking to his managers said: "Take care of your employees and they'll take care of your customers" (Marriott, 1988).

Various studies have confirmed Marriott's view. There is a clear and direct correlation between managers' relationships with their employees and the service behavior of those employees toward customers (Schneider, 1980). Such positive management–employee relationships can take various forms. For example, employees and managers at Marriott work together in identifying the specific needs of customers, and in seeking ways to satisfy those needs (Hubrecht & Teare, 1993). At Harvester Restaurants, employees function as "worker directors," assisting management to make decisions on matters that affect business policy and strategy (Barbee & Bott, 1991).

Superior service does not result from employees undertaking systemized tasks according to set procedures with management adopting a training role. Rather, excellence in service comes from employees showing initiative in a trusting work environment in which management assumes a supporting role. Management must therefore ensure that it establishes appropriate strategies and systems whereby employees will be able to exercise trust.

Wider effects of empowerment

A management philosophy of empowerment has a direct effect on organizational performance, with positive results in such variables as cost and productivity, quality, speed in responding to customer requests, innovation, and employee morale (Lawler, 1992). Other studies have confirmed these findings. For example, in the field of social work, it has been shown that empowerment practices enhance employees' satisfaction, morale, motivation, and productivity, with consequent improvement in consumer satisfaction (Shera & Page, 1995).

Two essential dimensions of empowerment

There are two essential dimensions of empowerment that are important in any organization:

* the personal dimension; and

* the organizational dimension.

The personal dimension

The personal dimension relates to the enrichment of employees by providing appropriate knowledge and skills to prepare them to take up responsibility and act on behalf of the organization (Zemke & Schaaf, 1989). The task of a service manager thus becomes that of a true *leader*—that is, someone who encourages and rewards employees for their initiatives, while tolerating their mistakes when well-intended efforts fail. Empowerment enhances the personal well-being of employees because they feel trusted, and because they believe that their opinions matter. In these circumstances, personal challenge becomes a positive experience rather than a negative one.

But personal empowerment has wider implications beyond that of personal satisfaction for the employee. At Sears, improved employee attitude not only improved customer satisfaction, but also substantially reduced employee turnover. In addition, Sears' employees assumed the role of true part-time marketers, promoting the retailer as the best place to work and the best place to shop (Rucci, Kirn, & Quinn, 1998). Empowerment thus encourages employees to undertake self-directed activities on behalf of the organization (see Table 8.1).

Table 8.1 *Potential benefits of empowerment*

Category	Benefits
Management	– creates good relationships with employees and customers – increased number of loyal customers – reduction in costs and employee turnover; increased productivity – increased market share, sales, and profitability – opportunities for growth – ultimately results in a competitive advantage
Employees	– increased self-esteem and confidence, when given the authority to decide – increased job satisfaction in an informal and friendly environment – sense of ownership – increased motivation – personal autonomy in daily tasks – prevention of burnout – receive management support, as opposed to management control – "feel-good factor" of resolving customers' problems
Customers	– needs readily satisfied – feel valued and important when personal attention is given – receive more than what is expected – a good relationship with the organization – approachable employees – alleviation of stress and frustration in the long term – reduce time delay

Author's presentation

The organizational dimension

The second dimension, the organizational dimension, refers to the creation of an appropriate environment by removing barriers (that is, structures, systems, and policies) that prevent employees' creative self-expression. Empowerment becomes really effective if its people, processes, and systems are designed to take on customer-oriented flexibility. That is, systems and processes in an organization should be designed to assist its people to serve customers better, and should be flexible enough to adapt as required in accordance with the needs of the customer.

To be effective, empowerment should thus span across all functions and activities of the organization. It is a holistic concept that initiates a learning climate and a culture of knowledge-sharing in which individuals are encouraged to use initiative and judgment in providing superior personal service to customers.

Benefits to management, employees, and customers

Empowerment strategy provides benefits to management, employers, and customers (see Table 8.1).

Real employee empowerment

The Ritz-Carlton Hotel chain has a policy whereby every employee has up to US$2,000 to enhance guest service. Whether the employee be an entry-level housekeeper or an experienced waiter in the fine-dining restaurant, this concept is explained to employees in their initial training program. One might ask what a housekeeper could do, apart from normal room-cleaning duties, that might be an example of employee empowerment.

A man and woman were guests at the Ritz-Carlton Hotel, Amelia Island, near Jacksonville, Florida. One day they were on the way to the beach with their young daughter when they passed two of the housekeepers in the hallway. The guests were warmly greeted, and one of the housekeepers commented on how adorable the child looked in her beach attire. The other housekeeper, agreeing, asked how old the child was. The couple nonchalantly replied that the child was turning 2 years old the next day, and the family then continued the trek to the beach. Upon returning to their room, they found a bright balloon and a big cookie on a plate. On the plate was written the greeting "Happy Birthday."

The child was delighted, and her parents told the hotel manager that the Ritz-Carlton would always have a special place in their hearts and would be their hotel of choice—and all because of the simple actions of two housekeepers who were empowered to make a real difference in caring for their guests.

Employee "empowerment" has been a "buzz phrase" for many years now. Many organizations purport to endorse and practice employee empowerment. But, in reality, it is often nothing more than the making of minor adjustments to minimize customer complaints—such as a front-desk receptionist being "empowered" to lower the room rate for a dissatisfied guest, or a waiter being "empowered" not to charge a customer for dessert because the customer was unhappy with the main course. But is employee "empowerment" limited only to situations of service recovery? If the intention is to build customer loyalty and employee commitment to the organization, empowerment should be proactive and should embrace countless other employee actions—like the actions of the two Ritz-Carlton housekeepers who delighted a little girl, and gained the loyal patronage of her parents for the hotel.

Debby Cannon

Suitability of empowerment

The goal of empowerment is the "best of all business worlds"—empowered employees confidently and capably addressing unique problems and opportunities as they occur. The concept of empowerment is best suited to organizations that embrace a creative philosophy that facilitates such a "best of all worlds." Such a firm is committed to:

* differentiating, customizing, and personalizing its services, and creating greater value to its customers through such services;

* forming long-term relationships with its customers;

* serving the complex, unpredictable, and nonroutine needs of customers;

* encouraging employees to make spontaneous decisions to assist customers; and

* seeking and retaining employees who have high aspirations, strong interpersonal skills, and a demonstrated ability to be self-motivated and self-managed.

If an organization can utilize its service personnel creatively and improve its service offerings, it has a critical competitive advantage. However, an empowerment strategy alone might not prove capable of providing an organization with a competitive advantage. Other strategies—service guarantee and service recovery—are also needed.

Service guarantees

Perceptions of risk

Every business encounter involves risk. And in every business encounter, one side of the transaction always assumes more of the risk than the other. This might occur explicitly or implicitly. Indeed, the participants might not always be consciously aware of the distribution of risk. However, in every business transaction, one party is always more at risk than the other, and some types of business transactions involve more risk than others.

When customers purchase a service, they usually take a relatively higher risk than when they purchase a physical object—and they know it. In purchasing an intangible service they cannot pretest the outcome, and there is, of course, no specific physical object to be examined before purchase (Zeithaml, 1981). The purchase of hospitality and tourism services are perfect examples—the services cannot be reworked or returned. In effect, the customer makes a purchase in the *trust* and *expectation* of receiving a good result.

To encourage prospective customers to avail themselves of its services, a service organization should therefore seek ways to reduce the perceived risk. Ideally, management should attempt to eliminate the perception of risk completely, and thus create a risk-free transaction. In effect, management offers the customer a *guarantee of service*.

Assurance of reliable service

A guaranteed service transaction will be seen by the prospective customers of hospitality and tourism organizations as an added bonus—something that adds value to the offer by increasing the likelihood that they will achieve what they wish to achieve.

What can you promise?

Service guarantees should strive to be as "unconditional" as possible, with a view to assuring the customer of service reliability.

In essence, a service guarantee is a twofold vow:

* that service delivery will meet company promises; and, if it does not . . .

* that the company will promptly compensate the customer.

Service guarantees can be "conditional" or "unconditional" (Hart, 1993; McDougal, Levesque, & Vanderplaat, 1998). Although the ideal objective is a completely risk-free offer, the reality is that no one can ever guarantee that mistakes will never be made. The best that can be done is a promise to make every effort to eliminate foreseeable and controllable error, together with an undertaking to make good any mistake that does occur—and to do so promptly. Service guarantees should thus strive to be as "unconditional" as possible, with a view to assuring the customer of service reliability. In essence, a service guarantee is a vow that service delivery will meet company promises; and if it does not, that the company will promptly compensate the customer (Zeithaml & Bitner, 1996).

Research into service quality shows that service reliability lies at the heart of excellent service; it constitutes the single most important factor in the estimation of customers, and is, in many ways, the *core* quality sought by most customers (Parasuraman, Berry, & Zeithaml, 1985). Service reliability thus constitutes the foundation on which a reputation for outstanding service quality is built; conversely, breaking the service promise is the single most important way in which service companies fail their customers (Berry, Zeithaml, & Parasuraman, 1990).

Prepurchase guarantees are especially important in the case of services. Services, by their very nature, offer few cues to assist service customers with their prepurchase decisions. Hospitality and tourism services are especially notable for not facilitating prepurchase evaluation, and customers are thus commonly forced to rely on the postpurchase evaluation of others (word of mouth) in making assessments about a service. Zeithaml (1981) noted that the purchase decision of services embodies a higher risk for the customer due to the fact that "services are intangible, non-standardised, and . . . usually sold without guarantees or warranties." As MacMillan and McGrath (1997) observed, the competitive advantage of service guarantees lies in *removing uncertainty,* thus making the buying process of customers more convenient and less irritating.

Guarantees and marketing

From a marketing perspective, a service guarantee thus has the potential to influence customers to avail themselves of the services on offer. Hospitality and tourism organizations that offer service guarantees command a substantially greater market share as compared with the competition (Sowder, 1996), thus enabling them to set a premium price for their services (Hart, 1988). For example, Promus Hotel Corporation's "100% satisfaction guarantee" elevated it to the top of the consumer ratings.

A guarantee reinforces a company's service promise to its customers, effectively making the promise "tangible" (Kandampully, 1998a). This, in turn, attracts new customers (Maher, 1991), enhances repeat business (Marvin, 1992), and retains customer patronage. Once established, service guarantees should constitute a permanent part of an organization's operating philosophy, and be supported by an advertising campaign to reinforce the fact.

Words of wisdom

Much has been spoken and written about empowerment, guarantees, and recovery. Here are some "words of wisdom" that, taken together, provide an overview of why these complementary strategies are so important in modern services management.

* "[Service guarantees] bring the customer loop right in to every employee in the company—the employees can literally hear the customer speaking to them through these guarantees" (Hunter, 1994).

* "By knowing what your customer's wants are, and meeting those wants, you create a unity of expectations between customer and employee, providing employees with a very clear focus" (Rose, 1990).

* ". . . it costs five times as much to attract a new customer as it does to retain an existing one" (Heskett, Sasser, & Schlesinger, 1997).

* ". . . except in a few rare instances, complete customer satisfaction is the key to securing customer loyalty and generating superior long-term financial performance" (Jones & Sasser, 1995).

Guarantees and service delivery

Service guarantees have the capacity to change the entire service-delivery system of an organization, and will substantially improve operational efficiency. A risk-aversive philosophy tends to permeate all aspects of organizational life, extending well beyond the limits of mere financial risk implied by the word "guarantee" (Albrecht, 1992).

The aim of service guarantees is "to bring the customer loop right in to every employee in the company—the employees can literally hear the customer speaking to them through these guarantees" (Hunter, 1994). Bringing the voice of the customer into an organization in this way is a matter of great importance for service companies, and various authors have discussed the need for effective tools and approaches to achieve this (Woodruff & Gardial, 1996). A service guarantee is one such effective strategy. It encourages customer feedback, and offers an organization the opportunity to take immediate corrective action—one of the crucial factors in converting dissatisfied customers into satisfied customers (Brendin, 1995).

Indeed, service guarantees are likely to be a more effective strategy for gaining customer feedback than traditional feedback questionnaires. For example, managers at Hampton Inn (a Promus Corporation hotel) adopted service guarantees, in association with rewards for employees for their commitment to such guarantees. These managers began to hear stories about their front-line staff members going out of their way to help and please customers (Sowder, 1996). The service-guarantee program at Hampton Inn thus assisted managers and staff to respond immediately when there was a need to improve the services on offer.

One of the important benefits of the service guarantee is, therefore, that it works as an effective conduit of feedback from customers (Kandampully & Butler, 1998). Such feedback enables employees to analyze situations and to take action to satisfy customers (Martin, 1995). Such a system thus enhances a firm's capacity to improve systems continuously, while simultaneously providing an opportunity to transform dissatisfied customers into lifelong loyal customers.

In an effort to encourage both positive and negative feedback, the use of a reward system—directed at both customers and employees—can be very useful (Kandampully & Butler, 1998). Such a reward system, by which customers are rewarded for their comments, and by which employees are rewarded for solving problems, effectively compels the organization to respond to customer feedback. And this is a great advantage to any firm. Research conducted by Sowder (1996) and by Evans, Clark, and Knutson (1996) showed that a powerful competitive advantage is available to any hospitality and tourism firm that is willing to offer a service guarantee and that proves capable of delivering on that promise.

Service guarantees thus provide benefits to the provider, as well as to the customer. For the provider, a service guarantee "lifts the game" of the whole organization and implicitly improves the whole service-delivery system.

Guarantees and mutual trust

Above all, customers appreciate such guarantees for the commitment to service that they represent. A service guarantee is essentially a way of demonstrating an organization's *trust in its customers*—in the full knowledge that some customers will attempt to take unfair advantage of the offer (Bell, 1993).

Such trust makes customers feel valued. It communicates one-half of a partnership reaching out to the other—thus facilitating a long-term partnership. The effect of this

Trust all around

A service guarantee encourages mutual trust—mutual trust between a firm and its external customers, and mutual trust between a firm and its internal customers. The overall effect is a general increase in cooperation and commitment among all stakeholders—essential in service organizations, which "live or die" on the basis of enduring personal relationships.

is that service guarantees create a commitment to the delivery of excellent service, and reciprocal trust on both sides, resulting in an impressive customer-retention rate (Davis & Baldwin, 1995).

Service guarantees create a customer-driven standard for service that defines the service promise of an organization to its internal and external customers simultaneously. That is, service guarantees not only set criteria by which customers can evaluate the quality of service they receive, but also establish the standard to which an organization needs to train its workers, so as to ensure that the staff are capable of delivering such quality service (Maher, 1991).

A service guarantee thus encourages mutual trust—mutual trust between a firm and its external customers, and mutual trust between a firm and its internal customers. The overall effect is a general increase in cooperation and commitment among all stakeholders—essential in service organizations, which "live or die" on the basis of enduring personal relationships.

The porter is working hard. The guest are ready to depart. The service guarantee is backed up by empowered employees with a commitment to delivering on the service ethos of their organization.

With kind permission of Blackwell Hotel, Columbus, Ohio

> ## *Real and effective service guarantees*
>
> Real and effective service guarantees must be:
>
> * unconditional;
>
> * easy to understand and communicate;
>
> * meaningful to the customer;
>
> * easy to invoke; and
>
> * easy to fulfill.

Effective service guarantees

It is not enough to offer a service guarantee as a public-relations exercise—cynically designed to attract attention and prospective customers—with no commitment to the concept of a *real* guarantee. An effective guarantee must be carefully designed and effectively organized as part of an overall commitment to a service-oriented culture.

Such a service-oriented guarantee should be:

* *unconditional*—when excuses are given, the customer feels cheated;

* *easy to understand and communicate*—specific and clear to both customers and employees;

* *meaningful to the customer*—promising something of real value if service is not delivered properly;

* *easy to invoke*—an unpleasant situation should not be exacerbated by a service guarantee that is difficult to invoke; and

* *easy to fulfill*—when a customer invokes a guarantee, the service provider should pay out immediately.

Incorporating these sorts of features into a service guarantee ensures that the guarantee is real and effective.

Benefits of service guarantees

It is apparent from the above discussion that service guarantees have benefits beyond the obvious benefit—assuring reliability and thereby encouraging doubtful customers. These wider benefits permeate through the whole organization.

In summary, service guarantees have the following benefits:

* assuring reliability and encouraging sales;

* enhancing customer feedback;

* improving service-delivery systems;

* identifying "fail points" in the service system;

* increasing customer satisfaction;

* improving employee performance;

* developing a general service-oriented culture in the business; and

* maintaining competitiveness in the marketplace.

Taking these points together, a service-guarantee strategy serves as a service standard that cannot be compromised. This strategy effectively coordinates every system in the organization to become focused on better serving the customer. It can thus be considered to function as an internal "auto-alignment" system.

The argument for a service guarantee

So why should a service organization go to the trouble of guaranteeing its service offering? The above discussion has canvassed various benefits that seem attractive enough in theory, but do such service guarantees really deliver in practice?

A service guarantee *does* deliver—it fulfills both an effective marketing function and an effective operational function (Kandampully, 1998a). That is, it simultaneously enhances an organization's (internal and external) marketing effectiveness and its operating competency (see Figure 8.1).

Figure 8.1 *Impact of a service guarantee on marketing and operations*

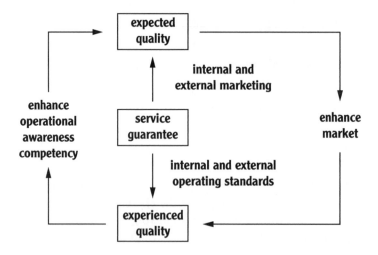

Author's presentation

This dual role (marketing and operational) reflects the fact that *customer satisfaction* is the ultimate measure of both marketing effectiveness and operational competency in any service organization. As Rose (1990) observed. "By knowing what your customer's wants are, and meeting those wants, you create a unity of expectations between customer and employee, providing employees with a very clear focus."

Such a strategy also helps to establish a learning relationship with each and every customer—an important concept if an organization is to improve (Peppers, Rogers, & Dorf, 1999). Even if conceived essentially as a marketing strategy, a guarantee is able to nurture what might be termed an "organizational learning process" as it focuses the whole organization on customer needs.

From the above discussion, it is apparent that a service guarantee *is* an effective and valuable management tool. All service organizations, especially hospitality services, should embrace the strategy of a service guarantee because:

* it forces an organization to focus on the customer's definition of good service, rather than relying on management's assumptions of what constitutes such service;

* it sets clear performance standards;

* it generates reliable data on poor performance (through records of complaints and payouts);

* it forces an organization to examine its entire service-delivery system for possible failure points;

* it builds customer loyalty and enhances positive word-of-mouth recommendation; and

* it encourages employees to show initiative and commitment to the firm and its customers.

Guarantees, empowerment, and recovery

Earlier in this chapter, we discussed the empowerment of employees. A service-guarantee strategy provides empowered employees with an opportunity to display their commitment to the customer, and to participate actively in the creation of an appropriate image for their own service, and for that of the whole organization. Indeed, the empowerment strategy discussed above is most effective in the presence of a complementary service-guarantee strategy.

It is the service-guarantee strategy that provides empowered and motivated employees with the authority to become actively involved in the third major subject of this chapter—*service recovery* (see below). The combination of empowered employees, a service guarantee, and a policy of service recovery transforms dissatisfied customers into satisfied and loyal partners.

Service recovery

Reliability as the core of service quality

In a competitive market economy, the ultimate goal of a business organization and the objective of its various marketing strategies is the provision of superior value to customers (Woodruff, 1997; Bateson, 1995; Batesen & Hoffman, 1999).

The consensus of the literature on management theory is that a firm's competitive advantage is due to organizational factors—primarily the firm's capability or core competencies (see, e.g., Prahalad & Hamel, 1990). However, in services, it is commonly these very core competencies that fail to meet customers' expectations. As we have noted in this book several times, research has shown that breaking the service promise is the single most important way in which service companies fail their customers (Berry, Zeithaml & Parasuraman 1990). From the customer's point of view, a service firm's capacity to deliver the core competencies is inextricably linked to reliability—that is, the ability to offer service without failure (Kandampully, 1998b). Reliability is the core of service quality (Berry & Parasuraman, 1992).

Retaining old customers or gaining new ones?

Although it might sometimes seem that there is an unlimited pool of potential customers for any given service firm, the primary goal of an organization must be to focus on maintaining the loyalty of its existing customer base (Slater, 1997). This is because recruitment is always more costly than retention. Indeed, it has been argued that "it costs five times as much to attract a new customer as it does to retain an existing one" (Heskett et al., 1997:9). In addition, the restless searching for new customers can mean that present customers are treated less well, with resultant loss of customer satisfaction and corporate reputation.

Various researchers have indicated that the loyalty, retention, and repurchase intentions of existing customers is inextricably linked to customer satisfaction (see, e.g., Patterson & Spreng, 1997). The main reason for customers leaving familiar service providers and seeking new ones has been repeatedly shown to be failure in the core service of the firm (Richman, 1996). And dissatisfied customers not only defect but also trigger a chain of negative word-of-mouth comments. As Jones and Sasser (1995:89) concluded: "except in a few rare instances, complete customer satisfaction is the key to securing customer loyalty and generating superior long-term financial performance."

This long-term perspective has produced a strong emphasis on orienting service strategy toward fulfilling service promise, increasing customer loyalty, and reducing customer dissatisfaction (Kandampully, 1998b).

A thriller in Manila—lessons in service recovery (1)

Two university lecturers were on their way to attend a conference in Manila, and booked to stay at the Mandarin Oriental Hotel—widely recognized as one of the finest hotels in the Asia–Pacific region. The hotel claims to have a personal approach to service that "reflects not only its own interests, but more importantly, that of its guests, staff, and shareholders." This service promise is in keeping with the parent group's aim to be "recognized as one of the top global luxury hotel groups, providing exceptional customer satisfaction in each of its hotels." Indeed, the group frequently receives international awards for outstanding service and quality management.

The two guests were informed that they would be met at the airport by the hotel valet service. Sure enough, upon arrival, they easily located the valet attendant who advised them of the charge and shuttled them promptly to the hotel in a luxury limousine.

Upon arrival at the hotel, the visitors were met by the concierge and escorted to the reception desk where a delightful young lady welcomed them and checked them in. She then escorted the guests to their room. On the way, she highlighted the many distinctive service features of the hotel and its rooms.

The first indication of any problem came during the young woman's description of the many hotel services. She inadvertently revealed that the two guests had been offered only the most expensive hotel limousine service for their ride from the airport. In fact, there had been an equally reliable (but much less expensive) hotel taxi service available as transport from the airport. Given their limited budget, and the fact that they had not been informed of this option, the two visitors began to wonder whether they had been "fleeced" when they had been offered only the limousine service. However, given the warmth of the welcome received, they decided to attribute this experience to bad luck.

The next day the visitors were due to set out on the 10-minute walk to the conference venue. Because it was raining they approached the concierge desk and requested a loan of a complimentary umbrella. After a 5-minute search and much fussing around, the staff apologized for the fact that all complimentary umbrellas were apparently out on loan. This explanation was accepted. However, conscious that it was typhoon season, the guests thought it would be a good idea to book two umbrellas for the remainder of their stay. This request was duly noted.

That evening, one of the guests decided to ring home using the in-room direct-dial telephone service. After carefully studying the information provided—including all surcharges, tariffs, taxes, and currency conversions—he calculated the cost to be around AUS$5.00. Having completed the call, he was anxious to check whether the correct rate had been charged to his account. Imagine his shock and dismay when he was advised that his account contained a fee of AUS$45.00 for the 4 minutes he had been on the telephone! He checked his previous calculations, decided that his initial total fee had been correct, and then related his concerns to the guest services manager. The manager investigated, acknowledged that there was potential for misinterpretation of the advice regarding telephone charges in the guest services directory, and reassured the guest that she would see what she could do.

Over the next three days, the rain continued and the guests continued to seek complimentary umbrellas with no success. They could not believe that a hotel such as the Mandarin Oriental would not have an adequate supply of complimentary umbrellas, and could not understand why their daily reservations for an umbrella were not honored. Upon confronting the concierge, they finally learned that their suspicions were correct—the concierge department did not have any complimentary umbrellas. The guests had been deceived all the time. However, they were advised that they could purchase a hotel umbrella at the hotel retail outlet!

Now determined to press their complaints with the management of the hotel, the guests drafted and delivered a letter of complaint outlining their discontent with the umbrella deception, the limousine deception, and the confusing advice regarding telephone charges. They also suggested possible solutions to prevent a recurrence of such incidents.

The letter set off a remarkable chain of efforts at service recovery that left an indelible perception of quality in the minds of both guests. To see what happened next, see the box "A Thriller in Manila—Lessons in Service Recovery (2)."

Martin O'Neill

"Doing it right the second time"

A customer's intention to repurchase is obviously an indication of whether that customer will remain loyal to the firm or switch to a competitor (Zeithaml, Berry, & Parasuraman, 1996) and, in a competitive environment, customers choose to maintain their patronage on the basis of a firm's ability to exhibit superior service with flawless performance (Berry, 1995). This creates a problem for service providers. In services, the human element is so prominent in both production and consumption that mistakes are unavoidable (Hart, Heskett, & Sasser, 1990). Given the inevitability of error, the way in which a service organization responds to mistakes becomes a crucial factor in customer retention.

When mistakes do happen, a firm's true commitment to service quality is displayed to the customer by the manner in which it responds (Zemke & Bell, 1990).

The title of Zemke and Bell's paper on this subject sums up the situation neatly: "Service Recovery: Doing It Right the Second Time." It is imperative that a firm goes out of its way to satisfy customers after a service failure. In contrast, if the firm *fails* to ensure customer satisfaction following a service failure, the result will be a decline in customer confidence and an increase in negative word-of-mouth comments. An initial failure might be tolerated, but if the firm fails to recover from the initial service failure, it has effectively failed *twice*–thus magnifying negative customer perception. Bitner, Booms, & Tetreault (1990) describe this as a "double deviation" from expectation.

A thriller in Manila–lessons in service recovery (2)

Having endured a number of annoying service failures (see "A Thriller in Manila–Lessons in Service Recovery (1)"), our friends in Manila finally wrote a constructive letter of complaint.

Within a short time a room service attendant arrived with a complimentary basket of exotic fruits and a letter from the floor manager. Then the concierge manager arrived and immediately took responsibility for the "umbrella problem." She apologized for the inconvenience and offered two free hotel umbrellas to the surprised guests, together with a courtesy limousine service for their return trip to the airport. Immediately afterward, the guest services manager arrived with news on the telephone problem. She courteously explained that the charge had been correct. However, she apologized for any confusion involved in the literature that described the charging structure. As a conciliatory gesture she offered a 10% discount on the charge. Soon after, another letter of apology arrived from the resident manager accepting full responsibility for the inability of the concierge department to supply complimentary umbrellas.

Everything about this effort at service recovery is impressive. The hotel admitted responsibility for its failings, the various managers took immediate "ownership" of the problems in their departments, and matters were followed through to a satisfactory resolution.

In addition, the hotel sought to prevent the problems occurring again. Later that evening, the guests witnessed concierge staff busily filling a cabinet with complimentary umbrellas for the future use of guests. Similarly, the hotel immediately advised airport transit staff that all guests were to be offered all transport options in the future. With respect to the telephone charges, the guest services directory was immediately rewritten to clarify the dialing fee structure.

It is apparent that the staff at the Mandarin Oriental looked upon the letter of complaint as a real opportunity to enhance customer service. Indeed, the guests agreed that the whole service-recovery process had been so impressive that their perception of the hotel was more positive than it would have been if the service had been faultless in the first instance!

Would they stay at the Mandarin Oriental again? Most certainly, YES!

Would they recommend it to friends and colleagues? Again, the answer is a resounding YES!

Martin O'Neill

Combining the strategies

Against this background, it is apparent that the establishment of the strategies of a *service guarantee* and *employee empowerment* are inextricably interwoven with the concept of *service recovery*. Effective service recovery involves a service guarantee to ensure an immediate response to failure, and employment empowerment to ensure effective corrective action to recover from that failure.

Service recovery is a systematic process undertaken by an organization in an effort to return aggrieved customers to a state of satisfaction after a service or product has

Recovery from someone else's service failure

When thinking of service recovery we usually equate recovery "systems" with specific plans to overcome definite in-house service failures. But sometimes, perhaps more frequently than we are aware, quality service firms help consumers to recover confidence when their faith in service quality has taken a "knock" as a result of adverse experiences elsewhere. Success in these cases is clearly not "system-dependent." Rather, it comes from an organizational culture in which quality of service is offered as a matter of course. The wife of a doctor attending a convention close to a small English market town describes her experience.

"I walked into the town alone. It was a Sunday. The shops were shuttered. There were no lights. The window 'displays' were lifeless. The whole scene was cold and forbidding. I vowed never to come here again. I returned to the hotel to spend a miserable evening alone. As soon as I walked in, the warmth of the welcome washed over me. People talked to me, showing genuine interest and concern. I felt special, cared for, and wanted. Nothing was too much trouble. I was treated with courtesy and respect, and spent a pleasant and memorable evening. I will most definitely return to this hotel."

Here was service recovery without a "system." Here was service recovery as part of a service culture in which quality is offered as a matter of course.

Gillian Lyons

failed to live up to expectations (Andreasson, 2000). Effective service recovery leads to enhanced perceptions of the firm's competence and a favorable image in terms of perceived quality and value (Zemke, 1995).

It is imperative to manage a customer's entire experience with the firm through numerous service encounters. Customer perceptions of so-called "moments of truth" play a major role in gaining customer satisfaction and in influencing future purchase decisions. Each of these encounters presents an opportunity for a firm to prove its superior quality of service or, alternatively, to lose its customers' trust and loyalty (Bitner, 1995). In addition, employees take note of how their firm handles problems. A service firm's ability to respond immediately to complaints of service failure can therefore communicate important signals about the firm to employees, as well as to its customers (Heskett, Sasser, & Hart, 1990).

The forgiving customer

Most customers are sympathetic to unforeseen service failures. They understand that these things do occur despite a service provider's commitment to offer superior service. Customers are, in fact, seldom unhappy about inadvertent service mishaps. Rather, they are unhappy if the service organization is unwilling to accept responsibility for the mishap. More importantly, they are especially unhappy if the service provider is unable (or, worse, unwilling) to take immediate action to fix the situation.

Tax and Brown (1998, 2000) found that the majority of customers are dissatisfied with the way in which companies resolve their complaints. Kelley, Hoffman, and Davis (1993) claimed that it is possible to recover from any failure—no matter what. They also found that, regardless of the type of failure experienced, customers will remain loyal to a service firm *provided that an effective recovery is executed.*

From a customer's perspective, recovering failed service demonstrates fulfillment of the firm's promise, and thereby confirms a firm's superior service.

Learning from the experience

Although the primary purpose of service recovery is to return the aggrieved customer to a state of satisfaction, a firm can gain additional benefit for itself if it makes use of the information gained from the experience to prevent future failure. Every service failure and recovery experience should trigger a learning process across the whole organization—to prevent a recurrence of the mistake.

This concept of "learning from failure" is crucial if an organization is to improve its people, its systems, and its procedures. Tax and Brown (1998) suggested the use of a database to record, categorize, and disseminate information to the entire organization to help everyone learn from the mistakes.

The importance of complementary strategies

The literature on service recovery and service guarantees stresses that recovery is most effective if a firm's response is focused on each customer's individual needs, and if employees have highly developed interpersonal skills that enable them to react flexibly to each situation that they encounter.

Empowerment shifts control of a situation to employees at the critical moment of contact with the customer. This is admittedly a potential area of concern for management, which might feel that it is losing control of a situation and ceding that control to more junior employees. However, if management has a complementary strategy of a service guarantee (effectively running in parallel with a strategy of empowerment), this imbues employees with a sense of the importance and urgency of their response. Service guarantee and employee empowerment are thus complementary strategies that reinforce one another in practice. Management can have confidence in employees who have confidence in management. The parallel strategies of employee empowerment and an overt service guarantee engender a spirit of mutual trust between management and employees—everyone is committed to the same goal of delivering quality service.

The integration of these three complementary strategies (of empowerment, guarantee, and recovery) within an organization results in an effective service culture that is not easily emulated by competitors, and thus constitutes a unique competitive advantage. But such a result is achievable only if the strategies are incorporated within a systemic infrastructure—a "service system." Such a system highlights the relationships of the respective strategies, and identifies the stages required in the delivery of superior service. We now turn to a consideration of such a coordinated service system.

Coordinating empowerment, guarantee, and recovery

Two types of competitive advantage

To be profitable in an industry, a company must have a sustainable competitive advantage. The literature on management theory is full of ideas on how to go about establishing such an advantage. Porter (1985, 1998) argued that these various theories could be classified into only two basic types of competitive advantage:

* lower costs than competitors; or

* superior quality than competitors.

With regard to the second of these—the ability to differentiate from others by offering the customer something unique in terms of superior quality and value—the modern service strategies of empowerment, guarantees, and recovery are of crucial importance. As noted above, these are best practiced within a coordinated and comprehensive service system. Figure 8.2 illustrates such a system.

Figure 8.2 *A service system showing links among empowerment, service guarantee, and service recovery*

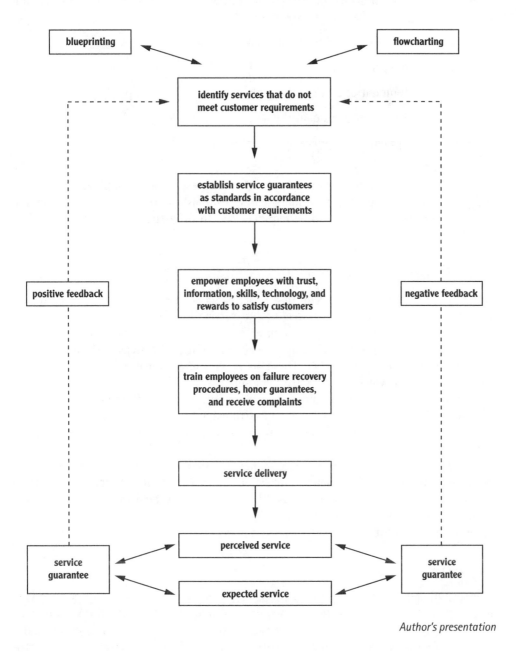

Author's presentation

Steps in establishing a service system

There are five basic steps in the design and establishment of an effective and coordinated service system. They can be summarized as follows:

* the identification of failure-prone areas;

* the obtaining of feedback;

* the establishment of service standards;

* ensuring that employees gain the requisite knowledge and skills; and

* the development of a service-failure strategy.

Each of these is discussed below.

The visual information contained in a blueprint, especially if employed during the design of a new service, will help managers to establish preventive support services as they are perceived to be likely to be required, and to offer special training for employees as appropriate.

Step 1: Identifying failure-prone areas

One of the first steps in the design of a superior service system involves the identification of failure-prone areas. In this regard, a service blueprint is a most effective resource in enabling managers to examine the entire service-delivery process visually (Walker, 1995). Using a blueprint, managers can identify the steps performed in view of or in contact with a customer. These steps represent critical points in the service-delivery process at which quality must be assured.

The visual information contained in a blueprint, especially if employed during the design of a new service, will help managers to establish preventive support services as they are perceived to be likely to be required, and to offer special training for employees as appropriate.

In addition to the use of blueprints, managers can also use other flowcharting techniques—such as "fishbone" analysis and Pareto analysis to examine factors influencing performance at quality-sensitive areas. This will not only help managers to identify problems and to find solutions, but also to prioritize action.

(See Chapter 5 for more on all of these subjects.)

Step 2: Obtaining feedback

The second step in designing a service system is the obtaining of feedback from customers. Service employees can also provide vital and reliable information about customers, especially with respect to customer needs and problems. It is essential that a firm establish a method to collect such customer feedback—both directly from customers, and indirectly via employees.

Five steps in designing a service system

There are five basic steps in the design and establishment of an effective and coordinated service system of empowerment, guarantee, and recovery. These are discussed in the text. They can be summarized as follows:

1. the identification of failure-prone areas;
2. the obtaining of feedback;
3. the establishment of service standards;
4. ensuring that employees gain the requisite knowledge and skills; and
5. the development of a service-failure strategy.

Too important to be left to chance

The coordination of the vital strategies of *empowerment, service guarantee,* and *service recovery* depends on an appropriate service system. Success in establishing this provides a service firm with a unique competitive advantage.

The establishment of such a system is thus too important a matter to be left to chance. It deserves and demands the full attention of committed management and staff.

In this regard, the use of service guarantees encourages customers to voice their dissatisfaction immediately. Moreover, if a guarantee is invoked, employees are required to recount and/or explain the incident to management. If this is complemented by an appropriate employee reward system, in which employees are acknowledged for their commitment and enthusiasm, managers will receive information on the positive experiences of customers also.

Such ongoing feedback is essential to the setting-up of an appropriate service system in the first place, and facilitates the review of any existing delivery processes.

Step 3: Establishing service standards

The third step in setting up an effective service system is to establish (or update) service standards that reflect customer requirements, and to ensure these are communicated to customers by close coordination between operational and marketing departments. In this regard, service guarantees explicitly define a firm's promise to the customer, thus effectively marketing both capability and commitment.

Step 4: Ensuring employee skills

The fourth step in the design of a service system is to ensure that the firm's employees gain the requisite knowledge and skills to render services commensurate with the agreed service standards. In this regard, it is important to recognize that superior service often requires employees to go beyond their job tasks if they are to serve the special needs of customers (Schweikhart, Strasser, & Kennedy, 1993). Adhering to structured job specifications and standards might not be sufficient in all situations.

In this regard, the strategy of empowerment is most useful. It allows employees the flexibility to be imaginative in finding alternative solutions for the myriad customer needs they encounter in their everyday jobs.

Step 5: Developing a service-failure strategy

The final step in the setting-up of a service system is the development of a service-failure strategy. This involves establishing procedures for employees to follow when service failure occurs—such as when customers register a complaint, or when a service guarantee is to be honored.

Recovery of service failure requires employees to possess special skills. It is at these moments that the touted service superiority of employees (and the whole organization) is most carefully scrutinized. It is imperative that every recovery of failed service is handled in a professional and courteous manner. This necessitates clearly established procedures to be followed by all employees, complemented by freedom to show initiative in special circumstances. Employees who can follow established procedures as required, but also show initiative in unusual circumstances, represent a valuable resource for any service firm. Their recruitment, training, and retention must be a top priority for any firm that wishes to be successful.

Summary of chapter

Although the nature of service products means that a service organization is especially vulnerable to duplication of its offerings by competitors, a firm that can consistently maintain and enhance customer satisfaction and loyalty will be able to sustain a superior market position. To achieve and maintain a competitive edge, it is imperative that a firm systematically identifies and manages the factors that influence service quality and customer satisfaction.

The intangible nature of services means that customer satisfaction depends, to a very large extent, on perceptions and personal judgments (rather than on predetermined standards set by management). And these perceptions and personal judgments are made throughout the entire service process—from prepurchase (e.g., communication with potential customers) to postpurchase (e.g., after-sale communication and conflict-handling).

The service experience in its entirety thus progresses through various stages, with a service strategy applicable to each stage:

* prepurchase communication (guarantee);
* service delivery (empowerment); and
* postpurchase relationship (recovery).

Of these, the service guarantee serves as a unique selling point that aims to promote the firm's customer orientation with real commitment. Such a service guarantee not only targets external customers but also employees—who become acutely aware of the firm's service philosophy and service vision (see Chapter 5). The service guarantee thus establishes and communicates the firm's image and market position to its customers, competitors, and employees. Ultimately, it will be reflected in customer satisfaction and loyalty.

To implement a service guarantee successfully, a firm also needs to implement the complementary strategies of service empowerment and service recovery. These provide the support necessary for the service guarantee to be operationally realistic and financially viable.

Although the theoretical and practical value of empowerment, service guarantee, and recovery have long been recognized, the implementation of these approaches has not always delivered the desired outcomes. In many cases, they have remained little more than management fads because managers have failed to recognize the organizational changes required to implement these strategies effectively. To realize the full potential of any service system, a firm must redesign its organizational structure and policies to accommodate, enable, and support such a system.

A service system of the type proposed in this chapter emphasizes the role of the human element in a service context. As such, it holds major implications for a firm's human resources policies—including employee training, communication, recognition, and reward. If the service system is to achieve its intended objectives, a firm needs to develop the necessary managerial attitudes and behaviors that can facilitate and promote the understanding, commitment, and participation of employees at all levels.

Review questions

1. Discuss the relationship between service loyalty and customer loyalty.

2. Discuss the implications of service empowerment, service guarantees, and service recovery on internal marketing and relationship marketing.

3. You are the operations manager of a first-class hotel. Identify the benefits and challenges of the strategies discussed in this chapter (empowerment, guarantee, recovery) as they pertain to your day-to-day operation.

Suggested reading for this chapter

This is a list of suggested further reading on topics covered in this chapter. For a separate list of full reference citations quoted in the chapter, see "References," Chapter 8, of the end of the book.

Barnes, J. G. 2001. *Secrets of Customer Relationship Management,* McGraw-Hill, New York.

Berry, L. L. 1999. *Discovering the Soul of Service,* Free Press, New York.

Gummesson, E. 1999. *Total Relationship Marketing,* Butterworth-Heinemann, Oxford, UK.

Wirtz, J., & Klein, J. 2001. "The Accellion Service Guarantee," *INSEAD Case Series,* INSEAD, Fontainebleau, France.

Wirtz, J., & Kum, D. 2001. "Designing Service Guarantees—Is Full Satisfaction the Best You Can Guarantee?," *Journal of Services Marketing,* vol. 15, no. 4, 282–299.

Wirtz, J., Kum, D., & Lee, K. S. 2000. "Should a Firm with a Reputation for Outstanding Service Quality Offer a Service Guarantee?," *Journal of Services Marketing,* vol. 14, no. 6, 502–512.

Zemke, R. 1995. *Service Recovery: Fixing Broken Customers,* Productivity Press, Portland, Oregon.

chapter nine
Global Strategies
for Hospitality Services

Study objectives

Having completed this chapter, readers should be able to:

✳ demonstrate an overall understanding of the factors that influence the internationalization of service organizations;

✳ understand the different internationalization strategies;

✳ understand the rationale behind international strategic alliances, and how to apply this understanding within the hospitality context.

The framework of this chapter

This chapter is set out as follows:

＊ Introduction

＊ The trend is global

＊ From inns to internationalization

  − Early days
  − The development of hotel "chains"
  − The impetus for globalization

＊ Choosing an international location

  − Macro factors to be considered
    Economic considerations
    Political considerations
    Cultural considerations
    Technological considerations
  − Special risks for physical assets
  − Cultural barriers to success
  − Technological barriers to success

＊ In search of global potential

  − Sales expansion
  − Product diversification
  − Resource acquisition
  − Brand recognition

＊ Strategies for globalizing hospitality firms

  − Five generic strategies
    Direct foreign investment
    Management contracts
    Joint ventures
    Franchising
    Strategic alliances

-   — Variations on the strategies
     Multisite and multicountry expansion
     Importing customers
     Following the customers
     Service "unbundling"
     Beating the clock
  — An overview of strategies for internationalization

* Globalization through partnerships and alliances

  — Why alliances?
  — Types and characteristics of alliances
  — Risks and success in alliances
     Undue influence
     Inefficient use of resources
     Loss of competitive position
  — The importance of trust
  — Choose well in the first place
  — Purpose of alliances
     Improved image and customer service
     Improved access
     Sharing and cost reduction
     Reduction in risks

* Summary of chapter

Introduction

From humble beginnings as individual establishments offering food and shelter to travellers, the hospitality business has developed into a diverse global industry that includes a range of establishments from the most humble to international conglomerates that cater to the complex and diverse needs of modern society. The changing nature of international commerce—brought about by increasing globalization, the explosion in information technology, and the emergence of many new markets in developing countries—provides a compelling incentive for firms to expand their operations internationally.

The process of globalization presents both opportunities and challenges to service firms that aspire to move beyond their national boundaries. Various strategies have been developed as organizations seek to minimize risks and increase their chance of success in foreign markets. In particular, international alliances and networks have proven to be very effective in assisting firms to acquire the skills and knowledge required to succeed in international markets. Strategic networks have allowed service organizations to capitalize on the knowledge, resources, and market share of their international allies to gain an advantage in the developing global market.

This chapter aims to equip readers with a broad understanding of the international development of the services industry, with special emphasis on the impact of globalization on the hospitality industry.

The trend is global

Hospitality is clearly a global industry today—not only because of the existence of global conglomerates that cross international boundaries in their own right, but also because of the plethora of international interrelationships within the hospitality sector itself, and between the hospitality sector and other sectors allied to hospitality. In every category of hospitality business—hotels, restaurants, hostels, and so on—the orientation today is clearly global. And within these individual services, the trend of all business functions is also global. In every business function—whether we look at facilities and services, customers, suppliers, employees, marketing, advertising, sales, management, ownership, or shareholders—the outlook is the same. Increasing internationalization is apparent in them all.

Hospitality and tourism, taken together, constitute the largest sector of the service economy in almost all developed countries. And services in general not only contribute the largest share of the gross domestic product (GDP) in most countries, but also serve as the major source of employment in both developed and developing countries (Dicken, 1998). In every country, services are the basis of the infrastructure on which effective manufacturing competition depends (McLaughlin & Fitzsimmons, 1996).

Hospitality businesses today offer a wide mix of services and products that are essential to the needs of society. The products and services offered by hospitality firms have become an integral part of everyday life for many people. As noted in Chapter 1, socializing outside the family circle has become more common, with gatherings in restaurants, pubs, bars, and so on becoming part of daily life for many people. Going out with friends and family has become a popular form of social entertainment. As a result, in the past 20 years or so, the demand for hospitality services, beyond those traditionally offered to travellers, has fuelled the growth of the hospitality industry globally. Changing habits in eating, drinking, and entertainment, along with increasing economic prosperity, have opened new markets for the hospitality industry worldwide. Numerous hotel and restaurant businesses have realized the growing opportunities that are available through access to the international market.

Service export has become a matter of major interest to economic planners in most countries. The international hotel industry effectively exports hospitality services on behalf of the host country, and generates export income for that country. Hospitality firms such as Hilton International, Marriott International, McDonald's, and Sheraton—all originally based in the United States—are just some of the companies that have come to command a major share of the international market.

The hospitality industry, by its very nature, was one of the first industries to become truly global. Other sectors of domestic economies all over the world are following the trend. Indeed, it might be said that, in following the increasing trend toward globalization, other sectors of domestic economies have imitated the global example provided by the hospitality industry (Go, 1999).

From inns to internationalization

Early days

The evolution of the hotel business down the ages has reflected the changing economic and industrial nature of the market it has served. The earliest hotels were established to serve the basic lodging and food requirements of travellers and their livestock. Early inns were little more than taverns that offered a bed in a corner of a large communal room shared by travellers (Weissinger, 1989, 2000). The introduction of coffee in the 17th and 18th centuries gave rise to the French café and the British coffee house—early examples of the expansion of hospitality industries beyond the immediate needs of travellers to a wider social role that included lively discussion, education, and entertainment (see box). The industrial revolution, and the need for accommodation away from home, led to the development of gentlemen's clubs offering accommodation to members (Medlik & Airey, 1978), and in the early 19th century hospitality continued to expand with the advent of the railway—which encouraged the establishment of new and larger hotels near train stations (Weissinger, 1989, 2000).

Coffee shops give "hospitality" a new meaning

The British coffee shops of the 17th and 18th centuries offered more than food and beverages. They were centers of political and philosophical debate, frequented by artists, philosophers, intellectuals, merchants, and financiers. Because the entry fee was set at one penny, the coffee houses were dubbed "penny universities" in which, it was said, a man could "pick up more useful knowledge than by applying himself to his books for a whole month."

The wide social influence of these coffee houses can be appreciated by two interesting examples. Jonathan's Coffee House in Change Alley, London, was one such popular coffee establishment. It was frequented by stockbrokers, and eventually became the London Stock Exchange. Similarly shipowners and marine insurance brokers visited Edward Lloyd's Coffee House on Lombard Street. It later became the center of world insurance and the headquarters of Lloyds of London.

It was the coffee houses of England that started the custom of "tipping" waiters. People who wanted good service and better seating would put some money in a tin labeled "To Insure Prompt Service" (TIPS). From this came our modern word "tips."

The coffee houses of Europe in the 17th and 18th centuries provided a new dimension to prevailing attitudes regarding "hospitality" and, in a sense, were the forerunners of our modern hospitality establishments offering a wider experience than the mere basic products of traditional innkeepers.

Source: <www.realcoffee.co.uk>

The development of hotel "chains"

In 1898, the Swiss hotelier César Ritz opened the Hotel Ritz in Paris and the Ritz-Carlton Hotel in the United States. The Ritz hotels were thus the first of what we now know, in various forms, as "franchise chains" in the hotel business.

Following World War II, economic progress within industrialized nations produced an increasing market of business travellers and tourists. The universal acceptance of a holiday as a fundamental right of every worker nurtured the growth of tourism as a commercial activity. Subsequently, hotel operations came to be pursued with the same vigor as that of other commercial businesses. American hotels such as Hilton, Sheraton, Marriott, and others established operations in various parts of the country—thus establishing hotel "chains," based on the concept of full-service lodging establishments focusing on the needs of the commercial market. In the past 30 years or so, many of these hotel chains have grown into major multinational firms (Olsen, West, & Tese, 1998).

The impetus for globalization

The impetus for hoteliers and restaurateurs to seek overseas markets was multifactorial. One of the primary reasons was, of course, the exponential growth of the tourism and hospitality industries worldwide in the second half of the 20th century. This phenomenal growth was essentially due to:

* the general economic prosperity of countries worldwide (in some cases due to technological advancement bringing about economic prosperity far greater than natural resources would normally have allowed—as, for example, in Japan, Korea, and Singapore);

* improved travel facilities (making it possible for people to travel long distances safely, and in a relatively short time); and

* technological advancement (improving travel and accommodation facilities and functions in innumerable ways).

As the lifestyle and habits of customers became more global, providers of hotel and restaurant services followed them to serve the changing market. Firms such as the U.S.-based Hilton and Sheraton hotel chains pioneered the development of overseas properties, initially to serve the increasing number of outbound American travellers.

Following the success of these ventures, many hotel firms choose to enter the international market in pursuit of new market opportunities, capitalizing on the experience and reputation they had gained in the domestic market.

Many firms chose market expansion to move away from what they perceived to be an intensely competitive and saturated local market (Lovelock, Patterson, & Walker, 1999). Other firms chose to pursue the international market to gain global economies of scale when they perceived that single-country markets were not large enough to allow them to achieve optimum scale, and that firms that remained in a single country would be restricted in their ability to compete (Lovelock & Yip, 1999).

Internationalization for these and other reasons has continued apace. A study conducted by Olsen and colleagues (1998) found that, among the top 25 hotel chains, 15 companies operate hotels in at least 18 countries, some of these having hotels in as many as 68 countries.

Choosing an international location

Macro factors to be considered

There are four major factors (or "macro factors") to be considered when a firm considers whether or not a country should be part of its internationalization strategy (see Figure 9.1). These four macro factors are:

* economic;

* cultural;

* political; and

* technological.

All four factors must be taken into consideration in assessing any given country. In some instances, even though market opportunities might seem to be superficially

Figure 9.1 *Macro factors in the choice of international location*

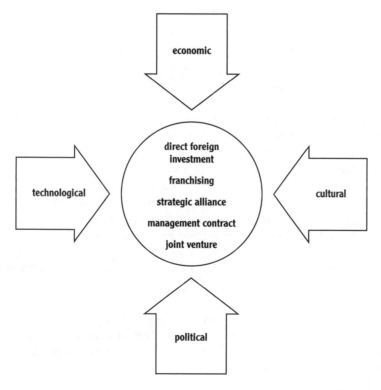

Author's presentation

appealing, a careful assessment of *all* of the above four factors is vital to avoid undue risk and unnecessary error. For example, moves toward economic deregulation in certain countries (East Europe, Russia, China, India, and New Zealand, for example) have lifted previous barriers to entry and made these countries more attractive for investors (Go & Pine, 1995). Firms contemplating expansion must be cognizant of these sorts of positive political and economic developments in making a proper assessment of potential expansion into various countries.

Internationalization factors

There are four major factors (or "macro factors") to be considered when a firm considers whether or not a country should be part of its internationalization strategy. These four macro factors are:

* economic;

* cultural;

* political; and

* technological.

All four factors must be taken into consideration in assessing any given country.

In contrast, negative factors might emerge from any such assessment. For example, what might be termed "political–legal distance" can have a negative effect on international entry (Berthon, Katsikeas, Constantine, & Berthon, 1999). According to a study conducted by Clark, Rajaratnam, & Smith (1996), governments sometimes use "mobility barriers" to control the flow of "contact-based services." These contact-based services are considered to be "pure" services because they exhibit all the distinctive characteristics of services—intangibility, heterogeneity, perishability, and inseparability. Consultancy services are a good example. In international contact-based services, producers and consumers often have to cross borders, personally and physically, to engage in transactions, and governments can impose barriers on the business (Clark & Rajaratnam, 1999). These "mobility barriers" include visa requirements, work permits, and demands for various other documents. Government policies and requirements can make trade in contact-based services difficult, or even impossible when conducted in person. However, many of these restrictions can be overcome, at least in part, by the use of advanced technologies including modern international telephony, network video, and the Internet.

These are just two examples of the sorts of assessments that must be made when a firm is considering a country as a prospect for its strategy of international expansion. In considering each country, a firm must assess the opportunities and barriers that exist—according to the four "macro factors" noted previously. Some of the opportunities and barriers to be considered include the following.

Economic considerations

Opportunities

* high growth in GDP;

* high standard of living;

* high average income for each family;

* high average disposable income of household; and

* developed information technology capability (or potential for this).

Barriers

* slow growth in GDP;

* low standard of living;

* low average income for each family;

* low average disposable income of household;

* undeveloped information technology (and poor potential); and

* economic uncertainty.

Political considerations

Opportunities

* political stability;

* government deregulation;

* a policy to encourage direct foreign investment; and

* friendly attitude of host country government.

Barriers

* political instability;

* unfair taxation;

* restrictions on repatriation of capital; and

* restrictive labor laws.

Cultural considerations

Opportunities

* rich cultural experiences;

* opportunities to modify services and products in a new cultural setting; and

* opportunities for service and products diversity.

Barriers

* language barriers;

* different local customs; and

* restrictions on consumption of certain products (e.g., cultural restrictions on consumption of certain foods).

Technological considerations

Opportunities

* enhancement of guest services;

* effective and efficient hotel operations and management;

* faster alternative forms of services delivery;

* closer relationship with key customers;

* improved ability to deal with intense rivalry;

* reduced costs and increased productivity;

* more effective communication; and

* downsizing of human resources.

Barriers

* incompatibility of technology in host country;

* lack of skilled staff;

* increased services might increase incidence of mistakes; and

* cost of installation (if required).

Special risks for physical assets

Because they have a "bricks-and-mortar" presence, hotels fall under the category of "asset-based" services (Clark & Rajaratnam, 1999). Asset-based service providers who rely on such physical assets are at greater risk than providers of "pure" services because the assets are also at the whim of host governments. Such measures as asset taxation, rules regarding the repatriation of capital, labor laws, restrictions on property acquisition by non-nationals, and manipulation of currency exchange rates can all have a negative effect on the business (Lovelock & Yip, 1999). Firms might therefore choose to seek out countries that have not imposed such restrictions on investors in the past.

Most industrialized countries have realized substantial revenue from service export (Dahringer, 1991). Hotels, restaurants, clubs, and all manner of hospitality services are offered in the world market by parent companies. They might be offered for outright sale as a real physical asset, but this business strategy exposes the company to the "asset risks" noted above. Alternatively, hospitality services might be offered as a "commercial idea"—in effect offering to sell the use of company name, or a particular brand name of the company, or even the technical or managerial "know-how" of the organization.

These various forms of exporting hospitality services represent creative attempts by companies to internationalize their product while reducing their risk of entry, reducing their risk of not being able to exit easily, and reducing other barriers to direct foreign investment. Such nonequity involvement in the international market—through franchising, management contracts, and alliances of various kinds—all represent creative attempts to minimize risk in various ways, especially the special risks to which physical assets are exposed (Olsen et al., 1998).

Cultural barriers to success

Hospitality services are "high-contact" services with a high degree of human involvement and face-to-face contact (Lovelock, Patterson, & Walker, 2001). Such direct interaction between customers of services and suppliers of services, if conducted internationally, involves intercultural contacts that have the potential to influence the sociocultural structures of host countries either positively or negatively (Go, 1999).

Difficulties in marketing services internationally due to such intercultural factors have been identified by Dahringer (1991). For example, in some cases "cultural distance" can create communication problems—both in personal verbal communication and in impersonal "external" communication such as advertisements (see also Gallois & Callan, 1997, for more on this).

Cultural differences can also create problems in appreciating unfamiliar ethical values, understanding various attitudes, and so on. In particular, if the service provider and the customer come from different cultural backgrounds, there can be serious implications with regard to that most important of hospitality issues—the perception of service delivery (Strauss & Mang, 1999). Because the perception of service delivery is of such importance in the hospitality industry, the modification of products and services to suit the ethos of the host community is vital for the survival and progress of international hotel companies in foreign countries (Olsen et al., 1998).

The hiring of local labor is an important strategy in decreasing cultural problems. Local staff members are not only familiar with local cultural mores, but also are well placed to overcome any language communication barriers that might exist (Contractor & Kundu, 1998).

Cultural pitfalls

A large hotel in Macau frequently recruited operational staff in mainland China. The rates of pay being offered (for food servers, room attendants, cleaners, and so on) were five or six times what the recruits could earn in China. Unfortunately, most of the mainland Chinese spoke Putonghua (Mandarin) whereas the language in Macau is Cantonese. Despite the language difference, the Macau hotel frequently received more than a thousand applicants seeking an interview.

To handle this large number, the hotel organized a team of 15 interviewers. Even with so many interviewers, the large number of applicants meant that each person received about 5 minutes. Upon this brief time, the person's future was decided.

As might have been anticipated, the hotel had a very poor retention rate among its staff.

This case study illustrates the cultural pitfalls that can lie in the path of an organization that embarks on an international strategy without due regard for all relevant local cultural factors. The company's desire for relatively cheap labor was understandable. But its lack of awareness of the language difficulties and its failure to put into place adequate interviewing techniques meant that the final result was far from satisfactory for both the hotel and its new employees.

International strategies must take into account all relevant local factors—including the very important cultural factors.

Based on Baker & Huyton (2001)

Technological barriers to success

It goes without saying that information technology (IT) has become one of the key strategic weapons for service organizations in recent years. Because IT is all about the rapid and effective exchange of information, often across international boundaries, the "technological revolution" has enormous implications for the internationalization of the service sector in general, and of the hospitality industry in particular. (See, for example, Wymbs, 2000.)

The topic is so vast that it is worthy of a separate chapter on its own, and these issues are discussed at greater length in Chapter 10, "Technology and Its Applications."

In search of global potential

Researchers have identified four factors that commonly motivate hospitality firms to expand globally. These are:

* sales expansion;

* product diversification;

* resource acquisition; and

* brand recognition.

Each of these is discussed below.

Sales expansion

Whether a firm is selling products or services, its sales are dependent on two related factors:

* the interest of customers in the firms' offerings; and

* the ability of customers to obtain those offerings.

In pursuing success in these objectives companies often seek economy of scale by increasing exposure in multiple markets. They might decide to enter international markets as a result of limitations in the home market—perhaps due to the small size of the market, or due to static or declining purchasing power among the people who comprise the market. Alternatively, a firm might decide to "go international" to avoid growing local competition in the home market (Kasper, Heldingen, & de Vries, 1999).

Many global hospitality firms derive more than half of their sales from outside their home countries. For example, the overseas sales of McDonald's are increasing at a greater rate than those in the United States (Yu, 1999).

The prospect of increasing sales is therefore a major consideration in prompting firms to seek opportunities through international expansion.

Motivations for global expansion

There are four factors that commonly motivate hospitality firms to expand globally. These are:

* ✻ sales expansion;

* ✻ product diversification;

* ✻ resource acquisition; and

* ✻ brand recognition.

These are discussed in more detail in the text.

Product diversification

By undertaking global diversification, a hospitality firm is able to diversify its services and products, and therefore its market portfolio, while simultaneously improving its competitiveness.

Because hospitality services are highly perishable in nature, the effect of cyclical and seasonal fluctuations can cause major concerns for hospitality businesses. However, firms that operate in multiple countries are able to offset the adverse consequences of fluctuations in any one country. Many firms take advantage of the varying business cycles and seasonal fluctuations in different countries around the world. For example, whereas winter is the slack season for hotels in the United Kingdom, winter is the peak season for warmer European countries such as Spain, Portugal, Italy, and Greece.

In addition, by gaining access to supplies from different countries, international firms can avoid price increases or shortages in vital supplies in any one country.

Finally, by diversifying into various geographical regions of the world, a firm is able to increase its overall market size, and thereby achieve economy of scale for its marketing initiatives.

Global product diversification is thus an important reason for internationalization in the case of certain companies. It offers advantages in terms of perishability, supplies, and economy of scale.

Resource acquisition

Firms often seek out all kinds of resources in other countries, with a view to gaining an advantage over their competition. The term "resources" in this context refers to all manner of assets that are valuable in some way to the company—including capital, materials, personnel, technology, knowledge, customers, the natural beauty of local attractions, and so on.

As a result of gaining these foreign resources, a firm might be able to reduce the costs of production and distribution, and thereby be able to offer cost savings to their customers. Alternatively, the new resources might enable the firm to offer a higher quality of products and services. Either way, the result should be increased sales and increased profits.

In seeking such resources, a firm might decide on a particular location to attract the talented workforce it requires to gain a competitive advantage and increased efficiency. Or a firm might recognize the benefit of expanding into a developing country to gain access to inexpensive land (and perhaps inexpensive labor). Even if the country in question has various political and economic limitations as compared with other countries, the acquisition of these valuable resources (in the form of cheap land and labor) might make the investment worthwhile.

In other cases, a firm might seek to acquire technology or "know-how" from a foreign country to give it the competitive advantage. For example, to produce decaffeinated coffee, Starbucks Coffee, an American coffee house based in Seattle, uses contractors with special technology and equipment located in Germany. This helps Starbucks not only to improve its product quality, but also to distinguish itself from its competitors (Daniels & Radebaugh, 1994).

The acquisition of valuable resources is thus another possible stimulus for global expansion, and this has particular appeal to certain companies.

Brand recognition

Some companies, such as McDonald's, use the same brand and logo globally. This gives the firm instant recognition, and reduces promotional cost. The loyalty achieved from global brands with a reputation for value is one of the most enduring of all competitive advantages.

In the service business, brands represent the "promise" of the firm (Berry 2000). An international hotel brand such as Marriott commands an advantage over others through its reputation as representing genuinely warm, friendly, and superior hotel service. Successful global service brands such as McDonald's, Club Med, Marriott, Disney, and Singapore Airlines convey clear values to both customers and employees around the world. Such brands therefore pose barriers for the entry of competitors to international markets.

By nurturing brand loyalty through familiarity and reliability of service, hospitality firms increase their brand recognition and ongoing brand awareness. And, once established, global brands are of great value in enabling the same firm to explore other opportunities by brand extension. For example, Marriott effectively extended its portfolio to include 11 brand extensions (Roberts, 2001) and to reduce threats from competition (Louro & Cunha, 2001).

Strategies for globalizing hospitality firms

There is a huge number of strategies for globalization in the hospitality industry. Through imagination and expertise, a wide range of such strategies has been devised. Moreover, many subtle variations on established strategies have been developed to accommodate the special needs of particular firms and particular circumstances.

It is therefore not possible to describe every conceivable scheme or strategy. We can only hope to describe such strategies in general terms. Strategies such as these, or variations on them, have proven successful for many international hotel firms, including such well-known names as Ramada, Hyatt, Four Seasons, Regent International, Forte, Club Med, and Accor (Lane & Dupré, 1997).

Five generic strategies

All hospitality projects should have a long-term focus, but this is especially so in undertaking an international project. To launch a successful international expansion with a long-term objective, a definite strategy is required. Five of the most commonly used international strategies are:

* direct foreign investment;

* management contracts;

* joint ventures (semi-ownership);

* franchising; and

* strategic alliances.

Each of these is discussed below.

Direct foreign investment

Because the intangible nature of services poses a higher risk for both investors and customers than does trading in physical goods, direct foreign investment is a common vehicle for the internationalization of hospitality services. In this strategy, firms use direct investment to gain access in the foreign market. Such a strategy is especially attractive for firms that do not possess a well-known corporate brand name.

A firm might choose to invest in a new operation or might choose to buy out an existing business, which is then absorbed into the original company. Depending on the particular country under consideration, such a strategy can have significant financial advantages. Buyouts are often favored when the goal is to gain rapid access to a new client base and personnel who are already experienced in operating in that market (Lovelock, Patterson, & Walker, 1998). Marriott International, for example, gained an immediate presence in Europe and Asia by acquiring Renaissance Hotels from New World in 1997 (Yu, 1999).

Table 9.1 *Direct foreign investment—characteristics, advantages, disadvantages, and examples*

Strategy	Direct foreign investment
Description	A hotel or firm directly invests in the host country's hotel industry and provides all the financial commitment, personnel arrangements, and technology required.
Advantages	Full ownership and direct control of the subsidiary
Disadvantages	(1) High risks depending on political and economic stability of host country; (2) difficult to find compatible local partners; (3) limitation on foreign investment or equity participation; (4) restrictions on import of special equipment, building materials, etc.; (5) lack of information on investing; (6) requirements for non-national employees.
Examples	(1) Singaporean investment in Brisbane Marriott Hotel; (2) Taiwanese investment in Sofitel Imperial Hotel in Mauritius.

Author's presentation

See Table 9.1 for a summary of the strategy of direct foreign investment—including its characteristics, advantages, and disadvantages, together with some examples of its use.

Management contracts

Some established hotel firms enjoy an excellent reputation for their management expertise worldwide. Investors understandably seek the assistance of such firms as part of their international strategy. In particular, investors seek their management "know-how" (obviously important for business success) and the use of their company name (with a view to gaining market acceptance). Examples include Marriott Brisbane (owned by investors from Singapore) and Sofitel Imperial in Mauritius (owned by Taiwanese investors).

A hotel management contract is often an agreement between a local hotel owner and a hotel corporation with an internationally known brand name. In this case, in return for paying a set management fee, the owner acquires the management expertise of the international firm to undertake responsibility for the efficient running of the hotel. In most cases, a portion of the management fee is a fee charged for using the brand name of the management company to market the host firm.

Many international hospitality firms use management contracts to gain market entry and gain international exposure for their global brand. Management contracts are popular as a vehicle for expansion into developing countries because the arrangement usually involves limited restrictions from the government and the local community.

See Table 9.2 for a summary of the strategy of management contracts—including its characteristics, advantages, and disadvantages, together with some examples of its use.

Table 9.2 *Management contracts—characteristics, advantages, disadvantages, and examples*

Strategy	Management contracts
Description	An agreement between a hotel management company and a hotel property owner whereby the management company takes responsibility for operating the hotel and managing its business
Advantages	*For the management company:* little or no capital required; *For the owner:* professional hotel consulting management.
Disadvantages	*For the management company:* less potential profit because no ownership of assets; *For the owner:* (1) additional management fees; (2) risks of investment (loan repayments and other financial obligations; (3) management company has little or no capital involvement and thus less incentive for creating value.
Examples (management companies)	(1) Marriott international; (2) Hilton international; (3) Hyatt international; (4) Accor; (5) Regent; (6) Holiday Inn.

Author's presentation

Joint ventures

Joint ventures involve part ownership or partnership between a foreign firm and a domestic firm. The agreement might include provision for joint interest in the development of the project or the management of it, or perhaps both.

Some host governments restrict the extent of the arrangements such that local firms hold a majority interest. Euro Disney in Paris is a good example. The French partners in this project maintain 51% of the stake, with the American partner being restricted to 49% (Daniels & Radebaugh, 1992).

If an international firm is not well equipped to cope with the political, economic, social, and cultural factors of a host country, firms might choose to use a joint venture to enter the new market. Conversely, host countries might seek foreign partners to gain access to capital, technology, "know-how," and brand name.

See Table 9.3 for a summary of the strategy of joint ventures—including its characteristics, advantages, and disadvantages, together with some examples of its use.

Franchising

A franchise is an arrangement under which a hospitality provider pays a franchiser to use an established brand name. The franchiser markets the brand, and often arranges reservations. Usually, franchisers have established a quality product, have marketed the

---

Five generic strategies for globalization

To launch a successful international expansion with a long-term objective, a definite strategy is required. Five of the most commonly used international strategies are:

* direct foreign investment;

* management contracts;

* joint ventures (semi-ownership);

* franchising; and

* strategic alliances.

These are discussed in more detail in the text.

Table 9.3 *Joint ventures—characteristics, advantages, disadvantages, and examples*

Strategy	Joint venture
Description	A multinational hospitality corporation provides partial equity involvement in joint business establishments in or with the host country and/or regional partners.
Advantages	(1) Joining with various industries to achieve high capability; (2) sharing the investment risks; (3) joining with local entrepreneurs to manage the cultural differences in the foreign countries.
Disadvantages	(1) Loss of flexibility to respond quickly to market demands and labor needs; (2) loss of control in hiring and firing staff and determining compensation packages; (3) loss of discretion over various other aspects of the hotel's management.
Examples	(1) Accor signed joint venture agreements with China, Korea, Vietnam, Malaysia, and Thailand for hotel development in the Asia-Pacific Rim; (2) Hyatt has joined with a computer company and SABRE to improve information technology operation.

Author's presentation

product widely, and have demonstrated their expertise in the field. The franchisee benefits from the marketing and management expertise of the franchiser, as well as from the bulk purchase of advertising and other goods.

Beginning in 1898 when the Swiss hotelier César Ritz linked the Hotel Ritz in Paris and the Ritz-Carlton Hotel in the United States, franchising has become one of the most commonly used strategies in the internationalization of hospitality services. Holiday Inn, for example, successfully used a franchising strategy to become the biggest international hotel chain in the world (Olsen et al., 1998). Similarly, through franchising, McDonald's has become the world's largest fast-food restaurant chain.

See Table 9.4 for a summary of the strategy of franchising—including its characteristics, advantages, and disadvantages, together with some examples of its use.

Table 9.4 *Franchising—characteristics, advantages, disadvantages, and examples*

Strategy	Franchising
Description	An arrangement under which a hospitality provider pays to use an established brand name, product, service, and business concept (including marketing strategy and plan, operating manuals and standards, quality control, and a continuing process of assistance and guidance).
Advantages	*For the franchiser:* (1) less capital investment; (2) fast growth and expansion; (3) additional revenue and profit; (4) potential for larger market share; (5) increased international customer recognition and brand loyalty.
	For the franchisee: (1) benefits of chain advertising; (2) access to the franchiser's international reservation referral system; (3) group purchasing arrangements; (4) regular inspections; (5) business advice; (6) employee training; (7) operating system manuals and procedures from franchiser; (8) assistance in obtaining financing.
Disadvantages	*For the franchiser:* (1) risk of conflicts between franchiser and franchisee; (2) high fixed costs of the reservations network over a large number of franchisees; (3) loss of day-to-day operation control; (4) potential liability exposure without control; (5) quality, service, and cleanliness control problems; (6) lack of control over pricing; (7) risk to hotel image.
	For the franchisee: (1) franchiser royalties and fees; (2) risk of conflicts between franchiser and franchisee; (3) excessive costs if incorrect franchiser chosen; (4) franchisers cannot offer owners guaranteed success; (5) difficulty and expense of transferring the franchise if the property is sold; (6) burden of adhering to various chain-wide standards that might be difficult in certain locations.
Examples	KFC
	McDonald's

Author's presentation

Strategic alliances

Strategic alliances are often formed between a hotel corporation and an associated service provider. See the box on page 300 for some examples.

In addition to these commercial arrangements, some service firms enter into alliances in the international market as a result of invitation (Lovelock et al., 1998). These invitations can come from governments, or from social organizations. The Taipei Hilton hotel (established by Hilton International) and the Westin Hotel Taipei (established by the Westin Group) are examples of such investment.

See Table 9.5 for a summary of the strategy of strategic alliances—including its characteristics, advantages, and disadvantages, together with some examples of its use.

For more on strategic alliances, see "Globalization through partnerships and alliances," this chapter.

Table 9.5 *Strategic alliances—characteristics, advantages, disadvantages, and examples*

Strategy	Strategic alliances
Description	Separate organizations share administrative authority and form social links through open-ended contractual arrangements as opposed to specific "arms-length" contracts.
Advantages	(1) Immense resources to compete worldwide effectively and efficiently; (2) minimization of capital investment; (3) increased market coverage; (4) economies of scope and scale; (5) increasing visibility of brand names; (6) cross-marketing; (7) avoids the creation of a subsidiary.
Disadvantages	(1) Conflicts among the parties as to what type of alliance they are consummating; (2) possibility of pitfalls and high divorce rates; (3) performance evaluation problems (difficulties on performance measurement).
Examples	(1) Telstra with Hilton International; (2) Marriott & Hilton with Pizza Hut; (3) Visa with Marriott, American Express with Accor, Sheraton and Hilton; (4) Holiday Inn with Thrifty Car Rental; (5) Westin with Japanese Airlines.

Author's presentation

Examples of strategic alliances

Strategic alliances can be formed between different sorts of service providers. These include:

* a hotel and an airline (e.g., the alliance between Westin and JAL);

* a hotel and a restaurant business (e.g., Marriott with Pizza Hut; Hilton with Pizza Hut);

* a hotel and a credit card company (e.g., Marriott with Visa; Accor with American Express; Sheraton with American Express; Hilton with American Express);

* a hotel and a car-rental firm (e.g., Holiday Inn with Thrifty Car Rental); and

* a hotel and a telecommunications company (e.g., Hilton with Telstra).

Variations on the strategies

As noted above, there are numerous strategies for the international expansion of hospitality enterprises. Apart from the five common generic strategies described above, McLaughlin and Fitzsimmons (1996) identified another set of five strategies, variations on the above, which service firms can use in globalizing service operations. They described these strategies in these terms:

* multisite and multicountry expansion;

* importing customers;

* following the customers;

* service "unbundling"; and

* beating the clock.

These are discussed, in brief, below and on the next page.

Multisite and multicountry expansion

Multisite expansion is often achieved by franchising, with the effect of "cloning" the pattern of service in multiple locations. However, direct cloning of a service operation from one culture to an alien culture is potentially hazardous. Because services require direct personal interaction between customers and employees, the exporting of a service concept to another country is limited by the cultural and social issues involved.

Importing customers

Rather than taking the service to another culture, a firm might attempt to entice foreign customers to come to it. This strategy—a strategy of effectively "importing customers"—is especially suitable for enterprises operating on a single site with a special attraction.

However, the marketing of single-site services is inevitably limited by time and distance because customers have to travel from all manner of places to the firm's single site. Tourist attractions—both natural and man-made—are constantly faced with such limitations of time and distance as they attempt to import their customers from around the world. Famous attractions such as the Egyptian pyramids, Niagara Falls, Disneyland, the Eiffel Tower, and the Taj Mahal are in this category, as are the myriad other places around the world that rely upon the attraction of visitors to a place of particular interest.

Internationalization by "importing" customers. The Hyatt Grand Champions is beautifully situated close to the mountains and scenic surroundings. Many of this international hotel's customers come specifically because of its location.

With kind permission of Hyatt Hotels Corporation

In these circumstances firms have to consider what is, effectively, a reverse conception of internationalization. Instead of internationalizing the firm, they internationalize their customers. This requires firms to plan carefully, with a view to managing transportation and other infrastructure to satisfy the accommodation needs and the various other needs of visiting international customers. And, in doing so, they must be sensitive to the cultural and social factors involved in attracting an international clientele.

Following the customers

Another approach to internationalizing hospitality services is to follow the customers as they leave one country and visit another. For example, in the 1970s and 1980s, hospitality firms based in the United Kingdom followed British tourists as they abandoned home resorts and flocked to the fashionable seaside resorts in the south of Spain. At first, the servicing of the needs of British tourists by British service providers, albeit in a foreign place, proved to be a flourishing success. However, overcrowding and a change in the interests of tourists (from sun and sea to nature and culture) considerably reduced the flow of U.K. tourists to the resorts of southern Spain, and the longer-term outlook of the strategy became less favorable.

Because the habits of tourists can change in this way, following the customers might not necessarily prove to be a viable strategy in the longer term. In addition, host communities are not always amenable to the influx of foreign competitors, and they might well take steps to resist what they perceive to be foreign firms "cashing in" on their local attractions.

Service "unbundling"

We have previously discussed the distinction between front-of-house functions and back-of-house functions (see Chapter 5). Because the back office is seldom seen by customers, service firms can effectively "unbundle" the back office to a location distant from the front office (Chase, 1978). For example, some restaurant firms operating several outlets in a single city use this strategy very effectively by moving most of their prepreparation to a separate location so as to serve more than one kitchen with ready-to-cook materials. This provides a restaurant firm with more efficient use of expensive space in downtown locations. Similarly, many hotel firms use the "unbundling" strategy to disassemble their back-office functions, and to subcontract various parts of these functions to professional firms. For example, many hotel firms subcontract their laundry, pest-control, fire, and security functions to professional firms.

International firms have taken this strategy further. They have "unbundled" various "back-of-house" functions from individual hotel properties and have set up functional centers around the world to service the entire group. For example, call centers, reservation systems, and marketing can all be handled in this way. This is an effective strategy for international firms to manage their resources around the globe, and provides economies of scale and efficiency, which can make the difference between success and failure in the international marketplace.

Beating the clock

In the past, distance and time zones posed a challenge to international management. However, in the developing era of advanced modern telecommunications, digital data transfer, and the burgeoning Internet, time differences between two locations have proved to be an advantage rather than a problem. Global firms can now utilize the new technology to combine demand from various locations in different time zones, and thus to improve the productivity of reservation departments, accounting departments, and so on.

In this way, internationalization becomes a useful strategy for producing economies of scale, and for maximizing the use of resources.

An overview of strategies for internationalization

Meeting the challenges of internationalization requires appropriate market-driven service strategies (Day, 1994). Handling the political, economic, cultural, and technological challenges involved can often prove to be very difficult. History provides us with examples of success—for instance, the success of McDonald's restaurants throughout the world, which has inspired many businesses to pursue international markets. But history also includes instances of failure—as, for example, the lack of success of the Euro Disney venture in France. Such failure reminds us of the challenges posed by internationalization, and the need for appropriate strategies to handle the specific challenges of each situation.

Each of the various generic strategies (and variations on them), as outlined above, can be useful in appropriate circumstances. Each has its place. However, one strategy deserves special consideration. The strategy of globalization through strategic alliance and partnerships is of increasing importance today, and is considered in further detail below.

Globalization through partnerships and alliances

Why alliances?

Cooperative alliances between competing companies have not been common in traditional business practice—unless some obvious and clearcut benefit has been apparent for both partners. However, globalization has changed the way in which businesses function and has fundamentally altered the nature of business relationships. Global competition has exposed firms to new challenges and forced them to consider strategies previously considered alien. The earlier sections of this chapter have examined some of these challenges and strategies.

However, despite the vast changes brought about by globalization, one thing remains constant—convincing the customer of the quality of the service on offer is essential if a firm is to survive in the new and challenging global environment.

It has thus become imperative for organizations to focus anew on strategies aimed at customer service and customer satisfaction. One such strategy is the formation of strategic alliances. Through strategic alliances, firms offering competing or complementary services form networks of services—with a view to gaining commercial strength and simultaneously delivering superior service and products to customers.

The rationale for strategic networking

The ability to offer customers superior value has become the modern business imperative.

Establishing strong links with customers and erstwhile competitors, serving the needs of all through strategic business networks, and thus gaining the long-term patronage of satisfied customers, has become more important than ever before.

Through strategic alliances, firms offering complementary services form networks of services—with a view to gaining commercial strength and simultaneously delivering superior service and products to customers.

This new business thinking recognizes the long-term advantages of collaborative arrangements among various complementary businesses, to the mutual benefit of all.

Types and characteristics of alliances

The term "strategic alliance" can refer to a variety of relationships between organizations. It can describe specific arrangements—short term or long term—between a supplier and a manufacturer for cooperation on particular matters. Alternatively, strategic alliances might be more diffuse and general, whereby partners tap into and learn from each other's capabilities in a range of activities. Irrespective of the exact nature of these "alliances," relationships of this kind are proliferating.

Thus various multinational companies share such resources as customer information, human resources, and logistical capital—with a view to enhancing the efficiency of both organizations. In the context of service operations, strategic alliances are essentially seen as tools for enhancing capability and efficiency in serving customers.

Definitions of a "strategic alliance"

The simple definition for a strategic alliance is that it is an interorganizational relationship of some type—usually developed to serve a specific purpose.

Palmer and Cole (1997) defined a strategic alliance as "an agreement between two or more organizations whereby each partner seeks to add to its competencies by combining its resources with those of a partner."

Howarth (1995) defined a strategic alliance as "a cooperative arrangement between two or more organizations in which the partners collectively agree on a group strategy that helps the individual partners to achieve their goals and objectives."

Although alliances vary in terms of details, Mockler (1999) suggested that strategic alliances are of three main types.

* Two or more entities unite to pursue a set of important agreed-upon goals. But the two entities remain essentially independent after the formation of the alliance.

* During the life of the alliance, the parties share both: (1) the benefits of the alliance; *and* (2) control over the performance of assigned tasks. This is the most common form of alliance, but it has significant management difficulties.

* Each of the partners contributes, on a continuing basis, one or more key strategic resources that are of particular importance to them—for example, technology or products.

Alliances are often multinational—indeed, one of the most common aims of firms that participate in alliances is to cross national boundaries (Harbison & Perkar, 1998).

Risks and success in alliances

Alliances can bring many advantages. However, if they are incorrectly planned, formed, and managed, many costs can also be incurred.

Because alliances require sharing of strategy, resources, and control, they are necessarily complex arrangements. One major critic of strategic alliances has been Porter (1998:66), who noted that:

> . . . alliances carry substantial costs in strategic and organizational terms. The very real problems of coordinating with an independent partner, who often has different and conflicting objectives, are just the start. Coordination difficulties impede the ability to gain the benefits of a global strategy.

Alliances can also suffer from inexperience, planning mistakes, failing to complete an adequate draft business plan, vagueness about objectives for the alliance, and

Air Canada's "Star Alliance"

A good example of a ground-breaking strategic alliance was Air Canada's "Star Alliance."

In establishing this arrangement, Air Canada developed partnerships with various other airline businesses, including some of their direct competitors. The aim of this alliance was to provide customers with significantly greater *flexibility* in air travel—considered by most travellers (especially business-class passengers) to be the single most important factor in assessing the relative value of competing air services.

"Star Alliance" thus established a service advantage that provided benefits to customers, and benefited all airlines comprising the partnership network.

Following the example of "Star Alliance," similar arrangements have become an integral part of the service strategy of airline businesses internationally.

incompatibility of processes and designs. In addition, because multinational alliances involve the cooperation and integration of companies from different corporate cultures, difficulty can arise when trying to manage the alliance successfully. Skills in conflict resolution, diversity integration, and crisis management are therefore essential to the success of strategic alliances (Mockler, 1999).

Howarth (1995) suggested that risks of alliances fall into three broad categories:

* the potential for undue influence of one strategic partner over the other in relation to goals and policies;

* the cost of the time and resources required for planning and coordinating alliance activities; and

* potential loss of competitive position by entering into an alliance with a competitor.

Each of these is considered below.

Undue influence

Control and effective management are important facets of any business. The potential loss of independence, flexibility, and position jeopardizes the autonomy of the individual firms involved. A firm entering into an alliance therefore needs to ensure that its own objectives and independence are not overshadowed by its partners. Tight regulation imposed by a dominant partner can easily reduce the flexibility and competitive position of inferior parties in an alliance arrangement.

Costs can accrue from conflicts between partners. If one partner fails to understand the corporate culture and ideology of the other partner, this can lead to dramatic differences regarding philosophies of business operation, and has the potential to undermine the overall stability of the alliance.

Inefficient use of resources

Another significant factor to be considered in any alliance is the use of resources. If not planned properly, financial and human resources can be used inefficiently, or simply wasted.

Loss of competitive position

Finally, a potential major cost from the formation of alliances is a loss of competitive position. This might occur if vital strategic information about one organization has to be revealed to another in the course of establishing the alliance.

Alternatively, competitive position can be lost if confidence in the forging of a stronger team is allowed to produce complacency. This can conceal the ongoing need for continuing innovation and caution in the business environment.

The importance of trust

Taking all of the above into consideration, it is evident that *trust* serves a crucial role in the formation of an alliance. However, trust in an alliance is not gained instantaneously. The complex subjective nature of personal relationships means that the development of trust is a lengthy process.

Howarth (1995) proposed that corporate trust is developed in three phases.

1. In the *first* stage, parties are required to cooperate and build early relationships. During this stage, initial uncertainties are quelled, and expectations are defined.

2. The *second* phase is characterized by a growth in trust, and the establishment of agreed arrangements regarding the interaction and control of parties involved in the alliance.

3. Finally, in the *third* stage, alliance partners are closely integrated, and a significant level of trust exists with which to forge stronger strategic objectives.

Usually this process evolves over some considerable time. However, this can be expedited if the personal qualities of the individual principals involved are compatible and harmonious. This allows personal relationships to facilitate the establishment of satisfactory trusting corporate relationships.

According to Child and Faulkner (1998), the development of trust is characterized by mutual benefit, predictability, conflict resolution, and mutual bonding. Commitments must be realistic and in accordance with the strategic goals of each partner— that is, there must be a "strategic fit." Conflict-resolution strategies must be agreed and predictable, and friendly personal contact must be regularly maintained between members of the alliance. With these initiatives in place, the interactions between alliance partners can be expected to run smoothly, and a sense of reciprocated reliability can be established between members.

Choose well in the first place

All of these ideas on the achievement of trust have merit. But a review of all the various hints and strategies for the achievement of trust reveals one indisputable fact—that the best method of ensuring ongoing trust and harmony is the selection of an appropriate partner in the first place. Trust can best be achieved when partners are selected on the basis of their exhibiting compatible characteristics, attitudes, and opinions. As Howarth (1995:27) observed: "lack of attention and effort in the search for a suitable partner can lead to the choice of an incompatible partner."

Even if firms in an alliance have prepared the best plans, analyzed all the costs, and formulated the strictest of objectives, the selection of an incompatible partner can ruin all hope of ultimate success.

Apart from these questions of personal compatibility, the choice of a potential partner is inevitably linked to technical questions of compatibility that go the question of why the alliance is being considered in the first place. For example, if technical expertise is missing in one firm, an alliance partner must be able to fill that gap by being technologically proficient. If financial resources are being sought, the prospective partner must be able to demonstrate financial stability. If a particularly specialized form of expertise is being sought, the potential partner must clearly have that expertise.

". . . precision tailoring and sharp focus"

A summary of the need to focus on the precise "fit" between potential partners was expressed by Harbison and Pekar (1998:13) in the following terms.

Through a strategic alliance, companies can select, build, and deploy the critical capabilities that will enable each of them to gain competitive advantage, enhance customer value, and drive markets. Their goal is to focus on the capabilities that they can use to renew their positions constantly. Competitive advantage in capabilities comes from precision tailoring and sharp focus, from using strategic alliances to fill critical capability gaps.

Purpose of alliances

The above discussion has covered various aspects of alliances as a strategy for internationalization. It is appropriate to draw the discussion together by summarizing the purposes and advantages of entering into such alliances. Figure 9.2 illustrates these factors. They can be summarized as follows.

Improved image and customer service

* improved image through international exposure

* meeting the holistic demands of customers

Improved access

* access to new markets

* access to new customers

* access to new resources, labor, technology, and knowledge

* access to new distribution channels

Sharing and cost reduction

* sharing research, design, and development costs

* extending life cycle of products

* general economies of scale

Reduction in risks

* reduction of insecurity of one market

* reduction of government, cultural, geographic, and trade barriers

* reduction in competition

* reduction in problem of lack of local resources (labor, raw materials, land)

Some brief summarizing notes on each of these follow.

Figure 9.2 *Reasons for collaboration*

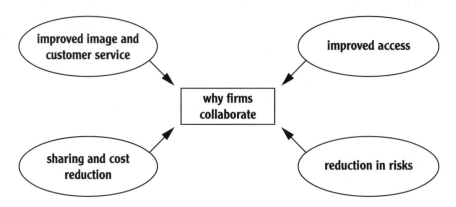

Author's presentation

Improved image and customer service

Alliance partners tend to measure the success of an alliance in monetary terms. However, a consistent theme of this book has been that customer satisfaction comes first, and profitably will follow. Customers judge the value of an alliance more subjectively and personally than the hotel accountants! They want good service and a pleasant hospitality experience, and they will judge an alliance on this basis.

Because a company's ultimate viability is judged on its ability to deliver quality service, which satisfies the holistic demands of customers, firms have a vested interest in forming successful alliances with firms of good reputation and proven service ability.

Improved access

Every company can improve its performance by improved access to new markets and new customers. And every firm, whatever its size and capacity, can benefit from improved access to new resources, labor, technology, and knowledge.

The gaining of new knowledge and resources through partnerships translates into new products and services to serve their expanded markets. This is clearly one of the major reasons for the growing popularity of strategic alliances in the highly competitive global environment (Mockler, 1999).

Sharing and cost reduction

A combination of strengths through partnerships can prove many times more beneficial then the individual capabilities of a firm standing alone. Sharing the costs of research, design, and development facilitates the development of new products, increases the likelihood of these products being appropriate and successful, and extends the life cycle of products.

In general, strategic alliances offer considerable advantages in economies of scale through sharing.

Reduction in risks

Strategic alliances reduce all manner of risk for partners. These include reduction of the insecurity of trying to survive in only one limited market, reduction of government, cultural, geographic, and trade barriers, and reduction in hostile competition by the formation of cooperative alliances. International strategic alliances can also reduce anxiety regarding potential scarcity of resources (such as labor, raw materials, and land) in a circumscribed local market.

Summary of chapter

The globalization of the modern marketplace presents business firms with both opportunities and challenges—*opportunities* to expand beyond national boundaries, and *challenges* from international competitors.

At the same time, the emergence of increasingly demanding customers has forced firms to improve the effectiveness of their operations to increase value to these customers.

Taken together, the move toward globalization and the emergence of more demanding customers has meant that, to succeed in today's turbulent market, firms need to enhance their competitive edge by improving their own competencies and by entering into alliances with other firms through the power of networking.

In the hospitality context, because hospitality services are based on fixed points of sale, whereas hotel customers are mostly travellers, the ability of a firm to cooperate with other hotels and service providers has always been a major advantage in strategies to improve service levels and retention of customers. Networking has thus been inherent in the nature of the hospitality industry long before the development of formal, structured international alliances.

Although internationalization and networking might, in theory, be effective strategies to protect and expand market share and to create a competitive advantage in the new economy, a practical decision to enter into a network agreement in a foreign market must involve a careful assessment of the potential benefits against the risks and costs. That is, although the factors and strategies discussed in this chapter are theoretically sound, individual firms should conduct their own research and design their own strategies—based on the actual circumstances they face in their own marketplace.

Review questions

1. Briefly describe the macro factors that must be taken into account when a firm assesses its plans for internationalization endeavors.

2. Outline the advantages and disadvantages of each of the internationalization strategies. Using examples, illustrate how a service firm might come to choose a particular strategy in preference to another.

3. Identify the potential risks and benefits present in a strategic alliance. What precautions should a hospitality firm take when joining such an alliance?

4. You are the manager of a resort hotel. What factors would you take into consideration before deciding to join a strategic alliance?

Suggested reading for this chapter

This is a list of suggested further reading on topics covered in this chapter. For a separate list of full reference citations quoted in the chapter, see "References," Chapter 9, at the end of the book.

McLaughlin, C. P., & Fitzsimmons, J. A. 1996. "Strategies for Globalizing Service Operations," *International Journal of Service Industry Management*, vol. 7, no. 4.

Olsen, M. D. 1999. "Macro-forces Driving Change into the New Millennium—Major Challenges for the Hospitality Professional," *International Journal of Hospitality Management*, vol. 18, no. 4.

Teare, R., & Olsen, M. D. (Eds.) 1996. *International Hospitality Management*, Longman, Harlow.

chapter ten
Technology and Its Applications

Study objectives

Having completed this chapter, readers should be able to:

✳ demonstrate an overall understanding of the role of modern technology in service industries;

✳ appreciate the potential benefits that technology can bring to the various aspects of a hotel operation; and

✳ understand the importance of utilizing technology to its best advantage.

The framework of this chapter

This chapter is set out as follows:

* Introduction
* The advent of technology
    - The technological boom
    - Services are different
    - "High-touch" and "High-tech"
    - Data collection empowers staff
* The shift of focus
    - Expectations of business customers
    - Translating information to strategies
    - The growth in alliances
* The internet
* Internal and external services
    - IT support for employees
    - IT support for customers
* Integration of marketing, operations, and human resources
* Applications of technology in the hospitality industry
    - Smart application is the key
    - Where technology works
    - Reservations and property management
    - IT networks
    - Guest facilities
    - Security and energy conservation
    - Conferences
    - Food and beverage services
    - Other services
    - Coordination
* Marketing and sales in the age of technology
    - Marketing and the internet
    - Smaller establishments
    - Electronic brochures
    - Versatility of electronic data
    - Database marketing
    - Supply and demand
    - Linking providers, distributors, and consumers
* Summary of chapter

Introduction

Traditionally, technology has always been viewed as the key to productivity in manufacturing industries. In recent years, however, technology has become an important catalyst in service firms also—stimulating innovation and adding value to the services received by customers.

The creative adaptation of technology as a distinctive strategic resource has had an enormous impact on the hospitality industry (Kandampully & Duddy, 2002). Service researchers have identified numerous ways in which technology has revolutionized service organizations, including the following:

* enhancing service quality;

* supporting service recovery;

* improving efficiency and productivity;

* offering convenience;

* augmenting the quality–value–loyalty chain;

* creating a competitive advantage;

* assisting customers; and

* improving the skills of management and staff.

All in all, modern technology has had a more profound effect on services in recent years than any other single external factor.

The use of technology in the hospitality industry obviously encompasses the technical aspects of the traditional hospitality business—that is, the use of computers, information technology (IT), the Internet, and various other technological innovations in providing accommodations, food, and beverages. But the use of technology in the hospitality industry also extends to all the peripheral processes and systems that produce an improved result—a better way of doing things.

It should be noted that the technology used might not be developed by, or be specific to, hospitality. It might well have been adapted from various other industries. But adapting "alien" technology to what has traditionally been a skills-based industry, is not without its difficulties.

Technology can play a powerful strategic role within a hospitality organization. It is potentially a functional arm that can traverse departments, and bring together various activities and people. The use of technology enhances the collective ability of employees by providing them with the support they require to offer superior service to customers.

There are numerous examples of leading service organizations that have creatively deployed technology to gain a competitive edge. One of the conclusions to be drawn from these examples is that technology does not, in itself, provide an advantage over competitors. Rather, it is the *innovative application of technology* that characterizes winning strategies.

Modern hospitality managers must therefore be technologically competent, and must possess an awareness of what technology can do here and now and how it might be deployed as a strategic instrument in the future.

The advent of technology

The technological boom

During the past 10 years or so there has been a massive increase in the application of new technology to almost every aspect of business enterprises. The exponential growth in the use of the Internet, for example, is enormous. Indeed, any estimates of user numbers are almost certainly out of date as soon as they are made. One researcher estimated user numbers in 2000 as being at least 550 million worldwide (Sweet, 2000) and, since then, according to one commonly cited estimate on the growth of the Internet (Greenstein & Feinman, 2000), we can assume that Internet traffic has doubled every hundred days.

This phenomenal growth in online customers has directly influenced the growth of service providers representing both business-to-business ("B2B") and business-to-consumer ("B2C") services (Wymbs, 2000). Again, estimates of numbers are likely to be outdated as soon as they are made. However, some idea of the size of the market can be gauged by the fact that, in 1999, it was calculated that more than 3 million traders worldwide were on the Internet, with this figure expected to increase fivefold in the following 3 years (Furnell & Karweni, 1999). And this in a market already counted in the trillions of dollars (Global Sight Corporation, 2001)! Little wonder that many believe that businesses without a presence on the Internet will lose vital business opportunities and jeopardize their competitive advantage (Van Hoff & Verbeeten, 1998).

Services are different

The impact of technology is pervasive throughout today's marketplace. In manufacturing industries, technology has gone beyond its role as a substitute for manpower to become a value-adding component for products. In the service sector, technology has assumed a different role. It certainly serves as a distinctive tool to improve the efficiency and effectiveness of services, but it also focuses and enhances the *collective effort of all aspects of a firm's endeavors*—whether these be operations, marketing, or human resources.

As has been argued many times in this book, the need for such a collective focus of the service firm in *all* aspects of its operations has never been as crucial as it is today, and technology has magnified this many times. Customers are aware of technological potential, and they demand that firms perform. To take a simple example, customers know that computerized reservation systems are available and should work. They are less likely to tolerate double-bookings, overlooked bookings, and similar errors that might have been accepted in the past as "human error." This is, admittedly, a simple example, but it serves as an illustration of the way in which technology has "raised the bar" in terms of customer expectations.

In addition, as competitors continue to improve their high-tech facilities to attract customers, even otherwise loyal customers become aware of what is available in the market, and are tempted to stray.

Customers know what is possible in the technological world of today. Modern technology thus presents challenges as well as opportunities.

"The bar has been lifted"

A recurrent theme of this book has been that hospitality firms today compete on the basis of *services*, and not so much on the basis of *physical products* (Grönroos, Heinonen, Isoniemi, & Lindholm, 2000). For example, there is often no apparent difference between the accommodation and other physical facilities provided by two international hotel firms. Rather, it is the *service* offered by a hotel that provides true value to the customer.

Earlier chapters of this book have repeatedly emphasized the importance of this theme—that hospitality providers today compete on the basis of *services*, not physical products.

The advent of modern technology complicates this basic issue. Modern technology makes superior service easier to achieve. But it also makes it more expected. And customers who are otherwise loyal are very much aware of what is on offer elsewhere from competitors who advertise widely on the Internet and through other media.

The "bar has been lifted" by modern technology, and successful hospitality service providers must rise to the challenge.

"High-touch" and "high-tech"

Adoption of various forms of technology has enabled hospitality firms to enhance customers' perceptions of the relative value of various service offers. The hospitality industry is being transformed from a traditional hands-on, low-tech industry into a global industry that utilizes technology to combine "high-touch" and "high-tech"—thus providing benefits to customers, employees, and the firm itself (Bitner, Brown, & Meuter, 2000).

A study of hoteliers from the United States, Asia, and Europe, conducted by *Hotels* magazine ("Technology Survey," 1998), found that an average hotel spent between US$50,000 and US$249,000 on technology during the preceding 5 years, and that this level of expenditure was expected to continue for at least the following 5 years.

Technology is thus playing, and will continue to play, an important role in customer-focused hospitality firms—to identify, communicate with, and evaluate customers and their needs (Cline, 1999). The personal touch will always be basic to quality hospitality service, but modern technology, deployed effectively, can make that personal touch all the more effective. "High-tech" augments "high-touch."

As noted above, customers today are becoming increasingly aware of the technological advances in the industry, and understandably expect higher levels of service. It has therefore become imperative for hotel firms to respond to this demand by seeking ways in which they can provide better value to their customers through the use of technology—both within the hotel's physical environment and in its cyber environment (Smith David, Grabski, & Kasavana, 1996). The relationships between a hotel and its customers, suppliers, retailers, and employees have been taken to a new level through the use of email and websites to communicate, seek information, and make reservations.

Data collection empowers staff

The collection, analysis, and digital storage of readily accessible information by hotels has become a powerful tool with myriad applications. Among other things, such data collection allows junior members of staff to assume responsibility for making on-the-spot decisions without the need to consult senior management. Junior members of staff who are empowered with decision-making initiative and customer information are able to meet the specific requirements of customers without delay (Kandampully & Duddy, 2002).

IT can also assist the sharing of important information between different departments of a hospitality firm, and between different levels of staff. This can effect faster and better decision making throughout the organization (Durocher & Niman, 1993). In the hotel industry, data collection, and its dissemination to the various properties within international chains, has become common practice in the pursuit of enhanced customer service.

Technology should thus be used as a tool to enhance the effectiveness of employees and the system in general—ultimately being reflected in increased customer satisfaction (Bensaou & Earl, 1998). But this requires employees who are encouraged and trained to collect relevant data. For example, at La Mansion del Rio Hotel in San Antonio, Texas, employees are trained to gather information about customer preferences for their database. This is further analyzed and put to use in customer-focused initiatives throughout the hotel (Peppers & Rogers, 2000).

As another example, the fast-food firm Taco Bell has a policy of using information technology with the express intention of creating an environment characterized by access to knowledge, a narrowing of management hierarchy, and enhanced employee empowerment. In utilizing IT in this way, Taco Bell aims to achieve productivity im-

"High-touch" and "high-tech" feed off one another

An Internet "visitor" clicks on a hotel chain's website. Why did she seek out this website from the virtually countless alternatives on offer? Perhaps she went to this particular website because of an enjoyable personal experience when staying at another hotel in the same group. And that enjoyable inter-personal experience might, in itself, have been facilitated by technology.

Perhaps this guest had been pleasantly surprised to have been welcomed by a well-informed receptionist who had greeted the new arrival as a valued returning guest—rather than as an unknown stranger. Perhaps the guest had been delighted to discover that the receptionist was able to make polite, in-formed conversation (without being intrusive) about the guest's home town, occupation, and journey to the hotel. Perhaps the receptionist had been aware that this guest preferred a king-size bed, and had anticipated that she would appreciate a copy of a particular newspaper and the booking of a par-ticular model of rental car for the next day.

But how was the receptionist able to do this? This personal "high-touch" service was, of course, facilitated by the hotel's "high-tech" database. Be-cause of modern technology, the receptionist was able to offer the best of traditional personal service (Zemke & Connellan, 2001).

So this satisfied guest, having been treated royally with traditional per-sonal service (made possible by technology), later makes contact with the hotel via its website (again made possible by technology), with a view to ex-periencing this superior personal service again (made possible by empowered service staff).

"High-tech" does not replace "high-touch"—they feed reciprocally off one another to the immediate benefit of the customer's service experience, and to the longer-term benefit of the hotel's profitability.

Hospitality firms are thus required to maintain a quality service that com-bines "high-touch" communication with "high-tech" communication—and one feeds off the other.

provement, product freshness, increased speed of service, and the delivery of services in the right way every time.

Technology can thus prove an effective means of supporting customer-focused hospitality organizations, and can empower its users to achieve what they wish to accomplish. But technology should always be the servant, and not the master (Berry, 1995).

> ## Marriott's huge database
>
> The reservation system of the Marriott hotel chain manages the booking of more than 355,000 hotel rooms globally. With 12 million customer profiles stored in its frequent-lodger program—probably the largest database in the travel industry—Marriott has collected an extensive store of information about the characteristics and habits of travellers.
>
> This information gives Marriott the opportunity to cross-reference the personal profiles of customers with their product preferences, and enables the targeting of incentives and promotions to be conducted with unprecedented precision ("The Wired Index," 2000).
>
> Staff members are empowered in their individual dealings with customers if they know that they are working in a corporate culture that emphasizes such a customer focus.

The shift of focus

Expectations of business customers

Due to changes in lifestyle—including changes in work patterns, travel needs, eating habits, and even the growth of multiculturalism—hospitality services have come to be considered a part of everyday life, rather than as luxuries. Hotels today do not represent a mere "home away from home" for customers. Hotels have also become a travelling office for business customers, a meeting place for conference customers, a sporting venue for leisure customers, a place of celebration for special occasions, and so on.

The traditional core offerings of a hotel—accommodation, food, and beverage—have thus come to represent only a small component of the package of experiences that customers seek. The newer service components (conference facilities, technology centers, in-room services, sporting facilities, and so on) present hotels with an opportunity to differentiate themselves from the competition using various service packages. Indeed, it has become critically important to identify and manage these new nontraditional service components because they constitute the value-adding elements within these packages.

Translating information to strategies

The change of focus from product to services, and the subsequent emphasis on customer satisfaction, have established a new paradigm that nurtures innovative strategies and approaches in the hospitality industry. In keeping with this, the enthusiastic adoption of modern technology in the hospitality industry results from its capacity to enhance the effectiveness and skills of the people who serve the customer (Blumberg,

1994). Information, in itself, is of no value. Rather, value comes from the insights gained from information collection, and the potential translation of these insights into effective strategies.

The growth in alliances

It has become increasingly common for hospitality organizations to enter the international arena through alliances and partnerships with various other sectors of the industry (see Chapter 9). Through these global networks, hotel firms are now able to enhance value as perceived by the customer, and thus are able to gain a competitive advantage. This reliance on strategic alliances has made it all the more imperative that hotel organizations secure global connectivity through information technology. Indeed, this has become one of the most pertinent factors in the success or otherwise of hotel companies (Cline, 1999). Porter (1985) has also emphasized the role of IT in a firm's "value chain" as a means of gaining competitive advantage.

The creative use of technology in various service firms thus has the potential to enhance capability, to reduce cost outputs, and to maximize personalization and customization (Quinn & Paquette, 1990), and is therefore an effective means of supporting customer-focused hospitality organizations (Siguaw & Enz, 1999; Siguaw, Enz, & Namasivayam, 2000).

The internet

The development of the global marketplace, especially through the burgeoning Internet, means that every hospitality business must improve its services. In effect, every organization, regardless of its size and location, is now competing in an international market. The competitive pressures of the global market and increasing customer expectations will force businesses to join the international electronic marketplace—irrespective of a firm's enthusiasm to do so (Gosh, 1998). The question is no longer *whether* to use the Internet, but *how* to deploy it profitably (Porter, 2001).

The introduction of self-service technology into service industries has changed the way in which customers communicate with firms to create service outcomes (Meuter, Ostrom, Roundtree, & Bitner, 2000). Some of the common applications of self-service technology in the hospitality industry include room reservations, food and beverage orders, and checkout procedures through interactive televisions (Bobbitt & Dabholkar, 2001). Internet organizations also invest in such modern interactive technologies to provide their customers with the latest options for two-way communication (Buress, 2000). This not only enhances communication with customers, but also enhances communication between firms (Grönroos et al., 2000).

It should also be noted that customers who choose to communicate through a particular medium usually expect the firm to respond in that same medium (Buress, 2000).

Internet retailers must recognize that the "instant" nature of the Internet means that customers who choose to communicate electronically are unwilling to tolerate delays. Indeed, many demand an information service that is more than prompt; they actually expect a service that is proactive (Richter, 1999). The proportion of customers who are comfortable using the Web for search and communication is increasing daily, and firms must be equipped to interact with these customers.

Not if ... but how!

The reach and influence of the Internet in the hospitality industry is huge. Every hospitality business, no matter how big or small, is part of the international marketplace.

Whether customers are seeking the grandest five-star hotel or the most modest bed & breakfast establishment, people from all over the world are using the Internet to seek information and make bookings.

For hospitality providers, the question is no longer *whether* to use the Internet, but *how* to deploy it profitably (Porter, 2001).

However, although the reach and influence of the Internet is huge and increasing, firms must still retain other effective means of communication. A variety of communication methods is still required (LaMonica, 1999). Indeed, the diversity of customers who use hospitality services means that a choice of communication options and delivery channels is still demanded (Porter, 2001). The tradition of personal interaction has been so prevalent for so long in the hospitality industry that it is unwise to rely solely on high-tech communication. The introduction of new channels of communication should therefore not entail the complete abandoning of traditional methods with which many customers are familiar and comfortable (Anton, 2000).

Apart from these general comments on the use of the Internet, more will be said about specific hospitality uses of the Internet (see "Applications of Technology in the Hospitality Industry," and "Marketing and Sales in the Age of Technology").

Internal and external services

IT support for employees

Previous chapters have discussed the concept of "internal" and "external" customers, and the related concept of "internal" and "external" marketing. In that context, the central role of employees in both service delivery and service marketing was emphasized. As in all aspects of the hospitality industry, modern technology has had a significant effect on service delivery and service marketing, both internally and externally.

The introduction of modern technology into these operations requires extensive planning and adaptation if it is to suit the customers of the firm and its employees (Bitner et al., 2000). Information, and timely access to it, is crucial in the effective functioning of various hotel operations. Information is especially pertinent in nurturing employee empowerment. Hotels can utilize IT to provide instantaneous access to vital information and, through this, to motivate hotel employees to embrace empowerment. This enables employees to serve both internal and external customers at an exceptional level by facilitating autonomous creative action by employees in any given situation.

Another major benefit associated with computerized systems is the reduction in time and money spent on training. The Promus Hotel Corporation in Memphis has built an integrated management system that facilitates training of staff and management throughout the hotel's various departments. The system is also designed to assist employees to clarify doubts in various situations, and thus offers online training and user support.

Apart from its role in advertising and reservations, the Internet is thus emerging as a useful training system for employees in chain hotels. Its real-time interaction is as effective as video-conferencing in allowing communication with a number of people simultaneously. Unlike video-conferencing, language differences can easily be overcome on the Internet. Training a large number of people simultaneously via the Internet also maintains the consistency sought by multinational companies, and provides definite cost benefits. For instance, using the Internet is less expensive than shipping training products (such as videos or printed materials) to an entire chain, especially if the chain includes properties in several countries. In addition, modern technology provides a means for training (one-on-one or group), without corporate trainers actually having to travel to distant locations.

The increasing use of technology in almost every functional area in hotels has added an IT component to every manual job. The ever-changing world of technology requires hotel organizations to seek employees who are technologically "literate", and who are willing to update their knowledge on an ongoing basis. Indeed, the need for proficiency in IT has elevated the general status of hospitality employees in the workforce.

Familiarity with information technology represents an important addition to the list of skills traditionally required in hoteliers (Miller & Cardy, 2000). The adoption of various forms of information technology in the hotel industry has increased the knowledge required by almost every hotel employee, and has become a prerequisite for success in the hospitality job market.

IT support for customers

Customers are often impressed when they encounter pleasant surprises—or moments of "spontaneous delight" (Bitner et al., 2000). To encourage such experiences, the Ritz-Carlton hotel chain utilizes technology to maintain a worldwide database of its customer preferences, and employees prepare themselves with pertinent customer information from the database. This might include such details as a customer's preferred name, preferred food and drinks, and preferred newspaper. Having this information allows employees to delight the customer with exceptional service encounters (Hart, 1996).

In a similar way, Marriott's guest-recognition system (see box) informs employees of frequent customers and their personal preferences. This system allows employees to offer special rates and to satisfy special requirements—such as a nonsmoking room, a king-size bed, an iron, a hairdryer, and so on (Berkley & Gupta, 1994).

Computer "games" yield "serious" data

Fairfield Inn (a Marriott property) uses simple personal computers and a check-out game "scorecard" to gain valuable feedback data from customers.

The game takes only 15 seconds to play, and encourages guests to "score" (and thus provide feedback) on issues such as the cleanliness of the room, check-in and check-out services, and the overall value of their experience.

Encouraging customers to play a "game," rather than completing a boring questionnaire, provides Marriott with customer feedback at a much higher rate than that obtained from traditional questionnaires. The "game" obtains feedback from 50% of customers, compared with a response rate of only 5% from questionnaires (Berkley & Gupta, 1994).

Integration of marketing, operations, and human resources

Although the use of IT in service organizations undoubtedly brings many advantages, the true potential of modern technology has not been fully realized because of a lack of cohesion among the various systems adopted. Although firms have utilized IT to enhance the separate functions of operations, marketing, and human resources, there has been limited effort to integrate these activities within a single technology to unify, simplify, and streamline activities. To gain the maximum advantage of IT, hospitality firms must:

* enhance the effectiveness of the individual functions of operations, marketing, and human resources; and

* utilize IT to link these functions together.

This will help management to streamline activities and to design processes that are compatible, interchangeable, and user-friendly (for both internal and external customers). See Figure 10.1.

In undertaking the first step—enhancing the effectiveness of the individual functions of operations, marketing, and human resources—management should seek IT op-

Figure 10.1 *Integrating marketing, operations, and human resources through IT*

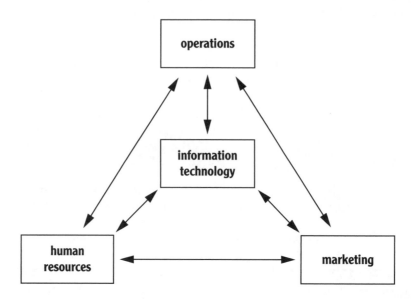

Author's presentation

portunities for innovation and improvement within each of these departments. Each of these areas should be viewed as being of equal importance, and management should aim to achieve a uniform improvement in the efficiency and capacity of each.

In undertaking the second step—utilizing IT to link these functions together—management should examine the interrelationships among operations, marketing, and human resources. The effectiveness of an organization is dependent on the efficiency of such interrelationships. Appropriate IT not only enhances the effectiveness of each individual function, but also coordinates the individual functions such that the collective output is greater than the sum total of the individual parts looked at separately. In effect, because they become linked (rather than functioning independently), each individual function pushes the others to the next level of excellence. The end result is a collective superiority of the network as compared with the individual activities of each department within the firm.

As an example of effective coordination between the traditionally separate functions of marketing and operations, consider the use of customer database information. Such information, which might have been collected primarily for marketing activities, is increasingly being used today to support daily service operations. The "marketing database" can become an "operations database," and can be used to inform operations staff about the specific requirements and needs of customers before their arrival. Apart from the use of this information in reception work (as previously discussed), the information can also be passed on to the food and beverage department to allow staff members to organize services in advance, thus surprising customers with personalized service. The creative use of technology to support employees in this way not only enhances their efficiency and productivity, but also enhances employee satisfaction and customer satisfaction.

In a similar way, information can be shared between operations and human resources. For example, information about service failure and recovery, as stored in the firm's operational database, can be effectively used by the human resources department for training purposes with both new and continuing employees.

Technology can thus serve an important function in hospitality firms in improving and coordinating the basic functions of marketing, operations, and human resources. This inevitably enhances the firm's overall effectiveness by converging the focus of the entire organization on its primary task of serving the customer better.

Applications of technology in the hospitality industry

Smart application is the key

Because of its capacity to offer creative benefits to both customers and service providers, technology has assumed a preeminent role in today's global world of business. Technology offers efficiency, consistency, and speed in the provision of all manner of hospitality services.

Consider the following examples.

∗ Technology is at the heart of McDonalds' worldwide success. The creative use of appropriate technology at all stages of the service chain allows McDonald's to serve food and drinks quickly, while maintaining high quality and consistency. It sounds simple in theory, but it is the creative and effective application of this simple strategy that is the secret of McDonalds' winning formula worldwide.

∗ The hand-held "SuperTracker" system gave Federal Express the edge over its competition. "Super Tracker" was able to assist the customer to track the status of a package in transit. Simultaneously, the technology helped the firm to meet its promise of delivering packets on time every time.

∗ American Airlines provided free computer terminals to travel agents, and then connected them with their own network. This move revolutionized its airline reservation system, effectively giving American its leading position in the industry.

In each of these examples, it was not the technology in itself that provided the edge to the organization. Rather, it was the creative idea and the smart application of the technology that provided the key advantage.

Where technology works

Various forms of technology have been used in this way to enhance the overall efficiency of hotels and other service providers, creating systems that are customer-friendly, and simultaneously facilitating procedures that have great marketing potential.

The use of technology in the hospitality industry has been especially effective in such areas as:

* marketing;

* reservations and booking;

* in-room services;

* security;

* communication;

* conference hosting; and

* billing and payments.

So she just walked out . . .

For many years, Ms. A has been a frequent and regular guest at a middle range city hotel. This hotel markets itself as providing a friendly, relaxed atmosphere in which guests can enjoy a "home away from home." Ms. A enjoys this style of service and has told many of her friends and professional colleagues about the personal service and relaxed atmosphere that makes this hotel more attractive to her than the more sophisticated offerings available from deluxe hotels in the city.

Unbeknown to Ms. A, the hotel has recently installed a new IT system, and is enthusiastically marketing its intention to use IT to ". . .enhance our already excellent customer services."

On arrival one day, Ms. A finds that she has not been booked into her usual "favorite" room. Her usual room has been allocated to someone else. Not only that, but when she arrives in her "new" room, she finds that the room has not been cleaned.

When she goes back to the front desk to complain, the receptionist, who has begun work in the hotel that very day, has no idea who Ms. A is, and clearly does not realize that she is a long-standing and valued client. As far as the receptionist is concerned, this is a problem for the housekeeping department, which has failed to clean the room on time. The receptionist tells Ms. A that the problem will be fixed, but Ms. A is left in no doubt that the receptionist thinks that this is really "someone else's problem." Ms. A is asked to wait in the lounge.

While waiting impatiently in the lounge, Ms. A discovers one of the hotel's new marketing brochures and begins to read about the "friendly, relaxed atmosphere in which guests can enjoy a home away from home," and discovers the new intention to use IT to ". . .enhance our already excellent customer services."

After waiting for a while, Ms. A returns to the front desk to enquire about progress on her room. She discovers the receptionist punching at a keyboard with increasing frustration.

"I really can't get this computer to work," complains the receptionist.

Ignoring this, Ms. A enquires about progress on cleaning her room.

"That's what I'm trying to arrange," replies the receptionist. "The housekeeper says that it won't be done until I enter it in the system."

Ms. A takes a deep breath, picks up her bag, turns on her heel, and walks out the front door . . .

Many lessons could be drawn from this story. As far as the use of technology in hospitality services is concerned, the following points emerge:

* the customer database of the hotel should have warned the reservations and reception staff that Ms. A was a regular and frequent guest with a favorite room;

* the "technological literacy" of the new employee should have been properly assessed *before* he was employed, not afterward;

* the hotel's marketing department, its various operations departments, and its human resources department could all use technology more efficiently within their own departments;

* the hotel's marketing, operations, and human resources departments could all use technology more efficiently for liaison among the various departments;

* in this hotel, technology appears to have become the master, not the servant; "high-tech" should never be allowed to replace "high-touch."

Hospitality firms must utilize IT to enhance the separate functions of operations, marketing, and human resources, and must then integrate these activities within a single technology to unify, simplify, and streamline service delivery with a personal touch. If they do not, more people like Ms. A will simply walk out!

Within these various departments and functions, the possibilities are almost endless. Consider this (admittedly incomplete) list of some commonly used technologies in the hospitality industry:

* yield-management systems;

* online reservation systems and automated guest records;

* computerized call accounting, message function, and wake-up call systems;

* smart cards for security and guest deposit tracking; in-room computers, email, voice mail, fax services;

* in-room check-out and customer feedback systems;

* in-room computerized mini-bar stock and billing systems;

* touch screens and electronic hand-held order-takers in restaurants (with a direct link to the kitchen and guest account);

* menu-planning and portion-control systems;

* inventory-control and purchase-ordering systems;

* performance-assessment, wages, and payroll systems;

* recruitment and training systems;

* customer, employee, and supplier database;

* customer-satisfaction surveys and research;

* ledger, financial statement, night audit, and daily and weekly reporting systems;

* cost-analysis, revenue-management, sales, and wages-information systems;

* online electronic locking, security, fire, and energy management systems; and

* Internet and intranet in all their forms and variations, including World Wide Web property-viewing systems.

This is a very long list—and yet it is incomplete! As with estimates of the number of users of the Internet, any list of technological applications in hospitality services is incomplete as soon as it is made. The growth in technological applications is exponential—a technological application in one area leads to the emergence of a new possibility, and this, in turn, spawns another new idea. The possibilities are endless!

Because it is impossible to list and describe every possible use of technology in hospitality services, attention must be directed to the most commonly used practical applications. The rest of this chapter explores some of these.

Reservations and property management

Of these many uses of technology in the modern hotel industry, probably the most important have been in the front office (especially reception and reservation) and in coordinated property management.

Mention has been made several times of the advantages of accurate databases that allow receptionists to streamline check-in procedures and to provide special moments of delight for a customer who discovers that he or she is not a mere "number," but a known and welcome individual guest. For example, Best Western International, in Phoenix, Arizona, computerized its reservation system and reduced the usually complex check-in procedure to a personalized welcome requiring little more than a signature from the guest (Hensdill, 1996c).

Computerized booking systems and property-management systems (as adapted from the airline industry) have enhanced the level of customer service and revolutionized the marketing strategies of most hotel organizations. Computerized property management facilitates access to information by personnel, and thus assists front-office staff to provide an immediate response to customer requirements. It also assists in decreasing or eliminating problems associated with human error and consistency of service by providing an easily accessible and consistent database from which to work.

Types of IT networks

There are, essentially, three sorts of IT networks:

* the *Internet*—which provides the firm the ability to interact with the external world:

* *intranets*—which are closed networks within an organization; and

* *extranets*—which are networks between associated firms to facilitate interactivity and transparency between trusted partners (airlines, travel agents, tour operators, and so on).

Sheraton Hotels in New York have recently introduced a property-management system that directly links their three hotels in the immediate area. This allows the hotels to integrate management and operational functions, and to maintain one accounting system. Other benefits derived from a common database include sharing of computer hardware costs, reduced staffing costs, and streamlined systems and operations (Hensdill, 1996b).

In addition, global distribution systems (GDSs) provide direct reservation access to third-party booking sources. Third-party reservation agents (such as airline and travel agents) can observe hotels' inventories, thus assisting the booking process by providing pertinent information direct to potential guests anywhere in the world (Mandelbaum, 1997).

IT networks

Hospitality providers use various types of IT network communication systems to facilitate communication—for example, between the head office and various hotels in a group. Such communication systems help hospitality providers to reduce costs, save time, and enhance efficiency. Many hotels (and other hospitality providers) also have network links with their own suppliers, and also with tour operators, airlines, and travel agents.

There are three generic types of networks:

* the *Internet*—which provides a firm with the ability to interact with the external world, both firms and individuals, through various visual and auditory representations; as has already been noted, with billions of users worldwide, the Internet is a burgeoning resource for hospitality providers;

* *intranets*—which are closed networks, using secure "firewalls," within an organization; such networks connect internal users, enhancing communication in all manner of business activities; and

* *extranets*—which utilize similar principles to those of external computer networks; such extranets are used by firms to create interactivity and transparency between trusted partners (airlines, travel agents, tour operators, and so on), helping to link alliance partners in the sharing of data and other operational information.

The real value of these networks lies not so much with advertising and marketing (the most obvious application), but rather as a new and exciting means of interpersonal communication (Murphy, Forrest, and Wotring, 1996). Networks allow internal and external communication with a variety of "stakeholders" on a range of subjects—including supplies, ordering, maintenance, recruitment, training, suggestions, complaints, forecasts, news, opinions, legal jeopardy, economic and political matters, health risks, environmental developments, dissemination of corporate information, and so on. The list of possibilities is limited only by human imagination. A huge number of interested persons can be simultaneously involved in appraisal of information, sharing ideas, and decision making. Or they can simply be kept informed of developments. The use of networks means that no one should be ignorant of what is happening. It is, of course, possible to "overload" people with useless information. However, if used with intelligence and discretion, networks should ensure the proper involvement of every person with a legitimate interest in new developments and decision making.

Nevertheless, although the primary value of these networks really lies in personal communication, it must be said that the Internet does offer hotels an unparalleled opportunity to market its facilities and services to the entire world. Prospective customers from anywhere in the world have an opportunity to interact with a hotel's website, including perhaps a "virtual tour" of the hotel and its facilities.

Websites can provide detailed information about hotels, including the room rates, various images (of the rooms, restaurant, conference, and entertainment facilities), and details of special features (e.g., the local beachfront). Some hotels provide map-based information featuring a searchable map and information on the infrastructure of the local city, perhaps with maps generated using sophisticated display technology. And all of this can be connected to local tourist information. The total presentation provides customers with a detailed visual image of the hotel and surrounding geography, and enables them to gain a useful perception of the hotel facility before they arrive.

Of course, Internet technology also offers customers the opportunity to make reservations easily and cheaply. This is becoming increasingly popular, and most major hotel companies are refocusing their technological resources in this direction (Hensdill, 1997a). All of the world's top international hotels have established Internet sites, each fully equipped with reservation capabilities. These websites have been phenomenally successful in terms of hits on the sites, bookings made, and customer feedback. For example, in the first 3 months of operating its website, Hilton Hotels exceeded US$1 million from online reservations alone, and Best Western International experienced a 100% return on investment within the first quarter of launching its website.

Front-line property-management systems and online reservation systems are therefore the biggest areas in which hotels have focused their investment in technology. It is

Selling distressed inventory

Wotif.com specializes in selling distressed inventory for hotels in Australia, New Zealand, and the United Kingdom. Using a simple business model, Wotif.com acts "virtually" like most traditional discount accommodation retailers—compiling special offers from various hotels and displaying them to the public.

The primary role of technology in this case is to facilitate speedy communication and to increase convenience for hotels and potential customers. Member hotels and customers communicate primarily through the Wotif.com website (www.wotif.com), which is designed in such a simple and straightforward manner that customers with even basic Internet skills can utilize it.

In this case, technology offers multiple benefits to all members of the supply chain, including:

* hotels—maximum yield, lower costs of distribution, and increasing operational effectiveness and efficiency by selling rooms 24 hours a day without increasing manpower;

* customers—low search costs because of minimum time and effort required; ability to compare and choose from offerings from several hotels; low risks with high information transparency; convenience and value for money; and

* Wotif.com itself—low investment with noncentral office space; low costs of operation due to low staffing level and communication costs; potential to expand the customer and hotel base.

Khanh La

important to note that whereas travel agents sell 75–80% of airline tickets, only 20% of hotel rooms are sold through such agencies (Chipkin, 2000). The services provided by online firms are therefore very useful to both hotels and to customers. Firms involved in this service include:

* leisureplanet.com—a business-to-business company that handles booking for more than 10,000 independent hotels; and

* LastMinuteTravel.com—a firm that offers hotels an opportunity to sell distressed inventory.

For more on the Internet and marketing, see "Marketing and Sales in the Age of Technology."

Guest facilities

Another major area of technological development is in services offered in guest rooms. Such facilities include in-room computing, shopping services, games, videos, and email. Many hoteliers believe that these developments are only the beginning. Again, it must be said that the possibilities are endless.

Being able to offer in-room fax and email services has become a necessity for many leading hotels around the world if they wish to attract and maintain the patronage of business travellers. A virtual email box allows guests, even those without computers, to receive email via infax. Through inmail, all guests who occupy an infax-equipped room

---

In-room "telecenters" in Kowloon

Business centers are becoming increasingly important in modern hotel operations.

The Kowloon Hotel in Hong Kong offers a large variety of in-room computing services through an interactive "telecenter" (Hensill, 1996d). Linked to a central computer, each in-room "telecenter" (essentially a personal computer) provides a variety of services, including:

* fax;

* printer;

* voice mail;

* external audio and video input;

* hotel services;

* shopping; and

* airline information.

---

automatically receive a personal email address—valid for the duration of their stay. It is estimated that infax has been installed in more than 45,000 hotel rooms in 17 countries. This technology is expected to expand rapidly in the coming years.

Security and energy conservation

As hotel crime has increased, the issue of safety and security has become an important concern of frequent travellers. An important innovation in guest room technology has been the development of integrated locking systems. These systems alleviate the anxiety of security-conscious customers, and assist management in streamlining operations and reducing costs. Most hotels use such computerized guest-room locking systems, in association with alarm-monitoring and energy-management programs.

With regard to energy conservation, sensors integrated into the locking systems can eliminate the problems commonly associated with control of room temperature when the guest is not in the room, or when rooms are unoccupied. At Comfort Suites in Nassau, for example, energy costs have been reduced by 50% (Hensdill, 1997b). Centralized locking systems can also assist in the tracking of guests, so that the cleaning of rooms can be arranged once guests have vacated the room.

Another innovation in technology that has become much more common is touch-screen control. This technology can be used effectively to control lighting, climate, radio, television, and drapes, as well as providing a complete telephone service.

Conferences

A special computer software program is used in many hotels to assist management with the organization of conferences and business meetings. The software reduces the

Some large hotels integrate marketing, operations, and human resources with the assistance of technology to host and manage conferences and exhibitions.

With kind permission of ONLA, Westerville, Ohio

amount of time devoted to managing event logistics at hotels. It provides a standard electronic template to assist managers with an operational plan for the conference.

As an adjunct to traditional conference business, modern technology allows for video-conferencing. This has become another valuable service offered by many hotels to their business customers.

IT at the Brisbane Hilton

At the Brisbane Hilton, "high-tech" and "high-touch" are combined to provide customer satisfaction. Information technology is utilized in four main contexts:

* for external communication with customers and suppliers;

* for internal communication among management and staff;

* for the provision of in-house services to customers; and

* in management and operational functions of various departments including front office, reservations, sales & marketing, and security & engineering.

All staff members employed in these functions and departments are required to demonstrate competence with the hotel's IT systems. This is complemented by the provision of routine training for IT skills acquisition and enhancement, with particular emphasis on front office, reservations, and sales & marketing departments. All staff members have access to computers and are encouraged to make use of the hotel's learning center, which facilitates personal development by providing access to the Internet and information on employment opportunities at other Hilton properties.

Email is used in conjunction with traditional hard copy for information dissemination between the various departments. The use of IT for communication has proved less effective in the context of the kitchen, restaurant, and housekeeping—where PC use by staff is not prevalent.

Managers at all levels rely on IT through PCs for communication and various other managerial activities including budgeting, forecasting, market plans, and so on.

Creative use of IT, integrated with a corporate culture of customer satisfaction and traditional hospitality good practice, enhances customer and staff satisfaction. The Brisbane Hilton thus views technology as a tool capable of assisting all staff members to enhance the quality of the services they offer to their guests, and to one another.

Food and beverage services

Food and beverage services are also becoming part of the technological revolution in hotels. The numerous problems related to food-service operations are universal. Today's hotel chefs are attempting to increase productivity and efficiency while, at the same time, cutting costs and improving the quality of cuisine.

Technology can assist in these objectives. For example, computerized combi-therm ovens can cook at much higher temperatures by pushing steam into the cooking box. This computer-guided system can maintain a consistent temperature using a self-monitoring probe that cuts power on and off, as appropriate, whenever the oven's internal temperature varies from the preset cooking temperature. Combi-therm ovens allow meals to be prepared close to the time of service, thus helping to eliminate over-production and waste (Hensdill, 1996a).

Other services

Other guest services have been significantly assisted by the technological revolution. Services as disparate as laundry services and children's game rooms have been revolutionized. Indeed, there is no limit to the ways in which technology can make customer services more attractive and efficient—for guests and management alike.

Coordination

Technology thus has a huge range of applications in the modern hotel industry. But the most important feature of modern technology is the way in which it has become the key that links various aspects of hotel operations, transcending all departmental boundaries (Olsen & Connolly, 2000).

Research conducted by Smith David and colleagues (1996) found that hoteliers believed that, as a result of such coordination, technology improved hotel operations across the board—including productivity, quality of business operations, accuracy, timeliness, guest services, and so on.

Marketing and sales in the age of technology

This chapter has already touched on some aspects of marketing and new technology in the hospitality industry. The advent of modern technology has led to considerable changes in communication and services distribution, and, of course, in marketing (Moncrief & Cravens, 1999). As previously noted, the World Wide Web has huge potential. It has the ability to communicate with, and offer information to, prospective customers all around the world. In addition, database marketing has become a vital tool in hospitality marketing. Some of the more important marketing implications of modern technology are discussed below.

Marketing and the internet

The use of the Internet has offered hospitality organizations a new marketing platform globally, through which businesses and consumers have the opportunity to exchange not only information, but also all kinds of products and services.

Meuter and colleagues (2000) defined the Internet market as "a virtual realm where products and services exist as digital information and can be delivered through information-based channels." The potential for global connectivity on the Internet empowers customers, and provides them with the necessary information, and a medium, to convert intentions into purchases (Wymbs, 2000). Moreover, the World Wide Web offers hospitality firms the opportunity to outsource their retailing of products and services, thus overcoming the constraints of traditional fixed points of sale. All in all, the emerging Web-centric business models offer numerous opportunities to hospitality firms while, at the same time, "raising the bar" with regard to customer expectations, speed, comparability, and price (La & Kandampully, 2002).

In recent years, an increasing number of Web-based businesses has specialized in selling service products such as airline seats and hotel rooms. As service intermediaries, these firms have successfully gained the interest and patronage of service customers because they are able to offer substantial benefits to the customers—such as a number of choices, convenience, and value for money. For the sellers, such as airlines and hotels, these firms help increase the effectiveness and efficiency of distribution, which, in a service context, are major determinants of the business success of a service provider. This is because the nature of service products increases the complexity of capacity management and makes timely distribution a vitally important aspect of the activity of service firms.

The effects of the Internet on the hospitality industry can be summarized as follows.

Strengths

* a flexible marketing tool;

* direct communication to ultimate customers;

* reduction in "no-show" bookings and cancellations;

* reduction of time required for transactions;

* reduction of promotional costs and brochure waste;

* reduction in workload;

* global distribution 24 hours a day, 365 days a year;

* interactivity with business alliances and potential customers; and

* provision of value-added products.

Weaknesses

* costs of design, construction, regular maintenance, and updating;

* increasing competition in the hotel marketplace;

* security issues (hackers and viruses); and

* customers cannot be filtered by hotels.

Smaller establishments

One of the advantages of the World Wide Web over other marketing media is its personal and interactive nature. When a "surfer" visits a site, that person is able to choose exactly what he or she wants—and all from the comfort of home. Having accessed the homepage, a prospective customer is able to proceed to select from various options—ranging from a skiing holiday, to visiting a major sporting event, to making a reservation at a modest hotel.

Indeed, smaller establishments such as bed & breakfast properties or guest houses stand to benefit enormously from a presence on the Internet. Most of these properties have no other means of communication with the wider market. In many ways, smaller firms gain much more than larger firms from a presence on the World Wide Web.

Electronic brochures

The use of "electronic brochures" to market travel and hospitality services is now commonplace. An electronic brochure is transmittable digital data about a product or place, with the capacity to capture interactive data, moving images, and sound—thus conveying the nature of the experience more fully. Once captured and stored digitally, data about a product or service can be transmitted over computer networks such as CompuServe, America Online, or to websites on the Internet.

There are several advantages to such online access. In particular, data can be updated when new services are added or taken off the market, and the hotel's costs are minimal because it is the user who normally pays the cost of online access. Moreover, electronic media have an intrinsically greater appeal because they trigger both visual and auditory sensation. It has been proven that sound and visual images, in combination, have a very stimulating effect on the customer.

Electronic data also provide users with the capacity to select and retrieve only what appeals to them. It is thus possible to produce what is effectively a "customized" brochure.

Versatility of electronic data

Electronic data have enormous versatility. Once the data have been captured, they can be accessed and distributed in a variety of ways—on a compact disk, through the mail as part of a direct marketing campaign, via the World Wide Web, or through interactive television (Pollock, 1996). From a management perspective, the most important feature of this medium is its potential for interactivity and, through this, its potential for allowing tracking of users.

Database marketing

Hotel organizations around the world have started to utilize various applications of database marketing. Database marketing affords hotels an excellent opportunity to learn more about their regular customers, and can be used to build customer loyalty very effectively (Schoenbachler, Gordon, Foley, & Spellman, 1997). Indeed, database marketing can provide a hotel with the critical edge in customer service. Customer records can be sorted and enhanced to produce useful information on target markets. Innovative applications have produced profitable new marketing programs for many hotels (Francese & Renaghan, 1991).

Database marketing creates new customer profiles and/or adds to existing customer profiles. Each customer has his or her own demographics and spending patterns. The objective of database marketing is to identify demographic patterns among a hotel's best customers, the aim being to build customer loyalty and to reduce the cost of marketing by increasing its precision. The database provides marketers with an understanding of the complex expectations and attitudes of customers. Hotels are therefore able to preplan services, even before the customers arrive, with a view to exceeding the expectations of the customer.

Customized service goes international

In some chain hotels, the customer database is used to ensure that preferred products and services are supplied at each and every hotel in the chain.

For example, among other things, Marriott offers customers a choice of rooms (smoking or nonsmoking), a choice of morning beverage (coffee or tea), and a choice of morning newspaper. Database marketing allows these and other offers to be targeted effectively to specific groups of customers, and even to specific individuals.

With regard to the choice of newspaper, modern technology can mean that if a guest stays at the San Diego Marriott and requests a copy of the London *Times*, the Miami Marriott should also have a copy of the *Times* available if the same guest later checks in there!

Supply and demand

To maximize their limited and time-sensitive capacity, hospitality managers are forced to consider several alternative strategies to facilitate the efficient management of the demand and supply (capacity) of services. To achieve the maximum yield from their inventory, hospitality industries have therefore employed various strategies (see Chapter 7). From a marketing perspective, service firms such as hotels and airlines are in the business of retailing their products and services either by themselves or through a third party.

Direct retailing can be undertaken through traditional methods (e.g., sales offices) or, more recently, through the companies' own websites. Alternatively, the distribution of services can be outsourced to third-party retailers (such as travel agents or tour operators or, more recently, e-business distributors). One of the widely acclaimed advantages of e-commerce is its ability to assist sellers in improving economic efficiency. Cost savings can be passed on to customers, thus increasing the ability of firms to compete in both price and service.

Linking providers, distributors, and consumers

Studies suggest that service outsourcing has increased rapidly in recent years (Kotabe & Murray, 2001), and technology has played a central role in this through its capacity to provide crucial links among service providers, distributors, and consumers (see Figure 10.2).

These developments have affected the hospitality industry just as much as they have altered the way that business is done in other services. Given the rapid development of the Internet market, and its equally rapid acceptance by consumers, it is likely that electronic distribution will continue to gain a very high market share compared with traditional methods. The convenience, efficiency, and low-cost benefits that can be achieved by customers and service firms alike ensure that modern technology has changed the marketing of hospitality services forever.

Figure 10.2 *Technology-based distribution channels*

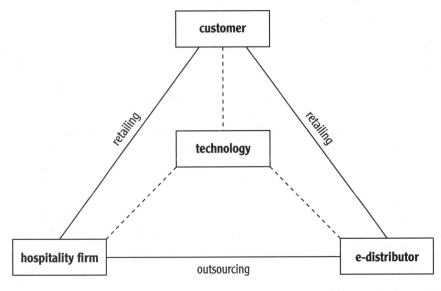

Adapted from La & Kandampully (2002)

Summary of chapter

The pervasive role of technology in modern society has had significant implications for business organizations of all types. In the service industry, which is traditionally viewed as a "high-touch" sector, technology is fast becoming a critical element in the competitive strategies of firms. In a tech-based competitive environment, firms are forced to update the technical aspects of their products and services on a continuous basis if they are to satisfy their increasingly demanding customers. As competitors continue to improve their high-tech facilities to attract customers, even otherwise loyal customers become aware of what is available in the market, and are tempted to stray. This increases customer expectations, and thereby effectively produces new industry norms and standards. In this regard, technology might not be a final determinant of business success or otherwise, but it is certainly an important factor in determining customer satisfaction and loyalty.

Firms in the modern marketplace therefore need to streamline their operations and increase business efficiency on a continuous basis if they are to maintain a competitive edge. In this respect, the role of technology is crucial in assisting firms to increase their service levels while reducing operating costs. In addition, technology removes the more mundane tasks from service employees, allowing them to focus more on customer service activities and professional development.

The application of technology can thus significantly influence the firm's marketing and management practices—with wider effects on various aspects of the business, including service quality, employee performance, and customer relationship. Technology, if properly managed, will reach out of its utilitarian functions and become a strategic tool that can assist firms to gain a competitive advantage. However, the strategic implementation of technology must be done with the utmost care so as not to jeopardize a firm's market position and financial resources.

Technology today is an integral part of hospitality services. The increasing application of technology in all areas of hotel functions means that the traditional perception of hospitality as a "low-tech" industry no longer holds true. As such, technological capability is becoming an imperative—not only for mid-level managers and front-line employees, but also for senior managers and back-of-house personnel. Therefore, hoteliers who are well versed in technological applications will be able to improve their managerial effectiveness and are thus more likely to succeed in their careers.

Review questions

1. Summarize the potential usefulness of technology in a hotel operation, both internally and externally.

2. Describe the concept of database marketing. What is the role of technology in database marketing?

3. The high-tech service environment greatly enhances the access of service staff to information, and the ability to make decisions. In your opinion, will this affect the role of mid-level managers? How?

Suggested reading for this chapter

This is a list of suggested further reading on topics covered in this chapter. For a separate list of full reference citations quoted in the chapter, see "References," Chapter 10, at the end of the book.

Bitner, M., & Meuter, M. 2000. "Technology Infusion in Service Encounters," *Journal of the Academy of Marketing Science,* vol. 28, no. 1, pp. 138–149.

Bobbitt, M., & Dabholkar, P. 2001. "Integrating Attitudinal Theories to Understand and Predict Use of Technology-Based Self Service; the Internet as an Illustration," *International Journal of Service Industry Management,* vol. 12, no. 5, pp 423–450.

Cusack, M. 1998. *Online Customer Care: Applying Today's Technology to Achieve World-Class Customer Interaction,* ASQ Quality Press.

Dabholkar, P. A. 2000. "Technology in service delivery: Implications for self-service and service support," in Swartz. T. A., & Iacobucci, D. (Eds.), *Handbook of Services Marketing and Management,* Sage Beverly Hills, California, pp. 103–110.

Fitzsimmons, J., & Fitzsimmons, M. 1998. *Service Management: Operation, Strategy, and Information Technology,* McGraw-Hill, Boston.

Olsen, M., & Connolly, D. 2000. "Experience-Based Travel: How Technology is Changing the Hospitality Industry," *The Cornell Hotel and Restaurant Administration Quarterly,* vol. 41, issue 1.

Piccolie, G., Spalding, B., & Ives. B. 2001. "The Customer-Service Life Cycle: A Framework for Improving Customer Service through Information Technology," *Cornell Hotel and Restaurant Administration Quarterly,* June, pp. 38–45.

chapter eleven

Implications of the New Paradigm in Hospitality

Earlier chapters in this book have examined various aspects of the new paradigm in hospitality—that the hospitality business is essentially a *services* business, and that the appropriate management philosophy is therefore one of *services management*.

This final chapter in the book reviews some of the major challenges facing hospitality managers today, and discusses the implications of these challenges for the future.

Evolving imperatives

The metamorphosis of the hospitality industry in the past decade has transformed the industry. In terms of the service offerings and business management now required, the changes have been quite profound. In the past, hospitality firms focused primarily on the sale of accommodation, food, and beverages—albeit with an awareness of a steadily growing demand for better service in delivering these basic products. The more recent transformation of the industry is in line with the general phenomenon of globalization in all industries—such that the international hospitality market now effectively constitutes a benchmark for all players in the industry. Hospitality firms have realized that a continuing focus on operations (i.e., the traditional hospitality skills involved in providing accommodation and in preparing and serving food) is inadequate against this international benchmark.

There is clearly a need for a new conceptual framework to support the business strategies and operational methods required to meet the emerging imperatives of a global hospitality industry. These emerging imperatives will be addressed briefly in this chapter under four broad, but interrelated, themes:

* the growing service element in product offerings;

* the increasing focus on the customer;

* the changing focus from price to value; and

* the growing importance of technology in hospitality operations.

The growing service element in product offerings

Almost all hospitality product offerings are being complemented by an increasing emphasis on the provision of service to fulfill the requirements of customers. In an effort to customize hospitality offerings to individual needs, it has become essential for firms to increase the service component of their offerings to enhance the value of the product.

Because hospitality products are difficult (if not impossible) to patent, competing firms are able to emulate one another's basic product offerings, and it is therefore the customer-focused service component of a product that provides a true competitive advantage. For example, the service component of a hotel's accommodation offer, personified by the staff who deliver that service, distinguishes one hospitality establishment from an essentially similar rival. The service component allows for flexibility and innovation in attending to customers' individual needs.

Thus it is that hospitality firms have increasingly recognized the importance of the service aspect of their products. This can only increase and intensify in the years ahead.

The increasing focus on the customer

Increasing competition has meant that most hospitality firms have had very little option other than to serve larger markets in an effort to remain viable. However, in the process, it has become increasingly difficult to maintain a personalized approach to the needs of individual customers. Despite the difficulties involved, it is essential in a highly competitive market that hospitality firms continue to develop close relationships with customers with a view to gaining their enduring patronage.

Hospitality establishments must appreciate that it is more efficient and profitable to nurture and maintain the loyalty of their present customers than it is to seek new customers. Hospitality managers must increasingly focus on developing and maintaining individual personal relationships with customers. In this regard, the adoption and creative use of technology can be of the utmost importance.

Technology can help firms to interact more effectively with customers in forming initial relationships, and to sustain these relationships through the acquisition of pertinent data on the present and changing needs of the customers involved. An effective customer database can help firms to make strategic customer-focused decisions, and can assist employees to provide appropriate personalized service.

The changing focus from price to value

The challenges of the hypercompetitive global market have convinced managers of the difficulty of competing in the marketplace on the basis of price alone. Because the marketplace can offer customers an almost unlimited number of options and prices, a choice on the basis of perceived quality will increasingly become the primary attraction for prospective customers.

Maintaining the quality of products requires significant ongoing financial invest-ment, and this inevitably brings increasing cost pressures. A strategy of competing on the basis of price alone is therefore a difficult strategy to maintain in the long term. It is therefore increasingly likely that a firm's market strength—in terms of value as per-ceived by customers—will increasingly depend on the quality of its relationships with various internal and external stakeholders.

Moreover, the notion of "value creation" will increasingly become a function of man-aging the "performance gap" by continuously improving a firm's performance in terms of quality, cost, cycle time, and productivity. In the future, customers will undoubtedly seek higher value in the form of greater benefit, rather than seeking higher value in the form of lower price. Firms are thus presented with a great opportunity to gain and maintain market share in terms of loyalty—value gained in return for value offered. And a firm's ability to add value on an ongoing basis will ultimately depend on the relationships it is able to nurture and maintain—both inside and outside the organization.

The growing importance of technology in hospitality operations

The advent of new technology has affected hospitality firms more than any other sin-gle external factor in recent times, and has changed the traditional concept of interac-tion forever. A hospitality firm's ability to interact effectively with its customers and its networks of partners ultimately determines the success of the firm.

In the past, technology has traditionally been viewed in terms of increased produc-tivity of goods. However, within the extended role of services in the hospitality indus-try, technology has become a primary catalyst in helping hospitality firms to innovate their service offers. Adoption of technology has provided hospitality firms with an op-portunity to enhance efficiency and add greater value to both internal and external networks of stakeholders. But the impact of new technology in the hospitality industry does not reside in the technology itself; rather, it lies in the *creative utilization* of that technology as a unique strategic functional resource.

The development of wide-ranging multiple networks of partners and customers has extended the traditional concept of "high-touch" hospitality interaction. Interaction and communication in the future will increasingly become "high-tech" as firms aim to ac-quire knowledge, gain expertise, build competency, and add value. Although the Inter-net, in particular, is a remarkably efficient means of customer communication, it is rather a more impersonal than traditional means of communication in the hospitality industry. To maintain a personal touch in these circumstances, hospitality firms will have to be especially aware of the importance of utilizing both "high touch" and "high-tech" techniques in delivering service if they are to continue to treat their customers as individuals.

Present directions and future predictions suggest that successful hospitality firms will have to operate globally within networks of operations. Although family-owned independent operations will undoubtedly continue to exist, the advent of the Internet has meant that every firm, no matter how small, is a player in the international marketplace. People from all over the world use the Internet to seek out even the most modest hospitality establishments. In that context, many smaller firms will seek partnership with larger firms or networks to gain access to a range of benefits.

These developments are also likely to see an acceleration in firms moving from a "generalist" approach to a more specialized niche in the industry, thereby gaining acceptance within the network, and globally, as a recognizable specialist provider. Direct competition among firms is therefore likely to diminish rapidly as firms seek to market themselves in particular niches. Similarly, large firms that previously maintained multiple operations and portfolios are likely to seek to distinguish their specialist niche skills under specific brands.

The development of new technology has thus led to considerable changes in hospitality business practices, particularly those that relate to marketing, communication, and distribution. Technology will play an increasing role in the direct and indirect retailing of services, and as a crucial link among service providers, distributors, and consumers. In particular, given the rapid development of the Internet market, and its ready acceptance by consumers, it is likely that electronic marketing and distribution will continue to grow exponentially.

Services management: the new paradigm in hospitality

This book has therefore addressed the need for hospitality managers to adopt a new management paradigm—in essence, the paradigm of services management. The fact is that hospitality establishments offer *services* to fulfill the needs of customers. They do not merely sell accommodations, food, beverage, and entertainment. Because the quality of hospitality services is constituted by *the experience of the customer,* a services management perspective is entirely appropriate for hospitality management. Hospitality providers are essentially in the business of providing services rather than goods; their management orientation should therefore be that of services management rather than that of goods management.

In adopting this new paradigm, the *human element* (both employees and customers) is absolutely crucial. In selling services, hospitality enterprises are "selling" personal relationships. Hospitality managers who conceptualize their hospitality offerings as being essentially *service offerings* conducted in a framework of human relationships will gain a new understanding of their business, and will be well placed to design, reengineer, and market their offerings to meet the demands of the new millennium.

References

ONE The Metamorphosis of Services

Albrecht, K., & Zemke, R. 1985, 1990. *Service America: Doing Business in the New Economy,* Dow Jones Irwin, Homewood, Illinois.

Aronsson, L. 2000. *The Development of Sustainable Tourism,* Continuum, London.

Aston, R. 2000. *Ecotourism: Sustainable Nature and Conservation Based Tourism,* Krieger Publishing, Melbourne.

Australian Bureau of Statistics (ABS) 2000. *Yearbook Australia,* Number 82, Canberra.

Bell, C. R., & Zemke, R. 1990. "Service Management: a Performing Art," paper presented at the "Quality in Services Conference 2," St John's University.

Berry, L. L. 1980. "Services Marketing is Different," *Business,* May–June, pp. 24–29.

Brunell, K., Kelley, E., & Ramesan, J. 1992. *A Framework for Using the "Voice of the Customer" to Design Services,* Center for Services Marketing and Management, Florida Atlantic University.

Edvardsson, B., & Gustavsson, B. 1992. *Problem Detection in Service Management Systems: A Consistency Approach to Quality Improvement,* QUIS-2, Business Research Institute at St John's University, New York, pp. 231–250.

Elliott, M. 1991. "Broadening the Mind: A Survey of World Travel and Tourism," *Economist,* vol. 318, March 23.

Engel, E. 1857. "Die Production–und Consumptionsverhaltnisse des Königreichs Sachsen," in *Zeitschrift der Statistischen Bureaus des Königlich Sachsischen Ministerium des Inneren,* Nos. 8 and 9, no. 22, 1857; republished in *Bulletin de l'Institute International de Statistique,* IX (1895).

Goeldner, C. R. 1992. "Trends in North American Tourism," *American Behavioral Scientist,* vol. 36, no. 2, November 1992.

Goeldner, C. R. 2000. *Tourism: Principles, Practices, Philosophies,* 8th ed., Wiley, New York.

Gourville, J. T., & Soman, D. 2001. "The Potential Downside of Bundling: How Packaging Services Can Hurt Consumption," *Cornell Hotel and Restaurant Administration Quarterly,* June, pp. 29–37.

Hall, C. M., & Page, S. J. 1999. *The Geography of Tourism and Recreation: Environment, Place and Space,* Routledge, London.

Hall, C. M., & Weiler, B. 1992. "What's Special about Special Interest Tourism?," in Weiler, B., & Hall, C. M. (eds.), *Special Interest Tourism,* Belhaven Press, London.

Kalinowski, M. K., & Weiler, B. 1992. "Educational Travel," Weiler, B. & Hall, C. M. (eds.), in *Special Interest Tourism,* Belhaven Press, London.

Lawrence, T. B., Wickens, D., & Phillips, N. 1997. "Managing Legitimacy in Ecotourism," *Tourism Management,* vol. 18, no. 5, pp. 307–316.

Lovelock, C. H., Patterson, P. G., & Walker, R. H. 1998. *Services Marketing,* Prentice-Hall, Sydney, Australia.

Normann, R. 1984, 2000. *Service Management: Strategy and Leadership in Service Business,* John Wiley, New York.

NZ 2000, *New Zealand Year Book,* 2000.

O'Rourke, B. 1990. *The Global Classroom,* An International Symposium on Educational Tourism, Department of Continuing Education, University of Canterbury, Christchurch, NZ.

Pearce, P. L. 1988. *The Ulysses Factors: Evaluating Visitors in Tourist Settings,* Springer-Verlag, New York.

Rust, R. T., Zahorik, A. J., & Keiningham, T. L. 1996. *Service Marketing,* HarperCollins, New York.

Shaw, G., & Williams, A. M. 1990. *Tourism and Development in Western Europe: Challenge and Change,* David Pinder (ed.), Institute of British Geographers, Belhaven Press, London.

Shostack, L. 1977. "Breaking Free from Product Marketing," *Journal of Marketing,* 41, April, pp. 73–80.

Smith, V. L., & Eadington, W. R. 1992. *Tourism Alternatives; Potentials and Problems in the Development of Tourism,* University of Pennsylvania Press, Philadelphia.

Williams, M. A., & Shaw, G. 1992. "Tourism Research," *American Behavioral Scientist,* vol. 36, no. 2, pp. 133–143.

Wood, C. 1992. "Australians Studying Abroad: A Private Sector Success Story in Educational Tourism, Weiler, B., & Hall, C. M. (eds.), *Special Interest Tourism,* Belhaven Press, London.

World Tourism Organization (WTO) 1991. *Tourism to the Year 2000: Qualitative Aspects Affecting Global Growth,* WTO, Madrid.

World Travel and Tourism Council (WTTC) 2001. "Building Human Capital," <www.wttc.org/resourcecentre/publications.asp>.

WTO *see* World Tourism Organization (WTO).

WTTC *see* World Travel and Tourism Council (WTTC).

Yu, L. 1999. *The International Hospitality Business, Management and Operations,* Haworth Hospitality Press, New York.

Zeppel, H. 1999. *Aboriginal Tourism in Australia: A Research Bibliography,* CRC for Sustainable Tourism, Gold Coast, Queensland.

Zeppel, H., & Hall, C. M. 1992. "Arts and Heritage Tourism," Weiler, B., & Hall, C. M. (eds.), *Special Interest Tourism,* Belhaven Press, London.

TWO The Nature of Services

Bateson, J. E. G. 1979. "Why We Need Service Marketing," in Ferrell, O. C., Brown, S. W., & Lamb, C. W., Jr. (eds.), *Conceptual and Theoretical Developments in Marketing,* Chicago: American Marketing, 131–146.

Bateson, J. E. G. 1992. *Managing Services Marketing, Text and Readings,* 2nd ed., Dryden Press, Orlando, Florida.

Farber, C. B. 1997. "Leveraging Customer Competency in Service Firms," *International Journal of Service Industry Management,* vol. 8, (no. 1), pp. 5–25.

REFERENCES

Grönroos, C. 2000. *Service Management and Marketing: A Customer Relationship Management Approach,* Wiley, Chichester & New York.

Hartline, M. D., & Ferrell, O. C. 1996. "The Management of Customer-Contact Service Employees: An Empirical Investigation," *Journal of Marketing,* vol. 60, pp. 52–70.

Kandampully, J. 1997. "Quality Service in Tourism," in Foley, M., Lennon, J., & Maxwell, J. (eds.), *Hospitality, Tourism and Leisure Management,* Cassell, London.

Kandampully, J. 2000. "The Impact of Demand Fluctuation on the Quality of Service: A Tourism Industry Example," *Managing Service Quality,* vol. 10, no. 1, pp. 10–18.

Kasper, H., van Helsdingen, P., & de Vries, W., Jr. 1999. *Services Marketing Management, an International Perspective,* John Wiley, West Sussex, UK.

Knisely, G. 1979. "Greater Marketing Emphasis by Holiday Inns Breaks Mould," *Advertising Age,* January 15, pp. 47–51.

Kurtz, D. L., & Clow, K. E. 1998. *Services Marketing,* John Wiley, New York.

Lovelock, C. H., & Wright, L. 1998. *Principles of Service Marketing and Management,* Prentice Hall, Upper Saddle River, New Jersey.

McLauglin, C. P. 1996. "Why Variation Reduction Is Not Everything: A New Paradigm for Service Operations," *International Journal of Service Industry Management,* vol. 7, no. 3, pp. 17–31.

Parasuraman, A., Zeithaml, V. A., & Berry, L. L. 1985. "A Conceptual Model of Service Quality and Its Implications for Future Research," *Journal of Marketing,* vol. 49, Fall 1985, pp. 41–50.

Rushton, A., & Carson, D. 1985. "The Marketing of Services: Managing the Intangibles," *European Journal of Marketing,* vol. 19, no. 3, p. 19.

Schuler, R. S. 1996. "Market-Focused Management: Human Resource Management Implications," *Journal of Market-Focused Management,* vol. 1, pp. 13–29.

Shostack, G. L. 1977. "Breaking Free from Product Marketing," *Journal of Marketing,* 41, April, 73–80.

Solomon, M. R., Surprenant, C., Czepiel, J. A., & Gutman, E. G. 1985. "A Role Theory Perspective on Dyadic Interactions: The Service Encounter," *Journal of Marketing,* vol. 49, Winter 1985, pp. 99–111.

Walker, J. L. 1995. "Service Encounter Satisfaction: Conceptualized," *Journal of Services Marketing,* vol. 9, no. 1, pp. 5–14.

THREE Quality—The Core Service

Baker, J. 1986. "The Role of the Environment in Marketing Services: The Consumer Perspective," in Czepiel J. A., Congram, C. A., & Shanahan, J. (eds.), *The Services Challenge: Integrating for Competitive Advantage,* AMA Services Marketing Conference Proceedings.

Berry, L. L. 1995. *On Great Service: A Framework for Action,* Free Press, New York.

Berry, L. L. 1999. *Discovering the Soul of Service.* Free Press, New York.

Berry, L. L., & Parasuraman, A. 1991. *Marketing Services: Competing Through Quality,* Free Press, New York.

Berry, L. L., Parasuraman, A., Zeithaml, V. A., & Adsit, D. 1994. "Improving Service Quality in America: Lessons Learned," *Academy of Management Executive,* vol. 8, pp. 32–52.

Berry, L. L., Zeithaml, V. A., & Parasuraman, A. 1985. "Quality Counts in Services Too," *Business Horizons,* May–June 1985.

Berry, L. L., Zeithaml, V. A., & Parasuraman, A. 1990. "Five Imperatives for Improving Service Quality," *Sloan Management Review,* September 1990.

Bessom, R. M. 1973. "Unique Aspects of Marketing of Services," *Arizona Business Bulletin,* November 1973.

Bessom, R. M., & Jackson, D. W., Jr. 1975. "Service Retailing: A Strategic Marketing Approach," *Journal of Retailing,* Summer 1975.

Brady, M. K., & Cronin, J. J. 2001. "Some New Thoughts on Conceptualizing Perceived Service Service Quality: A Hierarchical Approach," *Journal of Marketing,* vol. 65, July 2001, pp. 34–49.

Buzzell, R. D., & Gale, B. T. 1987. *The PIMS Principles: Linking Strategy to Performance,* Free Press, New York.

Conway, W. E. n.d. Conway Management, <www.conwaymgmt.com>, accessed March 2002.

Costin, H. I. (ed.) 1994. *Readings in Total Quality Management.* Reading 10 by Artemis March, "A Note on Quality: The Views of Deming, Juran, and Crosby," pp. 137–154, Dryden Press, Orlando, Florida.

Crosby, P. B. 1979. *Quality is Free,* McGraw-Hill, New York.

Crosby, P. B. 1984. *Quality Without Fears: The Art of Hassle-Free Management,* McGraw-Hill, New York.

Dabholkar, P. C., Shepherd, D., & Thorpe D. I. 2000. "A Comprehensive Framework for Service Quality: An Investigation of Critical Conceptual and Measurement Issues Through a Longitudinal Study," *Journal of Retailing,* vol. 76, no. 2, pp. 139–173.

Dabholkar, P. C., Thorpe, D. I., & Rentz, J. O. 1996. "A Measure of Service Quality for Retail Stores," *Journal of the Academy of Marketing Science,* 24, Winter, pp. 3–16.

Deming, W. E. 1982. *Out of the Crisis,* MIT Press, Cambridge, Massachusetts.

Deming Institute 2002. The W. Edwards Deming Institute, <www.deming.org>.

Department of Trade & Industry (UK) 2002. <www.dti.gov.uk>; information on Crosby accessed March 2002 at: <www.dti.gov.uk/mbp/bpgt/m9ja00001/m9ja0000114.html#23>.

Early, J. F. 1991. "Strategies for Measurement of Service Quality," *Quality Forum,* vol. 17, no. 1, March.

Easton, G. S., & Jarrell, S. L. 1998. "The Effects of Total Quality Management on Corporate Performance," *Journal of Business,* 71, April, pp. 253–308.

ecommerce-now 2002. <www.ecommerce-now.com>; information on Crosby accessed March 2002 at: <www.ecommerce-now.com/images/ecommerce-now/Crosby14steps.htm>.

Feigenbaum, A. V. 1956. "Total Quality Control," *Harvard Business Review,* 34, pp. 93–101.

Fisk, R. P. 1981. "Toward A Consumption/Evaluation Process Model for Services," in Donnelly, J. & George, W. (eds.), *Marketing of Services,* Proceedings of the American Marketing Association Conference, Chicago.

Gale, B. 1992. "Monitoring Customer Satisfaction and Market Perceived Quality," *Worth Repeating Series,* no. 922CS01, American Marketing Association, Chicago.

Garvin, A. D. 1983. "Quality on the Line," *Harvard Business Review,* Sept.-Oct., pp. 65–75.

Garvin, A. D. 1984. "What Does Product Quality Really Mean?," *Sloan Management Review,* Fall, pp. 25–43.

REFERENCES

Grönroos, C. 1980. "Designing A Long Range Marketing Strategy for Services," *Long Range Planning,* 13, April, pp. 36–42.

Grönroos, C. 1981. "Internal Marketing—An Integral Part of Marketing Theory," in Donnelly, J., & George, W. (eds.), *Marketing of Services,* Proceedings of the American Marketing Association Conference, Chicago.

Grönroos, C. 1982a. *A Service Quality Model and Its Managerial Implications,* Working paper presented at the Workshop of Research into the Management of Service Business, London Business School, January 1982.

Grönroos, C. 1982b. *Seven Key Areas of Research: According to the Nordic School of Service Marketing, Emerging Perspectives on Services Marketing,* Berry, L. L., Shostack, G. L., & Upah, G. D. (eds.), AMA Services Marketing Conference Proceedings.

Grönroos, C. 1984a. "A Service Quality Model and its Marketing Implications," *European Journal of Marketing,* vol. 18, no. 4, pp. 36–44.

Grönroos, C. 1984b. *Strategic Management and Marketing in the Service Sector,* Swedish School of Economics and Business Administration, Helsingfors.

Grönroos, C. 1990. *Services Management and Marketing,* Lexington Books, Lexington, Massachusetts.

Grönroos, C. 1991. "The Marketing Strategy Continuum: Towards a Marketing Concept for the 1990s," *Management Decision,* vol. 29, no. 1, pp. 7–13.

Grönroos, C. 1992. "Towards A Third Phase in Service Quality Research: Challenges and Future Directions," report presented at the "Frontiers in Services" conference at Vanderbilt University, Nashville, Tennessee, Sept. 1992.

Grove, S. J., & Fisk, R. P. 1982. "The Dramaturgy of Service Exchange: An Analytical Framework for Services Marketing," in Berry, L. L., Shostack, G. L., & Upah, G. D. (eds.), *Emerging Perspective on Services Marketing,* AMA Services Marketing Conference Proceedings.

Grove S. J., Fisk, R. P., & John, J. 2000. "Services as Theater: Guidelines and Implications," in Swartz, T. A., & Iacobucci, D. (eds.), *Handbook of Services Marketing and Management,* Sage, Beverly Hills, California.

Hartline, M. D., & Jones, K. C. 1996. "Employee Performance Cues in a Hotel Service Environment: Influence on Perceived Service Quality, Value and Word-of-Mouth Intentions," *Journal of Business Research,* vol. 35, pp. 207–215.

Hutchins, D. 1990. *In Pursuit of Quality,* Pitman, London.

Iacocca, L. 1988. *Talking Straight,* Bantam Books, New York.

Ittner, C., & Larcker, D. F. 1996. "Measuring the Impact of Quality Initiatives on Firm Financial Performance," in Ghosh, S., & Fedor, D. (eds.), *Advances in the Management of Organizational Quality,* vol. 1, Greenwich, CT: JAI, pp. 1–37.

Jacobson, R., & Aaker, D. A. 1987. "The Strategic Role of Product Quality," *Journal of Marketing,* vol. 51, pp. 31–44.

Juran Institute 2002. <www.juran.com/documentary/juranbio2.html>.

Juran, J. M. (ed.) 1989. *Quality Control Handbook,* 4th ed., McGraw-Hill, New York.

Kiechel, W. 1981. "Three (or Four or More) Ways to Win," *Fortune,* October 19, pp. 181–188.

Kordupleski, R. E., Rust, R. T., & Zahorik, A. J. 1993. "Why Improving Quality Doesn't Improve Quality (or Whatever Happened to Marketing?)," *California Management Review,* vol. 35, no. 3, pp. 82–95.

Lehtinen, J. R. 1983. "Customer Oriented Service System," Service Management Institute working paper, Helsinki, Finland.

Lehtinen, J. R. 1988. "Global Service Styles: Experimental Study on Service Production Process," in Bitner, M. J., & Crosby, L. A. (eds.), *Different Cultures, Designing a Winning Service Strategy,* AMA Services Marketing Conference Proceedings, 1988.

Lehtinen, U., & Lehtinen, J. R. 1983. "Service Quality: A Study of Quality Dimensions," unpublished working paper, Service Management Institute, Helsinki, Finland.

Maddox, R. N. 1981. "Two-Factor Theory and Consumer Satisfaction: Replication and Extension," *Journal of Consumer Research,* June 1981.

Marchese, T. 1991. "TQM Researches the Academy," *American Association for Higher Education Bulletin,* November, pp. 13–18.

Parasuraman, A., Berry, L. L., & Zeithaml, V. A. 1991. "Understanding, Measuring, Improving Service Quality Findings from a Multiphase Research Program," Brown, S., Gummesson, E., Edvardsson, B., & Gustavsson, B. (eds.), *Service Quality: Multidisciplinary and Multinational Perspectives,* Lexington Books, Lexington, Massachusetts.

Parasuraman, A., Zeithaml, V. A., & Berry, L. L. 1985. "A Conceptual Model of Service Quality and Its Implications for Future Research," *Journal of Marketing,* vol. 49, Fall, pp. 41–50.

Parasuraman, A., Zeithaml, V. A., & Berry, L. L. 1988. "SERVQUAL: A Multi Item Scale for Measuring Consumer Perception of Service Quality," *Journal of Retailing,* vol. 64, no. 1, Spring.

Peters, T., & Waterman, R., Jr. 1982. *In Search of Excellence,* Harper & Row, New York.

Porter, M. E. 1985. *Competitive Advantage,* Free Press, New York.

Porter, M. E., Takeuchi, H., & Sakakibara, M. 2000. *Can Japan Compete?,* Macmillan, Basingstoke, UK.

Rust, R. T., & Oliver, R. L. 1994. "Service Quality: Insights and Managerial Implications from the Frontier," in Rust, R. T., & Oliver R. L. (eds.), *Service Quality: New Directions in Theory and Practice,* Sage, Thousand Oaks, California, pp. 1–19.

Sasser, W. E., Olsen, R. P., & Wyckoff, D. D. 1978. *Management of Service Operations, Text & Cases,* Allyn and Bacon, Boston.

Shostack, G. L. 1977a. "Breaking Free From Product Marketing," *Journal of Marketing,* 41, April, pp. 73–80.

Shostack, G. L. 1977b. "Human Evidence: A New Part of the Marketing Mix," *Bank Marketing,* March, pp. 32–34.

Swan, J. E., & Comb, L. J. 1976. "Product Performance and Consumer Satisfaction: A New Concept," *Journal of Marketing,* April.

Woodruff, R. B., Cadotte, E. R., & Jenkins, R. 1983. "Modeling Consumer Satisfaction Process Using Experience-based Norms," *Journal of Marketing Research,* vol. 20, August, pp. 296–304.

Zeithaml, V. A. 1981. "How Consumer Evaluation Processes Differ Between Goods and Services," in Donnelly, J., & George, W. (eds.), *Marketing of Services,* Proceedings of the American Marketing Association Conference, Chicago.

Zeithaml, V. A. 2000. "Service Quality, Profitability, and the Economic Worth of Customers: What We Know and What We Need to Learn," *Academy of Marketing Science,* vol. 28, no. 1, pp. 67–85.

Zeithaml, V. A., Berry, L. L., & Parasuraman, A. 1993. "The Nature and Determinants of Customer Expectations of Service," *Journal of the Academy of Marketing Science,* vol. 21, Winter, pp. 1–12.

Zeithaml, V. A., Berry, L. L., & Parasuraman, A. 1996. "The Behavioral Consequences of Service Quality," *Journal of Marketing,* vol. 60, April, pp. 31–46.

Zeithaml, V. A., & Bitner, M. J. 2000. *Services Marketing,* McGraw-Hill, Burr Ridge.

FOUR Understanding Customer Needs

Albrecht, K., & Bradford, L. J. 1990. *The Service Advantage,* Dow Jones-Irwin, Homewood, Illinois.

Armstrong, P. K. 1992. "A Model for Analyzing Quality in the Service Delivery Process," paper presented at the Quality in Service Conference-3, University of Karlstad, Sweden.

Berry, L. L. 1992. "Improving America's Service," *Marketing Management,* Summer, p. 35.

Berry, L. L., & Parasuraman, A. 1992. "Prescriptions for a Service Quality Revolution in America," *Organizational Dynamics,* Spring, pp. 5–15.

Bitner, M. J., Booms, B. H., & Tetreault, M. S. 1990. "The Service Encounter: Diagnosing Favorable and Unfavorable Incidents," *Journal of Marketing,* vol. 54, January, pp. 71–84.

Bitner, M. J., Nyquist, J. D., & Booms, B. H. 1984. "The Critical Incident as a Technique for Analyzing the Service Encounter," *Services Marketing in a Changing Environment,* proceedings of the AMA Services Marketing Conference.

Bowen, D. E. 1996. "Market-Focused HRM in Service Organizations: Satisfying Internal and External Customers," *Journal of Market-Focused Management,* vol. 1, pp. 31–47.

Cronin, J. J., & Taylor, S. A. 1992. "Measuring Service Quality: A Reexamination," *Journal of Marketing,* vol. 56, July, pp. 55–68.

Crosby, L. A. 1991. "Integrating Customer Satisfaction Measurement (CSM) with Total Quality Management (TQM)," *Managing Service Quality,* March.

Crosby, A. L. 1992. "Customer Satisfaction Measurement and Service Quality Improvement," paper presented at Quality in Services Conference (QUIS-2), St John's University.

Czepiel, J. A. 1980. "Managing Customer Satisfaction in Consumer Service Business," research program working paper, Marketing Science Institute, Cambridge, Massachusetts.

Deming, W. E. 1982. *Quality, Productivity, and Competitive Position,* Massachusetts Institute of Technology Center for Advanced Engineering Study, Cambridge, Massachusetts.

Denzin, N. K., & Lincoln, Y. S. (eds.) 1998. *Strategies of Qualitative Inquiry,* Sage, Thousand Oaks, California.

Fisk, R. P., Brown, S. W., & Bitner, M. J. 1993. "Tracking the Evolution of the Services Marketing Literature," *Journal of Retailing,* vol. 69, no. 1, Spring.

Gale, T. B. 1990. "The Role of Marketing in Total Quality Management," paper presented at the Quality in Services Conference-2, St. John's University.

Gilly, M. C. 1987. "Postcomplaint Processes: From Organizational Response to Repurchase Behavior," *Journal of Consumer Affairs,* Winter, pp. 293–313.

Grönroos, C. 1984. *Strategic Management and Marketing in the Service Sector,* Swedish School of Economic and Business Administration, Helsinfors.

Hartline, M. D., & Ferrell, O. C. 1996. "The Management of Customer-Contact Service Employees: An Empirical Investigation," *Journal of Marketing,* vol. 60, pp. 52–70.

Heskett, J. L., Sasser, W. E., & Schlesinger, L. A. 1997. *The Service Profit Chain: How Leading Companies Link Profit and Growth to Loyalty, Satisfaction and Value,* Free Press, New York.

Hope, C., & Muhlemann, A. 1997. *Service Operations Management,* Prentice Hall, London.

Huckestein, D., & Duboff, R. 1999. "Hilton Hotels," *Cornell Hotel and Restaurant Administration Quarterly,* vol. 40, no. 4, pp. 28–39.

Kingman-Brundage, J. 1989. "The ABC's of service system blueprinting," in Bitner, M. J., & Crosby, L. A. (eds.), *Designing a Winning Service Strategy,* American Marketing Association, Chicago.

Klose, A., & Finkle, T. 1995. "Service Quality and the Congruency of Employee Perceptions and Customer Expectations: The Case of an Electric Utility," *Psychology and Marketing,* vol. 27, no. 7, pp. 637–646.

Marriott, J. W., Jr. 1988. foreword in Albrecht, K., *At America's Service,* Dow Jones-Irwin, Homewood, Illinois.

McAlexander, J. H., Kaldenberg, D. O., & Koenig, H. F. 1994. "Service Quality Measurement," *Journal of Health Care Marketing,* vol. 3, Fall, pp. 34–40.

Palmer, A., & Cole, C. 1995. *Services Marketing Principles and Practice,* Prentice Hall, Englewood Cliffs, New Jersey.

Parasuraman, A., Zeithamal, V. A., & Berry, L. L. 1988. "SERVQUAL: A Multi-Item Scale for Measuring Consumer Perception of Service Quality," *Journal of Retailing,* vol. 64, no. 1, Spring.

Pizam, A., & Ellis, T. 1999. "Customer Satisfaction and Its Measurement in Hospitality Enterprises," *International Journal of Contemporary Hospitality Management,* vol. 11, no. 7, pp. 326–339.

Reichheld, F. F., & Sasser, W. E., Jr. 1990. "Zero Defections: Quality Comes to Services," *Harvard Business Review,* Sept./Oct., pp. 105–111.

Rosander, A. C. 1985. *Application of Quality Control in Service Industries,* ASQC Press, Milwaukee, Wisconsin.

Rosander, A. C. 1991. *Deming's 14 Points Applied to Services,* ASQC Quality Press, New York.

Shapiro, R. R. 1992. "Retaining Profitable Customers: A Targeted Approach," paper presented at the Quality in Services Conference, QUIS-3, Karlstad University, Sweden.

Shostack, G. L. 1983. "Service Design in the Operating Environment," in George, W. R., & Marshall, C. (eds.), *Developing New Services,* American Marketing Association, Chicago, pp. 27–43.

Stauss, B. 1992. "Customer Service Problems: From Problem Detection to Problem Prevention, Service Problem Deployment," paper presented at the Quality in Service Conference, QUIS-3, University of Karlstad, Sweden.

Stauss, B. 1993. "Using the Critical Incident Technique in Measuring and Managing Service Quality," in Scheuing, E., & Christopher, W. (eds.), *The Service Quality Handbook,* Amacom, New York, pp. 408–427.

TARP *see* Technical Assistance Research Program (TARP).

Technical Assistance Research Program (TARP) 1979. *Consumer Complaint Handling in America: Final Report,* Office of Consumer Affairs, Washington, D.C.

Technical Assistance Research Program (TARP) 1986. *Consumer Complaint Handling In America: An Update Study,* Office of Consumer Affairs, Washington, D.C.

Thomas, J. M. 1988. "Getting Closer to the Customer." *MIP Journal,* vol. 6, no. 1, pp. 28–31.

Tschohl, J. 1991. *Achieving Excellence Through Customer Service,* Prentice Hall, Upper Saddle River, New Jersey.

Zeithaml, V. A., Berry, L. L., & Parasuraman, A. 1993. "The Nature and Determinants of Customer Expectations of Service," *Journal of the Academy of Marketing Science,* vol. 21, no. 1, pp. 1–12.

Zeithaml, V. A., Parasuraman, A., & Berry, L. L. 1990. *Delivering Quality Service: Balancing Customer Perception and Expectations,* Free Press, New York.

FIVE The Service Vision

Albrecht, K., & Zemke, R. 1985. *Service America: Doing Business in the New Economy,* Dow Jones Irwin, Homewood, Illinois.

Berry L. L. 1995. *On Great Service: A Framework for Action,* Free Press, New York.

Carlzon, J. 1987. *Moments of Truth,* Ballinger, Cambridge, Massachusetts.

Chase, R. B., & Garvin, D. 1990. "The Service Factory: A Future Vision," paper presented at the Quality in Services Conference QUIS-2, St John's University.

Costin, H. I. 1994. *Total Quality Management,* Dryden Press, Orlando, Florida.

Deming, W. E. 1982. *Quality, Productivity, and Competitive Position,* Massachusetts Institute of Technology Center for Advanced Engineering Study, Cambridge, Massachusetts.

Deming, W. E. 1986. *Out of the Crisis,* Massachusetts Institute of Technology, Cambridge, Massachusetts.

Eiglier, P., & Langeard, E. 1981. *A Conceptual Approach of the Service Offer,* working paper no. 217, iae, Aix-en-Provence, April.

Fitzsimmons, J., & Fitzsimmons, M. 1994 (2nd ed., 1998). *Services Management for Competitive Advantage,* McGraw-Hill, New York.

Grönroos, C. 1987. *Developing the Service Offering—A Source of Competitive Advantage,* AMA Services Marketing Conference Proceedings.

Gummesson, E. 1993. "Quality Management in Service Organizations," *International Service Quality Association Research Report,* no. 1, January.

Hosick, W. M. 1989. "The Use of Blueprinting to Achieve Quality in Service," *Service Excellence: Marketing's Impact on Performance,* Proceedings of the AMA 8th Services Marketing Conference.

Ishikawa, K. 1985. *What is Total Quality Control?—The Japanese Way,* translated by Lu, D. J., Prentice Hall, Englewood Cliffs, New Jersey.

Juran, J. M. 1989a. *Juran on Leadership for Quality,* Free Press, New York.

Juran, J. M. 1989b. *Quality Control Handbook,* 4th ed., McGraw-Hill, New York.

Kandampully, J. n.d., unpublished data; details available from author.

Kingman-Brundage, J. 1989. "The ABCs of Service System Blueprinting," in Bitner, M. J., & Crosby, L. A. (eds.), *Designing a Winning Service Strategy,* American Marketing Association, Chicago.

Lehtinen, U., & Lehtinen, J. R. 1983. *Service Quality: A Study of Quality Dimensions,* unpublished working paper, Service Management Institute, Helsinki, Finland OY.

Lovelock, C. H. 1994. *Product Plus: How Product and Service = Competitive Advantage,* McGraw-Hill, New York.

Lovelock, C. H. 1996. *Services Marketing,* 3rd ed., Prentice Hall, Upper Saddle River, New Jersey.

Lovelock, C. H., Patterson, P. G., & Walker, R. H. 2001. *Services Marketing: An Asia-Pacific Perspective,* 2nd ed., Pearson Education Australia, Sydney.

Normann, R. 1984. 3rd ed., 2000. *Service Management: Strategy and Leadership in Service Business,* John Wiley, New York.

Rust, R. T., Zahorik, A. J., & Keiningham, T. L. 1996. *Service Marketing,* HarperCollins College Publishers, New York.

Rust, R. T., Zeithaml, V. A., & Lemon, K. N. 2000. *Driving Customer Equity: How Customer Lifetime Value is Reshaping Corporate Strategy,* Free Press, New York.

Schuler, R. S. 1996. "Market-Focused Management: Human Resource Management Implications," *Journal of Market Focused Management,* vol. 1, pp. 13–29.

Senior, M., & Akehurst, G. 1990. *Perceptual Blueprinting in the United Kingdom,* QUIS-2, Business Research Institute, St John's University.

Shostack, G. L. 1981 (also 1982). "How to Design a Service," in Donnelly, J., & George, W. (eds.), *Marketing of Services,* Chicago American Marketing Association, pp. 221–229; (also appeared in *European Journal of Marketing,* 1982, vol. 16, 1).

Shostack, G. L. 1983. "Service Design in the Operating Environment," In George, W. R., & Marshall, C. (eds.), *Developing New Services,* American Marketing Association, Chicago, pp. 27–43.

Shostack, G. L. 1984a. "Designing Services that Deliver," *Harvard Business Review,* 62, January–February, pp. 133–139.

Shostack, G. L. 1984b. "Service Design in the Operating Environment," in George, W. R., & Marshall, C. E. (eds.), *Developing New Services,* American Marketing Association, Chicago, pp. 27–43.

Shostack, G. L. 1985. "Planning the Service Encounter," in Czepiel, S., & Surprenant, C. (eds.), *The Service Encounter,* Lexington Books, Lexington, Massachusetts.

Shostack, G. L. 1987. "Service Positioning through Structural Change," *Journal of Marketing,* 51, January, pp. 34–43.

Shostack, G. L. 1990b. "Why Do Service Firms Lack Design?," paper presented at the Quality in Services Conference, QUIS-2, St John's University, pp. 133–146.

Wyckoff, D. D. 1988. "New Tools for Achieving Service Quality," in Lovelock, C. H. (ed.), *Marketing Services: Marketing, Operations, and Human Resources,* Prentice Hall, New Jersey, pp. 226–39.

Zeithaml, V. A., Parasuraman, A., & Berry, L. L. 1990. *Delivering Quality Service: Balancing Customer Perception and Expectations,* Free Press, New York.

SIX Modern Marketing (1)—External Service Implications

Albrecht, K. 1988. *At America's Service,* Dow Jones Irwin, Homewood, Illinois.

Albrecht, K., & Bradford, L. J. 1990. *The Service Advantage,* Dow Jones Irwin, Homewood, Illinois.

Albrecht, K., & Zemke, R. 1985. *Service America: Doing Business in the New Economy,* Dow Jones Irwin, Homewood, Illinois.

Andreassen, T. W., & Lindestad, B. 1998. "The Effect of Corporate Image in the Formation of Customer Loyalty," *Journal of Services Research,* vol. 1, no. 1, pp. 82–92.

Berry, L. L., & Yadav, M. S. 1996. "Capture and Communicate Value in the Pricing of Services," *Sloan Management Review,* Summer, pp. 41–50.

Bitner, M. J. 1990. "Evaluating Service Encounters: The Effects of Physical Surroundings and Employee Response," *Journal of Marketing,* vol. 54, no. 2, pp. 69–82.

Bitner, M. J. 1992a. "Managing the Evidence of Service," paper presented at the Quality in Services Conference, QUIS-3, Karlstad University, Sweden.

Bitner, M. J. 1992b. "Servicescapes: The Impact of Physical Surroundings on Customers and Employees," *Journal of Marketing,* vol. 56, no. 2, April, pp. 57–71.

Bitner, M. J. 1996. "Evaluating Service Encounters: The Effects of Physical Surroundings and Employee Responses," *Journal of Marketing,* vol. 54, no. 2, pp. 69–89.

REFERENCES

Bitner, M. J., & Zeithaml, V.A. 1987. "Fundamentals in Services Marketing; Add Value to your Service," Surprenant, C. (ed.), *AMA Services Marketing Conference Proceedings,* Chicago.

Bitner, M.J., Booms, B. H., & Tetreault, M. S. 1988. "Critical Incident in Service Encounters," in Bitner, M. J., & Crosby, L. A. (eds.), *Designing a Winning Service Strategy,* proceedings of AMA Services Marketing Conference.

Booms, B. H., & Bitner, M. J. 1981. "Marketing Strategies and Organization Structures for Service Firms," in Donnelly, J. H., & George, W. R. (eds.), *Marketing of Services,* American Marketing Association, Chicago, pp. 47–51.

Bowen, D. E., & Lawler, E. E. 1992. "The Why, How and When of Empowerment: Farewell to the Production-line Approach to Service?," working paper no. 26, First Interstate Center for Services Marketing, Arizona State University.

Carlzon, J. 1987. *Moments of Truth,* Ballinger, Cambridge, Massachusetts.

Cina, C. 1989. "Five Steps to Service Excellence," in *Service Excellence: Marketing's Impact on Performance,* AMA 8th Services Marketing Conference Proceedings.

Czepiel, J. A., Solomon, M. R., Surprenant, C. F., & Gutman, E. G. 1985. "Service Encounters: An Overview," in Czepiel, Solomon, & Surprenant (eds.), *Service Encounter: Managing Employee/Customer Interaction in Service Business,* Lexington Books, Lexington, Massachusetts, pp. 3–16.

Davis, F. W. 1989. "Enabling is as Important as Empowering: A Case for Extended Service Blueprinting," *Service Excellence: Marketing's Impact on Performance,* AMA Services Marketing Conference Proceedings.

De Ruyter, K., Wetzels, M., Lemmink, J., & Mattson, J. 1997. "The Dynamics of the Service Delivery Process: A Value-Based Approach," *International Journal of Research in Marketing,* vol. 14, pp. 231–243.

Deming, W. E. 1982. *Quality, Productivity, and Competitive Position,* Massachusetts Institute of Technology Center for Advanced Engineering Study, Cambridge, Massachusetts.

Gould-Williams, J. 1999. "The Impact of Employee Performance Cues on Guest Loyalty, Perceived Value and Service Quality," *The Service Industries Journal,* vol. 19, no. 3, pp. 97–118.

Hartline, M. D., & Jones, K. C. 1996. "Employee Performance Cues in a Hotel Service Environment: Influence on Perceived Service Quality, Value and Word-of-Mouth Intentions," *Journal of Business Research,* vol. 35, pp. 207–275.

Knisely, G. 1979. "Greater Marketing Emphasis by Holiday Inns Breaks Mould," *Advertising Age,* January 15, pp. 47–51.

Lovelock, C. H. 1992. *Managing Services: Marketing, Operations and Human Resources,* Prentice Hall, Upper Saddle River, New Jersey.

Normann, R. 1984. (2nd and 3rd eds. 1991, 2000). *Service Management: Strategy and Leadership in Service Business,* John Wiley, New York.

Palmer, A., & Cole, C. 1995. *Services Marketing: Principles and Practice,* Prentice Hall/Simon & Schuster, Englewood Cliffs, New Jersey.

Peattie, K., & Peattie, S. 1995. "Sales Promotion: A Missed Opportunity for Service Marketers," *International Journal of Service Industry Management,* vol. 5, no. 1, pp. 6–21.

Rafaeli, A. 1993. "Dress and Behavior of Customer Contact Employees: A Framework for Analysis," *Advances in Services Marketing and Management,* vol. 2, pp. 175–211.

Rust, R. T., Zahorik, A. J., & Keiningham, T. L. 1996. *Services Marketing,* HarperCollins, New York.

Shostack, G. L. 1977. "Breaking Free from Product Marketing," *Journal of Marketing,* 41, April, pp. 73–80.

Shostack, G. L. 1985. "Planning the Service Encounter," in Czepiel, Solomon, & Surprenant (eds.), *The Service Encounter,* Lexington Books, Lexington, Massachusetts.

Surprenant, C. F., & Solomon, M. R. 1987. "Predictability and Personalization in the Service Encounter," *Journal of Marketing,* vol. 51, April, pp. 86–96.

Taylor, S., & Claxton, J. D. 1994. "Delays and the Dynamics of Service Evaluations," *Journal of the Academy of Marketing Science,* vol. 22, no. 3, pp. 254–264.

Zeithaml, V. A., & Bitner, M. J. 1996. *Services Marketing,* McGraw-Hill, New York.

SEVEN Modern Marketing (2)—Internal Management Implications

Achrol, R. S. 1991. "Evolution of the Marketing Organisation: New Forms for Turbulent Environments," *Journal of Marketing,* 55, October, pp. 77–93.

Antonacopoulou, E., & Kandampully, J. 2000. "Alchemy: The Transformation to Service Excellence," *The Learning Organisation,* vol. 7, no. 1, pp. 13–22.

Armistead, C. G., & Clark, G. 1994. The "'Coping' Capacity Management Strategy in Service, and the Influence on Quality Performance," *International Journal of Service Industry Management,* vol. 5, no. 2, pp. 5–22.

Barnes, J. 1989. "The Role of Internal Marketing: If the Staff Won't Buy It, Why Should the Customer?," *Irish Marketing Review,* vol. 4, no. 2, pp. 11–21.

Bell, C. R. 1993. "In Customers We Trust," *Executive Excellence,* vol. 10, issue 8, pp. 13–14.

Berry, L. L. 1981. "The Employee as Customer," *Journal of Retail Banking,* vol. 3, no. 1, pp. 33–40.

Berry, L. L. 1983. "Relationship Marketing," In Berry, L. L., Shostack, G. L., & Upah, G. D. (eds.), *Emerging Perspectives on Services Marketing,* AMA Services Marketing, American Marketing Association, Chicago.

Berry, L. L. 1987. "Big Ideas in Services Marketing," *Journal of Services Marketing,* vol. 1, no. 1, Summer.

Berry, L. L. 1995. *On Great Service: A Framework for Action,* Free Press, New York.

Berry, L. L., & Parasuraman, A. 1992. "Prescriptions for a Service Quality Revolution in America," *Organizational Dynamics,* Spring, pp. 5–15.

Berry, L. L., Zeithaml, V. A., & Parasuraman, A. 1990. "Five Imperatives for Improving Service Quality," *Sloan Management Review,* September.

Bitner, M. J. 1995. "Building Service Relationships: It's All About Promises," *Journal of the Academy of Marketing Science,* vol. 23, no. 4, pp. 246–251.

Buttle, F. 1996. *Relationship Marketing—Theory and Practice,* Chapman, London.

Cahill, D. 1995. "The Managerial Implications of the New Learning Organization: A New Tool for Internal Marketing," *Journal of Services Marketing,* vol. 9, no. 4, pp. 43–51.

Christopher, M., Payne, A., & Ballantyne, D. 1993. *Relationship Marketing: Bringing Quality, Customer Service, and Marketing Together,* Butterworth Heinemann, Oxford.

Colgate, M., & Danaher, P. 2000. "Implementing a Customer Relationship Strategy: The Asymmetric Impact of Poor versus Excellent Execution," *Journal of the Academy of Marketing Science,* vol. 28, no. 3, pp. 375–387.

REFERENCES

Cram, T. 1994. *The Power of Relationship Marketing—Keeping Customers for Life,* Pitman, London.

Evans, R. K., & Crosby, L. A. 1988. "A Theoretical Model of Interpersonal Relational Quality in Enduring Service Sales Relationships," AMA Services Marketing Conference.

Foreman, S., & Money, A. 1995. "Internal Marketing: Concepts, Measurement and Application," *Journal of Marketing Management,* vol. 11, no. 8, pp. 755–768.

Fournier, S., Dobscha, S., & Mick, D. G. 1998. "Preventing the Premature Death of Relationship Marketing," *Harvard Business Review,* vol. 76, no. 1, pp. 42–49.

Grönroos, C. 1981. "Internal Marketing—An Integral Part of Marketing Theory," in Donnelly, J., & George, W. (eds.), *Marketing of Services,* Proceedings of the American Marketing Association Conference, Chicago, pp. 236–238.

Grönroos, C. 1983. *Strategic Management in the Service Sector,* Chartwell-Bratt Ltd. Cambridge, Massachusetts.

Grönroos, C. 1990a. "Relationship Approach to Marketing in Service Contexts: The Marketing and Organisation Behavior Interface," *Journal of Business Research,* vol. 20, pp. 3–12.

Grönroos, C. 1990b. *Service Management and Marketing, Managing the Moments of Truth in Service Competition,* Lexington Books, Lexington, Massachusetts.

Grönroos, C. 1994. "From Marketing Mix to Relationship Marketing: Towards a Paradigm Shift in Marketing," *Management Decision,* vol. 32, no. 2, pp. 4–20.

Grönroos, C. 2000. *Services Management and Marketing: A customer relationship management approach,* 2nd ed., Wiley, West Sussex, UK.

Gummesson, E. 1994. "Making Relationship Marketing Operational," *International Journal of Service Industry Management,* vol. 5, no. 5.

Gummesson, E. 1996. "Relationship Marketing: From 4Ps to 30Rs," University of Stockholm, Sweden.

Hartline, M. D., & Ferrell, O. C. 1996. "The Management of Customer-Contact Service Employees: An Empirical Investigation," *Journal of Marketing,* vol. 60, pp. 52–70.

Heskett, J. L., Sasser, W. E., & Hart, C. W. L. 1990. *Service Breakthroughs; Changing The Rules of the Game,* Free Press, New York.

Heskett, J. L., Sasser, W. E., & Schlesinger, L. A. 1997. *The Service Profit Chain: How Leading Companies Link Profit and Growth to Loyalty, Satisfaction, and Value,* Free Press, New York.

Hirchman, O. A. 1970. *Exit, Voice, and Loyalty: Responses to Decline in Firms, Organizations, and States,* Harvard University Press, Massachusetts.

Holmund, M., & Kock, S. 1996. "Relationship Marketing: The Importance of Customer-Perceived Service Quality," *Retail Banking,* vol. 3, pp. 287–304.

Jackson, B. B. 1985. "Build Customer Relationships That Last," *Harvard Business Review,* November–December.

Kandampully, J. 2000. "The Impact of Demand Fluctuation on the Quality of Service: A Tourism Industry Example," *Managing Service Quality,* vol. 10, no. 1, pp. 10–18.

Kandampully, J., & Duddy, R. 1999. "Relationship Marketing: A Concept Beyond the Primary Relationship," *Marketing Intelligence and Planning,* vol. 17, no. 7, pp. 315–323. http://www.emeraldinsight.com/mip.htm

Kimes, S. E. 1989. "Yield Management: A Tool for Capacity Controlled Service Firms," *Journal of Operations Management,* vol. 8, no. 4, pp. 348–363.

Kotler, P. 1980, 1984. *Marketing Management: Analysis, Planning and Control,* 5th ed., Prentice Hall, Englewood Cliffs, New Jersey.

Levitt, T. 1983. "After the Sale is Over," *Harvard Business Review,* Sept.–Oct. pp. 88–89.

Lovelock, C. H. 1992. "Think Before You Leap in Services Marketing," in Berry, L. L., Shostack, G. L., and Upah, G. D. (eds.), *Emerging Perspectives on Services Marketing,* AMA Services Marketing Conference Proceedings.

Lovelock, C. H., Patterson, P. G., & Walker, R. H. 2001. *Services Marketing: An Asia-Pacific Perspective,* 2nd ed., Pearson Education Australia, Sydney.

McKenna, R. 1991. *Relationship Marketing: Successful Strategies for the Age of the Customer,* Addison Wesley, Reading, Massachusetts.

Parasuraman, A., Berry, L. L., & Zeithaml, V. A. 1991. "Understanding, Measuring, and Improving Service Quality: Findings from a Multiphase Research Program," in Brown, S., Gummesson, E., Edvardsson, B., & Gustavsson, B. (eds.), *Service Quality: Multidisciplinary and Multinational Perspectives,* Lexington Books, Lexington, Massachusetts.

Peppers, D., & Rogers, M. 1995. "A New Marketing Paradigm: Share of Customer, Not Market Share," *Planning Review,* vol. 2, pp. 14–18.

Reichheld, F. F., & Sasser, W. E. 1990. "Zero Defections: Quality Comes to Services," *Harvard Business Review,* Sept.–Oct., pp. 105–111.

Ries, A. 1997. *Focus: The Future of Your Company Depends On It,* HarperCollins, New York.

Rosen, E. D., & Surprenant, C. 1998. "Evaluating Relationships: Are Satisfaction and Quality Enough?," *International Journal of Service Industry Management,* vol. 9, no. 2, pp. 103–125.

Sasser, W. E. 1976. "Match Supply and Demand in Service Industries," *Harvard Business Review,* Nov.–Dec., pp. 133–141.

Schemwell, D. J., & Cronin, J. J. 1994. "Services Marketing Strategies for Coping with Demand/Supply Imbalances," *Journal of Services Marketing,* vol. 8, no. 4, pp. 14–24.

Sheth, J. N., & Parvatiyar, A. 1995. "Relationship Marketing in Consumer Markets: Antecedents and Consequences," *Journal of the Academy of Marketing Science,* vol. 25, no. 2, pp. 162–167.

Unzicker, D., Clow, K. E., & Babakus, E. 2000. "The Role of Organizational Communications on Employee Perceptions of a Firm," *Journal of Professional Services Marketing,* vol. 21, no. 2, pp. 87–103.

Zeithaml, V. A., & Bitner, M. J. 1996. *Services Marketing,* McGraw-Hill, New York.

EIGHT Empowerment, Guarantees, and Recovery

Albrecht, K. 1992. *At America's Service: How Your Company Can Join the Customer Service Revolution,* Warner Books, New York.

Andreasson, T. W. 2000. "Antecedents to Satisfaction with Service Recovery," *European Journal of Marketing,* vol. 34, nos. 1/2, pp. 156–175.

Barbee, C., & Bott, V. 1991. "Customer Treatment as a Mirror of Employee Treatment," *Advanced Management Journal,* vol. 5, p. 27.

Baron, S., & Harris K. 1995. *Services Marketing: Text and Cases,* Macmillan Business Press, London.

Bateson, J. E. G. 1995. *Managing Services Marketing: Text and Readings,* 3rd ed., Dryden Press, Chicago.

Bateson, J. E. G. 2000. "Perceived Control and the Service Experience," in Swartz, J., & Iacobucci, D. (eds.), *Handbook of Services Marketing and Management,* Sage, Thousand Oaks, California, pp. 127–144.

REFERENCES

Bateson, J. E. G., & Hoffman, K. D. 1999. *Managing Service Marketing: Text and Readings,* 4th ed., Dryden Press, Fort Worth, Texas.

Bell, C. R. 1993. "In Customers We Trust," *Executive Excellence,* vol. 10, no. 8, August, pp. 13–14.

Bell, C. R., & Zemke, R. 1998. "Do Service Procedures Tie Employees' Hands?," *Personnel Journal,* September, pp. 77–83.

Berry, L. L. 1995. *On Great Service: A Framework for Action,* Free Press, New York.

Berry, L. L., & Parasuraman, A. 1992. "Prescriptions for a Service Quality Revolution in America," *Organisational Dynamics,* Spring, pp. 5–15.

Berry, L. L., Zeithaml, V. A., & Parasuraman, A. 1990. "Five Imperatives for Improving Service Quality," *Sloan Management Review,* Summer.

Bitner, M. J. 1995. "Building Service Relationships: It's All About Promises," *Journal of the Academy of Marketing Science,* vol. 23, no. 4, pp. 246–251.

Bitner, M. J., Booms, B. H., & Mohr, L. A. 1994. "Critical Service Encounters: The Employee's Viewpoint," *Journal of Marketing,* 58, October, pp. 95–106.

Bitner, M. J., Booms, B. H., & Tetreault, M. S. 1990. "The Service Encounter: Diagnosing Favorable and Unfavorable Incidents," *Journal of Marketing,* vol. 54, January, pp. 71–84.

Bowen, D. E., & Lawler, E. E. III, 1992. "The Empowerment of Service Workers: What, Why, How and When," *Sloan Management Review,* vol. 33, no. 3, pp. 31–39.

Bowen, D. E., & Lawler, E. E. III, 1995. "Empowering Service Employees," *Sloan Management Review,* Summer.

Brendin, J. 1995. "Keeping Customers," *Industry Week,* vol. 244, no. 18, October 2, p. 2.

Czepiel, J. A., Solomon, M. R., Surprenant, C. F., & Gutman, E. G. 1985. "Service Encounters: An Overview," in Czepiel, Solomon, & Surprenant (eds.), *Service Encounter: Managing Employee/ Customer Interaction in Service Business,* Lexington Books, Lexington Massachusetts, pp. 3–16.

Davis, C., Jr., & Baldwin, L. 1995. "Put it in Writing," *American Agent & Broker,* vol. 67, no. 9, September, pp. 34–42.

Deming, W. E. 1982. *Quality, Productivity and Competitive Position,* Massachusetts Institute of Technology Center for Advanced Engineering Study, Cambridge, Massachusetts.

Evans, M. R., Clark, J. D., & Knutson, B. J. 1996. "The 100 Percent Unconditional Money Back Guarantee," *Cornell HRA Quarterly,* December, pp. 56–61.

Hart, C. W. 1988. "The Power of Unconditional Service Guarantees," *Harvard Business Review,* July–August, pp. 54–62.

Hart, C. W. L. 1993. *Extraordinary Guarantees: A New Way to Build Quality Throughout Your Company and Ensure Satisfaction for Your Customers,* Amacom, New York.

Hart, C. W. L., Heskett, J. L., & Sasser, W. E. 1990. "The Profitable Art of Service Recovery," *Harvard Business Review,* vol. 69, no. 4, July–August, pp. 148–156.

Heskett, J. L., Sasser, E. W., Jr., & Hart, C. W. L. 1990. *Service Breakthroughs,* Free Press, New York.

Heskett, J. L., Sasser, W. E., & Schlesinger, L. A. 1997. *The Service Profit Chain: How Leading Companies Link Profit and Growth to Loyalty, Satisfaction and Value,* Free Press, New York.

Hubrecht, J., & Teare, R. 1993. "A Strategy for Partnership in Total Quality Service," *International Journal of Contemporary Hospitality Management,* vol. 5, no. 3.

Hunter, R. 1994. "Learning from the Service Sector," *Industry Week,* vol. 243, no. 2, January 17, p. 12.

Jones, T. O., & Sasser, E. W., Jr., 1995. "Why Satisfied Customers Defect," *Harvard Business Review,* November–December, pp. 88–99.

Kandampully, J. 1998a. "Service Guarantees: Keep the Customers Coming Back," *Middle East Quality Review,* vol. 7, May, pp. 21–22.

Kandampully, J. 1998b. "Service Quality to Service Loyalty: A Relationship Which Goes beyond Customer Services," *Total Quality Management,* vol. 9, no. 6, pp. 431–443.

Kandampully, J. 2001. "Service Guarantee: An Organisation's Blueprint for Assisting the Delivery of Superior Service," In Kandampully, J., Mok, C., & Sparks, B. (eds.), *Service Quality Management in Hospitality, Tourism and Leisure,* Haworth Hospitality Press, New York.

Kandampully, J., & Butler, L. 1998. "Service Guarantee: A Strategic Mechanism to Enhance Feedback," *International Journal of Business Transformation,* vol. 1, no. 4, April, pp. 240–244.

Kandampully, J., & Duddy, R. 2001. "Service System: A Strategic Approach to Gain a Competitive Advantage in the Hospitality and Tourism Industry," *International Journal of Hospitality & Tourism Administration,* vol. 2, no. 1, pp. 27–47.

Kandampully, J., & Suhartanto, D. 2000. "Customer Loyalty in the Hotel Industry: The Role of Customer Satisfaction and Image," *International Journal of Contemporary Hospitality Management,* vol. 12, no. 6, pp. 346–351.

Kelley, S. W., Hoffman, D. K., & Davis, M. A. 1993. "A Typology of Retail Failures and Recoveries," *Journal of Retailing,* vol. 69, no. 4, Winter, pp. 429–452.

Lashley, C. 1996. "Research Issues for Employee Empowerment in Hospitality Organisations," *International Journal of Hospitality Management,* vol. 15, no. 4, pp. 333–346.

Lawler, E. E. III. 1992. *The Ultimate Advantage: Creating the High Involvement Organisation,* Jossey-Bass Management Series, Jossey-Bass, San Francisco.

Lovelock, C. H., Patterson, P. G., & Walker, R. H. 2001. *Services Marketing: An Asia–Pacific Perspective,* 2nd ed., Pearson Education Australia, Sydney.

MacMillan, I. C., & McGrath, R. G. 1997. "Discovering New Points of Differentiation," *Harvard Business Review,* July–August, pp. 133–145.

Maher, D. 1991. "Service Guarantees: Double-Barreled Standards," *Training,* vol. 28, no. 6, pp. 27–30.

Marriott, J. W., Jr. 1988. Foreword in Albrecht, K. *At America's Service,* Dow Jones, Irwin, New York.

Martin, F. 1995. "Putting Your Money Where Your Mouth Is," *International Journal of Retail and Distribution Management,* vol. 23, no. 8.

Marvin, B. 1992. "Exemplary Service Guaranteed," *Restaurants and Institutions,* vol. 102, no. 21, September, 9, pp. 108–121.

McDougal, G., Levesque, T., & Vanderplaat, P. 1998. "Designing the Service Guarantee–Unconditional or Specific?," *Journal of Service Marketing,* vol. 12, no. 4, pp. 278–293.

O'Brien, R. 1977. *The J. Willard Marriott Story,* Deseret Book Company, Salt Lake City, Utah.

Parasuraman, A., Zeithaml, V. A., & Berry, L. L. 1985. "A Conceptual Model of Service Quality and its Implications for Future Research," *Journal of Marketing,* vol. 49, Fall, pp. 41–50.

Patterson, P. G., & Spreng, R. A. 1997. "Modeling the Relationship between Perceived Value, Satisfaction and Repurchase Intentions in a Business-to-Business Service Context: An Emperical Examination," *International Journal of Service Industry Management,* vol. 8, no. 5, pp. 414–434.

Peppers, D., Rogers, M., & Dorf, B. 1999. "Is your Company Ready for One-To-One Marketing?," *Harvard Business Review,* January–February, pp. 151–160.

REFERENCES

Porter, M. E. 1985. *Competitive Advantage: Creating and Sustaining Superior Performance,* Free Press, New York.

Porter, M. E. 1998. *The Competitive Advantage of Nations: With a New Introduction,* Macmillan, Basingstoke, UK.

Prahalad, C. K., & Hamel, G. 1990. "The Core Competence of the Corporation," *Harvard Business Review,* May–June, pp. 79–91.

Richman, T. 1996. "Why Customers Leave," *Harvard Business Review,* January–February, pp. 9–10.

Rose, M. D. 1990. "No Strings Attached," *Chief Executive,* vol. 60, July/August, pp. 30–33.

Rucci, A. J., Kim, S. P., & Quinn, R. T. 1998. "The Employee–Customer Profit Chain at Sears," *Harvard Business Review,* January–February, pp. 83–97.

Schneider, B. 1980. "The Service Organization: Climate is Crucial," *Organizational Dynamics,* vol. 9, Autumn, pp. 52–65.

Schweikhart, S., Strasser, S., & Kennedy, M. 1993. "Service Recovery in Health Service Organisations," *Hospital and Health Service Administration,* vol. 38, no. 1.

Shera, W., & Page, J. 1995. "Creating More Effective Human Service Organizations through Strategies of Empowerment," *Administration in Social Work,* vol. 19, no. 4, pp. 1–15.

Sowder, J. 1996. "The 100% Satisfaction Guarantee Ensuring Quality at Hampton Inn," *National Productivity Review,* Spring, pp. 53–67.

Surprenant, C. F., & Solomon, M. R. 1987. "Predictability and Personalization in the Service Encounter," *Journal of Marketing,* vol. 51, pp. 73–80.

Tax, S. S., & Brown, S. W. 1998. "Recovering and Learning from Service Failure," *Sloan Management Review,* Fall, pp. 75–88.

Tax, S. S., & Brown, S. W. 2000. "Service Recovery: Research Insights and Practice," in Swartz, T. A., & Iacobucci, D. (eds.), *Handbook of Services Marketing and Management,* Sage, Thousand Oaks, California.

Vandermerwe, S. 1994. *From Tin Soldiers to Russian Dolls, Creating Added Value through Services,* Butterworth Heinemann, Oxford.

Walker, J. L. 1995. "Service Encounter Satisfaction: Conceptualized," *Journal of Services Marketing,* vol. 9, no. 1, pp. 5–14.

Wearne, N., & Baker, K. 2002. *Hospitality Marketing in the e-Commerce Age,* Hospitality Press/Pearson Education Australia, Sydney.

Woodruff, R. B. 1997. "Customer Value: The Next Source for Competitive Advantage," *Journal of the Academy of Marketing Science,* vol. 25, no. 2, pp. 139–153.

Woodruff, R. B., & Gardial, S. F. 1996. *Know Your Customer: New Approaches to Customer Value and Satisfaction,* Blackwell, Cambridge, Massachusetts.

Zeithaml, V. A. 1981. "How Consumer Evaluation Processes Differ Between Goods and Services," in Donnelly, J., & George, W. (eds.), *Marketing of Services,* American Marketing Association, Chicago, pp. 186–190.

Zeithaml, V. A., Berry, L. L., & Parasuraman, A. 1996. "The Behavioral Consequences of Service Quality," *Journal of Marketing,* vol. 60, April, pp. 31–46.

Zeithaml, V. A., & Bitner, M. J. 1996. *Services Marketing,* McGraw-Hill, New York.

Zemke, R. 1995. *Service Recovery: Fixing Broken Customers,* Productivity Press, Portland, Oregon.

Zemke, R., & Bell, C. 1990. "Service Recovery: Doing It Right the Second Time," *Training*, June, pp. 42–48.

Zemke, R., & Schaaf, D. 1989. *The Service Edge: 101 Companies That Profit from Customer Care*, NAL, Chicago.

NINE Global Strategies for Hospitality Services

Baker, K., & Huyton, J. 2001. *Hospitality Management—An Introduction*, Hospitality Press, Melbourne.

Berry, L. L. 2000. "Cultivating Service Brand Equity," *Journal of the Academy of Marketing Science*, vol. 28, no. 2, pp. 128–137.

Berthon, P. P., Katsikeas, L., Constantine, S., & Berthon, P. J. 1999. "Executive Insights; Virtual Services Go International, International Services in the Marketplace," *Journal of International Marketing*, vol. 7, no. 3, pp. 84–105.

Chase, R. B. 1978. "Where Does the Customer Fit in the Service Operation?" *Harvard Business Review*, November–December, pp. 137–142.

Child, J., & Faulkner, D. 1998. *Strategies of Cooperation: Managing Alliances, Networks, and Joint Ventures*, Oxford University Press, New York.

Clark, T., & Rajaratnam, D. 1999. "International Services: Perspective at Century's End," *Journal of Services Marketing*, vol. 13, nos. 4/5, pp. 298–310.

Clark, T., Rajaratnam, D., & Smith, T. 1996. "Toward a Theory of International Services: Marketing Intangibles in a World of Nations," *Journal of International Marketing*, vol. 4, no. 2, pp. 9–28.

Contractor, F. J., & Kundu, S. K. 1998. "Franchising versus Company Run Operations: Modal Choice in the Global Hotel Sector," *Journal of International Marketing*, vol. 6, no. 2, pp. 28–53.

Dahringer, L. D. 1991. "Marketing Services Internationally: Barriers and Management Strategies," *Journal of Services Marketing*, vol. 5, no. 3, pp. 5–17.

Daniels, J. D., & Radebaugh, L. H. 1992. "Disneyland Abroad: A Case Study," in *International Business: Environments and Operations*, 6th ed., Addison Wesley, New York.

Daniels, J. D., & Radebaugh, L. H. 1994. *International Business: Environments and Operations*, 7th ed., Addison Wesley, New York.

Day, G. S. 1994. "The Capabilities of Market-Driven Organizations," *Journal of Marketing*, vol. 58, October, pp. 37–52.

Dicken, P. 1998. *Global Shift: Transforming the World Economy*, 3rd ed., Guilford Press, New York.

Gallois, C., & Callan, V. J. 1997. *Communication and Culture: A Guide for Practice*, John Wiley, New York.

Go, F. M. 1999. "Internationalisation," in Brotherton B. (ed.), *The Handbook of Contemporary Hospitality Management Research*, John Wiley, Chichester, UK, pp. 477–491.

Go, F. M., & Pine, R. 1995. *Globalisation Strategy in the Hotel Industry*, Routledge, London, pp. 25–49.

Harbison, J. R., & Perkar, P., Jr. 1998. *Smart Alliances: A Practical Guide to Repeatable Success*, Booz-Allen & Hamilton.

Howarth, C. 1995. *Strategic Alliances: Resource Sharing Strategies for Smart Companies*, Pitman Publishing/Pearson Professional Australia, Melbourne.

Kasper, H., Helsdingen, P., & de Vries, W. 1999. *Services Marketing Management: An International Perspective*, Wiley, Chichester, UK.

REFERENCES

Lane, H. E., & Dupré, D. 1997. *Hospitality World!: An Introduction,* John Wiley, Toronto, Canada, pp. 60–67.

Louro, M. J., & Cunha, P. V. 2001. "Brand Management Paradigms," *Journal of Marketing Management,* vol. 17, pp. 849–875.

Lovelock, C. H., Patterson, P. G., & Walker, R. H. 1998. *Services Marketing: Australia and New Zealand,* Prentice Hall, Sydney, Australia.

Lovelock, C. H., Patterson, P. G., & Walker, R. H. 1999. "Developing Global Strategies for Service Business," in Bateson, J. E. G., & Hoffman K. D., *Managing Services Marketing: Text and Readings,* 4th ed., Dryden Press, Fort Worth, Texas, pp. 365–377.

Lovelock, C. H., & Yip, G. S. 1999. "Developing Global Strategies for Service Business," in Bateson, J. E. G., & Hoffman, K. D. (eds.), *Managing Services Marketing: Text and Readings,* 4th ed., Dryden Press, Fort Worth, Texas, pp. 365–377.

Lovelock, C. H., Patterson, P. G., & Walker, R. H. 2001. *Services Marketing: an Asia–Pacific Perspective,* 2nd ed., Pearson Education Australia, Sydney.

McLaughlin, C. P., & Fitzsimmons, J. A. 1996. "Strategies for Globalizing Service Operations," *International Journal of Service Industry Management,* vol. 7, no. 4, pp. 43–57.

Medlik, S., & Airey, D. W. 1978. *Profile of the Hotel and Catering Industry,* 2nd ed., Heinemann, London.

Mockler, R. J. 1999. *Multinational Strategic Alliances,* John Wiley, West Sussex, UK.

Olsen, M. D., West, J. J., & Tese, E. C. 1998. *Strategic Management in the Hospitality Industry,* 2nd ed., John Wiley, Toronto, Canada.

Palmer, A., & Cole, C. 1995. *Services Marketing: Principles and Practice,* Prentice Hall, Upper Saddle River, New Jersey.

Porter, M. E. 1998. *The Competitive Advantage of Nations,* Macmillan Business, London.

Roberts, C. 2001. "Consolidation in the International Hotel Industry," *Euro-CHRIE Conference Proceedings,* Brig, Switzerland, pp. 36–44.

Strauss, B., & Mang, P. 1999. "'Culture Shocks' in Inter-cultural Service Encounters." *Journal of Services Marketing,* vol. 13, nos. 4/5, pp. 329–346.

Weissinger, S. S. 1989. *Hotel/Motel Operations: An Overview,* South Western, Ohio.

Weissinger, S. S. 2000. *Hotel/Motel Operations: An Overview,* 2nd ed., Delmar/Thomson Learning, Albany, New York.

Wymbs, C. 2000. "How E-commerce is Transforming and Internationalizing Service Industries," *Journal of Services Marketing,* vol. 14, no. 6, pp. 463–478.

Yu, L. 1999. *The International Hospitality Business: Management and Operations,* Haworth Press, New York.

TEN Technology and Its Applications

Anton, J. 2000. "Customer Connections," *Electric Perspectives,* Jul./Aug., pp. 15–21.

Bensaou, M., & Earl, M. 1998. "The Right Mind-Set for Managing Information Technology," *Harvard Business Review,* September–October, pp. 119–128.

Berkley, B. J., & Gupta, A. 1994. "Improving Service Quality with Information Technology," *International Journal of Information Management,* April, vol. 14, pp. 109–121.

Berry, L. L. 1995. *On Great Service: A Framework for Action,* Free Press, New York.

Bitner, M. J., Brown, S. W., & Meuter, M. L. 2000. "Technology Infusion in Service Encounters," *Journal of the Academy of Marketing Science,* vol. 28, issue 1, pp. 138–149.

Blumberg, D. F. 1994. "Strategies for Improving Field Service Operations Productivity and Quality," *The Service Industries Journal,* vol. 14, no. 2, p. 262.

Bobbitt, M. L., & Dabholkar, P. A. 2001. "Integrating Attitudinal Theories to Understand and Predict Use of Technology-Based Self-Service: The Internet as an Illustration," *International Journal of Service Industry Management,* vol. 12, no. 5, pp. 423–450.

Buress, K. 2000. "Online Customer Care," *Business Perspectives,* Summer, pp. 4–9.

Chipkin, H. 2000. "Generation-e Checks in," *Lodging,* June, pp. 61–66.

Cline, R. S. 1999, "Hospitality 2000," *Lodging Hospitality,* June, pp. 18–28.

Durocher, F. J., & Niman, B. N. 1993. "Information Technology: Management Effectiveness and Guest Services," *Hospitality Research Journal,* vol. 17, no. 1, pp. 121–131.

Francese, A. P., & Renaghan, L. M. 1991. "Finding the Customer," *American Demographics,* January, pp. 48–51.

Furnell, S. M., & Karweni, T. 1999. "Security Implications of Electronic Commerce: A Survey of Consumers and Business," *Internet Research,* vol. 9, no. 5, pp. 372–382.

Global Sight Corporation 2001. <www.internetindicators.com>.

Gosh, S. 1999. "Making Business Sense of the Internet," *Harvard Business Review,* March–April, pp. 126–135.

Greenstein, M., & Feinman, T. 2000. *Electronic Commerce: Security, Risk Management and Control,* Irwin McGraw-Hill, New York.

Grönroos, C., Heinonen, F., Isoniemi, K., & Lindholm, M. 2000. "The NetOffer Model: A Case Example from the Virtual Marketspace," *Management Decision,* vol. 38, no. 4, pp. 243–252.

Hart, C. W. 1996. "Made to Order," *Marketing Management,* vol. 5, no. 2, pp. 11–23.

Hensdill, C. 1996a. "Kitchen Technology," *Hotels,* September, pp. 71–74.

Hensdill, C. 1996b. "New CRSs Enhancing Marketing Power," *Hotels,* July, p. 86.

Hensdill, C. 1996c. "Sheraton Complexing PMS," *Hotels,* vol. 30, November, p. 122.

Hensdill, C. 1996d. "Touring the Guestroom of the Year 2000," *Hotels,* vol. 30, February, p. 62.

Hensdill, C. 1997a. "Hoteliers Find Initial Success on the Web," *Hotels,* vol. 31, February, p. 64.

Hensdill, C. 1997b. "Integrated Locks and Automated Security," *Hotels,* vol. 31, April, p. 78.

Kandampully, J., & Duddy, R. 2002. "The Impact of Technology on Human Resources in the Hospitality Industry," in Watson, S., D'Annunzio-Green, N., & Maxwell, G. A. (eds.), *Human Resource Management: International Perspectives in Tourism and Hotel Management,* Continuum Publishing, London, pp. 64–73.

Kotabe, M., & Murray, J. 2001. "Outsourcing Service Activities," *Marketing Management,* Spring, pp. 41–45.

La, K. V., & Kandampully, J. 2002. "Electronic Retailing and Distribution of Services: Cyber Intermediaries that Serve Customers and Service Providers," *Managing Service Quality,* vol. 12, no. 2, 100–116. http://www.emeraldinsight.com/msq.htm

LaMonica, M. 1999. "Stuck in the Web: Don't Leave Customers Hanging While You Untangle Your Online Customer Service," *Infoworld,* vol. 21, no. 2. pp. 75–76.

REFERENCES

Mandelbaum, R. 1997. "Hotel Sales-and-Marketing Management," *Cornell Hotel and Restaurant Administration Quarterly,* December, pp. 46–51.

Meuter, M. L., Ostrom, A. L., Roundtree, R. I., & Bitner, M. J. 2000. "Self-Service Technologies: Understanding Customer Satisfaction with Technology Based Service Encounters," *Journal of Marketing,* vol. 64, pp. 54–60.

Miller, J. S., & Cardy, R. L. 2000. "Technology and Managing People: Keeping the "Human" in Human Resources," *Journal of Labor Research,* vol. 21, no. 3, pp. 447–461.

Moncrief, W. C., & Cravens, D. W. 1999. "Technology and the Changing Marketing World," *Marketing Intelligence and Planning,* vol. 17, no. 7, pp. 329–332.

Murphy, J., Forrest, E., & Wotring, C. 1996. "Restaurant Marketing on the World Wide Web," *Cornell Hotel & Administration Quarterly,* February 1996, p. 63.

Olsen, M. D., & Connolly, D. 2000. "How Technology is Changing the Hospitality Industry," *Cornell Hotel & Restaurant Administration Quarterly,* February, vol. 41, issue 1, pp. 30–43.

Peppers, D., & Rogers, M. 2000. *One-To-One Manager: Real-World Lessons in Customer Relationship Management,* Capstone Publishing, UK.

Pollock, A. 1996. "The Role of Electronic Brochures in Selling Travel: Implications for Business and Destinations," *Australian Journal of Hospitality Management,* vol. 3, no. 1, pp. 25–30.

Porter, M. E. 1985. *Competitive Advantage: Creating Sustaining Superior Performance,* Free Press, New York.

Porter, M. 2001. "Strategy and the Internet," *Harvard Business Review,* March, pp. 62–78.

Quinn, J. B., & Paquette, P. C. 1990. "Technology in Services: Creating Organizational Revolutions," *Sloan Management Review,* Winter, pp. 67–77.

Richter, R. 1999. "Minding Your Own E-business," *Association Management,* September 1999, pp. 48–55.

Schoenbachler, D. D., Gordon, G. L., Foley, D., & Spellman, L. 1997. "Understanding Consumer Database Marketing," *Journal of Consumer Marketing,* vol. 14, no. 1, pp. 5–19.

Siguaw, J. A., & Enz, C. A. 1999. "Best Practices in Information Technology," *Cornell Hotel and Restaurant Administration Quarterly,* October, pp. 58–71.

Siguaw, J. A., Enz, C. A., & Namasivayam, K. 2000. "Adoption of Information Technology in US Hotels: Strategically Driver Objectives," *Journal of Travel Research,* vol. 39, pp. 192–201.

Smith David, J., Grabski, S., & Kasavana, M. 1996. "The Productivity Paradox of Hotel-Industry Technology," *Cornell Hotel & Restaurant Administration Quarterly,* vol. 37, no. 2, pp. 64–70.

Sweet, P. 2000. "Strategic Value Configuration Logics and the New Economy: A Service Economy Revolution?," in Edvardsson, B., Brown, S. W., Johnston, R., & Scheuing, E. E. (eds.), *Service Quality in the New Economy: Interdisciplinary and International Dimensions,* QUIS-7, ISQA International Service Quality Association.

"Technology Survey," 1998. *Hotels,* June.

Van Hoff, H., & Verbeeten, M. 1998. "Email, Web Site Most Commonly Used Internet Tools," *Hotel & Motel Management,* vol. 213, no. 11, p. 34.

"The Wired Index–40 Companies Driving the Future," 2000. *Wired,* June, pp. 230–266.

Wymbs, C. 2000. "How E-commerce is Transforming and Internationalising Service Industries," *Journal of Services Marketing,* vol. 14, no. 6, pp. 463–478.

Zemke, R., & Connellan, T. 2001. *e-Services: 24 Ways to Keep Your Customers When the Competition Is Just a Click Away,* AMACOM, New York.

Index